European and Global Governance: Key Topics

European and Global Governance: Key Topics

Edited by
Santiago Christian

STATES
ACADEMIC PRESS
www.statesacademicpress.com

Published by States Academic Press,
109 South 5th Street,
Brooklyn, NY 11249, USA

ISBN: 978-1-63989-193-1

Cataloging-in-Publication Data

European and global governance : key topics / edited by Santiago Christian.
p. cm.
Includes bibliographical references and index.
ISBN 978-1-63989-193-1
1. European Union. 2. International cooperation. 3. Administrative law--European Union countries. 4. Law--European Union countries. 5. Public administration.
I. Christian, Santiago.

KJE947 .E87 2022
341.242 2--dc23

For information on all States Academic Press publications visit our website at www.statesacademicpress.com

STATES
ACADEMIC PRESS

Contents

Preface

This book aims to highlight the current researches and provides a platform to further the scope of innovations in this area. This book is a product of the combined efforts of many researchers and scientists, after going through thorough studies and analysis from different parts of the world. The objective of this book is to provide the readers with the latest information of the field.

The movement of translational actors towards political cooperation, which is aimed to negotiate responses to problems which affect more than one state or region is termed as global governance. The four stages in which global governance is broadly classified are agenda-setting, policymaking, implementation and enforcement, and evaluation, monitoring, and adjudication. Under the umbrella of European governance, many areas of policy are federalised into common institutions which are capable of making law and deals with competences to control foreign policy, defence policy or the majority of direct taxation policies. European governance analyzes the European and global economic structures, the effects of economic incentives on the national and international scale and the processes of growth and development. This book is compiled in such a manner, that it will provide in-depth knowledge about European and global governance. It presents this complex subject in the most comprehensible and easy to understand language. This book will serve as a valuable source of reference for graduate and post graduate students.

I would like to express my sincere thanks to the authors for their dedicated efforts in the completion of this book. I acknowledge the efforts of the publisher for providing constant support. Lastly, I would like to thank my family for their support in all academic endeavors.

Editor

1

The Constitution of Estonia: The Unexpected Challenges of Unlimited Primacy of EU Law

Madis Ernits, Carri Ginter, Saale Laos, Marje Allikmets, Paloma Krõõt Tupay, René Värk and Andra Laurand

Abstract The report informs that due to historical ties to the German legal culture, the most influential model for reconstruction of the Estonian legal order after the restoration of independence was German law, including when drafting the 1992 Constitution. However, with regard to EU law, a different approach was chosen: a

Madis Ernits is Judge at the Tartu Court of Appeal, and Visiting Lecturer of Constitutional Law at the Faculty of Law, University of Tartu. e-mail: madis.ernits@kohus.ee.

Carri Ginter is Associate Professor of European Law at the Faculty of Law, University of Tartu. e-mail: carri@ginter.ee.

Saale Laos is Justice of the Supreme Court of Estonia. e-mail: saale.laos@riigikohus.ee.

Marje Allikmets is Legal Advisor, Supreme Court of Estonia; at the time of writing Adviser to the Chancellor of Justice. e-mail: marje.allikmets@riigikohus.ee.

Paloma Krõõt Tupay is Lecturer in Constitutional Law at the Faculty of Law, University of Tartu; at the time of writing Legal Expert on Constitutional Law at the Ministry of Justice. e-mail: palomakreet.tupay@ut.ee.

René Värk is Associate Professor of International Law at the Faculty of Law, University of Tartu. e-mail: rene.vark@ut.ee.

Andra Laurand is a student assistant to the Estonian report, stud. iur., Universität Hamburg. e-mail: andra.laurand@studium.uni-hamburg.de.

M. Ernits (✉) · C. Ginter
Faculty of Law, University of Tartu, Tartu, Estonia
e-mail: madis.ernits@kohus.ee

C. Ginter
e-mail: carri@ginter.ee

P. K. Tupay
Faculty of Law, University of Tartu, Tallinn, Estonia
e-mail: palomakreet.tupay@ut.ee

blanket clause in a self-standing constitutional act that suspends the Constitution, in order to give full supremacy to EU law. The Supreme Court and its Constitutional Review Chamber have adopted an unconditionally EU-friendly approach. However, the report documents the widespread concerns that have emerged amongst Estonian lawyers with regard to setting aside the Constitution, as well as the practical difficulties in constitutional adjudication by the Supreme Court. The tensions peaked in the process of ratification of the ESM Treaty, which was approved by 11 judges against 8, with the latter submitting strongly worded dissenting opinions expressing concerns about the impact of the very large financial liabilities on the rule-of-law-based, democratic and social state. Concerns by lawyers were also raised with regard to the European Arrest Warrant system, which led to review proceedings initiated by the Chancellor of Justice based on defence rights. The report also explores the excess sugar stocks cases concerning the principles of legitimate expectations and non-retroactivity, and issues regarding publication of laws in the context of EU law. The report finds that broadly speaking, any strains on constitutional values have been justified, given the benefits of EU integration. It nevertheless recommends introducing a German *Solange*-style limitation clause into the Constitution.

Keywords The Estonian Constitution · Constitutional amendments regarding EU integration · The Estonian Supreme Court and the Constitutional Review Chamber Fundamental rights and the *Rechtsstaat* approach to the rule of law Influences of the German constitutional tradition · Constitutional review statistics and grounds · ESM Treaty · European Arrest Warrant and defence rights *Balbiino* · *Excess Sugar Stocks* cases and publication of laws · The principles of legal certainty, legitimate expectations and non-retroactivity · Justiciability of social rights · Data Retention Directive · Unconditional supremacy of EU law Referendum · Parliamentary reservation of law

R. Värk
e-mail: rene.vark@ut.ee

S. Laos
Supreme Court of Estonia, Tartu, Estonia
e-mail: saale.laos@riigikohus.ee

M. Allikmets
Supreme Court of Estonia, Tartu, Estonia
e-mail: marje.allikmets@riigikohus.ee

A. Laurand
Universität Hamburg, Hamburg, Germany
e-mail: andra.laurand@studium.uni-hamburg.de

1 Constitutional Amendments Regarding EU Membership

1.1 Constitutional Culture

1.1.1 At the top of the Estonian norm hierarchy stands the *Põhiseadus*[1] (Constitution), which was adopted by a referendum on 28 June 1992 and came into force on the following day, as prescribed by § 1(1) of the *Eesti Vabariigi põhiseaduse rakendamise seadus*[2] (The Constitution of the Republic of Estonia Implementation Act, hereinafter CREIA). The Estonian Constitution is a typical example of a constitution adopted after the fall of an authoritarian regime – it is fully binding and enforceable in courts. The Estonian constitutional order is determined by five fundamental principles of the Constitution: human dignity,[3] democracy,[4] the rule of law,[5] the social state[6] and the Estonian identity[7].[8] The Estonian legal order is part of the continental legal culture with a strict hierarchy of norms, the principle of reservation of law provided by § 3(1) of the Constitution that requires a specific enactment of a statute for every specific exercise of state power, and the fundamental division of the legal order into public and private law. Historically bound to the German legal culture, old ties awoke from hibernation after the restoration of independence in 1991. The most influential model for reconstruction of vast parts of the Estonian legal order was again German law. In first order this applies to the central parts of private law, but also to criminal law and general administrative law.

1.1.2 The rationale of the Constitution is best defined in its preamble, according to which the Constitution is created to protect the peace and defend the people against aggression from outside, to form a pledge to present and future generations for their social progress and welfare, and to guarantee the preservation of the Estonian

---

[1] *Riigi Teataja* [State Gazette] (RT) RT 1992, 26, 349; RT I, 27.04.2011, 2. Estonian legislation in Estonian and English is available at: https://www.riigiteataja.ee/en/. Some revisions have been made to the translations by the editors of this volume.

[2] RT 1992, 26, 350.

[3] E.g. Judgment of the Constitutional Review Chamber of the Supreme Court (CRCSCj) 21.01.2004, 3-4-1-7-03, para. 14; 05.05.2014, 3-4-1-67-13, para. 49. Selected decisions of the Constitutional Review Chamber and the Administrative Law Chamber are available in English at http://www.riigikohus.ee/?id=823 and http://www.riigikohus.ee/?id=719. Some revisions have been made to the translations by the editors of this volume.

[4] E.g. Judgment of the Supreme Court *en banc* (SCebj) 01.07.2010, 3-4-1-33-09, paras. 52 and 67.

[5] E.g. Order of the Constitutional Review Chamber of the Supreme Court (CRCSCo) 07.11.2014, 3-4-1-32-14, para. 28.

[6] E.g. CRCSCj 21.01.2004, 3-4-1-7-03, para. 14; 05.05.2014, 3-4-1-67-13, para. 49.

[7] CRCSCj 04.11.1998, 3-4-1-7-98, para. III.

[8] On the debate about fundamental principles of the Constitution, see Drechsler and Annus 2002, p. 473 et seq.; Ernits 2012, p. 126 et seq.; Maruste 2007, p. 8 et seq.; Maruste 2000, p. 311 et seq.; Laffranque 2007, p. 528 et seq.; Narits 2009, p. 56 et seq. For a compilation of the sources in Estonian and presentation of the debate, see Ernits 2011, p. 5 fn. 9, p. 6 et seq. and p. 23 et seq.

people, the Estonian language and the Estonian culture through the ages. The Constitution is organised as follows. It opens with an introductory chapter of seven sections (§), which includes a rather strict sovereignty clause in § 1. This chapter is followed by a detailed catalogue of constitutional rights with 48 sections. The Constitution also contains fundamental principles in § 10: human dignity, democracy, social state and the rule of law. The rule of law principle has complex elements, which are relatively frequent grounds of adjudication. The organisation of the state is regulated in Chapters III–XIII: The People, The *Riigikogu* (Parliament), The President of the Republic, The Government of the Republic, Legislation, Finance and the State Budget, Foreign Relations and International Treaties, National Defence, The State Audit Office, The Chancellor of Justice and The Courts. The Supreme Court (SC) is the highest court and also has powers of constitutional review.

1.2 The Amendment of the Constitution in Relation to the European Union

1.2.1–1.2.2 On 1 May 2004, Estonia, together with nine other European countries, joined the European Union. Before accession, the Constitution was amended by the *Eesti Vabariigi põhiseaduse täiendamise seadus* (The Constitution of the Republic of Estonia Amendment Act, hereinafter CREAA),[9] which provides as follows:

> In a referendum held on 14 September 2003 pursuant to section 162 of the Constitution of the Republic of Estonia, the people of Estonia adopted the following Act to amend the Constitution:
>
> § 1. Estonia may belong to the European Union, provided the fundamental principles of the Constitution of the Republic of Estonia are respected.
>
> § 2. When Estonia has acceded to the European Union, the Constitution of the Republic of Estonia shall be applied taking into account the rights and obligations arising from the Accession Treaty.
>
> § 3. This Act may only be amended in a referendum.
>
> § 4. This Act shall enter into force three months after the date of its promulgation.

As noted in the preamble of the Act, the CREAA was adopted by a referendum. It entered into force on 6 January 2004. The draft CREAA was submitted to the *Riigikogu* on 16 May 2002. The draft presented had one important difference compared with the final version of the CREAA: § 1 of the initial version laconically provided that 'Estonia may accede to the European Union'.[10] As a result of

---

[9] RT I 2003, 64, 429; RT I 2007, 43, 313.

[10] Draft Act No. 1067 SE (16 May 2002). Draft Acts are available in Estonian at http://www.riigikogu.ee//?s=&checked=eelnoud.

parliamentary debates and criticism from legal scholars, § 1 of the draft CREAA was amended on the recommendation of the then Chancellor of Justice Allar Jõks, to provide as follows: 'Estonia may belong to the European Union, provided the fundamental principles of the Constitution of the Republic of Estonia are respected'.[11] On 18 December 2002, the *Riigikogu* adopted a resolu-tion[12] on holding a referendum on accession to the EU and on amending the Constitution by the CREAA, by a vote of 88 for and 1 against out of 101. The referendum was held on 14 September 2003 and is to date the only referendum that has been held under the Constitution of 1992. The turnout was 64% of all citizens eligible to vote, and 67% of all voters gave their consent to the amendment.

1.2.3 The aims of the amendment and idea behind the amendment On 28 November 1995, Estonia applied for membership of the EU. Becoming a member of the EU was one of the most important aims of the post-Soviet independence period for many reasons. First and foremost, a new isolation and seclusion from western societies which are based on the principle of individual freedom – as had occurred in the 1940s – was feared. Moreover, Estonia wished to guarantee that the principles of democracy, the rule of law and human rights that had once again been enforced would remain the fundamental principles of its legal order, regardless of possible geopolitical challenges that could lie ahead in the future. Bearing those aims in mind, the *Riigikogu* together with the Government began with preparations for joining the EU soon after the restoration of independence in 1991.

Conceptual background to the choice of wording and key factors influencing the decision on the scope and content of the amendment In 1991, the *Põhiseaduse Assamblee* (Constitutional Assembly, hereinafter Assembly) gathered with the task of drafting a new Constitution for Estonia. The members of the Assembly were aware of the wish of the population of Estonia to become a member of the EU in the future; however, at the time this aim was still so far out of reach that the assembly scarcely touched upon the issue. However, one foreign legal expert, Peter Germer, did point out that 'the draft contains no provision concerning the transferral of power to supranational organizations like the European Community', and that even though it may not happen in the near future, some day Estonian may join the European Community and might need a special provision to that effect, as in most other countries.[13]

In March 1995 the Constitutional Committee of the *Riigikogu* proposed that the Government prepare a legal expert analysis on the Constitution; this resulted in a landmark report of 1998 by the Legal Expertise Committee, which aimed to analyse, *inter alia*, whether the Constitution contained any conflicts of norms or

---

[11] List of amendment proposals to the CREAA Draft Act No. 1067 SE II (12 December 2002).

[12] RT I 2002, 107, 637.

[13] Peep 1997, p. 331; Laffranque 2003, p. 181.

legal gaps and whether the Constitution – also in the light of possible accession to the EU – required amendment.[14]

The present report will now explore the amendment proposals and debates in greater detail, as several issues have resurfaced in result of more recent cases, and have prompted calls to change the EU provisions in the Estonian Constitution. In the above-mentioned 1998 Report, the Expert Committee concluded that in order to become a Member State of the EU, the Constitution had to be amended. The committee first proposed the addition of § 1(3) to the Constitution, according to which Estonia may accede to the European Union by a referendum and on the conditions laid down in a new § 123[1]. Secondly, the committee proposed the addition of § 123[1] to the Constitution, with the following wording:

> Estonia may, based on the principles of reciprocity and equality, delegate state powers stemming from the Constitution to the institutions of the European Union for the purposes of joint realisation by the Member States of the European Union to the extent necessary to implement the agreements underlying the union and on the condition that this does not contradict the fundamental principles as established in the preamble of the Constitution.
>
> The Government shall inform the *Riigikogu* as early and comprehensively as possible in matters concerning the European Union and shall take the positions of the *Riigikogu* into account upon participating in the European Union legislative process. Upon membership, a more detailed procedure shall be provided by law.[15]

The report also contemplated on the question of what the EU 'is'. The Expert Committee took the view that the Constitution would theoretically allow Estonia to accede to the EU if it were a confederation, however it also affirmed that the EU is an international organisation *sui generis.*[16]

Sixteen foreign legal experts also participated in the drafting of the expert report. Amongst some of the views, Professor Robert Alexy elaborated in his expert opinion on the fundamental rights catalogue of the Estonian Constitution that § 1 hinders accession to the EU and should be amended by the addition of a third paragraph in the following wording: 'The independence and sovereignty of Estonia do not exclude membership in the European Union'.[17] From the report of McKenna & Co it can be concluded that in order to ensure conformity between Estonia's legal order and the principle of primacy of EU law, amending the Constitution would be inevitable.[18] Several amendments were proposed, for example to complement § 1 (2) with permission to transfer a part of sovereignty to an international organisation

---

[14] The resulting report is entitled *Võimalik liitumine Euroopa Liiduga ja selle õiguslik tähendus Eesti riigiõiguse seisukohalt* (Possible accession to the European Union and its legal meaning from the perspective of Estonian constitutional law), Final Report of the Legal Expertise Committee for the Constitution of the Republic of Estonia (1998), (available in Estonian) http://www.just.ee/et/eesti-vabariigi-pohiseaduse-juriidilise-ekspertiisi-komisjoni-lopparuanne, hereinafter referred to as 'The 1998 Report of the Legal Expertise Committee'. See also Varul 2000.

[15] The 1998 Report of the Legal Expertise Committee, supra n. 14 (translation by the authors).

[16] Ibid.

[17] Alexy 2001, p. 93.

[18] McKenna & Co 1996, p. 17 and para. 3.1.

in accordance with § 3 of the Constitution, and to amend § 3 such that it would also allow for the exercise of governmental authority pursuant to EU law.[19] Professor Guy Carcassonne proposed the addition of a separate chapter on the EU in the Constitution.[20] This Chapter would have consisted of three paragraphs allowing Estonia to become a member of the EU, every new treaty would have had to be submitted to the SC before ratification by Parliament, and the Government would have been required to introduce a specific procedure for informing Parliament.

In Estonian domestic discussions that followed the conclusions and proposals of the Expert Committee, Anneli Albi suggested an alternative wording for the constitutional amendment. Albi suggested that the two provisions proposed in the report, § 1(3) and § 123[1], be merged and that the amendment be added as a separate paragraph to § 1 of the Constitution.[21] A further contribution to the discussion on whether/how to amend the Constitution was made by Julia Laffranque, who in an article in 2001 listed possible ways to amend the Constitution for the purpose of EU membership; the list also summarised proposals presented by other legal experts, *inter alia* the possibility of introducing a third supplementing act to the Constitution.[22]

In 2002, a working group comprised of experts and members of the political factions in the *Riigikogu* was formed.[23] It should also be stressed that during the time the working group held its sessions, a public opinion survey showed that more than half (51%) of the citizens who had the right to vote were against joining the EU, and only 37% supported accession.[24] The solution later found by the working group was presumably to some extent influenced by this survey.[25]

In January 2002, the Minister of Justice at the time, Märt Rask, asserted that the legal scholars had not reached a conclusion on whether and, if so, how exactly and to what extent the Constitution should be amended. Subsequently, Rask published the preferred form for the amendment – a laconic supplementing act to the Constitution – and its possible content.[26] The reasoning behind this choice was the desire not to amend the base text of the Constitution, since the Constitution itself was considered a 'sacred' text, and the Minister of Justice did not want the

---

[19] Ibid., pp. 18–19.

[20] Carcassonne 1998, p. 10.

[21] Albi 2000, p. 164.

[22] Laffranque 2001, p. 215 et seq.

[23] According to Mart Nutt, the following experts played a central role in the drafting process of the future CREAA, submitted to the *Riigikogu* on 16 May 2002: Kalle Merusk, Jüri Põld, Ülle Madise, Julia Laffranque and Märt Rask, see minutes of the IX Riigikogu, VII session (11 June 2002), (available in Estonian) http://stenogrammid.riigikogu.ee/et/200206111000#PKP-2000008924.

[24] For the period January 2000 to March 2001, see Mattson, T. (2001, March 28). *Üle poole kodanikest on euroliidu vastu* (More than half of all citizens oppose the EU). Postimees. http://www.postimees.ee/1858647/ule-poole-kodanikest-on-euroliidu-vastu. See also Albi 2005, p. 89.

[25] Albi 2005, p. 89.

[26] Rask, M. (2002, January 15). *Kas muuta põhiseadust või mitte?* (To amend the Constitution or not?) Postimees. http://arvamus.postimees.ee/1914493/kas-muuta-pohiseadust-voi-mitte.

Constitution to become a pile of amendments and insertions, losing its clarity and simplicity.[27]

The critique and advice of legal scholars A wave of criticism from legal scholars followed. Rait Maruste, at the time Judge of the European Court of Human Rights (ECtHR), conceded that the Minister of Justice's proposal was one possible solution – and definitely a politically convenient one; however, he expressed doubt whether the Third Act (as the supplementing act came to be widely known) could maintain the clarity and simplicity of the Constitution.[28] He insisted that the Constitution had to reflect the actual mechanisms of exercising power. The Third Act with its few sentences would not be able to do so. According to Maruste:

> It is as clear as day that upon joining the EU the actual ways in which power is exercised change, and change significantly. They change, in my opinion, to such an extent that this cannot be overcome through simple interpretation, by establishing a general rule or, in the worst case, by tacitly looking past any incompatibilities. It would be a rape of the Constitution and constitutional nihilism.[29]

The criticisms by Maruste were followed by the Chancellor of Justice, Allar Jõks,[30] who also pointed out several shortcomings of the Third Act solution. For example, Jõks stated that without establishing clear rules on changes brought upon by the EU, it would be impossible to foresee problems that might arise from the Third Act.[31] Furthermore, by raising EU law above the Constitution, Estonia would give up too much and, moreover, the Constitution does not permit entry into an international treaty that is not in accordance with the Constitution. Jõks proposed following the German example by adding a clause which would bind membership in the EU with adherence to the fundamental principles of the Constitution. Among further scholars, Lauri Mälksoo, now Professor of International Law at the University of Tartu, argued that amending the Constitution with a separate addendum which, in addition, modifies the contents of the Constitution itself, would

---

[27] Ibid.

[28] Maruste, R. (2002, January 29). *Põhiseadust tuleks siiski muuta* (The Constitution should nevertheless be amended). Postimees. http://arvamus.postimees.ee/1917325/pohiseadust-tuleks-siiski-muuta.

[29] Ibid., (translation by the authors).

[30] The monocratic institution of the Chancellor of Justice is unique, with a tripartite division of its functions. The first is to exercise supervision over the constitutionality and legality of the proceedings of the legislative and executive powers. To perform this function, the Chancellor of Justice has the right to speak before the *Riigikogu* (the Estonian Parliament) and during the sessions of the Government, to lodge a complaint against any state organ, to submit a direction to the *Riigikogu* to initiate an Act and also to appeal to the SC, if this request is not fulfilled. The second function is the ombudsman function, which includes the right to receive individual complaints, and to analyse and make suggestions to improve administrative governance. Thirdly, the Chancellor of Justice has the right to decide whether to bring a question of removal of immunity before Parliament.

[31] Jõks, A. (2002, April 16). *Põhiseadus muutuste künnisel* (The Constitution on the brink of change). Postimees. http://arvamus.postimees.ee/1933583/pohiseadus-muutuste-kunnisel.

be harmful for the clarity of the Constitution.[32] In addition, Mälksoo stated that the 'neutral' route of the CREAA was being used in an attempt to avoid some essential questions on the extent to which the rights and obligations arising from the Accession Treaty will change the Constitution. The irony of this 'legal masquerade' was that the Estonian Constitution provided one of the strictest sovereignty clauses in Europe.[33] Mälksoo insisted that the core of the Constitution should be respected, and the Third Act should not become a Trojan horse which would allow the fundamental principles of the Constitution to be turned upside down; he proposed the addition of reference to the fundamental principles of Estonian statehood and of the Constitution in the text of the CREAA.

In the summer of 2002, six scholars – Anneli Albi, Michael Gallagher, Indrek Koolmeister, Rait Maruste, Lauri Mälksoo and Peeter Roosma – published a joint statement concerning the Third Act.[34] The statement stressed that the Third Act would not describe the actual way power is exercised, and that accession to the EU must be regulated in accordance with constitutional law. By choosing the supplementing act solution, the text of the Constitution would cease to be as clear and easily applicable as it was before the Third Act. Moreover, the Constitution itself does not foresee the possibility to change the Constitution by means of a separate act: Chapter XV of the Constitution only permits amendment of the Constitution by amending its text. The six scholars concluded that the draft CREAA was not in accordance with the principle of a democratic state based on the rule of law, and that the Act might lay a foundation for a risky precedent in future. As an alternative, the scholars proposed that the text of the Constitution be amended by adding Chapter IX^1 on the European Union. The proposed chapter would have included Article § 123^1 ('Estonia may delegate state powers stemming from the Constitution to the European Union according to the conditions laid down in the Treaties of the European Union and to the extent that this does not harm the fundamental principles of Estonian statehood'), and provisions regarding the participation of the *Riigikogu*, application of EU law in cases of conflict, equal treatment of EU citizens, and a revision regarding the Bank of Estonia with a view to participation in the Monetary Union.

In April 2002, the Minister of Justice recognised that many legal scholars wanted to change the Constitution in detail, so that exactly what would change after joining the EU would be clear.[35] The Minister proposed that the changes should be explained and clarified in the explanatory memorandum to the draft CREAA; however the draft itself, he maintained, should remain 'short, simple and clear'.[36]

---

[32] Mälksoo, L. (2002, May 13). *Kuidas muuta põhiseadust*? (How should the Constitution be amended?) Postimees. http://arvamus.postimees.ee/1938787/kuidas-muuta-pohiseadust.

[33] Ibid.

[34] Albi et al. 2002, pp. 352–353.

[35] Rask, M. (2002, April 19). *Ühinemise otsustab rahvas* (Accession will be decided by the people). Postimees. http://arvamus.postimees.ee/1936071/uhinemise-otsustab-rahvas.

[36] Ibid. (translation by the authors).

A more comprehensive justification for the Third Act was presented in an academic article by the working group.[37]

Amendment procedure and obstacles The procedure for amending the Constitution is set out in Chapter XV of the Constitution.[38] Notably, § 162 provides that Chapter I (General Provisions) and Chapter XV (Amendment of the Constitution) may only be amended by referendum. Since the CREAA would in principle have changed the first chapter of the Constitution (particularly § 1 and § 3), the amendment could only be adopted by a referendum.

1.2.4 With regard to EU-related amendment proposals, two different periods can be distinguished: the first period up to the decision by the *Riigikogu* to hold a referendum on the CREAA, and the second period starting from this decision and continuing to this day.

The question of further amendment of the Constitution was in particular revived by the discussions on the Treaty Establishing a Constitution for Europe, which ultimately never came into force. During the debates on the CREAA, it had been stressed on several occasions (including in the above-mentioned justification article by the working group that initiated the Third Act) that the next time the EU Member States amended the fundamental treaties of the EU, Estonia would need to amend the CREAA accordingly, and therefore a new referendum would have to be held.[39]

In the context of the European Constitutional Treaty, some legal experts proposed a total revision of the Constitution. Märt Rask, who meanwhile in 2004 had been appointed Chief Justice of the SC, asserted that it would be very difficult for the Constitutional Review Chamber of the SC (CRCSC) to interpret the Constitution, considering that both the European Constitutional Treaty and the Estonian Constitution were applicable.[40]

The subsequent developments in the *Riigikogu*, however, took a completely different direction. In December 2004, a working group to analyse the European Constitutional Treaty was formed with the task of, *inter alia*, analysing whether the Constitution and the CREAA allowed for ratification of the European Constitutional Treaty in the *Riigikogu* without amending the Constitution.[41]

---

[37] Laffranque et al. 2002, pp. 563–568. Cf. Ginter and Narits 2013, p. 60.

[38] The right to initiate amendments rests with one-fifth of the members of the *Riigikogu* and with the President (§ 161(1) of the Constitution).

[39] E.g. in Laffranque et al. 2002, p. 567.

[40] Piirsalu, J. (2004, 21 September): *Märt Rask: põhiseadus vajab lähiajal kindlasti revideerimist* (Märt Rask: The Constitution must definitely be revised in the near future). Eesti Päevaleht. http://epl.delfi.ee/news/eesti/mart-rask-pohiseadus-vajab-lahiajal-kindlasti-revideerimist?id=50993275.

[41] See *Riigikogu* press release of 14 December 2004 and *Riigikogu* press release of 4 February 2005.

In March 2005, Chancellor of Justice Allar Jõks warned in a press article that in the interests of at least the formal constitutionality of the changes brought about by the European Constitutional Treaty, the reference to the Accession Treaty in § 2 CREAA should be replaced with 'Treaty Establishing a Constitution for Europe'.[42] For this minimum change, a new referendum should be held, since according to § 3 CREAA, the Act can only be amended by referendum. In the beginning of 2005, Uno Lõhmus, Judge of the European Court of Justice, referred *inter alia* to the standpoints of the legal experts who had drafted the CREAA[43] and stated that a new EU Treaty would have to be adopted by a referendum, since the CREAA only applies to the Accession Treaty explicitly named in the CREAA.[44]

However, the report of the working group of the *Riigikogu* published subsequently concluded that the European Constitutional Treaty should be treated as a normal international treaty and therefore requires no referendum. The report stated:

> The Treaty Establishing a Constitution for Europe ... is by its nature in a wider sense a constitutional act, which in the meaning of the Constitution must be considered as an international treaty.[45]

The conclusions were not reached unanimously.[46] Insofar as the European Constitutional Treaty never came into force, the report did not have any significant impact on the decisions relating to amendment of the Constitution in 2005. However, some years later, the Lisbon Treaty was approached in a similar way as the European Constitutional Treaty: no amendments were introduced in either the Constitution or the CREAA.

In September 2010 the issue of amending the Constitution was once again brought to the forefront. Rait Maruste proposed a revision of the Constitution in the light of the changes that had taken place during the previous years.[47]

---

[42] Jõks, A. (2005, March 7). *Põhiseaduse leping ja põhiseadus õiguslikke küsimusi* (Legal Questions regarding the Constitutional Treaty and the Constitution). Postimees. http://www.postimees.ee/1460167/allar-joks-pohiseaduse-leping-ja-pohiseadus-oiguslikke-kusimusi.

[43] Laffranque et al. 2002, p. 566.

[44] Lõhmus 2005, p. 78.

[45] *Euroopa põhiseaduse lepingu riigiõigusliku analüüsi töörühma seisukohad lepingu ratifitseerimise küsimuses* (Report of the working group on the European Constitutional Treaty) 2005, para. II 1. (translation by the authors). http://www.riigikogu.ee/v/failide_arhiiv/Riigikogu/epsl_20051211_ee.pdf.

[46] Ibid.

[47] Although Maruste's proposal was no different from his earlier statements, his proposal caused a passionate debate (possibly also because he had embarked on a political career). See Maruste, R. (2010, September 17). *(Päris) vaba Eesti põhiseadus* (The (truly) free Estonian Constitution). Postimees. http://pluss.postimees.ee/314169/rait-maruste-paris-vaba-eesti-pohiseadus.

1.3 Conceptualising Sovereignty and the Limits to the Transfer of Powers

1.3.1 The delegation of powers to the EU is regulated in § 2 CREAA. There are no clear limits to the transfer or delegation of powers to the EU. The brief wording of the CREAA has left several major questions open, e.g. the effect of EU law, for interpretation by the judiciary.

The SC ruled on this issue in 2012. Although in this case concerning the constitutionality of the Treaty Establishing the European Stability Mechanism (ESM Treaty) the SC held that the ESM Treaty is not part of EU law, it included an *obiter dictum* on the potential limits to transfer of competences to the EU.[48] The Court referred to the CREAA and stated that in the view of the Court, 'the CREAA is not an authorisation to legitimise the integration process of the European Union or to delegate the competence of Estonia to the European Union to an unlimited extent'.[49] It can be derived from the reasoning of the SC that any further amendment which leads to deeper integration of the EU and any additional delegation of competences, would need additional approval by referendum. According to the SC:

> If it becomes evident that a new founding treaty of the European Union or amendment to a founding treaty of the European Union gives rise to a more extensive delegation of the competence of Estonia to the European Union and a more extensive interference with the Constitution, it will be necessary to seek the approval of the holder of supreme power, i.e. the people, and presumably to amend the Constitution once again.[50]

1.3.2 The SC has not given much attention in its case law to the concept of sovereignty. The SC has addressed this concept directly only in the case concerning the constitutionality of the ESM Treaty in 2012:[51]

> [T]he Constitution does not require, despite the strict wording of the sovereignty clause, observation of absolute sovereignty. ... [M]embership of the EU and in international organisations has become a natural part of sovereignty in this day and age.[52]

In the reasoning that followed, the SC treated sovereignty as a principle that can be weighed against other principles. In fact, Estonian doctrine has never known a prevailing theory of absolute sovereignty. Instead, already in 1936 the leading professor of international law, Ants Piip, observed that the contemporary concept of sovereignty had changed significantly; it was only understood as a leeway within

---

48 SCebj 12.07.2012, 3-4-1-6-12, paras. 217–233.

49 Ibid., para. 223.

50 Ibid., para. 223. See also Sect. 2.7. for a discussion regarding potential limits arising out of principles such as the budgetary autonomy of Parliament.

51 SCebj 12.07.2012, 3-4-1-6-12.

52 Ibid., paras. 128 and 130. See on this judgment: Ginter 2013, p. 335 et seq.

the limits deriving from international law. Sovereignty, according to Piip, was at that time already used in this sense in interstate relations.[53] In contemporary writings, sovereignty was no longer considered an absolute concept.[54] On the other hand, the SC also stated in the ESM case: 'The core essence of sovereignty is the right of discretion in all matters, irrespective of external influences'.[55] This can be considered as an expression of the classic concept of sovereignty.

In Estonian constitutional doctrine, the classic Kelsenian distinction between internal and external sovereignty is deep-rooted.[56] The former refers to the state's power competences; the latter bears the connotation of independent statehood in the international arena.[57] Kelsen's disciple Artur-Tõeleid Kliimann introduced this distinction to Estonian doctrine, re-naming internal sovereignty as independence (*sõltumatus*) and external sovereignty as self-determination (*iseseisvus*).[58] However, according to the Government's translation of the Constitution (and as used in the work of e.g. Albi[59]), '*iseseisvus*' equals independence and '*sõltumatus*' equals sovereignty. In this way the translators have put sovereignty on an equal footing with independence and the similarity of this distinction with the Kelsenian approach is no longer recognisable.

These two concepts can be found again in the wording of § 1(1) of the Constitution, and e.g. the Legal Expertise Committee for the Constitution of the Republic of Estonia adopted this dualistic definition of sovereignty in its expert report.[60] However, the significance of the two elements is not entirely clear. The author suggests that internal sovereignty ought to be considered as identical with democracy because it refers to the unimpeded exercise, by the people, of the highest inner-state decision-making competence that lies in a democratic state. The SC proclaimed in 2012: 'The sovereignty of the people gives rise to the sovereignty of the state and thereby all state institutions obtain their legitimation from the people.'[61] External sovereignty, on the other hand, concerns rather the commitment of the state in international relations and means simply the right of the state to govern itself.

Thus, the concept of sovereignty remains classic but the approach to the concept has been influenced by modern legal theory – the SC considers sovereignty to be open to restrictions and weighing. Therefore, not every infringement of sovereignty necessarily constitutes a violation, and an infringement may be justified by

[53] Piip 2007, p. 415 et seq. Cf. Kalmo and Luts-Sootak 2010, p. 14.

[54] See also two Estonian edited volumes: Kalmo, Luts-Sootak 2010; Loone et al. 2004.

[55] SCebj 12.07.2012, 3-4-1-6-12, para. 127.

[56] Kelsen 1925, p. 110.

[57] Ibid.

[58] Kliimann 1935, p. 49 et seq.

[59] Albi 2005, pp. 25, 30 et seq., 126.

[60] The 1998 Report of the Legal Expertise Committee, supra n. 14.

[61] SCebj 12.07.2012, 3-4-1-6-12, para. 127.

weightier reasons, e.g. by the financial stability of the euro area, including of Estonia, like in the case concerning the ESM Treaty.

1.3.3 Whilst there is no clear articulation of any limits on EU law, the fundamental principles of the Constitution have been articulated in the case law of the SC. The current interpretation of the Constitution implies that potential limits could indeed be surpassed by referendum. It could be argued that the fundamental values of the Constitution, such as the right to national self-determination, preservation of the Estonian nation and culture, etc., are inalienable and therefore cannot be forsaken.

1.3.4 The Constitution does not directly proclaim the supremacy of the Estonian Constitution, although § 3(1) provides that state authority shall be exercised solely pursuant to the Constitution and laws which are in conformity therewith. Currently, the Constitution is interpreted in a Europe-friendly manner, and Estonia, with a liberal approach to the economy and law, has shown a remarkable willingness to adapt to EU principles, led by its SC, with the suspension of Constitutional provisions in the event of a conflict with EU law.[62] According to the SC:

> Proceeding from of § 2 of the Constitution of the Republic of Estonia Amendment Act …, pursuant to which when Estonia has acceded to the European Union, the Constitution of the Republic of Estonia shall be applied taking into account the rights and obligations arising from the Accession Treaty, the result of the adoption of this Act is that only that part of the Constitution which is in conformity with European Union law or which regulates the relationships not regulated by European Union law can be applied. The effect of those provisions of the Constitution that are not compatible with European Union law and are thus inapplicable, is suspended.[63]

On 11 May 2006 the SC, this time performing constitutional review, adopted an opinion regarding the interpretation of the Constitution (the *Transition to the Euro* case).[64] According to the opinion:

> In the substantive sense this [i.e. § 2 CREAA] amounted to a material amendment of the entirety of the Constitution to the extent that it is not compatible with European Union law. … only that part of the constitution is applicable, which is in conformity with European Union law or which regulates relationships that are not regulated by the European Union law. The effect of those provisions of the constitution that are not compatible with the European Union law and are thus inapplicable, is suspended.[65]

The decisions of the SC have been criticised in the dissenting opinions of two justices. Primarily the existence of limitations to this interpretation as well as to the binding nature of the opinion on further practice have been questioned. In a dissenting opinion, Justice Kõve expressly stated that when analysing the implications

---

[62] Ginter 2008. The process of accepting the supremacy and direct effect of EU law in Estonia has been analysed in detail in Ginter 2007, pp. 337–345.

[63] CRCSCo 26.06.2008, 3-4-1-5-08, para. 30.

[64] CRCSC Opinion 11.05.2006, 3-4-1-3-06.

[65] Ibid., para. 16.

of § 2 CREAA, the Court should have also clarified the meaning of § 1 as well as the meaning of Chapter I of the Constitution in its entirety.[66] Dissenting Justice Kergandberg equally pointed to the need for an analysis of the nature and impact of § 1 CREAA.[67]

In the absence of a decision by the SC, it is currently not clear whether § 1 CREAA should be seen as what it says grammatically – a limitation to Estonia's membership in the EU – or as an interpretative tool, to the benefit of the fundamental principles of the Estonian Constitution in the case of a conflict with EU law. The grammatical text of the CREAA seems to favour the first interpretation. On the other hand, the practice of the supreme courts of 'old' Member States, including but not limited to the famous *Solange* saga,[68] would rather support the second alternative. Indeed the court may even find that both solutions can be applied simultaneously.

1.4 Democratic Control

1.4.1 There are no specific rules in the Constitution concerning the participation of the Estonian Parliament in the EU decision-making processes. In 2004 the *Riigikogu* Rules of Procedure Act (RRPA)[69] was amended and a new standing committee, the European Union Affairs Committee (EUAC), was introduced.[70] The EUAC is unique since it is comprised of members who at the same time are members of other committees of the *Riigikogu*. The EUAC has the right to compose, in the name of the entire *Riigikogu*, opinions concerning draft EU acts. This position of the *Riigikogu* is in general binding for the Government. However, the Government has also been left a certain amount of discretion in negotiations: the Government is allowed to deviate from this position, but only on exceptional grounds.[71] One exceptional ground would be for example a change of situation during the discussions at the EU level. If the Government does not follow the official position of the *Riigikogu*, it is bound to appear before the EUAC or the Foreign Affairs Committee to provide an explanation.

1.4.2 On the EU accession and constitutional amendment referendum of 2003.

---

[66] Dissenting Opinion of Justice Kõve to CRCSC Opinion 11.05.2006, 3-4-1-3-06, para. 2.

[67] Dissenting Opinion of Justice Kergandberg to CRCSC Opinion 11.05.2006, 3-4-1-3-06.

[68] *Entscheidungen des Bundesverfassungsgerichts* (BVerfGE) 37, 271 (*Solange* I); BVerfGE 73, 339 (*Solange* II).

[69] RT I 2003, 24, 148; RT I, 05.11.2014, 5.

[70] See also Kundla in Mõttus et al. 2012, Introduction to Chapter § 18^1, comm. 5.

[71] Ibid., § 152^4, comm. 5.

1.5 *The Reasons for, and the Role of, EU Amendments*

1.5.1–1.5.2 On the reasons behind the amendments and the factors that influenced the content of the amendments.

1.5.3 The CREAA, introduced by a referendum in 2003, unfortunately entails more problems than it solves. As pointed out above, it was heavily criticised already in the course of the *travaux préparatoires*. The application of the CREAA has shown that some of that criticism was justified. The following proposal is therefore another attempt to point out the key issues regarding the CREAA and to offer a suitable solution to these problems.

Delegation of powers clause Sovereignty and the partial delegation of powers are the key aspects of all international cooperation clauses. The Constitution in § 1(2) establishes a particularly strong sovereignty clause: 'The independence and sovereignty of Estonia are timeless and inalienable.' It is one of the strongest accentuations of sovereignty in Europe[72] and perhaps even the world. It should also be stressed that the fear of a rollback to a Soviet Union-type organisation was the main consideration behind the wording of § 1(2).[73]

Amending the Constitution by a separate act has been sharply criticised. Even if it is not explicitly prohibited by the Constitution, this practice does not constitute a welcome way to amend a legal document of central importance. Amending the text of the Constitution should be preferred in order to preserve legal clarity and to avoid unnecessary interpretation issues. What is more, both of the relevant sections, § 1 and § 2 CREAA, introduced problems that could have easily been avoided by simply amending the text of the Constitution.

It is not only the EU that restricts sovereign statehood in the globalised world, but also the Council of Europe, NATO, the UN, etc. In 2012 the question of international organisations other than the EU reached the SC in a case regarding the ESM Treaty. The delegation of powers to the ESM was found to be outside of the regulative effect of the CREAA.[74] The SC *en banc* identified an infringement of the principle of sovereignty but found by an extremely narrow majority of ten votes to nine that this was proportionate and justified by substantial considerations.[75] This tactic of reasoning has been sharply criticised, particularly by Justice Luik in his dissenting opinion. Justice Luik clearly held that 'due to the existence of the prohibition on partial waiver of sovereignty, the Constitution does not permit ratification of the Treaty',[76] with reference to § 1(2) of the Constitution.

Indeed, this was perhaps the most problematic point in the reasoning of the SC. Section CREAA does not permit the delegation of powers to any international

---

[72] Albi 2002, p. 42; cf. the table in Albi 2005, p. 26 et seq. and its summarised background p. 30.

[73] Cf. Peep 1997, p. 68.

[74] SCebj 12.07.2012, 3-4-1-6-12, para. 110.

[75] SCebj 12.07.2012, 3-4-1-6-12, paras. 176–203 and 207–210.

[76] Dissenting Opinion of Justice Luik to SCebj 12.07.2012, 3-4-1-6-12, para. 14.

organisation other than the EU and, in the light of this conclusion, the restriction of sovereignty for any other purpose is in fact questionable in the light of § 1(2) of the Constitution. Taking the aforementioned aspects into consideration, it would seem appropriate to amend the sovereignty clause with an exception that would also allow the delegation of powers to other international organisations, instead of restricting its application solely to the EU. Simultaneously, the minimum requirements for such organisations should be established to exclude the legality of any potential attempt to incorporate Estonia into any organisation that does not respect human rights, democracy or the rule of law.[77] A good example of such a clause is Art. 3a of the Constitution of Slovenia (see the Slovenian report in this Volume).

European Union clause In addition to a more detailed delegation of powers clause, (a) revised provision(s) concerning the functioning and aims of the EU should be introduced. The author of this section recommends the introduction of a set of conditions for the EU in the Constitution. The freedom that was regained in 1991 is based on respect for human dignity, democracy, the rule of law, a social state and the national identity of Estonia. These fundamental principles should be respected both nationally and within the EU. The guarantee of equally effective protection of fundamental rights on the EU level should also be mentioned. These criteria are necessary to stress the objectives of the EU for Estonian political decision-makers and to guarantee an effective constitutional review of future amendments to the EU treaties. An example of such a clause is Art. 23(1)1 of the German *Grundgesetz* (see the German report in this Volume). In the Estonian Constitution, the systematic position for this type of article could be in the preamble or in Chapter I or IX of the Constitution; the preferable position, however, would be a new § 120(1) of the Constitution.

Qualified majority clause There are three possible procedures for delegating powers to the international level. The first and probably most democratic procedure would be the holding of a referendum for any delegation of powers. The second possibility would be to follow the regular legislative procedure in Parliament, i.e. powers could be delegated by a simple majority. The third alternative, in a sense the golden mean, would be to introduce a legislative procedure which requires a qualified parliamentary majority.

Compared to other possibilities, referendums are usually financially more onerous, more time-consuming and often politically unpredictable. Furthermore, powers are delegated through international treaties and, according to § 106(1) of the Constitution, no ratification of any international treaty shall be submitted to a referendum. However, a mere simple majority would not correspond to the importance of the decision. Therefore, in order to stress the importance of a delegation of powers, a qualified majority of two-thirds of all the members of the

[77] The best solution would be to add a new section § 1(3) to § 1. Such clause would determine legally that Estonia will remain part of the free world, and Soviet-type organisations would thus be precluded.

Riigikogu, which is presently foreseen in four instances in the Constitution, would seem appropriate. A comparable rule can also be found in Art. 3a of the Slovenian Constitution.

Exercise of power clause According to § 3(1), of the Constitution, state authority shall be exercised solely pursuant to the Constitution and laws which are in conformity therewith. According to § 2 CREAA, when Estonia has acceded to the EU, the Constitution shall be applied taking into account the rights and obligations arising from the Accession Treaty. As the SC asserted in its opinion of 11 May 2006,[78] § 2 CREAA led to a suspension of a large part of the Constitution and to a redefinition of § 3(1) of the Constitution. This has been described as one of the most significant (legal) changes caused by accession to the EU.[79] The SC has even relinquished its competence to perform constitutional review if EU law collides with the Constitution, with reference to the competence provision: '§ 152(2) of the Constitution, as well as the Constitutional Review Court Procedure Act passed for the implementation thereof, must not be applied to the extent that these enable to declare invalid, due to unconstitutionality, a provision relating to EU law of any Act or other legislation, which is in conformity with the EU law on the basis of which it was enacted'.[80]

The main argument in support of the view of the SC is that the SC does not have competence to exercise judicial review over national legislation transposing EU law into national law.[81] This restrictive interpretation of the SC's competence has been sharply criticised with overweighing arguments.[82] Since the Constitution gives the SC universal competence to review all laws that might contradict the Constitution, there can be no doubt that the SC is competent to review all laws that are applied in Estonia. If the SC thereby comes to the conclusion that the object of the review is national legislation transposing EU law, it should take the primacy of EU law into consideration in deciding the case. Otherwise, by suspending some of the norms of the Constitution, the SC would decide on the validity of the norms on which its own competence for constitutional review is based. Pursuant to the Constitution, however, this would be *ultra vires*.[83]

---

[78] See Sect. 1.3.4, CRCSC Opinion 11.05.2006, 3-4-1-3-06, para. 16. Cf. CRCSCj 26.06.2008, 3-4-1-5-08, para. 30.

[79] Madise et al. in Madise et al. 2012, Introduction to the CREAA.

[80] CRCCo 26.06.2008, 3-4-1-5-08, para. 30.

[81] Kalmo 2008, p. 583 et seq.; Laffranque 2007b, p. 535 et seq.; Laffranque 2009, p. 498. Cf. the discussion in Ernits 2011, p. 49 et seq.

[82] Lõhmus 2011, p. 24 et seq.; Mälksoo 2010, p. 147 et seq.; Ernits 2011, p. 37 et seq. and 61 et seq.; Ernits 2012, p. 137 et seq. (See also Sect. 2.9)

[83] Ernits 2011, p. 49 et seq.; cf. Lõhmus 2011, p. 25. In 2015, the SC revised partially its earlier far-reaching position, cf. SCebj 15.12.2015, 3-2-1-71-14, para. 81, 83: 'The fact that any provisions are compatible with European Union law cannot lead to the conclusion that the same provisions are also compatible with the Estonian Constitution or that declaring a provision unconstitutional and repealing it would constitute a breach of European Union law. The connection of a legal act with EU law, or an opinion of any other institution on the compatibility of

It is well established that after accession to the EU, state powers can be exercised not only on the basis of parliamentary laws but also on the basis of directly applicable EU law. However, instead of declaring a conflict between the Constitution and EU law, suspending the Constitution[84] and relinquishing competence for constitutional review, it would be advisable to re-interpret the relevant provisions of the Constitution (and thus still apply them) in conformity with EU law, and thus to apply EU law on the basis of the Constitution to the extent possible. As long as there is no violation of the fundamental constitutional principles, it would be the legitimate way to achieve both: conformity with the EU Treaties and preservation of the Constitution, including the constitutional review competence of the SC.[85] This concept is not new in the context of other EU Member States.[86] It would, however, be an innovation in the Estonian context.

Since § 2 CREAA serves as the basis for the current interpretation of the SC, it would be recommendable to abandon the present text of § 2 CREAA and to choose a solution that better fits the system of the Constitution. Instead of integrating § 2 CREAA into the text of the Constitution, § 3 of the Constitution should be amended with a new para. 2, whereas the existing para. 2 would become the new para. 3. A good example of such a clause is Art. 8(4) of the Constitution of Portugal (see the Portugal report in this Volume). This would help to avoid the erosion of the Constitution and at the same time systematically guarantee that EU law is applied in accordance with the Constitution.

Parliamentary participation and information clause The 1998 legal expert report on the Constitution proposed *inter alia* a further clause introducing the obligation of the Government to inform the *Riigikogu* as early as possible and comprehensively of matters relating to the EU. Although a similar procedure is foreseen in § 152[1] RRPA, no such guarantee is provided by the Constitution. As this question concerns the checks and balances on state powers, it is a constitutional matter. According to the present regulation, the Government is not obliged to involve the Riigikogu in matters concerning the EU and Parliament is not able to effectively demand information and compliance with the parliamentary opinion by the Government. It would therefore be necessary to include such provisions in a

domestic legislation with EU law cannot in itself preclude review of the constitutionality of the legal act within the meaning of § 152 of the Constitution. [...] Within the boundaries set by EU law, including state aid guidelines, the national legislator is bound by the requirements arising from the Estonian Constitution, and the national courts by the duty under § 152 of the Constitution to check the constitutionality of the measure(s) chosen for achieving the aim. By no means does EU law prohibit member states from ensuring domestic fundamental rights to the extent that the exercise of the rights does not endanger the supremacy, uniformity and effectiveness of EU law.' However, it still remains unclear how far would the SC go in recognising the primacy of the EU law over the Constitution.

[84] CRCSC Opinion 11.05.2006, 3-4-1-3-06, para. 16; CRCSCo 26.06.2008, 3-4-1-5-08, para. 30.

[85] Cf. Ernits 2011, p. 61 et seq.

[86] Cf. Ehricke 1995, p. 598 et seq.; Nettesheim 1994, p. 261 et seq.; Heukels 1999, p. 313 et seq.

future reform package (e.g. in Chapter VI of the Constitution). Comparable rules can also be found in Art. 23(2) and Art. 45 of the German *Grundgesetz*.

Further issues The list of the aforementioned problems is not exhaustive. There are further questions, for example whether there should be a parliamentary committee authorised to exercise the rights of the Parliament in matters concerning the EU, whether § 111 and/or § 112 of the Constitution should be amended with a euro clause and/or European Central Bank clause, and whether the Constitution needs to contain an equal rights clause for European citizens. There are, moreover, other issues that should be analysed in depth, e.g. the often-cited § 58 of the Constitution that allows for the restriction of the right to vote of imprisoned Estonian citizens only.

Furthermore, there has been a call for a general renovation of the Constitution of 1992.[87] The need for a general renovation is questionable, since there is no constitutional crisis in Estonia and the Constitution of 1992 has proven, beyond the CREAA, to be well-functioning and, in a historical perspective, the most successful Constitution for Estonia ever.

2 Constitutional Rights, the Rule of Law and EU Law

2.1 The Position of Constitutional Rights and the Rule of Law in the Constitution

2.1.1 Constitutional rights are provided in Chapter II of the Constitution. Five general rights can be identified: a general right to liberty in § 19(1), general right to equality in § 12(1), general right to state protection in § 13(1), general right to organisation and procedure in § 14[88] and a general social right in § 28(2).[89] The chapter on constitutional rights is otherwise rather comprehensive and detailed.[90] Constitutional rights and fundamental principles like the rule of law are enforceable in courts. They are procedurally guaranteed by the general right to address a court in the case of an alleged violation of a right, provided for in § 15(1).

---

[87] Maruste's written report for *Eesti Õigusteadlaste Päevad* (Congress of Estonian lawyers) 2004, cited in Maruste, supra n. 47.

[88] 'The guarantee of rights and freedoms is the duty of the legislative, executive and judicial powers, and of local governments.'

[89] This division was first introduced by Robert Alexy in the first systematic monograph concerning fundamental rights in the Estonian Constitution: Alexy 2001, pp. 51 et seq., 56 et seq., 68 et seq., 73 et seq., 76 et seq.

[90] It contains classic rights and liberties such as the right to privacy in § 26, freedom to choose an occupation in § 29(1), right to property in § 32, inviolability of the home in § 33, right to free movement in § 34, freedom of religion in § 40, secrecy of correspondence in § 43, freedom of expression in § 45, freedom of assembly in § 47, etc., as well as special social rights such as the right to education in § 37.

However, the enforceability of constitutional rights has not been fully developed. It remains disputable in Estonian constitutional law theory whether there is a right to an individual constitutional complaint to the SC on the grounds of the Constitution or whether all courts have the obligation to enforce constitutional rights with no room for a direct complaint to the SC. It can be noted that the Constitutional Review Court Procedure Act (CRCPA)[91] does not foresee an individual constitutional complaint.

2.1.2 Section 11 of the Constitution states: 'Rights and freedoms may be restricted only in accordance with the Constitution. Such restrictions must be necessary in a democratic society and shall not distort the nature of the rights and freedoms restricted'. The aforementioned § 3(1) and § 11 define the general minimum requirements for every restriction: every infringement of a constitutional right requires a legal basis and must be proportional. However, these provisions cannot be considered as sufficient authorisations to restrict a particular constitutional right. If the legislator wants to restrict a particular constitutional right, it must consider the statutory reservation of the particular constitutional right. For example, the second sentence of § 26 of the Constitution states: 'State agencies, local governments and their officials shall not interfere with the private or family life of any person, except in the cases and pursuant to procedure provided by law to protect health, morals, public order, or the rights and freedoms of others, to combat a criminal offence or to apprehend a criminal offender'. This is an example of a clause that states a qualified statutory reservation. Beyond this, there are constitutional rights with a simple statutory reservation (e.g. § 29(1), second sentence: 'Conditions and procedure for the exercise of this right may be provided by law') and rights without any statutory reservation (e.g. § 38(1)). A simple statutory reservation does not add anything substantial to the general minimum requirements, whereas the SC has specified that only other fundamental rights or constitutional values can provide a legitimate justification for an infringement of a fundamental right established without reservations.[92] In every case the state has a duty to justify all infringements of rights and liberties.[93]

2.1.3 The rule of law can be considered as one of the fundamental principles of the Constitution anchored in § 10 and determining the rules and principles for the exercise of state power.[94] The rule of law is the most complex principle in the Constitution, containing further sub-principles such as the separation of powers and due checks and balances, the supremacy of law, the reservation of law and certainty of law, non-retroactivity, legitimate expectations, the principle of proportionality, access to courts, judicial review and judicial independence.

---

[91] *Põhiseaduslikkuse järelevalve kohtumenetluse seadus*. – RT I 2002, 29, 174; RT I, 23.12.2013, 57.

[92] SCebo 28.04.2004, 3-3-1-69-03, para. 28; SCebj 03.07.2012, 3-3-1-44-11, para. 72.

[93] Cf. Ernits in Madise et al. 2012, Introduction to Chapter 2 of the Constitution, comm. 8 et seq.

[94] Cf. CRCSCj 19.03.2009, 3-4-1-17-08, para. 26.

In the Estonian legal commentary, five key elements of the rule of law principle have been identified:[95] (1) restriction of state power by constitutional rights and the principle of proportionality; (2) separation of powers and due checks and balances; (3) legal certainty; (4) legality; and (5) access to courts and judicial review.

Legal certainty is one of the five central postulates of the rule of law principle and is intended to create order and stability in society.[96] The SC has stated:

> The principle of legal certainty is based on § 10 of the Constitution …. In the most general sense this principle should create certainty in regard to the current legal situation. Legal certainty means clarity in regard to the content of valid norms (principle of legal clarity) as well as certainty that the established norms shall remain in force (principle of legitimate expectations).[97]

Legal clarity Legal clarity has a double nature in the Constitution. First, it is a fundamental right guaranteed by § 13(2), according to which 'the law shall protect everyone from the arbitrary exercise of state authority'.[98] Already in its early case law, the SC proclaimed that 'insufficient regulation upon establishing restrictions on fundamental rights and freedoms fails to protect everyone from the arbitrary treatment of state power'.[99] The classic meaning was given to subjective legal clarity by the SC *en banc* in 2002:

> Legal norms must be sufficiently clear and comprehensible, so that an individual can foresee the conduct of public power with a certain probability and can regulate his or her conduct. A citizen must be able – if need be with appropriate advice – to foresee, to a degree that is reasonable in the circumstances, the consequences which a given action may entail. Those consequences need not be foreseeable with absolute certainty: experience shows this to be unattainable.[100]

Secondly, according to the SC, legal clarity also derives as an objective principle directly from the rule of law set out in § 10.[101]

Legitimate expectations Legitimate expectations include three subcategories: *nulla poena sine lege*, non-retroactivity and legitimate expectation in a narrower sense.[102]

---

[95] Ernits in Madise et al. 2012, p. 93, § 10 of the Constitution, comm. 3.4. et seq.

[96] CRCSCj 30.09.1994, III-4/1-5/94; 23.03.1998, 3-4-1-2-98, para. IX.

[97] CRCSCj 02.12.2004, 3-4-1-20-04, para. 12; 15.12.2005, 3-4-1-16-05, para. 20; 20.03.2006, 3-4-1-33-05, para. 21; 31.01.2007, 3-4-1-14-06, para. 23.

[98] SCebj 28.10.2002, 3-4-1-5-02, para. 31; CRCSCj 20.03.2006, 3-4-1-33-05, para. 21; Judgment of the Criminal Law Chamber of the SC (CLCSCj) 28.02.2002, 3-1-1-117-01, para. 12.

[99] CRCSCj 12.01.1994, III-4/1-1/94. See also Alexy 2001, p. 36.

[100] SCebj 28.10.2002, 3-4-1-5-02, para. 31.

[101] SCebj 10.12.2003, 3-3-1-47-03, para. 30; CRCSCj 31.01.2007, 3-4-1-14-06, para. 22.

[102] Ernits in Madise et al. 2012, § 10, comm. 3.4.3.2.

The second element is non-retroactivity which derives from the constitutional interpretation of the SC. The SC proclaimed already in its early case law in 1994: 'One of the general principles of law is that as a rule, laws must not have retroactive effect.'[103] Later the SC, referring to its earlier case law, specified that the legislator is entitled to issue legislation with retroactive effect in areas other than criminal law, but it must thereby take into account the will of the people expressed in the Constitution, bear in mind the general interests of the state, and consider the actual situation as well as the principle of legality.[104] The administrative law chamber of the SC has stated even more precisely that the legislator may give retroactive force to a law if there is a well-founded need, it does not cause disproportionate harm to legitimate expectations and the law is not surprising for the person concerned.[105] Recently, the SC has restricted its point of view: 'It is generally inadmissible to increase obligations with a genuine legal instrument of retroactive force, which means that no legal consequences may be established on actions already performed in the past.'[106]

The third element of legitimate expectations is legitimate expectation in a narrower sense, concerning 'non-genuine retroactive force', which arises 'if it concerns an activity that has started, but has not yet ended by the time of the adoption of a legal instrument, to be more exact, if it establishes prospectively legal consequences for an activity that has started in the past'.[107] The most important definition was provided in 2004:

> Pursuant to the principle of legitimate expectations everyone must have the possibility to arrange his or her life in reasonable expectation that the rights given to and obligations imposed on him or her by the legal order shall remain stable and shall not change dramatically in a direction unfavourable for him or her.[108]

Thus, according to the principle of legitimate expectation in a narrower sense,

> [e]veryone has a right to conduct his or her activities in the reasonable expectation that applicable Acts will remain in force. Everyone must be able to enjoy the rights and freedoms granted to him or her by law at least within the period established by the law. Modifications to the law must not be perfidious towards the subjects of the law.[109]

If something is promised by law, the legitimate expectation is that the promise shall be applied to those who have started to exercise their rights.[110] However,

> [t]he principle of legitimate expectations does not mean that the restriction of persons' rights or withdrawal of benefits is impermissible. The principle of legitimate expectations

103 CRCSCj 30.09.1994, III-4/1-5/94.

104 CRCSCj 20.10.2009, 3-4-1-14-09, para. 50.

105 ALCSCj 17.03.2003, 3-3-1-11-03, para. 33.

106 CRCSCj 16.12.2013, 3-4-1-27-13, para. 61.

107 Ibid.

108 CRCSCj 02.12.2004, 3-4-1-20-04, para. 13; 31.01.2012, 3-4-1-24-11, para. 49.

109 E.g. CRCSCj 30.09.1994, III-4/1-5/94; 31.01.2012, 3-4-1-24-11, para. 49 et seq.

110 CRCSCj 17.03.1999, 3-4-1-2-99, para. II.

> does not require fossilisation of the valid regulatory framework – the legislator is entitled to re-arrange legal relationships according to changed circumstances and, by doing so, inevitably deteriorate the situation of some members of society. The legislator is competent to decide which reforms to undertake and which groups of society to favour with these reforms.[111]

Prohibition of secret laws The rule that only published laws can be valid or the prohibition of secret law plays a central role in the Estonian Constitution – § 3(2), second sentence states explicitly: 'Only published laws have obligatory force'. This norm can be considered as a reaction to the tendency of the Soviet occupation regime to apply secret laws from time to time. In particular, the deportations of March 1949 during which more than 20,000 persons were expatriated and transported to Siberia were based on secret Soviet regulations.[112] Furthermore, since § 3 of the Constitution is located in Chapter I, it not only belongs formally to the core elements of the rule of law principle, but it can also be amended only by a referendum. Beyond this, the *vacatio legis* principle can be considered as part of the principle of prohibition of secret law: 'The requirement arising from the *vacatio legis* principle is that, prior to the entry into force of amendments, persons concerned must have sufficient time to examine the new legislation and take it into account in their activities.'[113]

Legality The rule that the imposition of obligations, administrative charges or penalties and criminal punishments is only permissible on the basis of a parliamentary statute derives from § 3(1) of the Constitution, according to which: 'State authority shall be exercised solely pursuant to the Constitution and laws which are in conformity therewith'. Several sub-principles derive from this norm; the two most important in the present context shall be presented briefly.

According to the principle of parliamentary reservation, the legislator is obliged to regulate essential questions in law itself: 'What the legislator is … obliged to do under the Constitution cannot be delegated to the executive, not even temporarily and on the condition of judicial review'.[114] This defines the separation of powers principle, or, more specifically the division of powers between the legislator and the Government as the issuer of regulations: 'The reservation of law principle delimits the competence of the legislative and executive powers'.[115] Robert Alexy has called this aspect the democratic dimension of the principle of legislative reservation.[116] The SC has stated that in regard to issues concerning fundamental rights, all

---

[111] E.g. CRCSCj 02.12.2004, 3-4-1-20-04, para. 14; cf. CRCSCj 31.01.2012, 3-4-1-24-11, para. 49.

[112] See Jäätma 2006, p. 31.

[113] CRCSCj 16.12.2013, 3-4-1-27-13, para. 51.

[114] CRCSCj 12.01.1994, III-4/1-1/94. See also: CRCSCj 26.11.2007, 3-4-1-18-07, para. 36; 20.10.2009, 3-4-1-14-09, para. 32.

[115] CRCSCj 26.11.2007, 3-4-1-18-07, para. 36; 20.10.2009, 3-4-1-14-09, para. 32.

[116] Alexy 2001, p. 36.

decisions that are essential from the point of view of the exercise of fundamental rights must be taken by the legislator.[117]

According to the principle of legal basis, every infringement of any constitutional right needs a legal basis. According to the SC, '[p]ursuant to this principle an authorisation by the legislator is required for the restriction of fundamental rights by a body ranking lower than the legislator'.[118] Public authority is only entitled to act if there is a legal basis or enabling act permitting it to do so. The law must determine the conditions for and extent of every infringement.

Access to courts and the right to judicial review Access to courts and the right to judicial review result from § 15(1) of the Constitution: 'Everyone whose rights and freedoms are violated has the right of recourse to the courts. Everyone has the right, while his or her case is before the court, to petition for any relevant law, other legislation or procedure to be declared unconstitutional'. This guarantee – a constitutional right in itself – is broad and strong and must be regarded as a core element of the rule of law.[119] It enables the rule of law to be rendered fully justiciable through a constitutional right, i.e. if there is an infringement of any constitutional right which constitutes a violation of any of the sub-principles of the rule of law, the constitutional right is also violated. The SC has also stressed the close tie between Art. 6(1) of the European Convention on Human Rights (ECHR) and § 15(1) of the Constitution: 'The violation of Art. 6(1) of the Convention, found by the European Court of Human Rights, also constitutes a violation of § 15 of the Constitution'.[120]

2.2 *The Balancing of Fundamental Rights and Economic Freedoms in EU Law*

In Estonia, the balancing of fundamental rights with economic free movement rights has not raised substantial constitutional issues or discussion. There have, however, been some cases where such a discussion would have been merited.

In 2009, the media covered the case of Aivo Piirsoo,[121] a truck-driver from a small Estonian village who had been detained in Germany on the accusation of smuggling cigarettes. He had been released due to his innocence. Approximately nine years later, he discovered that his Estonian bank account had a negative

[117] SCebj 03.12.2007, 3-3-1-41-06, para. 21; 02.06.2008, 3-4-1-19-07, para. 25; cf. CRCSCj 24.12.2002, 3-4-1-10-02, para. 24.

[118] CRCSCj 13.06.2005, 3-4-1-5-05, para. 9; 20.10.2009, 3-4-1-14-09, para. 34.

[119] Cf. CRCSCo 05.02.2008, 3-4-1-1-08, para. 3.

[120] SCebj 06.01.2004, 3-3-2-1-04, para. 27.

[121] Henno, E. (2009, November 4). *Saksamaa nõuab eestlaselt miljoneid kroone* (Germany is demanding millions of kroons from an Estonian). Postimees. http://www.postimees.ee/183910/saksamaa-nouab-eestlaselt-miljoneid-kroone.

balance of 6.7 million Estonian kroons (approx. 430,000 EUR). The Estonian Tax and Customs Board had frozen the bank account upon the request of the German authorities due to a claim for tax and interest on the illegal cigarettes. With interest, the total claim amounted to more than 10 million Estonian kroons (i.e. approx. 640,000 EUR). The case made apparent the fact that there is no judicial involvement in administrative cooperation, i.e. authorities can cause a significant change in a person's financial standing without prior judicial review in the Member State of residence of the person. It became apparent that in cases of such cooperation, there is no effective remedy for an ordinary citizen (in this particular case with a monthly salary of ca. 700 EUR) without sufficient funds for a cross-border legal battle. It is at minimum debatable whether this is in line with the requirements of Art. 47 of the Charter of Fundamental Rights of the European Union (the Charter) and the equivalent provisions of the Estonian Constitution.

A similar series of events unrolled when a truck driver, Neeme Laurits, was jailed in Finland for nine months, accused of organising international drug-trade.[122] He was picked up by the Estonian police from his home in Estonia and delivered to the Finnish authorities pursuant to a court order issued by an Estonian judge to execute a European Arrest Warrant (EAW). The accusations related to events in February of the same year. However, Mr. Laurits had not in fact travelled to Finland within the five years before his detention. The main evidence against him in Finland appeared to be the fact that three traffickers arrested in Finland all had his mobile phone number in their phones. Hence, he was treated as the mastermind of the criminal scheme. The actual explanation was that Mr. Laurits had worked in Estonia conducting vehicle roadworthiness tests years ago – and thus they had his number as that of an ordinary service provider. He was later released and acquitted by a Finnish appeals court.

There has been no extensive discussion about the above cases in the Estonian academia. A prominent attorney, Kaido Pihlakas, sharply criticised the system of European arrest warrants in an article published in the media, referring to the fact that Estonia is too eager to trust foreign authorities when executing their requests.[123] He proposed that the relevant procedure be expanded to include the right of a person to be heard before being extradited and that a simpler procedure for obtaining compensation for having been detained should be established. A Member of Parliament and former judge of the ECtHR opined that there is a strong need for local judicial supervision and stated that '[d]omestic control must be

[122] Randlaid, S. (2012, February 1) *Narkoparuniks tembeldatud eestlane pisteti 9 kuuks Soome vanglasse* (Estonian labelled as drug baron and thrown into Finnish jail for 9 months). Estonian National Broadcasting. http://uudised.err.ee/v/eesti/242d45bc-0425-415a-b986-4163decf25dc.

[123] Loonet, T. (2012, February 29). *Advokaat: Eesti täidab Euroopa vahistamismäärusi liiga püüdlikult* (Attorney: Estonia executes European Arrest Warrants too eagerly). http://www.postimees.ee/756124/advokaat-eesti-taidab-euroopa-vahistamismaarusi-liiga-puudlikult.

substantive and not only formal'.[124] The fact that this is not the case with the European arrest warrant is obvious.

Indeed, there seems to be a strong imbalance between the effectiveness of the extradition process and the mechanisms available for obtaining compensation. At a minimum, individuals should be able to initiate compensation mechanisms with their domestic authorities. Thus, the requesting Member State would still obtain full and efficient cooperation from other Member States during the extradition process and at the same take into account that those very same authorities would later be entitled to order compensation measures equally effectively. This would most likely reduce the moral conflict involved, as the risk of actually having to pay compensation would most likely increase significantly.

The third example of a shift in the protection of fundamental rights concerns the excess stocks cases.

2.3 *Constitutional rights, the European Arrest Warrant and EU Criminal Law*

2.3.1 The Presumption of Innocence

2.3.1.1 The first two paragraphs of § 22 of the Constitution stipulate as follows:

> No one may be deemed guilty of a criminal offence before he or she has been convicted in a court and before the conviction has become final.
>
> No one is required to prove his or her innocence in criminal proceedings.

The principle of the presumption of innocence is closely related to the right to liberty and security guaranteed by § 20 of the Constitution ('No one may be deprived of his or her liberty except in the cases and pursuant to a procedure provided by law') and to the grounds for lawful deprivation of liberty listed in § 20.

There has been no significant constitutional debate covering the presumption of innocence in the context of surrender procedures. Instead, more general questions concerning the right to defence during surrender proceedings – in the situation where the courts do not examine evidence for or against the suspicion of a criminal offence set out in a European arrest warrant – have been raised both in the media and in professional discussions in recent years (mainly from 2012 onwards, after media coverage of the Laurits case). However, the legal commentary has found that e.g. in the case of a valid alibi, the surrender of a person should be refused on grounds of conflict with the general principles of Estonian law, whereby

[124] Krjukov, A. (2012, February 5). *Maruste: kodanike väljaandmisel peab olema tugev siseriiklik kontroll* (Maruste: Strong domestic control is needed when extraditing citizens). Estonian National Broadcasting. http://uudised.err.ee/v/eesti/4cd69e51-2204-498c-8d0b-b4aa1377166e.

suspicion of guilt is a precondition for surrender.[125] Until 1 January 2015, it was not possible to refuse a request for surrender due to the general grounds for refusal in international cooperation in criminal matters (*inter alia* conflict with the general principles of Estonian law) specified in § 436(1) CCP, except if there was reason to believe that the request had been issued for the purpose of bringing charges against or punishing a person on account of his or her race, nationality or religious or political beliefs, or if the situation of the person may have deteriorated for any such reasons. Due to the restrictions on the right to appeal an EAW, the SC has not had enough opportunities to rule upon matters regarding surrender. The constitutional aspects of surrender proceedings have not been successfully raised before the courts as of yet. However, the evaluations given by SC to the regulation of extraditions under international treaties could, by analogy, be in some aspects relevant.

Domestic criminal procedure requires that in order to take a person into custody, a reasonable suspicion and legal (constitutional) ground for deprivation of liberty has to be present. The same applies when an EAW is issued by Estonia. In the context of extradition under international treaties, the SC has, in response to the defence's argument that extradition to and the conduct of criminal proceedings in the USA would infringe the fundamental rights of the defendant, acknowledged the limitation of fundamental rights. The SC concluded that the fundamental rights of a person in domestic proceedings were guaranteed since the defence had, during the court proceedings, a possibility to effectuate the right to protection of fundamental rights[126] and, in addition, there was an option to contest the extradition decision (either adopted by the Government or the Ministry of Justice) in an administrative court.[127]

The legal situation of the protection of fundamental rights in the framework of surrender between EU Member States differs from that in domestic criminal proceedings by virtue of the essence of surrender. In EAW proceedings, the right to appeal is restricted, as a ruling made by a county court can be contested only in the circuit court, whose judgment is final (§ 504(4) CCP). In order to ensure the uniform application of law, the SC has only explained that restrictions of basic rights may occur prior to the issue of an EAW as well as during execution of the EAW in the requesting state, but not through issue itself. Therefore, disputes concerning the existence of a legal ground for deprivation of liberty in Estonia do not include the right to contest an EAW by the requested person in Estonia. If there was no legal ground for detention, the person is entitled to claim compensation.[128]

Interpreting the evaluation of the SC by analogy, it can be concluded that the constitutional ground for arrest for surrender is § 20(1)6) of the Constitution. The SC has found that arrest for extradition is different from taking a person into custody in domestic criminal proceedings, because in extradition proceedings the

[125] Plekksepp in Kergandberg and Pikamäe 2012, § 492, comm. 7.1.

[126] The legal admissibility of the extradition of a person shall be verified by a court in extradition proceedings pursuant to international treaties.

[127] CRCSCo 29.05.2013, 3-4-1-10-13, para. 11.

[128] CLCSCo 19.09.2011, 3-1-1-93-11, paras. 17 and 18.

decision to deprive the person of liberty has already been made by a court of the requesting state. The principle of mutual recognition in international co-operation in criminal procedure means that the executing state is not allowed to question such a decision. In addition, the grounds for deprivation of liberty may to some extent vary from state to state.[129] The same limitation upon the courts therefore applies accordingly in the case of surrender.

From a wider perspective of a right of defence, in April 2012 the Estonian Bar Association submitted a proposal to the Legal Affairs Committee of the Estonian Parliament to amend the regulation of surrender in the CCP, by way of a brief summary, as follows: (1) refusal to surrender a person on the ground of a conflict with the EU Charter should be provided for; (2) the list of the rights of a person arrested for surrender should be stipulated, including the right to be heard immediately by a judge; (3) the requirements for formalising voluntarily consent to surrender should be defined; (4) there is a need for more specific regulation in cases where a party requests that additional information be sought from a requesting state. The committee forwarded the proposal to the Minister of Justice. As the Minister of Justice did not support the amendments,[130] in November 2012 the Estonian Bar Association asked the Chancellor of Justice to verify the conformity of the surrender regulation with the Constitution. The Chancellor of Justice initiated the respective proceedings in April 2013.

Although the legal analysis of the Chancellor of Justice is still pending, he expressed his preliminary opinion in the request for information sent to the Minister of Justice.[131] He found that in addition to the legal interpretations, how the regulation governing surrender procedures is applied in practice, in other words, what kind of problems have been raised in protecting the fundamental rights of the persons affected and how these problems have been handled, must inevitably be explored. The Chancellor of Justice also established that there is no such overview on the Ministry of Justice website or in the explanatory memorandum to the latest

---

[129] CLCSCo 19.12.2013, 3-1-1-101-13. In this case the defence lawyer claimed that the CCP is unconstitutional to the extent that it does not provide for alternatives (bail, electronic surveillance) to custody in extradition proceedings, as are provided for in domestic criminal proceedings. According to the SC decision, there is no unlawful unequal treatment because of the different legal situation: in extradition proceedings the decision to take a person into custody has already been made by the requesting state, whereas in domestic proceedings it is decided by the domestic court. Furthermore, the legislator has not expanded the domestic regulation of imposing bail or electronic surveillance instead of taking a person into custody to the regulation of international co-operation in criminal procedure.

[130] Minister of Justice letter No. 8-2/8349 (23 October 2012), http://adr.rik.ee/jm/.

[131] Chancellor of Justice letter No. 6-1/130507/1301793 (16 April 2013), http://adr.rik.ee/okk/. The opinion of the Chancellor of Justice is based on the same document. Both co-authors of Sect. 2.3 were involved in preparing this preliminary opinion. After this report was written, the new Chancellor of Justice, Ülle Madise, took office in March 2015. She issued a final opinion in which she found in an abstract review of constitutionality that the provisions of the Code of Criminal Procedure relating to the EAW are not in conflict with the Constitution. See Chancellor of Justice Letter No. 6-1/130507/1601468 (7 April 2016), http://adr.rik.ee/okk/dokument/4680282.

draft law dealing with international co-operation in criminal matters.[132] Some individual cases have been discussed in the media as well as in legal commentary.[133]

In short, the Chancellor of Justice focused his analysis on two main topics: (1) can the person affected and his/her counsel effectively exercise the right of defence in surrender proceedings, considering the short time limits foreseen by the CCP; this includes the question of how the clause enabling a court to obtain additional information from a requesting state is applied in practice; (2) how the state reacts or should react if subsequently it becomes evident that the person surrendered has been acquitted or released on other grounds (the issue of compensation for damage).

The Estonian legal literature has pointed out that the exercise of some procedural rights in surrender proceedings is problematic, e.g. the right to notify a person close to the detainee of his/her detention.[134] Additionally, the question of the conformity of the CCP with Art. 12 of the EAW Framework Decision (FD)[135] has been raised, as § 503(4) of the CCP (mandatory detention until factual surrender) excludes the use of alternatives to detention in surrender proceedings.[136] Another issue that has raised concerns is the conformity of § 492(3) of the CCP (Estonia will surrender its citizens who reside permanently in Estonia for the period criminal proceedings are conducted, provided that the punishment imposed in the requesting state will be executed in Estonia), with the prohibition of discrimination.[137]

From the perspective of the right of defence, it is important to keep in mind the readiness and willingness of defence lawyers to request, if needed, clarification of foreign law from the requesting state or a preliminary ruling from the Court of Justice (CJEU). The Chancellor of Justice has also addressed the Estonian Bar Association and raised the question of the need for training for defence lawyers. Additionally, the Chancellor of Justice has requested examples of problematic practices of surrender.[138] In its reply, the Bar Association advised that in the course of its supervision, it has discovered no misgivings on the part of advocates regarding surrender proceedings.

2.3.1.2 Estonian law guarantees the right to be heard in court before surrender to all persons, irrespective of consent to surrender (§ 502(4)3) CCP). An analysis of Estonian court practice has confirmed this.[139]

---

[132] Draft Act No. 578 SE, adopted 12 June 2014.

[133] E.g. Albi 2015.

[134] Plekksepp in Kergandberg and Pikamäe 2012, § 502, comm. 3.4.

[135] Council Framework Decision of 13 June 2002 on the European arrest warrant and the surrender procedures between Member States (2002/584/JHA), [2002] OJ L 190/1.

[136] See CLCSCo 19.12.2013, 3-1-1-101-13. By analogy, the alternatives to detention are excluded also in surrender proceedings, although once in the practice of the county courts, bail was imposed instead of detention (Order of the Harju County Court 12.09.2008, 1-08-4553).

[137] Plekksepp in Kergandberg and Pikamäe 2012, § 504, comm. 4.1. and § 492, comm. 3.2.

[138] Chancellor of Justice letter No. 6-1/130507/1301794 (16 April 2013), http://adr.rik.ee/okk/.

[139] The summary of court practice (2004–2012) is based on the MA thesis by Marje Allikmets 2013.

Estonian courts have on several occasions been faced with claims on the part of the defence that the person has an alibi, that the person was not aware of the allegations or that the respective circumstances set out in the EAW were superficial. In contesting an EAW, requested persons and their counsel have sought to prove the existence of an alleged alibi, although they have often been unsuccessful for different reasons. In court practice from 2002–2012, there were at least two cases where the court, in order to refute reasonable suspicion, decided to request additional information from the requesting state.[140] In general, an analysis of court practice indicates that overall, no preliminary review of evidence takes place and, as a rule, Estonian courts follow the principles of mutual recognition and mutual trust strictly.

In connection with the right to be heard, it is worth mentioning that the Estonian Bar Association has proposed that a person's right to be heard by a judge immediately after his/her arrest should be included in the CCP. However, in a reply to the Chancellor of Justice, the Minister of Justice held that such amendment would have no added value.[141] A requested person has the opportunity to express his/her opinion on three occasions: upon arrest, at the court hearing in which detention before surrender is decided and at the court hearing in which surrender is decided. According to the Minister of Justice, additional questioning would not in any way support the possibility of the Estonian court to evaluate the decision of the requesting state to issue an EAW in respect of a particular person objectively, if the evidence reviewed by the requesting state is unknown to the Estonian court. The Minister of Justice also referred to cases where a person has claimed his/her innocence and has managed independently to obtain essential supportive evidence within 24 hours, in result of which the EAW has been withdrawn.[142] However, the Minister of Justice also noted that a refusal to surrender a person to a Member State does not entail the obligation of the requesting state to withdraw the EAW and to remove the notice of a wanted person in the Schengen Information System (SIS). According to the Minister of Justice, it has happened that after an Estonian court has refused surrender, the person has been arrested based on an SIS notice in some other Member State and has nevertheless been surrendered.

The Chancellor of Justice is of the opinion that a person's right of defence can be seen as a right to get explanations from his or her defence lawyer with regard to

[140] Harju County Court Order 22.12.2011, 1-11-13412 and Tallinn City Court Order 21.11.2005, L-15/05.

[141] Minister of Justice letter No. 10-2/13-4291 (4 June 2013), http://adr.rik.ee/jm/. Here and subsequently, the opinion of the Minister of Justice is based on same document if not shown otherwise.

[142] (2007, April 26) Itaalia nõudis Eestist välja süütu mehe (Italy demanded extradition from Estonia of innocent man). Eesti Ekspress. http://ekspress.delfi.ee/news/paevauudised/itaalia-noudis-eestist-valja-suutu-mehe.d?id=69107847; see also Plekksepp in Kergandberg and Pikamäe 2012, § 490, comm. 1.2.

surrender proceedings and the related documents, as well as the use of defence tactics such as presenting evidence in order to preclude or restrict surrender. Considerable weight should be attributed to the right to consent or refuse to consent to surrender. According to § 499(3) CCP, consent, once given, cannot be withdrawn. The Chancellor of Justice has therefore proposed that the Minister of Justice consider elaborating the requirements for how consent is obtained and formalised. Statistical data show that the majority of surrendered persons consent to surrender.[143] However, it is notable that Neeme Laurits, who was surrendered to Finland and acquitted after 9 months of detention and whose case was extensively discussed in the Estonian media, is among those who have consented to surrender. According to Laurits, he had agreed to surrender because the police told him that if he did, even if the request was groundless, then at least he could be back from Finland in a couple of days. If he did not agree, he would be thrown in jail for several months in Tallinn and then would be surrendered to Finland anyway.

At the same time no data exists on the number of cases in which consent has been given but the initial suspicion has turned out to be unsubstantiated or the criminal proceedings have been terminated for some other reason. The Chancellor of Justice has emphasised that even if it can be assumed that protection of the fundamental rights of the requested person will be endangered only in exceptional cases, it is the obligation of the state to guarantee a fair trial to everyone. Therefore, in his opinion, the factual application of the regulation of surrender proceedings has to be explored.

The Chancellor of Justice also recalled that the time limits in surrender proceedings are tight and, because of this, it is of practical importance to evaluate whether the exercise of the right of defence is at all effectively possible within these time limits. The true aim of the right to be heard and its impact on the decision taken in surrender proceedings is also relevant.

If a surrender decision cannot be made within the prescribed term, the time period for making the surrender decision shall be extended by thirty days (§ 502(7) CCP). A court may set a term for the submission of additional information (§ 502 (5) CCP) by the requesting state, although it may extend the length of detention. The right of a court to acquire additional information and the right of the parties to request it from the court are relevant first and foremost in cases of incomplete or ambiguous EAWs, e.g. if there are doubts concerning the identity of the person requested or the facts relating to or classification of the criminal offence (i.e. check of double criminality, if allowed).[144] The SC has acknowledged the need for additional information where there is uncertainty whether the limitation period for the criminal offence has expired or it is unclear whether the person requested has absconded from criminal proceedings.[145]

---

[143] According to the summary of court practice 2004–2012, consent was given to 226 (74.3%) of the total of 304 surrender requests.

[144] Plekksepp in Kergandberg and Pikamäe 2012, § 502, comm. 5.

[145] CLCSCo 18.03.2009, 3-1-1-9-09, para. 8.3.

In the above-mentioned preliminary opinion, the Chancellor of Justice noted that in the case of reasonable doubt, a request for additional information may be of critical importance. Surrender of a person may be refused if additional information has not been submitted by the deadline determined by the court. Additional information may, and as previously mentioned has, in (rare) individual cases resulted in the withdrawal of an EAW.

In practice, defence lawyers seek to convince the court of the need to request additional information, especially when the substance of the charge is incomplete or unclear. In reply to one such request, a county court explained that in surrender proceedings there is no room for disputes in respect of the substance of the charge.[146] In most cases such request will not be satisfied. Based on the court practice, it is possible to conclude that in deciding on a request for additional information, the court will primarily rely on the opinion of the prosecutor.[147]

In the preliminary opinion, the Chancellor of Justice categorised the potential problems in exercising the right of defence in surrender proceedings as follows: (1) defective regulation (e.g. insufficient time limits); (2) officials violating their duties (e.g. not allowing examination of respective documents; not explaining a person's rights to them); (3) incompetent defence lawyers; (4) concurrence of these reasons. In domestic court proceedings there is the additional factor of the understanding of judges of the role and competence of courts in surrender proceedings.

Overall, an analysis of court practice reveals that, as a rule, Estonian courts do not carry out preliminary judicial review in order to evaluate the factual basis of an EAW, although the right to be heard is guaranteed to all requested persons. On several occasions, the courts have *expressis verbis* found that the court hearing the EAW case does not have any competence to deal with the substance of the charge, and is allowed only to check whether circumstances exist which preclude or restrict the surrender of the person. Therefore, the majority of court rulings deciding on surrender are laconic in their formulation. The same applies to decisions on detention for the purposes of surrender. In the latter case, the courts usually write in their decisions that the court has no reason to doubt the information sent by the requesting state and, in order to ensure the execution of the EAW, the person has to be detained. Courts have sometimes additionally explained that it is reasonable to assume that upon issuing an EAW, the requesting state has ascertained the relevant facts on which the charge is based and that this is sufficient for arrest as a precondition for surrender.[148]

In legal commentary, however, it has been remarked that the examination of an EAW is not always formalistic and, in the case of reasonable doubt, certain substantial requirements have to be followed to control the validity of relevant information.[149] The SC has, in the context of the expiry of the limitation period of the

[146] Harju County Court Order 21.03.2012, 1-12-2617.

[147] E.g. Harju County Court Order 29.05.2012, 1-12-73 and 03.01.2011, 1-10-16977.

[148] E.g. Harju County Court Order 03.12.2012, 1-12-11375.

[149] Plekksepp in Kergandberg and Pikamäe 2012, § 492, comm. 7.1.

offence, noted the following: if an EAW does not contain information that the person requested has absconded from the criminal proceedings, the court must hold that this has not happened. If the court still has doubts concerning the circumstances on which an EAW is based (including expiration of the limitation period), the court has to acquire additional information from the requesting state.[150]

2.3.2 *Nullum crimen, nulla poena sine lege*

This principle is stipulated in § 23(1) and (2), first sentence of the Constitution:

> No one may be convicted of an act which did not constitute a criminal offence under the law in force at the time the act was committed.
>
> No one may be sentenced to a penalty that is more severe than the one that was applicable at the time the offence was committed.

The principle of legality in criminal matters derives from this provision, in conjunction with § 13(2) of the Constitution, which provides that everyone is entitled to protection by the state and of the law.

As far as it is known to the Experts, in practice no problems with the application of the *nulla poena sine lege* rule have arisen. Estonia has on one occasion refused the surrender of a person to Sweden due to the fact that the act committed (infringement of the Swedish law regulating the collection of debts) was not punishable in Estonia and it was not an offence in the list of 32 offences in the EAW FD.[151] In legal literature, there has been no additional discussion on this subject. The legal commentary only refers to the decision of 18 July 2005 of the German Constitutional Court and to the CJEU *Advocaten voor de Wereld* decision.[152]

In the view of the Experts, there is a justified concern regarding the legal regulation of surrender, as the 32 crimes stipulated in the EAW FD include offences that are not harmonised in EU law. In addition, this may cause problems relating to the proportionality of the offence on which an EAW is based. The SC has stated in *obiter dictum* that in the case of an offence other than one stipulated in the EAW FD, the court may not solely rely on the qualification of the act stated in the EAW by the requesting state, and must therefore verify whether the facts of the case correspond to the necessary elements of an offence stipulated in Estonian law.[153]

---

150 CLCSCo 18.03.2009, 3-1-1-9-09, para. 8.3.

151 Harju County Court Order 21.11.2007, 1-07-14422.

152 Plekksepp in Kergandberg and Pikamäe 2012, § 491, comm. 2.2.

153 CLCSCo 18.03.2009, 3-1-1-9-09, para. 8.2.

2.3.3 Fair Trial and *In Absentia* Judgments

Everyone's right to attend all hearings held by a court in his/her case is stipulated in § 24(2) of the Constitution. The CCP provides some grounds for a court hearing without the participation of the accused. As an exception, a criminal matter may be heard in the absence of the accused if his/her whereabouts in Estonia cannot be established, there is sufficient reason to believe that he/she is outside the territory of Estonia and is absconding from the court proceedings, reasonable efforts have been made to find him/her and the court hearing is possible without the accused (§ 269(2) CCP). If an *in absentia* hearing is not possible due to the facts of the case, there may be grounds for issuing an EAW.

2.3.4 The Right to a Fair Trial – Practical Challenges Regarding a Trial Abroad

2.3.4.1 Estonia does not provide any practical assistance to surrendered citizens or permanent residents. In the view of the Chancellor of Justice,[154] it would be important to explore the practical aspects of implementing EAWs and, if necessary, to learn from any mistakes.

In response to the Chancellor of Justice, the Minister of Justice has stated that the rare, negative cases covered by the media have not been caused by any miscarriage of justice by Estonian law enforcement authorities, but by a reappraisal of the evidence in the requesting state.

In response to the question whether the state should be obliged to give necessary contact information to persons surrendered, the Minister of Justice responded that Estonia does not have information about the authorities a person could turn to in order to get more information about one's rights in another Member State.

The Minister of Justice replied to the Chancellor of Justice that the state does not have any information concerning the criminal proceedings of surrendered persons in other Member States. Thus, there is no plan to analyse 'the fate' of surrendered persons. Likewise, Estonia does not give information to other states about criminal proceedings in which Estonia has issued an EAW. According to the Minister of Justice, there have only been a few cases in one Member State where, figuratively speaking, the person surrendered has come to the Estonian embassy on the following day asking for help in returning to Estonia.

In practice, individuals themselves and their defence lawyers have sometimes claimed that they do not have any information about the proceedings in another Member State and that Estonia should protect and help its citizens in surrender

[154] Preliminary opinion of the Chancellor of Justice, Chancellor of Justice letter No. 6-1/130507/1301793 (16 April 2013), http://adr.rik.ee/okk/.

proceedings.[155] Estonia, however, does not have any public or non-governmental organisations that provide assistance to surrendered persons.

Unquestionably, several problems arise when participating in criminal proceedings in another Member State, e.g. starting with the need for translation. Questions regarding the guarantee of fundamental procedural rights equally to citizens and permanent residents do not arise only in the case of surrender, but also in all other cases involving foreigners. Freedom of movement within the EU has raised the number of alien suspects and accused persons. Ideally, the state should provide additional help for its citizens and permanent residents in proceedings in other Member States, even though under recent EU directives defence rights in the requesting state are now more clearly regulated.

2.3.4.2 According to information from the Minister of Justice, 8,508 criminal convictions entered into force in 2013, 94 (1.1%) persons were partially acquitted and 73 (0.86%) were fully acquitted (this data may include cases where the prosecutor withdrew the charges or the proceedings were terminated on grounds other than acquittal). In 2012, the percentage of partially or fully acquitted persons was 1.62% (156 of 9,638).[156]

Between 2011–2013 only one of all the persons surrendered to Estonia was partially acquitted. According to the official data,[157] during these years 67, 61 and 88 EAWs, respectively, were issued in Estonia. At the time of the compilation of this data, during those years, 31, 39 and 45 persons, respectively, were surrendered to Estonia (including surrenders on the basis of EAWs issued in earlier years). Therefore, the percentage of surrendered persons who have been acquitted cannot be reliably compared to the percentage of individuals who have been acquitted in domestic criminal proceedings.

There is no information on how many of the individuals surrendered from Estonia have subsequently been found innocent.

The legal literature has pointed out a problem which arises from a so-called negative conflict of competency, i.e. a situation where none of the Member States involved foresee any rules for compensation for violations that occur in surrender proceedings.[158] One of the reasons may be the absence of such rules in the EAW FD.

With regard to compensation for damage, the Chancellor of Justice has made a proposal to analyse whether the Minister of Justice could help surrendered

[155] Harju County Court Order 27.03.2012, 1-12-2397.

[156] Urvo Klopets (adviser in the Criminal Policy Department of the Ministry of Justice) in response (e-mails of 13 and 17 June 2014) to the enquiry of Saale Laos (6 June 2014). For statistical data see also '*Kuritegevus Eestis 2012*' (Crime in Estonia in 2012), p. 29. http://www.kriminaalpoliitika.ee/sites/krimipoliitika/files/elfinder/dokumendid/17._kuritegevus_eestis_2012_0.pdf.

[157] Webpage of the Ministry of Justice, statistics on international legal aid. http://www.just.ee/et/eesmargid-tegevused/rahvusvaheline-oiguskoostoo/rahvusvahelise-oigusabi-statistika.

[158] Plekksepp in Kergandberg and Pikamäe 2012, § 490, comm. 6.2.2.

individuals by publishing overviews of the rules on state liability and pertinent court practice in the Member States that submit the most EAWs to Estonia.

The Minister of Justice is of the opinion that Estonia could compensate for damage only in cases where Estonia is the requesting state. The SC has stated that the state's obligation to pay fair compensation even in the case of a lawful restriction in an extraordinary manner of some fundamental right (obligation to endure the performance of criminal procedural acts in respect of a person, as criminal proceedings serve the public interest) arises from the Constitution.[159] In the opinion of the Chancellor of Justice, the same principle applies to international co-operation in criminal procedure, including surrender. The Compensation for Damage Caused in Offence Proceedings Act (entered into force 1 May 2015) includes rules on compensation for damage caused by measures applied in the course of international co-operation in criminal proceedings.[160]

Publication in the media of the Neeme Laurits case in Finland brought about public debate and calls for a more thorough control of EAWs by the domestic courts, including from politicians (e.g. statement of the head of the Constitutional Committee of the *Riigikogu*).[161]

In another case, a person surrendered to Italy who had been accused because he had been a passenger in the same bus as the actual criminals, was released three months later.[162] There has also been at least one negative case concerning identity theft, in which a person was surrendered to France, although the accused claimed that his passport had been stolen; he was released soon after the surrender.[163] In this case, it was problematic that the court had not requested any necessary supplementary information.

2.3.5 The Right to Effective Judicial Protection: The Principle of Mutual Recognition in EU Criminal Law and Abolition of the Exequatur in Civil and Commercial Matters

2.3.5.1 The above-mentioned *Piirsoo* case[164] is remarkable, but unfortunately there is no public information as to whether the topic has been discussed any further in Parliament or at the Governmental level.

---

[159] E.g. SCebj 31.03.2011, 3-3-1-69-09, paras. 60 and 64.

[160] RT I, 20.11.2014, 1, Compensation for Damage Caused in Offence Proceedings Act § 2(4), see also explanatory memorandum to Draft Act No. 635 SE, paras. 12 and 13.

[161] See supra n. 124.

[162] Filippov, J. (2008, December 18). Itaalia vaikib Eesti juveeliröövlitest (Italy silent on Estonian jewel thieves). http://ekspress.delfi.ee/news/paevauudised/itaalia-vaikib-eesti-juveeliroovlitest.d?id=27684285; see also supra n. 142.

[163] Plekksepp in Kergandberg and Pikamäe 2012, § 492, comm. 4, with reference to Harju County Court Order 06.06.2008, 1-08-6004.

[164] Also reflected in the paper by Albi 2015, p. 176.

2.3.5.2 There has been no extensive debate on the move to mutual recognition in criminal matters. However, related issues have arisen in the context of specific cases. In legal commentary, Plekksepp has criticised the shift to mutual recognition in criminal matters, stating that unlike the free movement of goods, penal law is a societal and cultural construction, based on agreements and values recognised in the particular Member State.[165]

2.3.5.3 From a critical point of view it could be concluded that it is largely unclear what the role of the courts is in safeguarding individual rights in surrender proceedings, what level of protection is guaranteed by the Constitution and what, in addition to the formal prerequisites for surrender, the courts can assess. There is no relevant CJEU case law as of yet and it is not clear how the Charter can and will be applied in practice.

In short, Estonia tends to satisfy all EAWs. Court practice indicates that courts in Estonia operate exactly pursuant to the regulation in the CCP (and therefore pursuant to the EAW FD) and, as a rule, they have not established any new grounds for refusal to execute an EAW.

As of 31 December 2012, courts in Estonia have refused to execute 8 (i.e. 2.6% of all) EAWs. Only in one notable case did a court refuse surrender on the grounds of a general provision of international co-operation, as the accused had a valid alibi.[166] However, it has to be said that in many other similar cases, courts have satisfied the request to surrender. On three occasions, Estonia has refused surrender on the grounds that the double criminality requirement was not fulfilled.[167] On one occasion, the EAW was considered to be an international rogatory letter.[168] A requesting state has twice annulled an EAW after Estonia asked for additional information,[169] and Estonia has once refused surrender due to expiry of the limitation period.[170]

[165] Plekksepp in Kergandberg and Pikamäe 2012, § 490, comm. 1.2.

[166] Harju County Court Order 29.03.2007, 1-07-3718; see also Plekksepp in Kergandberg and Pikamäe 2012.

[167] Tartu County Court Order 24.04.2012, 1-12-3543 (causing damage to a person's health did not constitute a criminal offence under Estonian law, as the health disorder caused persisted less than four weeks); Harju County Court Order 25.09.2008, 1-08-12380 (theft of a CD-player is a misdemeanour under Estonian law because of the low value of the object) and 21.11.2007, 1-07-14422 (infringement of the Swedish law regulating collection of debts).

[168] Harju County Court Order 31.03.2008, 1-08-4051.

[169] Harju County Court Order 22.12.2011, 1-11-13412 and Tallinn City Court Order 21.11.2005, L-15/05.

[170] Tallinn Circuit Court Order 17.11.2008, 1-08-13649.

2.3.5.4 The question of proportionality arises in the context of deprivation of liberty (detention for surrender), as this constitutes an intensive restriction of a fundamental right. To date, the European handbook on how to issue a European arrest warrant,[171] which also introduces a proportionality test, is just an advisory guideline.

The Minister of Justice has explained that even though the CCP does not provide any requirement of a proportionality test, various guidelines and trainings have emphasised that authorities conducting proceedings should consider proportionality. The Minister of Justice has confirmed that Estonia has not submitted any EAWs that have been in conformity with the EAW FD but not proportionate.

In the Experts' view, application of the EAW FD needs to be assessed and problems that arise should be resolved through amendments to the EAW FD (if application of the EAW FD on the national level is problematic). If the competence of the local courts is to be reinstated, the problems this aims to resolve (e.g. re-establishment of the requirement of double criminality, pre-evaluation of evidence, etc.) must first be identified. It is therefore difficult to support a general proposal to widen the jurisdiction of the courts of the executing state to expand preliminary judicial review. It is clear that the amount and quality of evidence may vary depending on the stage of the pre-trial procedure, and the prerequisites for suspicion of guilt (e.g. for arrest) may differ among the Member States. As a starting point, it may be reasonable to reassess the time-limits for proceedings and to focus on requesting additional information without having false modesty about distrusting the judicial authorities of another Member State.

2.4 *The EU Data Retention Directive*

2.4.1 The implementation of the Data Retention Directive 2006/24/EC[172] (DRD) has not raised any serious constitutional concerns in Estonia. The Directive was implemented in national law by amendment of the Electronic Communications Act (ECA) in 2007.[173] According to § 111^1 ECA, communication data is generally retained for one year. Requests submitted and information given to specific authorities is retained for two years. In the interest of public order and national security, the Government can extend these terms of retention.

[171] Council of the European Union, 17195/1/10 REV 1 (17 December 2010).

[172] Directive 2006/24/EC of the European Parliament and of the Council of 15 March 2006 on the retention of data generated or processed in connection with the provision of publicly available electronic communications services or of public communications networks and amending Directive 2002/58/EC, [2006] OJ L 105/54.

[173] Draft Act No. 62 SE (28 May 2002).

By the amendment of 2012,[174] the legal classification of requests submitted by law enforcement agencies to communication services providers was downgraded from 'measures of surveillance activities' to 'general investigative activities'. This means that certain special legal requirements for surveillance activities, *inter alia*, the agencies' obligation to notify the person subjected to surveillance measures after their completion, no longer apply to the requests concerned. Additionally, through this amendment, the right of request was no longer restricted to criminal proceedings exclusively, and was extended to misdemeanour proceedings. This right, which had been exclusive to the specific prosecution authorities, was extended to other authorities entitled to process administrative offences (e.g. the Environmental Inspectorate, the Financial Supervisory Authority and the tax and customs authorities). Aware of the European Commission's critical approach to the vague term 'serious crime' used in the Directive, the legislator defended the amendment by declaring that the right to define the term 'serious crime' lies with the national legislator.[175]

The explanatory memorandum to the amending act did not consider questions concerning the compatibility or proportionality of the measures envisaged, rather the motivation for their adoption was based particularly on the necessity to reassess the needs of internal security after the terror attacks in Madrid and London in 2004–2005.[176]

According to the Estonian legislator[177] and the prevailing legal opinion,[178] the statutory duties provided for in the DRD did not interfere with the right to secrecy of correspondence guaranteed in § 43 of the Estonian Constitution,[179] as the retention obligation refers only to connection data but not to its content. Although the retention of connection data does encroach on the right to the inviolability of private life guaranteed in § 26 of the Constitution, the latter is seen as less entitled to protection than the right to secrecy of correspondence.[180] The general diagnosis is that these topics are not in the awareness of the Estonian public at large.[181] At the same time, the practical realisation of an e-state – including e-governance, e-healthcare and e-voting, to name only a few areas – has long become reality in Estonia.

---

[174] Draft Act No. 175 SE (6 February 2012).

[175] Explanatory memorandum to Draft Act No. 175, supra n. 174, p. 6.

[176] See explanatory memorandum to Draft Act No. 62, supra n. 173, pp. 11 and 13.

[177] Ibid., p. 12.

[178] Kask et al in Madise et al. 2012, § 43, comm. 6.

[179] 'Everyone has the right to confidentiality of messages sent or received by him or her by post, telegraph, telephone or other commonly used means. Derogations from this right may be made in the cases and pursuant to a procedure provided by law if they are authorised by a court and if they are necessary to prevent a criminal offence, or to ascertain the truth in criminal proceedings.'

[180] See explanatory memorandum to Draft Act No. 62, supra n. 173, p. 12.

[181] See also Tigasson's critical remarks on the lack of public awareness concerning the topics of eavesdropping and surveillance in Estonia. Tigasson, K.-R. (2013, October 30). *Klaasist maailm* (Glass world). Eesti Päevaleht. http://epl.delfi.ee/news/arvamus/kulli-riin-tigasson-klaasist-maailm.d?id=66999970.

Concerning the disclosure of personal information, the Estonian SC has without further consideration approved the Estonian lawmaker's general decision to disclose the identity of the defendant in court decisions (the latter are generally made public via the Internet).[182] It has also approved the right of creditors to publicly disclose their debtors, arguing that this constitutes an appropriate instrument to protect the legitimate interests of the former.[183] These judgments exemplify the Court's disposition to accept restrictions to the right to privacy and/or the secrecy of correspondence where it finds the given grounds justifiable.

In a recent ruling of February 2015, the Criminal Law Chamber of the SC also delivered its opinion on the invalidation of the DRD and its legal impact on national law.[184] In its decision, the Chamber acknowledged that the invalidation of the DRD does not automatically lead to the unconstitutionality of the respective national law, and upheld the constitutionality of the Estonian rules on data retention discussed above as in force prior to the amendments of 2012. According to the Chamber's majority view, the classification of insurance fraud as a 'serious crime' was up to the legislator, while the proportionality of the measure was ensured in particular by the requirements applicable to surveillance activities.[185] Two out of the six justices of the Chamber presented a dissenting opinion. Among other issues, they challenged the adequacy of the procedural guarantees under the measures, and questioned the Chamber's view concerning the proportionality of the general one-year data retention period.[186]

There is another aspect that has in the past made data retention an unlikely topic for particular concern in Estonia. This is the issue of national security. Due to its historical experience and geo-political position, since the restoration of independence in 1991, Estonia has regarded NATO and therewith the U.S. as the strongest guarantors of its sovereignty and security interests.[187] For this reason, Estonia unequivocally supported – rhetorically and militarily – the U.S. invasion of Iraq, notwithstanding the strong opposition of e.g. Germany and France.[188] This may help explain Estonia's willingness to prioritise security matters over aspects of personal freedom.

Based on the above, it seems rather unlikely that the SC would have considered declaring measures on data retention – even if they were not part of the EU legal order – unconstitutional prior to the CJEU's decision to annul the DRD.

---

182 See, e.g., CLCSCo 10.09.2007, 3-1-1-35-07.

183 E.g. Judgment of the Civil Chamber of the Supreme Court (CiCSCj) 21.12.2010, 3-2-1-67-10, para. 22.

184 CLCSCj 23.02.2015, 3-1-1-51-14.

185 Ibid.

186 CLCSCj 23.02.2015, 3-1-1-51-14, dissenting opinion of Justices Kergandberg and Laos para. 5 et seq. Furthermore, the judges underlined that if the Criminal Chamber had doubts concerning the conformity of the regulations with the Constitution, it would by law be obliged to refer the decision on the constitutionality of the legal norms to the SC *en banc* (ibid., paras. 1 and 3).

187 See also: Sprūds 2012, p. 60 et seq.; Kaldas 2006, pp. 97 and 107 et seq.

188 Ibid.

The author's view is corroborated by the Estonian answers to the Questionnaire on the Area of Freedom, Security and Justice and the Information Society for the FIDE Congress in Tallinn 2012.[189] Concerning the question of the impact of the Data Retention Directive on the legal order of the Member State, Estonia's answers focus on the Directive's vital role in the fight against terrorism and serious crime and reiterate the importance of every Member State to implement the Directive as soon as possible.[190] Equally, the invalidation of the DRD by the CJEU did not attract any special interest at societal level in Estonia. However, the Ministry of Justice in cooperation with the Ministry of Economic Affairs and Communications decided in spring 2014 to conduct a legal analysis on the rules in question. Additionally, the Estonian Chancellor of Justice has asked the Ministries of Justice, of the Interior and of Economic Affairs and Communications for their opinion on the constitutionality of the national regulation in force. The Government's official conclusions are still pending at the time of writing in May 2015.

2.5 Unpublished or Secret Legislation

2.5.1 In the context of EU law, the issue of unpublished or secret measures has arisen in case law on the applicability of measures adopted immediately before EU accession.

In 2006, the SC was confronted with the question of whether EU legislation, which had not been published in Estonian, was binding on individuals. In two decisions of the Administrative Law Chamber of the SC of 10 May 2006, the applicants argued that they were not to be blamed for incorrectly declaring their goods to the customs authorities. The case related to customs declarations filed immediately after the accession of Estonia to the EU. According to the applicants, they did not knowingly submit false data to the customs authorities as 'they did not and could not have known it, as the EU rules were hard to access and the relevant Estonian regulations were passed, so to speak, at the last minute'. The SC stated that ignorance of the law does not release the declarant from the duty to submit correct data to the authorities. The court also decided that since the applicant acted as a professional customs broker, it was irrelevant whether the EU acts had been published in Estonian.[191]

Curiously enough, this decision relies on a number of cases from the CJEU regarding substantive rules. Yet the decision makes no reference to the obligation of the court of last instance to refer matters of EU law for a preliminary ruling (Art. 267 TFEU). Almost exactly at the same time, namely on 24 March 2006, a Czech court, faced with a similar dilemma of EU legislation having to be published in the

---

[189] Antonova et al. 2012, p. 319 et seq.

[190] Ibid., p. 325 et seq.

[191] ALCSCj 10.05.2006, 3-3-1-65-05 and 3-3-1-66-05.

official language of the Member State, referred a question to the CJEU, which led to the famous *Skoma-Lux* decision.[192]

Consequently, the SC had to revisit its earlier position. As an example of creative judicial writing, the Court placed the responsibility on the CJEU, stating that '[a]t the time of the processing of the current administrative matter, the CJEU has in its more recent practice expressed a clear position regarding the central importance to the rights of individuals of the requirement to publish EU legal acts in the language of the Member States, which is why in solving of the current case it is not appropriate to take into account the positions of the chamber expressed in the 10 May 2006 decisions'.[193]

In the *Pimix* case, the CJEU, responding to a request from the Estonian SC, confirmed that 'the relevant provisions of Regulations Nos 1789/2003 and 1972/2003 could not be enforced against individuals in Estonia with effect from 1 May 2004, since they had not been properly published in Estonian in the Official Journal of the European Union or reproduced in Estonian national law'.[194]

The Constitution foresees that laws have to be published and that only published legislation can have mandatory force; this is also a key part of the rule of law. According to Estonian legal doctrine, publication of laws is a necessary precondition for their legal existence as such.[195] Accordingly, the prevailing opinion is that unpublished legislation cannot be binding and valid laws cannot be declared secret. The Estonian rule is stricter, and the law is considered non-existent instead of merely 'not enforceable'.

Another question relates to secret regulations of a minister (or of the Government). Such regulations mainly concern national security, e.g. regulations concerning the methods used by that authority to secretly gather information, but also e.g. the requirements for encrypted materials and processing and protection thereof. Section § 3(2) of the Constitution, which states that only published laws may have binding force, does not explicitly mention 'regulations'. Non-publication of some regulations is *expressis verbis* allowed by § 4(2) of the *Riigi Teataja seadus* (the Estonian State Gazette Act)[196] and is based on the understanding that 'law' in the sense of § 3(2) of the Constitution must be interpreted to mean only Acts of Parliament. In these cases, the State Gazette publishes only the title, date and number of the regulation together with its unclassified provisions. However, this interpretation of § 3(2) is not mandatory: the SC has not yet answered the question whether the word 'law' in the meaning of § 3(2) of the Constitution only refers to Acts of the Parliament or also to regulations of the Government or a minister. Although Acts of Parliament are the only 'laws' in the formal sense, 'law' in the substantive sense includes all acts that are addressed to an undetermined number of addressees. Thus, in the substantive sense, regulations are also

[192] Case C-161/06 *Skoma-Lux* [2007] ECR I-10841, para. 37.

[193] ALCSCj, 13.10.2008, 3-3-1-36-08, para. 21.

[194] Case C-146/11 *Pimix* [2012] ECLI:EU:C:2012:450, para. 42.

[195] Merusk et al in Madise et al. 2012, § 3, comm. 4.

[196] *Riigi Teataja seadus*. – RT I 2010, 19, 101.

'laws'.[197] Furthermore, there are good reasons to treat regulations as laws in the sense of § 3(2) of the Constitution. First, there is neither a theoretical nor a practical need to enact secret regulations because everything that must remain secret may also be adopted by an administrative act that will be classified according to the State Secrets and Classified Information of Foreign States Act.[198] Secondly, it is questionable whether a universal legal norm can be valid at all without prior publication, since an unpublished act cannot be followed by the public and cannot therefore be socially effective.[199] Thus, there is no consensus among Estonian scholars whether § 3(2) excludes secret regulations of the Government or a minister or not.

A practical example of unpublished documents having a character similar to unpublished legislation is the question of references to national or international standards, such as e.g. CEN and CENELEC as well as ISO and IEC. For instance in construction related disputes, the standards form a part of the rules relevant to solving disputes. As the standards are not available without charge, they may be considered similar to unpublished legislation *de facto*. So far the Estonian courts have not addressed this issue and the standards have been accepted as relevant in litigation. For example in civil litigation, a county court has referred to standard EN 976-2 regarding underground tanks of glass-reinforced plastics when dismissing a buyer's damage claim that relied on a lack of installation instructions in the documents handed over with a purchased underground tank.[200]

2.6 *Rights and General Principles of Law in the Context of Market Regulation: Property Rights, Legal Certainty, Non-retroactivity and Proportionality*

The Estonian SC has taken a relatively liberal approach towards accepting EU law as interpreted by the CJEU.[201] There have been very few cases in the SC in which the argument of EU law being contrary to national constitutional law has arisen.

Such cases have primarily concerned the taxation of excess stocks (of e.g. sugar) that took place at the time of the accession of Estonia to the EU in 2004.[202] There

[197] Cf. Merusk 1995, p. 13.

[198] *Riigisaladuse ja salastatud välisteabe seadus*. - RT I 2007, 16, 77.

[199] The concept of legal validity, according to Gustav Radbruch, includes three elements: a legal, a social and a legal philosophical element, see Radbruch 1914, p. 158 et seq. The publication of a universal act can be considered as a precondition for social effectiveness. If it is lacking, the validity of the act is questionable.

[200] Harju County Court Judgment 16.03.2011, 2-06-11240, para. 7; upheld on appeal by the Tallinn Circuit Court 20.03.2012.

[201] For an analysis of the practice of the SC, see Ginter 2008.

[202] For a detailed discussion, see Albi 2009, pp. 46–69 and Albi 2010, pp. 791–829. Albi's analysis suggests that the standard of protection of e.g. legitimate expectations and property rights by the CJEU in these cases was significantly lower than in the established Estonian case law.

were many issues with constitutional implications in the matter, however only two will be mentioned here: the issue of legal certainty and the right to property. Undertakings were requested to make payments for excess stocks of certain products as of 1 May 2004. Up until the last minute, it was not clear which products would be subject to the tax and how it would be determined what stock would be considered normal and what would be considered to be in excess of that normal. The relevant regulations were, however, not adopted by the European Commission in due time. EU Regulation 1972/2003 entered into force only on 1 May 2004, and the draft was amended immediately before its enactment – i.e. on 10 April 2004 and 20 April 2004. In Estonia, the Surplus Stocks Act, implementing the EU regulations, was published on 27 April 2004 and took effect on 1 May 2004. This gave the relevant undertakings nowhere near enough time to adjust their behaviour or dispose of excess stocks.

The most famous case where property rights were invoked is the 5 October 2006[203] decision of the SC (the excess stocks case). The applicant challenged the administrative prescriptions ordering it to pay a fee on its excess stock of sugar at the time of the accession of Estonia to the EU. The applicant (unsuccessfully) argued, *inter alia*, that the challenged administrative acts as well as the legislative provisions which formed the legal basis for those acts breached provisions of the Estonian Constitution protecting the rights of enterprise and property. The applicant also requested that the relevant regulations of the European Commission be set aside because they breached the Estonian Constitution.

In the light of the SC's stringent rule of law case law, it is very doubtful that in a wholly internal situation such a significant financial impact, imposed over such a short period of time, would have been acceptable under national constitutional rules.[204]

2.7 *The ESM Treaty, Austerity Programmes and the Democratic, Rule-of-Law-Based State*

2.7.1 In Estonia, the ESM Treaty was subject to a constitutional challenge by the Estonian Chancellor of Justice. In his legal challenge to the Estonian SC, the Chancellor of Justice pointed out that the unprecedented magnitude of the financial commitment could potentially seriously limit the very ability of the state to ensure the functioning of state institutions, including the judicial system, and the protection

---

[203] ALCSCj 05.10.2006, 3-3-1-33-06, http://www.juradmin.eu/docs/EE01/EE01000007.pdf.

[204] In Case C-146/11 *Pimix*, n. 194, the CJEU decided that the regulations could not be enforced against individuals due to the fact that they had not been published in Estonian. No consideration regarding the temporal scope of application was expressed in the decision.

of the rights and social welfare benefits envisaged under the Constitution.[205] The case has been analysed in detail in other publications.[206]

According to the treaty framework, after the 'temporary correction period', the contribution of Estonia, if the maximum capital calls allowed under the ESM Treaty were to be made, would amount to 1.79 billion EUR.[207] In 2013, the GDP at current prices of Estonia was 18.4 billion EUR.[208] Accordingly, the maximum contribution would amount to approximately 9.7% of the GDP. Estonia's commitment to the European Financial Stability Facility (EFSF) is close to 2 billion EUR.

The issue of whether those amounts would be added together or absorbed was of central focus during the parliamentary debate, where the reporting Member of Parliament (MP) was unable to provide a consistent response.[209] The debate is best illustrated by the following question of MP Igor Gräzin:

> You have heard that they are not summed. I have heard that they are. You have heard one thing, I have heard another. Hasn't the thought crossed your mind that if we are talking about billions, it would be wise to check if they are or are not summed?

The fact that the contribution of Estonia is very large was also one of the central arguments of the national constitutional challenge, where the constitutionality of the 'emergency voting' mechanism set out in Art. 4(4) of the ESM Treaty was questioned.

It was argued that the emergency voting provisions render this mechanism contrary to the principle of parliamentary democracy, the principle of parliamentary prerogatives, parliamentary control over public finances and the principle of a democratic state subject to the rule of law. More generally, the delegation of responsibility over public finances from Parliament to the executive branch would, according to the petition, break the chain of legitimation and political responsibility; it would greatly impact the budgetary powers of Parliament and its ability to use funds to guarantee the rights and liberties of the people.

The constitutional challenge also focused on the issue of 'incalculable risks' and the Parliament no longer being able to exercise overall budgetary responsibility. In the German ESM case, the German Constitutional Court noted the ambiguities in the Treaty's wording about whether a maximum limit exists, and thus requested Parliament to address this issue in the ratification process. In Estonia, the SC was confident in deciding that the amount set in the Treaty 'is the maximum limit of the obligations of Estonia, which cannot be changed without its consent and without

[205] SCebj 12.07.2012, 3-4-1-6-12 on the ESM Treaty.

[206] Ginter 2013, pp. 335–354; Ginter and Narits 2013, pp. 55–76.

[207] See Art. 42 of the ESM Treaty.

[208] Press release by Statistics Estonia 'Economic growth slowed down in 2013' (11 March 2014), http://www.stat.ee/72427.

[209] Minutes of the XII Riigikogu (30 August 2012), (available in Estonian) http://stenogrammid.riigikogu.ee/et/20120830/.

amending the Treaty'.[210] However, Justice Kõve, one of the dissenting justices, argued along the same lines as the *Bundesverfassungsgericht*, stating that

> I deem it necessary to note that I am not convinced that the opinions of the SC *en banc* on the interpretation of the Treaty are correct. Namely, I am not convinced that the maximum limit of the possible obligations of Estonia according to the Treaty does not in any case exceed 1.302 billion euros and that obligations larger than that may arise for Estonia only through amendment of the [Treaty].[211]

This is evidence of the fact that the existence or absence of an upper limit was discussed in the deliberation room.

The same issue was addressed in the parliamentary debate. When the head of the parliamentary Finance Committee was asked whether the maximum amount of the contribution could be increased under the emergency procedure, the chairperson responded that '[t]his is the information I have at the moment and what I will base my decisions on in today's voting. Should you have different information be sure to let me ... know. ... I suppose it is so'.[212] In a press conference, the Prime Minister of Estonia was quoted as saying '[f]irst the ESM must be ratified and then we can discuss the details'.[213]

The fact that under Arts. 8(4) and 9(3) of the ESM Treaty the capital calls have to be met 'irrevocably and unconditionally', within seven days, was not analysed from the point of view of the Constitution. In a dissenting opinion, six justices proclaimed that '[t]his is the most important case in the history of [Estonian] constitutional review'.[214] In the same dissenting opinion, the six justices pinpointed the very same issue, writing that '[w]e find that in addition to Art. 4(4) of the Treaty referred to by the Chancellor of Justice, also the irreversible and unconditional nature of the financial obligations to be assumed by the Treaty ... and the limited nature of judicial review of the operations of the ESM ..., as referred to by Anneli Albi ..., should have been addressed as related provisions'. In the opinion of the dissenting judges, this condition also should have been taken into account when analysing the seriousness of the interference with the Constitution. According to the dissenting judges, as the obligations are irrevocable and unconditional, '[c]onsequently, the *Riigikogu* cannot, without breaching the Treaty, alleviate the effect of

---

210 SCebj 12.07.2012, 3-4-1-6-12, para. 144.

211 Dissenting Opinion of Justice Kõve to SCebj 12.07.2012, 3-4-1-6-12. Estonian law does not recognise the term 'concurring opinion' which is why, although justice Kõve supported the final decision, the opinion is titled 'dissenting'.

212 Quoted text by MP Sven Sester, see minutes of the XII Riigikogu, VIII session (18 December 2014), (available in Estonian) http://stenogrammid.riigikogu.ee/et/201412181000. The final comment by MP Sester was edited out of the revised version of the official transcript.

213 Quote by Andrus Ansip as provided by Kuusik, I. (2012, August 14). *Ansip: kõigepealt tuleb ESM ratifitseerida, siis räägime detailidest* (Ansip: First the ESM must be ratified, then we can discuss the details). Postimees. http://majandus24.postimees.ee/939704/ansip-koigepealt-tuleb-esm-ratifitseerida-siis-raagime-detailidest.

214 Dissenting Opinion of SC Justices Jõks, Järvesaar, Kergandberg, Kivi, Kull and Laarmaa to SCebj 12.07.2012, 3-4-1-6-12.

possible negative consequences for Estonia arising from the application of Art. 4(4) of the Treaty'. Dissenting Justice Luik added along the same lines:

> Now it is time to ask: what is/will be left of the *Riigikogu*'s financial sovereignty besides a merely formal competence to decide on the ratification of the Treaty in question and on the post-ratification obligation to establish a legal environment necessary for the fulfilment of the financial obligation assumed irrevocably and unconditionally, and to reserve 1,153,200 million euros to ensure the satisfaction of a claim filed at any given time? Perplexed, I place three question marks here.

The narrow majority of the SC concluded that Art. 4(4) of the ESM Treaty does not breach the Constitution of Estonia. The Court confirmed that the ESM Treaty affected the financial competences of Parliament, including those of future parliaments and thereby also the financial sovereignty of the state. The Court recognised that budgetary powers are one of the core competences of Parliament. The essence of this competence is the right and duty of Parliament to decide on the revenue and expenditure of the state. It added that, 'the state must use public assets in a manner which enables the performance of the duty … to guarantee the protection of fundamental rights and freedoms'.[215] The Court decided that the interference with the parliamentary powers was justified.

The Court expressly excluded the possibility that the seriousness of the interference could be derived from the fact that it constitutes a vast financial obligation.[216]

Differently from the German *Bundesverfassungsgericht*, which relied on the fact that the *Bundestag* remains in control of decision-making, the Estonian court accepted the reduction of the powers of Parliament in order to provide financial stability. The SC decided that 'the economic and financial sustainability of the euro area is contained in the constitutional values of Estonia as of the time Estonia become a euro area Member State'.[217] According to the Court,

> [e]conomic stability and success ensure the planned receipt of state budget revenue. Incurring necessary expenditure ensures constitutional values. The obligation to guarantee fundamental rights arises from § 14 of the Constitution. Extensive and consistent guarantee of fundamental rights is extremely complicated, if not impossible, without a stable economic environment.[218]

The Estonian decision was very much focused on the close connection between fundamental rights and having the necessary finances available to secure their existence.

While the ESM Treaty is not considered as EU law,[219] in an *obiter dictum* the Court considered it necessary to point out potential constitutional limitations for further EU integration.

---

[215] SCebj 12.07.2012, 3-4-1-6-12, para. 139.

[216] Ibid., para. 190.

[217] Ibid., para. 163

[218] Ibid., para. 166.

[219] As was confirmed later by the CJEU in Case C-370/12 *Pringle* [2012] ECLI:EU:C:2012:756.

2.7.2 There has been no substantial discussion about the constitutionality of other proposed measures, such as Eurobonds and the Banking Union, from the point of view of the potential of exposing the country's citizens and residents to unlimited liability for bank failures in other European countries.

2.7.3 Not applicable; Estonia has not been subject to a bailout programme.

2.8 Judicial Review of EU Measures: Access to Justice and the Standard of Review

2.8.1 We have no information of any cases where the applicants would have challenged the validity of secondary EU law via the preliminary ruling procedure. It is possible that such arguments have arisen within the context of national proceedings, but there have been no references for a preliminary ruling that pose such questions.[220] However, the possibility to invoke EU regulations against individuals was addressed in the so-called 'sugar saga' vis-à-vis rules regulating the imposition of financial duties on excess stocks at the time of EU accession.

2.8.2 It is the impression of the Experts that there seems to be a discrepancy between the strict application of the principle of proportionality to the legislation of the Member States when compared to the methodology applied when reviewing the legality of secondary EU law. In the context of the free movement of goods, for example, it is not uncommon for the CJEU to point to an abundance of more lenient alternatives available to the legislator as sufficient grounds to declare national measures illegal. In judicial review of secondary EU law, however, such an approach is rarely to be seen, and the Court focuses more narrowly on issues such as the existence of a proper legal basis for the measure. Accordingly, the author would suggest that a stricter standard of judicial review of EU measures could be argued for. For example, the CJEU could in fact exercise a stricter review of concepts such as subsidiarity. Although subsidiarity is a core concept of EU law that is prominently displayed in the first chapters of any respectable EU law textbook, one has to look carefully to find any cases where it has been considered by the CJEU in the context of review of EU legislation. As a rare example, in *Vodafone*, referring back to *Imperial Tobacco*,[221] the CJEU analysed the conformity of an instrument of secondary EU law with the principle of subsidiarity, confirming that the measure's objective could best be achieved at EU level.[222]

The rarity of such review has in fact led to statements such as echoed by the spokesperson of the European Commission, stating that '[t]he issue here is that

[220] A full list of references from Estonia can be found on the page *Eesti kohtute eelotsusetaotlused* (available in Estonian) http://www.riigikohus.ee/?id=872.

[221] Case C-491/01 *Imperial Tobacco* [2012] ECR I-11453.

[222] Case C-58/08 *Vodafone* [2010] ECR I- 04999, paras. 72–79.

subsidiarity is a political concept rather than a judicial one. Every proposal we make, we believe, respects subsidiarity'.[223] This may be interpreted as a sign of confidence that subsidiarity is something for the Commission to assess without fear of judicial review.

2.8.3 In Estonia, the SC is rather open towards review of constitutionality/legality of legislation, regulatory acts of the executive branch and administrative action. Judgments of the CRCSC establishing the unconstitutionality of national laws and regulations are quite regular.[224] By way of recent examples, in June 2014 the SC declared legislative measures regarding pensions for judges to be unconstitutional.[225] In January 2014, the court declared unconstitutional a law establishing differentiated state fees depending on whether an applicant used digital means to address the court.[226] In many cases, the annulment of a law has been based on fundamental principles of law, such as legitimate expectations, equal treatment and proportionality.

2.8.4–2.8.5 In its 25 April 2006 ruling (in the case related to the effects of the Polish challenge to the excess stock rules), the SC recognised the exclusive competence of the European Court to decide on the invalidity of secondary Community law, as was established in *Foto-Frost*, and the obligation of a domestic court to make a reference, where doubts as to such validity arise.[227]

The SC has accepted that in the case of a contradiction between Estonian and EU law, the Estonian law should be disapplied without initiating constitutional review proceedings.[228] It is not clear what the approach of the SC would be should a contradiction with the fundamental principles of Estonian constitutional law arise. The Court has so far not adopted a position similar to that in the German Constitutional Court's *Solange II* judgment[229] or the ECtHR's *Bosphorus* judgment[230] that would assume that the EU standard of protection of rights is equivalent

[223] Quoted in Mahony, H. (2012, May 29). National parliaments show 'yellow card' to EU law on strikes. EU Observer. http://euobserver.com/social/116405.

[224] In the period 1993–2004 the CRCSC declared an act or a provision unconstitutional in 75.5% cases (68 out of 90 cases), see Aaviksoo 2005, pp. 295–307. According to another source, in the period 2010–2013, the SC declared a norm or absence of a norm unconstitutional on 72 occasions. See information provided by the SC in 2014, (available in Estonian) http://www.riigikohus.ee/vfs/1712/Lisa%202_PS%20jarelevalve%20lahendite%20taitmine.pdf. In 2014, the SC heard 48 constitutional review cases and in 23 cases declared the relevant provisions unconstitutional, see: Teeveer et al. 2014, (available in Estonian) http://www.riigikohus.ee/vfs/1885/Kohtute%20aastaraamat%202014.pdf.

[225] SCebj 26.06.2013, 3-4-1-1-14.

[226] SCebj 21.01.2014, 3-4-1-17-13.

[227] ALCSCo 25.04.2006, 3-3-1-74-05, para. 21; Case C-314/85 *Foto-Frost v. Hauptzollamt Lübeck-Ost* [1987] ECR I-04199.

[228] ALCSCo 07.05.2008, 3-3-1-85-07, para. 38.

[229] *Entscheidungen des Bundesverfassungsgerichts* (BVerfGE) 37, 271 (*Solange* I); BVerfGE 73, 339 (*Solange* II).

[230] *Bosphorus Hava Yolları Turizm ve Ticaret Anonim Şirketi v. Ireland* [GC], no. 45036/98, ECHR 2005-VI.

to the ECtHR or national standard, unless the applicant proves a significant fall of standards.

2.8.6 In Estonia, the issue of reverse discrimination has not been reflected in case law.

2.9 *Other Constitutional Rights and Principles*

In Estonia, discussions regarding constitutional rights and the rule of law in relation to EU law, beyond the issues explored in the preceding sections, are overall rather scarce.

One example would be the issue of imposing duties on traders for excess stocks accumulated up until the time of accession of Estonia to the EU. The Estonian SC has a long line of case law confirming the principle that taxes can only be imposed by a law enacted by Parliament. A constitutional issue could have arisen vis-à-vis the question of whether regulations such as Commission Regulation (EC) No. 1972/2003 of 10 November 2003 on transitional measures relating to accession of new Member States could in fact impose financial obligations on individuals. The question is further complicated considering that the regulations could not traditionally produce effects in states that were not yet in the EU (e.g. the day before accession). However, the issue remained undecided in the context of the 2004 enlargement, as the possibility to apply the regulations against individuals was excluded by the CJEU on other grounds, namely that they had not been published in the Official Journal in Estonian.

The issue of whether the suspension of large parts of the Constitution by the SC[231] was a good solution[232] or not[233] has been the subject of a passionate debate. Supporters of the SC's approach argue that it would be pointless and useless for the constitutional court of any Member State to have constitutional review competence with regard to EU law. They warn that a deviation from the primacy of EU law in a particular case could lead to a withdrawal from the EU by the Member State in question or even to a collapse of the EU.[234] Critics argue that the material amendment of the entirety of the Constitution that was claimed by the SC lacks a mainstay in the text of the Constitution as well as the relevant will of the people to abandon sovereignty. On the contrary, a clear intention not to abandon sovereignty can be identified in the explanatory memorandum to the CREAA.[235] Furthermore, such an interpretation is an imperative neither from the point of view of the

[231] See Sect. 1.3.4.

[232] Laffranque 2009, p. 483 et seq.; Kalmo 2008, p. 583 et seq.

[233] Mälksoo 2010, p. 132 et seq.; Lõhmus 2011, p. 15 et seq.; Ernits 2011, p. 35 et seq.; Ernits 2012, p. 137 et seq.

[234] Cf. the discussion in Ernits 2011, p. 46 et seq.

[235] Explanatory Memorandum to the CREAA.

Constitution nor because of the primacy of EU law. There are weighty reasons supporting the thesis that the SC did not act on the basis of the competence conferred on it by the Constitution. Neither the Constitution nor any other act confers on the SC competence to rule on the validity of constitutional provisions.[236] On the contrary, the Constitution provides the legal basis for the existence of the SC itself, and gives it the task and the competence to act as the Constitutional Court. If the SC does not perform this function, it endangers not only its own existence but also the continuity of the entire Constitution.[237] This situation has been referred to as the 'erosion of the Constitution' by Uno Lõhmus.[238]

2.10 Common Constitutional Traditions

2.10.1 The SC relied on the central importance of the practice of the EU in determining the principles of law long before Estonia's accession to the EU. Already in September 1994, the SC declared that general principles of law developed by European institutions are incorporated into the fundamental principles of Estonian law.[239] According to the SC,

> [i]n developing the general principles of Estonian law, in addition to the Constitution, the general principles of law developed by the institutions of the Council of Europe and the European Union must also be considered. These principles have their origin in the general principles of law of the highly developed legal systems of the Member States.[240]

A contradiction with those principles would constitute a violation of the Constitution.[241] A norm contrary to the Constitution will be declared null and void by the SC. Such semi-automatic extension of the vast catalogue of general principles of law represents a strong willingness to develop the Estonian legal system in harmony with the European legal system. It may be seen as a demonstration of the general openness and trust of the SC towards European institutions.

As arguments of interpretation, general principles of law provided an impetus for the SC to develop the following principles in the 1990s: legality, non-retroactivity, legitimate expectations and legal certainty more broadly, and the principle of equality.[242] In a certain sense the general principles of law served as a catalyst for a constitutional leap from a post-communist transformation society to a modern democratic rule-of-law-based state of Western European character.

---

236 Lõhmus 2011, p. 18.

237 Ernits 2011, pp. 44, 62 and 69 et seq.

238 Lõhmus 2011, p. 24.

239 CRCSCj 30.09.1994, III-4/A-5/94; 17.02.2003, 3-4-1-1-03.

240 CRCSCj 30.09.1994, III-4/A-5/94.

241 Cf. Ernits 2011, p. 11 et seq.

242 ALCSCo 24.03.1997, 3-3-1-5-97, para. 4.

Accordingly, we consider it likely that 'common constitutional traditions' may indeed exist among the Member States of the EU as well as within the EU itself. It is of course difficult to come up with a list that could claim universal legitimacy.

As an example of the practical difficulties, one can take the different positions adopted by the German *Bundesverfassungsgericht*[243] and the Estonian SC in their respective ESM cases. In the German case, the Court focused on the importance of the fact that Parliament remains the central decision-maker over the budget and that it retains a veto over the decisions of the ESM with Germany's shares. In the Estonian case, the court accepted the need to limit the budgetary autonomy of Parliament for the greater good of having the ESM functional.[244] However, it is our hypothesis that the fundamental principles, even budgetary autonomy, should essentially have a very similar substance throughout the 28 Member States of the EU. There may be differences in the value attributed to each and every one of the principles depending on local geographical, ethnic, religious, cultural or other reasons. For example, the value attributed to the protection of small languages such as Estonian or Gaelic may well be different due to the need to take into account the very real risk of these languages diminishing.

From the Estonian perspective, we would indeed argue that many principles could be regarded as a part of the 'common constitutional traditions', such as the principle of the democratic legitimation of policy-makers, *nulla poena sine lege*, the right to be heard, access to courts, judicial independence, etc. We believe that the Estonian constitutional interpretation would support the interpretation of the German Constitutional Court in the Data Retention Case, and would conclude that it is part of the constitutional identity that the citizens' enjoyment of freedom may not be totally recorded.

2.10.2 It would certainly facilitate identification of the common constitutional traditions if the courts highlighted the long-standing constitutional rights or safeguards for the rule of law in the national constitutions, along with comparative case law on the established standards in different Member States (as suggested separately by Torres Perez and Albi, cited in the Questionnaire).

2.11 Article 53 of the Charter and the Issue of Stricter Constitutional Standards

We appreciate the controversy surrounding the approach adopted by the court in the *Melloni* case and the wording of Art. 53 of the Charter.[245]

---

[243] BVerfGE 131, 152, 194 ff.

[244] For the relevant discussion, see Ginter 2013, pp. 335–354.

[245] Case C-399/11 *Melloni* [2013] ECLI:EU:C:2013:107, paras. 59 and 63.

In the case of Estonia, we do not foresee any substantial controversy concerning the standard of protection of fundamental rights at the national and EU level.[246] The reason for this can be found in the very pro-European approach to interpretation of national constitutional principles by the SC and in the existence of social rights in the Constitution. Already in September 1994, only a year after its establishment, the SC declared that general principles of law developed by the Council of Europe and EU institutions are incorporated into the fundamental principles of Estonian law. A contradiction with those principles would constitute a violation of the Constitution. Such semi-automatic extension of the vast catalogue of general principles of law represents a strong willingness to develop the Estonian legal system in harmony with the European legal system. The pro-European approach of the SC is further evidenced by its willingness to refer to European sources even in cases where the substance of the case is not directly based on European law. For example, the ambiguous legal status of the Charter did not prevent the SC from referring to the Charter several times even before Estonia's accession to the EU.

On 17 February 2003, the SC referred to the Charter as one of the most recent international documents on fundamental rights evidencing the existence of the general principle of good administration.[247] Other pre-accession references to the Charter include the principle that if, subsequent to the commission of a criminal offence, the law provides for a lighter penalty, that penalty shall be applicable,[248] and that the EU recognises the right to social and housing assistance so as to ensure a decent existence for all those who lack sufficient resources.[249] Since EU membership, references to the Charter have included the right to bequeath property (Art. 17).[250] On 28 March 2006,[251] the SC referred to Art. 1 of the Charter when confirming that human dignity is inviolable, the basis for all of the fundamental rights of the individual and the goal of protecting fundamental rights and freedoms.[252]

A clear parallel between the practice of the SC and that of the CJEU in establishing pan-European fundamental rights can thus be seen. Accordingly, we do not predict that the Charter or practice of the CJEU would lead to a lowering of the existing constitutional guarantees vis-à-vis fundamental rights. However, for discussion on some areas where the standards under the Estonian Constitution may be higher (the judicial protection of the rule of law, especially legiti-mate expectations).

---

246 Ginter 2008.

247 CRCSCj 17.02.2003, 3-4-1-1-03, para. 15.

248 SCebj 17.03.2003, 3-1-3-10-02.

249 CRCSCj 21.01.2004, 3-4-1-7-03, para. 20.

250 SCebj 22.02.2005, 3-2-1-73-04.

251 ALCSCj 28.03.2006, 3-3-1-14-06, para. 11.

252 Case C-377/98 *Netherlands v. Parliament and Council* [2001] ECR I-07079.

2.12 *Democratic Debate on Constitutional Rights and Values*

2.12.1 The adoption of the European Arrest Warrant was not surrounded with substantial scholarly debates; the debate primarily emerged in 2012 after some problematic cases were highlighted in the media. The explanatory memorandum to the implementing law briefly dealt with the constitutional conflict concerning the prohibition of extradition of Estonian citizens. According to the document, as accession to the EU was approved by a referendum in 2003 and the EAW system was foreseen in the existing *acquis*, the Constitution must be interpreted taking into account this obligation of Estonia arising from EU law.[253] Thus, the conclusion that the adoption of the EAW Framework Decision was marked by 'the lack of public engagement in the area of defence rights and the almost total absence of political debate on the subject' (see the Questionnaire) is fully applicable also to Estonia. The same applies to the adoption of the EU Data Retention Directive.

There have been no cases where important constitutional issues have arisen and have been referred to the SC at the stage of implementing EU law. The case relating to the implementation of the ESM Treaty is excluded here, as the treaty was considered to be non-EU law.

2.12.2–2.12.3 Considering the long line of case law of the CJEU referring to the system of protection of fundamental rights on the EU level being related to the common constitutional traditions of the Member States, if important constitutional issues have been identified by a number of constitutional courts, it would be appropriate for the application of the questioned measure to be suspended and a review of the measure initiated on the EU level.

The authors have differing opinions in regard to the recommendation to recognise, as a defence on the part of the Member State in an infringement procedure, that unconstitutionality has been identified in accordance with the domestic system of control of constitutionality. On the one hand, there are some cases where the need for more effective protection of fundamental rights, also in the face of EU law, is hard to deny.[254] In such cases the Estonian system of control of constitutionality would be in a position to grant the necessary protection properly and responsibly. Furthermore, as long as the Member States remain the only genuine bearers of sovereign power in the EU, the supremacy of the fundamental principles of their constitutions and the sovereignty of their interpretation by national constitutional courts are also hard to deny.[255] If an infringement procedure were initiated in a case like *Piirsoo* or *Laurits* because of a refusal to deliver the person to another Member State on the grounds that the delivery would violate at least one of the fundamental

---

[253] Explanatory memorandum to the amendment of the Code of Criminal Procedure (RT I 2004, 54, 387).

[254] Cf. e.g. the *Piirsoo* and *Laurits* cases in Sect. 2.2.

[255] Cf. Ernits 2011, p. 60 et seq.

principles of the Constitution (e.g. the rule of law), it would seem to be a good solution to allow the state to defend itself with the argument that unconstitutionality has been identified in accordance with the domestic system of control of constitutionality. On the other hand, we see the danger of undermining the uniform application of EU law that could at one point lead to a fragmentation of the EU along national lines. From this point of view, a procedure whereby the validity of the EU measure is checked by the CJEU with reference to a potential breach of common constitutional principles would be preferable.

2.13 Experts' Analysis on the Protection of Constitutional Rights in EU Law

2.13.1–2.13.2 It is extremely difficult to provide an accurate conclusion regarding whether or not there has been an overall reduction in the standard of protection of constitutional rights and the rule of law in the context of EU law. In our opinion the balance would inevitably have to take into account the significant positive impacts of EU law in the fields of free movement, non-discrimination, gender equality and other areas noted in the Introduction to Part 2 in the Questionnaire. It is perhaps appropriate to refer to the English idiomatic proverb, 'you can't have your cake and eat it'. Accordingly, we have to consider the concept of trade-offs.

For instance, the internal market freedoms regarding free movement of persons or goods provide a considerable benefit to the persons exercising those freedoms. In exchange, the risk of cross-border crime inevitably increases. Accordingly, as a trade-off, a measure is needed which in the case of cross-border crime appears e.g. in the form of the European Arrest Warrant. Thus if one were to examine the concept of the arrest warrant in a vacuum, one could establish a significant reduction in the protection of constitutional rights by the national court. However, considering it in context with a person's increased mobility, one could conclude that the reduction is proportional to the increased opportunities for the person and the increased impact of his or her activities in the jurisdictions of other Member States.

It is likely that in some areas a reduction in the level of protection of constitutional rights has taken place. At times, this has been inevitable given the objectives of European integration, and at times this may have resulted from a lack of wider awareness and debate given issues such as the complexity of multilevel governance.

In the light of e.g. the decision of the CJEU in the EU Data Retention case, we are of the opinion that the CJEU is in principle equipped to deal with issues relating to the guarantee of a higher level of protection of fundamental rights. We do not consider that EU accession to the ECHR would significantly increase the level of protection of fundamental rights within the EU, as it is common knowledge that the ECtHR is overburdened with cases and has difficulty providing decisions in due time as it is.

2.13.3 An increased dialogue between the national constitutional courts and the CJEU in cases dealing with fundamental rights could provide a potential improvement. If the CJEU, when faced with the need to decide on a matter of interpretation of fundamental rights, were able to engage the national constitutional courts by asking for an opinion on the matter, the legitimacy of the interpretations provided might be increased.

3 Constitutional Issues in Global Governance

3.1 Constitutional Rules on International Organisations and the Ratification of Treaties

3.1.1 There is no explicit provision in the Estonian Constitution nor does the Constitution regulate the general transfer of powers to international organisations. Indirectly, however, § 123(1) of the Constitution states that Estonia may not enter into international treaties which are in conflict with the Constitution. If laws or other legislation of Estonia are in conflict with an international treaty ratified by the *Riigikogu*, the provisions of the international treaty shall apply (§ 123(2)). If, however, an international treaty is not in accordance with the Constitution, § 65, clause 4, of the Constitution gives the *Riigikogu* the right to denounce the treaty. It follows that the limit to the delegation of powers is the Constitution itself – no international treaty may be in conflict with constitutional norms.

The procedures concerning international treaties are regulated in detail in the *Välissuhtlemisseadus*[256] (Foreign Relations Act (FRA)). According to § 6(1)2) FRA, the *Riigikogu* has the competence to ratify treaties by passing Acts concerning accession, approval, acceptance, ratification or other Acts, and to denounce ratified treaties by passing Acts concerning the denunciation of, withdrawal from or termination of the agreement or other Acts. The Ministry of Foreign Affairs (MFA) has the right to initiate the conclusion of a treaty. The MFA shall review the materials specified in § 14 submitted thereto for compliance with legislation (§ 15 (1) FRA). If the materials of a treaty contain deficiencies, the MFA shall set a reasonable term for the elimination of deficiencies (§ 15(2) FRA). A treaty prepared for conclusion has to be approved by the Government (§ 16 FRA). According to § 121 of the Constitution, ratification by the *Riigikogu* is required if (1) state borders are altered by the treaty; (2) the implementation of the treaty requires the passage, amendment or repeal of Acts of the Republic of Estonia; (3) the Republic of Estonia joins an international organisation or union according to the treaty; (4) the Republic of Estonia assumes military obligations by the treaty; (5) by the treaty, the Republic of Estonia assumes proprietary obligations in relations in public law for the performance of which no funds have been designated in the state budget, or which

[256] RT I 2006, 32, 248; RT I, 21.06.2014, 10.

exceed the limits for proprietary obligations established by the state budget within which the Government of the Republic is authorised to conclude the treaty; (6) ratification is prescribed in the treaty.

The instrument of agreement of a treaty ratified by the *Riigikogu* shall be signed by the President of the Republic. The instrument of agreement of a treaty concluded by the Government of the Republic shall be signed by the Prime Minister or the Minister of Foreign Affairs (§ 21 FRA).

3.1.2 Not applicable.

3.1.3 No amendments concerning international law and global governance have been made or debated on the parliamentary or Governmental level.

3.2 The Position of International Law in National Law

3.2.1 The Constitution contains a special section (§ 123) with two paragraphs addressing the applicability of treaties and their relationship in domestic law. The first paragraph provides that '[t]he Republic of Estonia shall not enter into international treaties which are in conflict with the Constitution'. This provision is usually understood to mean that in the domestic hierarchy of legal sources, the Constitution takes the highest position. In practice, it requires the authorities to analyse the constitutionality of a treaty in the course of its preparation and conclusion. The Constitution does not explain what happens if there is a collision between the Constitution and a treaty in force. Such collisions are overcome, to the extent possible, by interpretation. As the Constitution cannot release Estonia from its international obligations, the courts should adopt an international law friendly approach in this regard. The Constitution does not provide for the judicial review of treaties; however the CRCPA authorises the SC to verify the conformity of international agreements with the Constitution.

Within the Constitution, § 123(2) provides: 'If laws or other legislation of Estonia are in conflict with international treaties ratified by the *Riigikogu*, the provisions of the international treaty shall apply'. The status of treaties depends on whether they have been approved by Parliament or some other state organ. In the former case, the Constitution confirms that the treaties are directly applicable domestically, provided that they are able to regulate domestic relations and are detailed enough for that purpose. Parliament does not rewrite treaties into domestic legislative acts, which means that treaties remain connected to their international 'background' (e.g. text, interpretation, practice), which consequently affects their application. If a domestic legislative act is in conflict with a treaty, it is not unconstitutional and does not become null and void. Instead, the treaty is applied as a practical solution. When it comes to treaties approved by other state organs (e.g. agreements between ministries), such treaty may be directly applicable, although its position in the domestic hierarchy of legal sources depends on the state organ which concluded the treaty.

3.2.2 Estonia is often considered monistic, as the Constitution and the practice of the different state organs are international law friendly. The supporters of the monistic approach point to the fact that treaties are not rewritten into domestic legislative acts, meaning that their original texts are applied, i.e. international law is applied domestically. However, as was explained above, this logic applies fully only to treaties which have been approved by Parliament. The monistic view is also supported by § 3(1) of the Constitution, which provides that '[g]enerally recognised principles and rules of international law are an inseparable part of the Estonian legal system'. Regardless of the actual wording, this section refers to customary international law and general principles of law. It should be noted that the Constitution does not similarly provide that treaties form an inseparable part of the Estonian legal system.

3.3 Democratic Control

3.3.1 Estonian law entrusts the primary responsibility for initial international negotiations to the Government, first and foremost to the Ministry of Foreign Affairs. According to § 9(3) FRA, the MFA initiates the conclusion of treaties, participates in negotiations concerning treaties, prepares or approves and submits to the Government draft treaties or the texts of treaties adopted, and organises the preparation, signing and exchange or submission to the depositary of the instruments of agreement.

The competency of the *Riigikogu* and its Foreign Affairs Committee (FAC) primarily relates to the procedure of ratification. However, the FAC regularly discusses foreign policy, discusses the report from the Government on the foreign policy of the state and presents its report at a plenary sitting of the *Riigikogu*, and also discusses the bases of security policy and the principles of development co-operation and humanitarian aid presented by the Government.

The detailed procedure is regulated in the RRPA. Section 115 RRPA provides that drafts concerning international treaties undergo two readings in the *Riigikogu,* if the leading committee does not propose otherwise.

Subsequent involvement in scrutinising an international organisation beyond the initial ratification of a related treaty has not been regulated in detail. The MFA is, however, obliged to regularly inform the President, the President of the *Riigikogu*, the Prime Minister and the FAC of the implementation of foreign policy. Also, once a year the MFA prepares a report of the Government on foreign policy.

3.3.2 The ratification and denunciation of international treaties may not be subjected to a referendum as stems from § 106(1) of the Constitution. Thus, the referendum on amending the Constitution and accession to the EU was in this respect constitutionally debatable.

3.4 *Judicial Review*

The competence of the SC to review treaties and measures adopted under international law derives from § 2 clause 2 and § 4(1) CRCPA. Further, the Chancellor of Justice may submit a request to the SC to declare an international agreement which has been signed or a provision thereof to be in conflict with the Constitution.[257] The SC further may, on the basis of a reasoned request of a participant in the proceedings or on its own initiative, suspend, with good reason, the enforcement of a contested legislative act or a provision thereof or the enforcement of an international agreement until the entry into force of the judgment of the SC.

In the adjudication of cases, the SC may declare an international agreement which has entered into force or has not yet entered into force or a provision thereof to be in conflict with the Constitution (§ 15(1) No. 3 CRCPA). Further, § 15(3) CRCPA adds that if an international agreement or a provision thereof is declared to be in conflict with the Constitution, the body which entered into the agreement is required to withdraw from it, if possible, or commence denunciation of the international agreement or amendment thereof in a manner which would ensure its conformity with the Constitution; an international agreement which is in conflict with the Constitution shall not be applied domestically.

3.5 *The Social Welfare Dimension of the Constitution*

3.5.1 The social state dimension is mentioned in § 10, whereas the general social right is embedded in § 28(2) of the Constitution.[258] According to the SC, the social state is a fundamental, core principle of the Constitution.[259] The SC stated in 2004:

> The concepts of a social state based on social justice and the protection of social rights contain an idea of state assistance and care to all those who are not capable of coping independently and sufficiently. The human dignity of those persons would be degraded if they were deprived of the assistance they need for satisfaction of their primary needs.[260]

---

[257] The SC *en banc* held that § 6(1)4) CRCPA gives the Chancellor of Justice the right to challenge a signed international agreement or a provision thereof both before the ratification of the international agreement, i.e. by way of preliminary review, and after ratification, i.e. by way of *ex-post* review. The SC held that the competence arising from § 6(1)4) CRCPA is in accordance with the Constitution, see SCebj, 12.07.2012, 3-4-1-6-12.

[258] 'An Estonian citizen has the right to state assistance in the case of … need.' According to § 28 (2), citizens of foreign states and stateless persons who are in Estonia have this right equally with Estonian citizens, unless otherwise provided by law.

[259] CRCSCj 21.01.2004, 3-4-1-7-03, para. 14; 05.05.2014, 3-4-1-67-13, para. 49.

[260] CRCSCj 21.01.2004, 3-4-1-7-03, para. 14.

The SC has declared a number of laws unconstitutional on the ground of social rights, and has stressed that 'the right to receive state assistance in the case of need is a subjective right, in the case of violation of which a person is entitled to go to court, and the courts have an obligation to review the constitutionality of an Act granting a social right'.[261] However, the SC has stressed several times: '[u]pon ensuring social rights, the legislator has an extensive right of discretion and the courts must not make social policy-related decisions in lieu of the legislator. The exact extent of social fundamental rights also depends on the state's economic situation'.[262]

The potential impact of the policies of global institutions on the social state has not been a matter of discussion in Estonia.

However, the concern of the dissenting judges that the financial commitments undertaken under the ESM Treaty may undermine the social state.

3.6 *Constitutional Rights and Values in Selected Areas of Global Governance*

There are many further theoretical constitutional issues arising in the context of constitutional rights and values in global governance, e.g. the transfer of a part of sovereign powers to the International Criminal Court. However, due to the space restriction, they shall not be addressed here.

References

Aaviksoo B. (2005) Kohtulik aktivism põhiseaduslikkuse järelevalve funktsioonina. Kui aktivistlik on Eesti põhiseaduskohus? (Judicial activism as a function of constitutional review. How activist is the Estonian constitutional court?) Juridica 5:295–307.

Albi A. (2000) Euroliit ja kaasaegne suveräänsus. Üks võimalikke vastukajasid põhiseaduse ekspertiisikomisjoni üleskutsele aruteluks (The European Union and contemporary sovereignty. One possible response to the call for a discussion by the Constitutional Expert Committee) Juridica 3:160–171.

Albi A. (2002) Estonia's Constitution and the EU: How and to What Extent to Amend It? Juridica International 7:39–48.

Albi A. (2005) EU Enlargement and the Constitutions of Central and Eastern Europe. Cambridge University Press, Cambridge.

Albi A. (2009) Ironies in human rights protection in the EU: pre-accession conditionality and post-accession conundrums. ELJ 15:46–69.

---

[261] CRCSCj 21.01.2004, 3-4-1-7-03, para. 16; reiterated in CRCSCj 05.05.2014, 3-4-1-67-13, para. 31.

[262] E.g. SCebj 07.06.2011, 3-4-1-12-10, para. 58.

Albi A. (2010) From the Banana saga to a Sugar Saga and Beyond: Could the Post-communist Constitutional Courts Teach the EU a Lesson in the Rule of Law? CML Rev. 47:791–829.

Albi A. (2015) Erosion of constitutional rights in EU law: A call for 'substantive co-operative constitutionalism', Part 1. Vienna Journal of International Constitutional Law 9(2):151–185.

Albi A., Gallagher M., Koolmeister I., Maruste R., Mälksoo L., Roosma P. (2002): Ühispöördumine seoses nn Põhiseaduse Kolmanda akti riigiõiguslike probleemidega (Joint appeal regarding constitutional law problems relating to the so-called Third Act of the Constitution). Juridica 5:352–353.

Alexy R. (2001) Põhiõigused Eesti põhiseaduses (Fundamental rights in the Estonian Constitution). Juridica Eriväljaanne:5–96.

Allikmets M. (2013) Loovutatava isiku õigused loovutamismenetluses – kohtupraktika analüüs (Rights of the requested person in surrender proceedings – Analysis of judicial practice). Master's Thesis, University of Tartu. http://dspace.utlib.ee/dspace/bitstream/handle/10062/31813/allikmets_marje.pdf?sequence=1.

Antonova J., Pardla M., Markus I. (2012) Estonia. In: Laffranque J (ed.) The Area of Freedom, Security and Justice, Including Information Society Issues. Reports of the XXV FIDE Congress Tallinn 2012, Vol. 3. Tartu University Press, Tallinn, pp. 319–331.

Carcassonne G. (1998) Kommentaarid Euroopa Liiduga ühinemisega seotud uue paragrahvi kohta Eesti põhiseaduses (Commentary on the new section in the Estonian Constitution relating to accession to the European Union). www.just.ee/sites/www.just.ee/files/elfinder/article_files/prof_guy_carcassone._kommentaarid_euroopa_liiduga_uhinemisega_seotud_uue_paragrahvi_kohta_eesti_pohiseaduses.pdf.

Drechsler W., Annus T. (2002) Die Verfassungsentwicklung in Estland von 1992 bis 2001. Jahrbuch des öffentlichen Rechts der Gegenwart 50:473–492.

Ehricke U. (1995) Die richtlinienkonforme und die gemeinschaftsrechtskonforme Auslegung nationalen Rechts. RabelsZ 59:598–644.

Ernits M. (2011) Põhiõigused, demokraatia, õigusriik (Fundamental rights, democracy, the rule-of-law-based state). Tartu Ülikooli Kirjastus, Tartu.

Ernits M. (2012) 20 Jahre Menschenwürde, Demokratie, Rechtsstaat, Sozialstaat. In: Hülshörster S., Mirow D. (eds.) Deutsche Beratung bei Rechts- und Justizreformen im Ausland: 20 Jahre Deutsche Stiftung für Internationale Rechtliche Zusammenarbeit (IRZ). Berliner Wissenschafts-Verlag, Berlin, pp. 123–140.

Ginter C. (2007) Effective Implementation of the Trade Mark Directive in Estonia. ECLR 28 (6):337–345.

Ginter C. (2008) Application of principles of European Law in the Supreme Court of Estonia. PhD Thesis. University of Tartu. http://dspace.utlib.ee/dspace/handle/10062/6494.

Ginter C. (2013) Constitutionality of the European Stability Mechanism in Estonia: Applying Proportionality to Sovereignty. EuConst 9(2):335–354.

Ginter C., Narits R. (2013) The Perspective of a Small Member State to the Democratic Deficiency of the ESM. Review of Central and East European Law 38(1):55–76.

Heukels T. (1999) Von richtlinienkonformer zur völkerrechtskonformen Auslegung im EG-Recht: Internationale Dimensionen einer normhierarchiegerechten Interpretationsmaxime. ZeuS (3): 313–333.

Jäätma J. (2006) Salajane õigus – "kas õigus?" (Secret law – 'is it law?'). Bachelor Thesis, University of Tartu.

Kaldas K.-H. (2006) The Evolution of Estonian Security Policy. In: Kasekamp A. (ed.) The Estonian Foreign Policy Yearbook 2006, pp. 95–117.

Kalmo H. (2008) Mis on järel põhiseadusest? Veel kord Euroopa Ühenduse õiguse ülimuslikkusest (What is left of the Constitution? Once more about the supremacy of European Community Law). Juridica 9:583–597.

Kalmo H., Luts-Sootak M. (2010) Suveräänsus: iganenud või igevene? (Sovereignty: obsolete or eternal?). Kalmo H., Luts-Sootak, M. (eds.) Iganenud või igavene? Tekste kaasaegsest suveräänsusest (Obsolete or eternal? Texts on contemporary sovereignty). Tartu Ülikooli Kirjastus, Tartu, pp. 9–37.

Kelsen H. (1925) Allgemeine Staatslehre. Springer, Berlin.

Kergandberg E., Pikamäe P. (eds.) (2012) Kriminaalmenetluse seadustik: Kommentaar (Code of Criminal Procedure: Commentary). Juura, Tallinn.

Kliimann A.T. (1935) Eesti iseseisvuse areng (The development of Estonian independence). Õigus, Tartu.

Laffranque J. (2001) Constitution of the Republic of Estonia in the Light of Accession to the European Union. Juridica International 6:207–221.

Laffranque J. (2003) Eesti põhiseaduse ja Euroopa õiguse kooselu (The cohabitation of the Estonian Constitution and European law). Juridica 3:180–190.

Laffranque J. (2007) Pilk Eesti õigusmaastikule põhiseaduse täiendamise seaduse valguses Euroopa Liidu õigusega seotud võtmeküsimused põhiseaduslikkuse järelevalves (A Glance at the Estonian Legal Landscape in View of the Constitution Amendment Act on key issues relating to EU law in constitutional review). Juridica 8:528–536.

Laffranque J. (2009) Sõltumatu ja demokraatlik õigusriik Riigikohtu praktikas Eesti Euroopa Liidu liikmesuse kontekstis (An independent and democratic rule-of-law-based state in the practice of the Supreme Court Estonia in the context of European Union membership). Juridica 2009 8:483–499.

Laffranque J., Madise Ü., Merusk K., Põld J., Rask M. (2002) Põhiseaduse täiendamise seaduse eelnõust (On the draft Constitution Amendment Act). Juridica 8:563–568.

Lõhmus U. (2005) Mida teha põhiseadusega? (What to do about the Constitution?). Juridica 2:75–83.

Lõhmus, U. (2011) Põhiseaduse muutmine ja muutused põhiseaduses (Amendment of the Constitution and amendments in the Constitution). Juridica 1:12–26.

Loone E., Järvik M., Loone K.O. (2004) Suveräänsus, seadus, immigratsioon (Sovereignty, law, immigration). Altex, Tallinn.

Madise Ü., Aaviksoo B., Kalmo H., Mälksoo L., Narits R., Pruks P., Vinkel P. (eds.) (2012) Eesti Vabariigi Põhiseadus. Kommenteeritud väljaanne (The Constitution of the Republic of Estonia. Commentary), 3rd edn. Juura, Tallinn.

Mälksoo L. (2010) Eesti suveräänsus 1988–2008 (Estonian sovereignty 1988–2008). In: Kalmo H., Luts-Sootak M. (eds.) Iganenud või igavene? Tekste kaasaegsest suveräänsusest (Obsolete or eternal? Texts on contemporary sovereignty). Tartu Ülikooli Kirjastus, Tartu, pp. 132–156.

Maruste R. (2000) Democracy and the Rule of Law in Estonia. Review of Central and East European Law 26(3):311–327.

Maruste R. (2007) The Role of the Constitutional Court in Democratic Society. Juridica International 13:8–13.

McKenna & Co (1996) Seadusandluse ühtlustamine: konstitutsioonilised parandused (Harmonising legislation: constitutional amendments). www.just.ee/sites/www.just.ee/files/elfinder/article_files/mckenna_co._seadusandluse_uhtlustamine_-_konstitutsioonilised_parandused.pdf.

Merusk K. (1995) Kehtiv õigus ja õigusakti teooria põhiküsimusi (Applicable law and the fundamentals of the theory of legal acts), 2nd edn. Juristide Täienduskeskus, Tartu.

Mõttus, A., Ernits M., Oja L. (eds.) (2012) Riigikogu kodu- ja töökorra seadus. Kommentaarid, (Riigikogu Rules of Procedure and Internal Rules Act. Commentary). Riigikantselei, Tallinn.

Narits R. (2009) About the Principles of the Constitution of the Republic of Estonia from the Perspective of Independent Statehood in Estonia. Juridica International 16:56–64.

Nettesheim M. (1994) Auslegung und Fortbildung des nationalen Rechts im Lichte des Gemeinschaftsrechts. Archiv des öffentlichen Rechts 119:261–293.

Peep V. (ed.) (1997) Põhiseadus ja Põhiseaduse Assamblee (The Constitution and the Constitutional Assembly). Juura, Tallinn.

Piip A. (2007) Suveräänsuse mõiste (The concept of sovereignty). In: Piip A., Pärna, P. (eds.) Õiguse jõud (The force of law). Ilmamaa, Tartu, pp. 413–422. (Original work published in 1936).

Radbruch G. (1914) Grundzüge der Rechtsphilosophie. Quelle & Meyer, Leipzig.

Sprūds A. (ed.) (2012) Friendship in the Making: Transforming Relations between Germany and the Baltic-Visegrad Countries. Latvian Institute of International Affairs, Friedrich Ebert Stiftung, Riga.

Teeveer R., Anton T., Lapimaa V., Narits R., Pappel T., Saar T., Saarmets V. (eds.) (2014) Kohtute aastaraamat 2014 (Yearbook of Estonian courts 2014).

Varul P. (2000) Põhiseaduse juriidiline ekspertiis: eesmärgid, töökorraldus ja tulemused (Legal expert analysis of the Constitution: objectives, method and results). Riigikogu Toimetised 1:65–76.

2

The Cypriot Constitution Under the Impact of EU Law: An Asymmetrical Formation

Constantinos Kombos and Stéphanie Laulhé Shaelou

Abstract The Constitution of Cyprus (1960) is described in the report as unique and as a hybrid model. On the one hand, it has been seen as one of the world's most rigid and detailed constitutions; on the other hand, some parts are governed by the doctrine of necessity, given the division of the country. Special features include a strong protection of social rights and of the right to property; the protection granted to these and some other rights goes beyond the protection afforded by the ECHR. Cyprus has a mixed model of constitutional review. Fundamental rights based review is strong, with provisions interpreted in favour of the individual in cases of doubt. Resorting to constitutional amendments has become a tool for addressing issues related with the idiosyncrasies of the Cypriot Constitution. The use of this approach has become more frequent in the last two decades, whereas there had been a persistent refusal to amend the Constitution in the previous years. With regard to EU law, the Constitution has been amended to remove conflicts, including by virtue of Art. 1A, modelled loosely on the blanket EU clause of the Irish Constitution. At times, the amendments have even proved to be excessive, e.g. as regards an amendment pertaining to the EU Data Retention Directive that was subsequently annulled. The Constitution has also been amended to remove barriers to the European Arrest Warrant, alas in an incomplete way, at least initially; in parallel,

---

Constantinos Kombos is Associate Professor of Public Law, Law Department, University of Cyprus. e-mail: c.c.kombos@ucy.ac.cy.

Stéphanie Laulhé Shaelou is Professor of European Law and Reform and Head, School of Law, University of Central Lancashire, Cyprus. e-mail: SLaulhe-Shaelou@uclan.ac.uk.

Constantinos Kombos wrote Part 1 and Sects. 2.1, 2.4, 2.7, 2.9–2.13. Stéphanie Laulhé Shaelou wrote Sects. 2.2, 2.3, 2.5, 2.6, 2.8 and Part 3.

C. Kombos (✉)
Law Department, University of Cyprus, Nicosia, Cyprus
e-mail: c.c.kombos@ucy.ac.cy

S. Laulhé Shaelou
School of Law, University of Central Lancashire, Pyla, Cyprus
e-mail: SLaulhe-Shaelou@uclan.ac.uk

the initially rights-protective approach of Cypriot courts has gradually been watered down. The cases regarding EU sugar stocks measures raised issues regarding the principles of legitimate expectations and non-retroactivity of charges. The report raises the issue of a lack of debate about constitutional limits to EU law. It highlights the merits of a dissenting judicial opinion in the so-called 'bail-in' case that cautioned against elimination of the rule of law and judicial protection.

Keywords The Constitution of Cyprus · Constitutional amendments regarding EU and international co-operation · The Supreme Court of Cyprus · The 'necessity' doctrine · Judicial review · Fundamental rights and the rule of law
Data Retention Directive and excessive constitutional amendment
European Arrest Warrant · Defence rights · Judicial review and the statute of limitations · Property rights · Judicial dialogues and absence of constitutional limits
Supremacy · 'Bail-in' case · *Sugar stocks* cases and the principles of legitimate expectations and non-retroactivity of charges · International extradition treaties

1 Constitutional Amendments Regarding EU Membership

1.1 Constitutional Culture

1.1.1 The Cypriot constitutional paradigm is unique in content and atypical in character, and it can be argued that as such it has no comparative parallel at the international level. That is manifested in two main ways.

First, there is the peculiarity of the constitutional setting whereby there is a stark and material difference between the provisions of the Constitution of 1960 and their actual application since 1964, when the doctrine of necessity was introduced by the Supreme Court in the landmark judgment *Ibrahim*.[1] The doctrine of necessity has redefined constitutional law and created two parallel constitutional worlds. On the one hand, there are the constitutional provisions that remain in full formal force; they provide for a bi-communal structure that assumes the presence and participation of both Turkish and Greek Cypriots and for a constitutional system with organs of the state that are reflective of bi-communalism and with a plethora of strict checks and balances on the same basis. This can be called 'the silent Constitution'. On the other hand, there is the *ad hoc* suspension of the invalidity rule that attributes hierarchical supremacy to the Constitution of 1960 in those instances that can be justified under the doctrine of necessity. This can be called 'the pragmatic Constitution'.

Therefore, the primary peculiarity of the Cypriot constitutional system is that both 'Constitutions' coexist to the point where a constitutional provision and

---

[1] *The Attorney General of the Republic v. Mustafa Ibrahim* [1964] CLR 195. For analysis see Kombos 2015a, b; Polyviou 2013, pp. 26–64; Polyviou 2015a, pp. 32–124; 2015b.

constitutional reality are two completely different things. For example, Art. 1 provides for a Turkish-Cypriot Vice-President, but no such official has assumed duties since 1963. Moreover, the Constitution in Art. 133(1) provides for a Supreme Constitutional Court composed of three members (a Turkish-Cypriot, a Greek-Cypriot and a presiding non-Cypriot). Since 1964, there is instead a Supreme Court that was founded on the basis of Law 33/64, which included provisions that were in direct contradiction with Art. 133. Nonetheless, the Supreme Court continues to function regardless of the rule in Art. 179 of the Constitution that attributes hierarchical supremacy to the constitutional provisions.

At this point, it is useful to elaborate on the doctrine of necessity, which was introduced on the basis of the founding premise that the Constitution exists for the state and when the state is in grave danger of collapse, constitutional provisions have to give way. In response to this dilemma, the Supreme Court enabled the suspension of the application of certain fundamental constitutional provisions yet without in any way altering any of those provisions in the formal sense. The doctrine of necessity is an atypical response to an atypical constitutional situation and is now in its fifth decade in Cyprus.[2] Therefore, the constitutional provisions remain fully effective in theory but where the doctrine of necessity is applied, their content and effectiveness is numbed, neutralised and non-applicable. The preceding approach can be explained by reference to the German theoretical perception that distinguishes between the concept of hierarchical supremacy leading to invalidity (*Geltungsvorrang*) and the concept of priority in application (*Anwendungsvorrang*). Where the doctrine of necessity applies, the constitutional norm is rendered non-applicable in an exceptional and extraordinary manner, thus removing the invalidity (*Geltungsvorrang*) function and, as a corollary, the contested legal norm acquires a *de facto* priority in application (*Anwendungsvorrang*).[3]

Therefore, the classic perception that emphasises the distinction between 'Constitution' and 'constitutional law' is especially relevant to the Cypriot context, given the fact that the Constitution of 1960 must be read in the light of the doctrine of necessity that, since 1964, offers the pillar on which the Constitution relies for its preservation. In this vein, 'Constitution' refers to the constitutional provisions of the Constitution of 1960, while 'constitutional law' refers to the application of those provisions through the filter of the doctrine of necessity. Through the *Ibrahim* judgment, the doctrine of necessity in effect redefined the scope, content, structure and philosophy of the Constitution, yet without formally amending any of its provisions.[4]

The second distinctive character of the Cypriot constitutional context relates to the judicial approach that is characterised by cosmopolitanism and by a traditional reliance on the comparative methodology.[5] It can be argued that the national system

[2] Loizou 2001, pp. 12–31; Nicolaou 2000, pp. 105–34; Evriviades 1975; Tornaritis 1980, pp. 54–77.

[3] Kombos 2015a, Chap. 2.

[4] Kombos 2015a.

[5] Kombos 2015b, Chap. 3; Hatzimihail 2013.

was developed with direct references to foreign jurisdictions. The nexus with comparative law as a special feature of the Cypriot legal order has been explained with reference to historical factors.[6] These relate to the organic evolution of the legal system, thus classifying Cyprus as part of 'the mixed-jurisdictions sub-genre'.[7] This argument is supported with reference to the areas of family law and contract law[8] where there is a considerable body of evidence pointing to a strong presence of common law principles. For example, Hatzimihail argues that the three main Codes of the Cypriot legal system are directly derived from common law and especially from the Nigerian Criminal Code, the Indian Contract Code and also the Indian Civil Wrongs Code.

In the field of public law, the creation and evolution of administrative law has been marked by the strong influence of the Greek *droit administratif*.[9] This is evident in the form of frequent reliance on Greek academic works and on the case law of the Greek *Conseil d'Etat*, to the point where it is reasonable to argue that it is rare to find a decision in the area of administrative law where reference is not made either directly or indirectly to Greek academic works and/or Greek jurisprudence. It must be noted that the codification of administrative law took place in 1999, and thus until that point the evolution of administrative law by the Supreme Court took place on a case-by-case basis.

The Cypriot legal system has also more generally used the comparative method either as an independent source of law or as an auxiliary tool for supplementing existing constitutional provisions. Reference to foreign jurisdictions extends beyond the Greek context.[10]

The use of the comparative method – strong in intensity and dense in frequency – is indicative of a willingness of the Supreme Court to be open to external sources of influence. This characteristic of the judicial approach represents a benchmark for analysing the degree and form of receptiveness that the Supreme Court has illustrated in relation to EU law. The peculiarity relates to the scale and intensity of the use of the comparative method on the one hand, and to the unjustified entrenchment of EU law concepts and principles on the other.

As a corollary, the rather bold opening statement about the uniqueness of the Cypriot constitutional system is not an exaggerated claim influenced by an inherent 'need' to give priority and importance to the national constitutional idiosyncrasies and peculiarities. Moreover, the preceding statement is not an expression of constitutional patriotism dictated by an anachronistic inward approach to public law

---

[6] Hatzimihail 2013.

[7] Ibid., p. 39.

[8] Ibid.

[9] Hatzimihail 2013, p. 79.

[10] Kombos 2015b, Chap. 3; Hatzimihail 2013.

that is dictated by a pre-existing familiarity with national legal doctrines and thought.[11]

Overall, the Cypriot constitutional culture reflects the normative and conceptual modifications that have affected the system after the application of the above-mentioned doctrine of necessity that has redefined constitutional law in pragmatic terms.[12] Accordingly, the Cypriot example can be classified in a hybrid category that falls between classical and evolutionary constitutions.[13] The former tend to have a strict and pure legal character that is founded on rigidity, normative hierarchy and effective judicial protection, while the latter tend to be more evolutionary, historic and political in nature.[14] In the case of Cyprus, the Constitution of 1960 is founded on strict adherence to the hierarchical supremacy of the constitutional provisions (Art. 179), combined with a permanency of the system that is reflected in the long list of unamendable provisions (Art. 182 and Annex III) whereby 48 out of the 199 constitutional provisions have perpetual status. It must be noted that in that list, only one article relates to fundamental human rights (Art. 23 on the right to property). To that effect, De Smith has argued that the Constitution of 1960 is 'the most rigid, detailed and complicated constitution in the world',[15] and has also stated that

> [t]he Constitution of Cyprus is … weighted down by checks and balances, procedural and substantive safeguards, guarantees and prohibitions. Constitutionalism has run riot in harness with Communalism. The Government of the Republic must be carried on, but never have the chosen representatives of a political majority been set so daunting an obstacle course by the constitution makers.[16]

Therefore, the Cypriot constitutional system is inherently a classical Constitution yet with certain important and influential special features. First, the Constitution is the outcome of international law applied in an unusual form. Specifically, the nature of the process of decolonisation and the actual method for the transfer of power to a newly formed independent state in 1960 were decided in principle and also in detail in Zurich, by Greece and Turkey, in the physical absence of the legally responsible entity that was the colonial power (Great Britain). That paradox is significant, as Great Britain within days of the conclusion of the international agreement between Greece and Turkey stated its acceptance of all the terms with just one single addition in relation to the status of the military bases that it was to retain on the island. The Zurich agreement had 17 points that would form the organisational core of the new state, and those were to create the framework and the content of the new Constitution. Thus, the right of self-determination and, more importantly, the right to exercise primary constitutive power found no expression in the case of Cyprus.

[11] Legrand 2002, pp. 246 and 255.

[12] Soulioti 2006.

[13] Birkinshaw and Kombos 2009; Kombos 2010a.

[14] Besselink 2006, p. 113 et seq.; Albi 2005, p. 22 et seq.

[15] De Smith 1964, p. 285.

[16] Ibid.

No referendum was called and no constituent assembly was formed. Secondly, the Cypriot example is also characterised by the attribution of the role of guardian to Great Britain, Greece and Turkey through the Treaty of Guarantee. Their role included the safeguard of the constitutional status quo, thus creating an impasse in the event of the need to modify the Constitution and its philosophy because of functionality problems. Thus the Cypriot Constitution is simultaneously a classical constitution and also deviates from that blueprint due to the restriction of the exercise of constitutive power at the moment of inception and at any later stage.

At the same time, the Cypriot constitutional system is undoubtedly also an evolutionary constitution because the application of the doctrine of necessity after *Ibrahim* has created a parallel constitutional world, as explained above. Nonetheless, the maintenance at a formal and normative level of the original Constitution, even after the application of the doctrine of necessity, has the effect of excluding the characterisation of the system as purely evolutionary.

By way of summary, the Cypriot paradigm thus represents a hybrid model that does not fall in either of the two categories in a mutually exclusive manner, but rather belongs to both categories.

1.1.2 The position of the Constitution in such an open and evolving constitutional system that has been redefined in a fundamental way by the doctrine of necessity remains central with regard to the rationale of the judiciary. The rationale and the role of the Constitution remain paramount in the sense of ensuring full effective judicial protection, the rule of law, separation of powers and the principle of legality. The concept of sovereignty and the organisation of the state take a subsidiary role in the approach of the Court for different reasons. As regards the organisation of the state, the doctrine of necessity has an important impact, since it enables the restructuring of state organs in order to ensure functionality. In terms of the concept of sovereignty, the Supreme Court has in the past placed emphasis on the need to preserve the formal status of constitutional provisions by restricting the possibility of amendments as a way to ensure the preservation of the Republic at the level of public international law. Overall, the emphasis is on the rule of law and effective judicial protection, and these can be considered to be the foundations for the judicial approach towards the Constitution.

The Courts have to strike a delicate balance between the actual constitutional provisions and the application of the doctrine of necessity; in general, two categories of cases can be identified. First, there are the cases where the full application of a constitutional provision is not possible due to the withdrawal of the Turkish-Cypriot Community, thus triggering the application of the doctrine of necessity. Secondly, there are the cases where a constitutional provision has remained unaffected by the withdrawal of the Turkish-Cypriots and, in those instances, the Constitution remains the paramount guiding source. One such area is the protection of fundamental rights that the Constitution fully provides for in Part II.[17] In such cases the doctrine of necessity has remained non-applicable almost

[17] Kombos and Pantazi 2012; Kombos et al. 2015.

entirely[18] because the Court places the centre of gravity on the protection of fundamental rights.

One special feature of the Cypriot Constitution in relation to fundamental rights that can be seen as part of the national constitutional identity is the protection of social rights. The Constitution by a series of articles guarantees the individual certain social and economic rights, which are to be exercised within the framework of the public interest and common good.

1.2 *The Amendment of Constitution in Relation to the European Union*

1.2.1–1.2.4 Prior to EU accession, the Constitution was amended in relation to the EU only as regards the independence of the Central Bank. The Fourth Constitutional Amendment, introduced by Law 104 (I)/2002, amended Arts. 147, 118 and 119 of the Constitution to ensure the independence of the Central Bank in terms of restricting the dismissal of the Governor and also to exclude any political supervision of the Bank.

After EU accession, the Constitution was amended in 2006 by the Fifth Amendment of the Constitution Law[19] in order to accommodate the introduction and application of the basic principles of EU law.

By way of the history of its introduction, during the lengthy process of implementation of the *acquis communautaire*, the need to amend the Constitution was considered, and a formal recommendation was made to extensively amend the Constitution in order to facilitate accession to the European Union.[20] However, at first the decision was taken that such a course of action was not necessary for three main reasons that are related to the external recognition of the Republic, to the limits of the doctrine of necessity and to the complexity of the provision governing constitutional amendments. In particular, the Supreme Court initially,[21] in the 1980s, rejected attempts to amend the Constitution on the basis that the votes of the Turkish-Cypriot Members of Parliament were required under Art. 182(3) of the Constitution. This could have been remedied through the doctrine of necessity. Nonetheless, the approach of the Supreme Court was to reject the use of the doctrine, which is deemed an exceptional measure to be used in the most extreme situations where the existence of the state is endangered. As such, its application

---

[18] For the rare examples where the opposite applied see Kombos 2015a, Chap. 6.

[19] Law No. 127(I)/2006, Official Gazette No. 4090, 28.7.2006, Annex I(I), p. 1372, available in English at http://www.olc.gov.cy/olc/olc.nsf/all/EC240D2A9413ABBB4225793A00403484/$file/The%20Fifth%20Amendment%20of%20the%20Constitution%20Law%20of%202006.pdf?openelement.

[20] Lycourgos 2010, pp. 102–03.

[21] *President of the Republic v. House of Representatives* [1985] 3 CLR 2224; *President of the Republic v. House of Representatives* [1986] 3 CLR 1439.

must have a temporary effect. A constitutional amendment would have a permanent effect, and hence the doctrine of necessity cannot be used to enable the enactment of a constitutional amendment.[22] Although that approach was subsequently reversed, the crucial point is that the rationale against constitutional amendments remained relatively strong and influential.

In relation to EU accession, it was thought that a solution would be found through a judicial method whereby the provisions of the Constitution would be interpreted in the light of Art. 169 of the Constitution that refers to the status of international treaties and also in the light of the doctrine of necessity. As a result, it was hoped that the courts would enable the effective and efficient participation of the Republic in the EU by harmoniously construing the obligations arising from EU membership with national constitutional law.

The key in the preferred approach was Art. 169(3) of the Constitution that grants superior force against any conflicting municipal law to ratified Treaties. This basic rule was supplemented by the adoption of Law No. 35(III)/2003, with which the House of Representatives approved the ratification of the Accession Treaty. The Law contained the important Art. 4, which stated in clear terms that '[t] he rights and obligations deriving from the Treaty [of Accession] are directly applicable in the Republic and take precedence over any contrary legal or regulatory provision'. The formula used secured the primacy of EU law against all conflicting acts originating from national law, yet it fell short from regulating the relationship between national constitutional law and EU law.

This obvious shortcoming emerged in *Attorney General of the Republic v. Costas Constantinou*.[23] The case concerned the implementation of the European Arrest Warrant (EAW) Framework Decision (FD)[24] by Law 133(1)/2004, and the issuing of an order to surrender Mr. Constantinou to the United Kingdom. The Supreme Court held that the Framework Decision could not prevail over Art. 11 of the Constitution that expressly prohibits the extradition of Cypriot nationals,[25] despite the fact that the Supreme Court acknowledged the case law of the Court of Justice of the European Union (CJEU) on the principle of primacy of EU law. Accordingly, the Supreme Court declared the incompatibility of the national implementing law with the Constitution, which according to Art. 179 of the Constitution renders the law invalid. Moreover, the Supreme Court in effect indirectly dictated the need for a constitutional amendment without stating so, thus giving the impression that the solution remains within the exclusive powers of the other branches of the state. This approach is in line with the principle of separation of powers, but it also creates an understanding that the subsequent normative accommodation of the primacy of EU

[22] Kombos 2015a, Chap. 6.

[23] [2005] 1 CLR 1356.

[24] Council Framework Decision of 13 June 2002 on the European arrest warrant and the surrender procedures between Member States (2002/584/JHA), [2002] OJ L 190/1.

[25] *Attorney General v. Afamis* 1 R.S.C.C 121.

law with regard to the Constitution must be full in order to ensure future compliance with the yardstick that the Court applied in *Constantinou*. It is in this light that one must read the subsequent Fifth Constitutional Amendment that, as will be explained below, had an unnecessarily extensive scope.

The Court on first sight safeguarded the hierarchy of the Constitution, but at the same time it opened the door for the redefinition of that hierarchical position. This was perhaps a clear outcome dictated by express constitutional provisions that limited the room for harmonious interpretation, but at the same time the open-ended invitation to amend the Constitution without defining the limits of what could be acceptable represents a serious shortcoming. Such an approach contradicts the traditional vigilance that the Supreme Court has shown with regard to constitutional amendments. In addition, the decision could be contrasted with that of the German *Bundesverfassungsgericht* in the *Lisbon Judgment*,[26] which provides an interesting example of the 'proactive approach', representing a judicial pronouncement – at the earliest possible opportunity – on what would interfere with the Constitution and the separation of powers.

In terms of the content and character of the Fifth Constitutional Amendment, which, as noted earlier, was introduced (two years) after EU accession in 2006, the original idea was to ensure the primacy of EU law in one single article of the Constitution that would then function as the point of reference for any incompatibility arising between EU law and national constitutional law. This is now Art. 1A of the Constitution. Nonetheless, it must be noted that despite the fact that introduction of an umbrella provision was the selected model, the provisions of the Fifth Constitutional Amendment took a completely different form in terms of methodology and approach. There were instead a nexus of constitutional provisions that were amended in addition to the introduction of the single umbrella provision: in addition to Art. 1A, a paragraph was added to Arts. 140 and 169, and alterations were made to Arts. 11(2) and 179 of the Constitution.

Specifically, Art. 1A states:

> No provision of this Constitution shall be considered as invalidating laws enacted, acts done or measures adopted by the Republic necessitated by its obligations as a Member State of the European Union or shall prevent Regulations, Directives or other acts or binding measures of a legislative character adopted by the European Union or by the European Communities or by their institutions or by their competent bodies under the provisions of the treaties founding the European Communities or the European Union, from having legal effect in the Republic.

It is submitted that there is a crucial problem with Art. 1A, and that problem has both formal and substantial aspects. Formally, as explained above, Art. 182(1) of the Constitution, read in combination with Annex III of the Constitution, creates a long list of non-amendable articles of the Constitution, which includes Art. 1. The addition of para. A to Art. 1 is only indirectly justified in the Preamble of the Fifth Constitutional Amendment Law as not amounting to a constitutional amendment of

[26] BVerfG, Judgment of 30 June 2009 - 2 BvE 2/08 - Rn. (1-421).

a basic constitutional provision. It is submitted that this approach is not correct and is at best playing with formalism, because an addition to any article of the Constitution cannot be construed as anything other than a constitutional amendment. At the same time, the insertion in Art. 1 was deliberate in order to pre-empt any future constitutional amendment. Moreover, it is submitted that the issue is made clear by Art. 182 of the Constitution:

> 1. The Articles or parts of Articles of this Constitution set out in Annex III hereto which have been incorporated from the Zurich Agreement dated 11th February, 1959, are the basic Articles of this Constitution and cannot, in any way, be amended, whether by way of variation, addition or repeal.
>
> 2. Subject to para. 1 of this Article any provision of this Constitution may be amended, whether by way of variation, addition or repeal, as provided in para. 3 of this Article.
>
> 3. Such amendment shall be made by a law passed by a majority vote comprising at least two-thirds of the total number of the Representatives belonging to the Greek Community and at least two-thirds of the total number of the Representatives belonging to the Turkish Community.

Accordingly, there is a clear question about the constitutionality of the Law introducing the Fifth Constitutional Amendment. There has never before or since been any amendment of a basic constitutional provision.

Moreover, besides Art. 1A, further amendments were introduced to other parts of the Constitution – Arts. 11(2), 140, 169 and 179.

Lastly, it would have been expected that the Supreme Court would have at least examined even as *obiter* the nature and even validity of the introduction of Art. 1A; this has never happened so far. Yet, it is imperative that the Supreme Court take a position on the matter, as the issue exceeds by far the matter of primacy of EU law.

Furthermore, it would have been preferable to implement the choice of introducing an umbrella clause by amending Art. 179, which guarantees the supremacy of the Constitution and, in terms of structural coherency, it would have represented the obvious place for such a clause. As to the possible argument that Art. 179 could be further amended in the future and thus it would not present a permanent solution, the answer has three parts. First, it is not axiomatic that the Republic should make the acceptance of the principle of primacy of EU law perpetually permanent, as it can theoretically decide to exit the Union. Secondly, the introduction of the principle of primacy of EU law in Art. 179 would have the same permanency as that of Art. 1A, since nothing would restrict the House of Representatives from repealing that paragraph. Thirdly, one must balance the importance of accommodating the principle of primacy of EU law in a permanent way with the need to safeguard the non-amendable nature of the fundamental constitutional provisions, which is by far and without question the most important consideration.

The next step in the normative solution was to complement Art. 1A with the amendment of the non-basic provisions to be found in Arts. 169, 179, 140 and 11 of the Constitution. Article 179, in its amended form, reads as follows:

> 1. Without prejudice to the provisions of Art. 1A, the Constitution shall be the supreme law of the Republic.
>
> 2. No law or decision of the House of Representatives or of any of the Communal Chambers and no act or decision of any organ, authority or person in the Republic exercising executive power or any administrative function shall in any way be repugnant to, or inconsistent with, any of the provisions of this Constitution or any obligation imposed on the Republic as a result of its participation as a Member State in the European Union.

In terms of the effect of the preceding provision, Lycourgos correctly observes that:

> [t]he combined effect of the new Art. 1A and of Art. 179 as amended, is that not only Community law but also EU law has been recognized as taking precedence over the Constitution. In that respect, the principle enshrined in the Constitution of the Republic of Cyprus preceded even the case law of the ECJ, which never expressly held that the acts adopted under the Union's third pillar – as it was at the time the fifth constitutional amendment – had precedence over national constitutional provisions.[27]

However, from the preceding approach arises a serious substantive problem: it had, at the time, the effect that *the Republic of Cyprus gave a more extensive scope and effect to the principle of primacy of EU law than what the jurisprudence of the ECJ required*. Although the issue has lost its relevance since the entry into force of the Lisbon Treaty, before that, the EU and the EC dimension had clearly been distinguished under Union law, with the ECJ jurisdiction having been limited in relation to the Second and Third Pillars. This in a comparative perspective is perhaps unprecedented. The Supreme Court remained silent on the issue.

The remaining amendments concerned Art. 11(2) in relation to extradition under the European Arrest Warrant. 140 and 169, which will subsequently be explored here.

Under Art. 140, as applied after 1964, the President of the Republic may, prior to the promulgation of any law or decision of the House of Representatives, refer to the Supreme Court for its opinion as to whether such act is inconsistent with the Constitution. With the Fifth Constitutional Amendment, this power was extended to the compatibility of a law or decision of the House of Representatives with the 'law of the European Communities or of the European Union'.

The difficulty arises from the way in which the power of the President is exercised in practice. Traditionally, the Art. 140 power was exercised in instances of a clear difference of opinion between the President and the Parliament and on matters having a non-negligible political dimension and/or affecting the balance of powers and/or impacting on the proper interpretation of the Constitution. In addition, the Attorney General advises the President on the propriety of making use of Art. 140 and in practice, the view of the Attorney General is crucial. Compliance with the often technical requirements of the obligations arising from EU law creates a different setting, where the advisory role of the Attorney General is expected to be

---

[27] Lycourgos 2010, p. 105.

broadened; it marks a considerable shift towards a stronger advisory role of the Attorney General.

As regards the extension of this jurisdiction to compatibility with EU obligations, it must be stressed that the point of reference for the exercise of the jurisdiction by the Supreme Court changes. The issue could very likely become one of interpretation of what the EU obligations entail, thus opening the way for a preliminary reference to the CJEU. In the event of a preliminary reference, the status of the law will remain pending until the CJEU responds, thus creating, as Lycourgos correctly argues, an issue of propriety and compliance with the principle of separation of powers.[28] The alternative for the Supreme Court would be to deliberately avoid making a preliminary reference, thus distancing the Court from the correct application of Art. 267 TFEU. Therefore, the amendment of Art. 140 of the Constitution seems to be creating more problems than it solves.

One such notable example was evident in *President of the Republic v. House of Representatives,*[29] which concerned non-compliance with Directive 2000/13/EC on the approximation relating to the labelling, presentation and advertising of foodstuffs,[30] which required that all national implementing measures relating to the sale of genetically modified foodstuffs in supermarkets had to be notified to the European Commission and the other Member States. Moreover, only after three months following that notification and only if the Commission did not issue a negative opinion could the national measures be introduced. An amendment to the Foodstuffs (Control and Sale) Law came within the scope of the Directive, but the notification procedure had not been followed. As a result and on the advice of the Attorney General, the President proceeded to refer the Law via the amended Art. 140 of the Constitution. The Supreme Court found that there was an apparent procedural error that resulted in non-compliance with the EU obligations. The finding in this case was relatively straightforward, as the issue was one of apparent procedural infringement; however the same cannot be said in relation to more complex situations.

One such complex situation arose in *Reference 2/2013, President of the Republic v. House of Representatives.*[31] The case concerned a conflict between a Law adopted in 2012 on the protection of the seaside and the Services Directive.[32] The national Law, in which priority was given to the owner or operator of a seaside hotel or recreational business in relation to the tender procedure for leasing the relevant part of the beach, went against the Directive's requirement that the licensing system should not be discriminatory and disproportionate. In this case the President referred the

[28] Ibid., p. 107–08.

[29] [2008] 3 CLR 118.

[30] [2000] OJ L 109/29.

[31] 9 May 2014.

[32] Directive 2006/123/EC of the European Parliament and of the Council of 12 December 2006 on services in the internal market, [2006] OJ L 376/36.

incompatibility to the Supreme Court under Art. 140 of the Constitution. The decision of the Supreme Court made note of the CJEU case law that the Attorney General cited in his argumentation, but at the same time the Court did not make any specific reference to those cases. Moreover, the issue concerned the application of the principle of proportionality, which by nature has an element of subjectivity and creates room for different approaches. However, the Supreme Court was unanimous in deciding that there was an apparent incompatibility between the Law and the Directive. The matter in this case was one of substance rather than procedure, and the Court made the correct assessment. Nevertheless, the assessment was much more complex than that necessitated in the earlier case, which gives rise to concerns relating to the selection of instances where Art. 140 is used and the manner of deciding such cases in the context of a preliminary reference.

Finally, there is also a technical issue regarding a gap that has emerged in relation to secondary legislation (i.e. regulations, etc., introduced by the executive but the approval of which is to be decided by the legislature) that is often the means used for completing the implementation of directives. Such measures cannot be the subject of a reference under Art. 140, since under Arts. 51 and 140 of the Constitution, the President is not required to sign them. The issue came to the surface in the aftermath of the Supreme Court decision in the same case, *Reference 2/2013*. The House of Representatives had modified regulations submitted by the executive that were intended to comply with the provisions of the Services Directive in the context of the licensing system that would apply for seaside establishments wishing to take commercial advantage of the seaside (sunbeds, water sports, etc.). The relevant regulations that the House of Representatives had adopted introduced a discriminatory scheme whereby it was considered an advantage if an applicant for a license had experience (5 years) in providing services in the specific area. Therefore, despite the earlier ruling of the Supreme Court and the clear provision of the Directive, the adopted regulations reintroduced a discriminatory system. According to Cypriot constitutional law, secondary legislation cannot be the subject of a reference under Art. 140. Consequently, the problem of incompatibility arose and resulted in the Ministry of Interior asking the local authorities to not comply with the regulations on the basis of the ECJ decision in *Fratelli Costanzo*.[33] There the ECJ held that 'administrative authorities, including municipal authorities, are under the same obligation as a national court to apply the provisions of… [a] Directive and to refrain from applying provisions of national law which conflict with them',[34] provided that the relevant provision has direct effect.[35] According to related case law of the ECJ, the scope of application must be construed in the light of the principles of national procedural autonomy and national institutional autonomy. Therefore, an interesting gap in relation to Art. 140 of the Constitution exists that creates further doubts as to its effectiveness,

[33] Case C-103/88 *Fratelli Costanzo v. Commune di Milano* [1989] ECR 01839.

[34] Ibid., para. 33.

[35] Ibid., paras. 29–32.

given its non-applicability to secondary legislation. Moreover, attempts are made to fill the gap in by relying on the *Fratelli Costanzo* rule which has, as its basic precondition, the direct effect of the EU law provision. But the issue then arises as to who has the authority to make such a complicated determination, since the obligation to apply such secondary legislation often rests on administrative authorities. This creates issues of legal certainty, expertise and separation of powers. All of these matters surfaced in the example in question and, at the time of writing, the outcome is uncertain.

To summarise, it must be questioned whether the constitutional amendment of Art. 140 of the Constitution was necessary given the problems arising from its application and the rarity of its use.

The Fifth Constitutional Amendment additionally added a new para. 4 to Art. 169 to the Constitution, which reads as follows:

> 4. The Republic may exercise every choice and discretion provided for in the Treaties establishing the European Communities and the Treaty on European Union and in any Treaties which amend or replace the above and which are concluded by the Republic.

This provision and its rationale are once again forward-thinking. The provision shields the national act related with the exercise of the option from scrutiny as to its constitutionality. The question is whether it should, given that there is a clear distinction between obligation and option. The ECJ founded the creation of primacy of EU law on the basis of a paramount need for the effectiveness, uniformity and structural coherence of the legal system of the Union. The justifying rationale for the principle of primacy of EU law, however, does not apply to the exercise of options by Member States before they decide to make use of their discretion. Therefore, the amendment of Art. 169 cannot be justified with reference to the need to comply with the principle of primacy of EU law.

The Constitution was subsequently further amended in 2010 (Sixth Amendment, of Art. 17 of the Constitution) with regard to the Data Retention Directive[36] in the aftermath of the Supreme Court judgment in *Alexandrou.*

Finally, Art. 11 of the Constitution was amended on a further occasion in 2013 by introducing the Seventh Amendment of the Constitution via Law 68(I)/2003, in order to allow the extradition of Cypriot citizens in connection to events that took place at any time even before accession to the EU.

In general, the opinions of legal scholars were not requested during the process of introducing the above amendments, with the exception of the Fifth Constitutional amendment for which consultation took place, at an earlier stage of the discussion, about the need for a full revision of the Constitution. At the time of writing, no

[36] Directive 2006/24/EC of the European Parliament and of the Council of 15 March 2006 on the retention of data generated or processed in connection with the provision of publicly available electronic communications services or of public communications networks and amending Directive 2002/58/EC, [2006] OJ L 105/54.

other constitutional amendments relating to EU law are being discussed; however there are areas where such discussion could be useful. For instance, the whole logic of the Fifth Constitutional Amendment, as explained previously, needs to be re-examined since it is problematic and overly expansive. In addition, the Sixth Constitutional Amendment is now equally problematic given that the Data Retention Directive has been annulled by the CJEU.

1.3 Conceptualising Sovereignty and the Limits to the Transfer of Powers

1.3.1 The provisions on supremacy of EU law were provided.

1.3.2 The issue of the transfer or delegation of powers to the EU has not been at the epicentre of the debate in Cyprus because the prevailing view sees participation in the EU as a matter of political determination that was expressed through accession to the Union. Therefore, any delegation or transfer of competences is understood as an expression of the will of the sovereign state and as a matter of choice that attracts the full accommodation of the international obligations of the Republic. If such membership requires the effective transfer or delegation of powers and if that in practice commands the amendment of the Constitution, then any such adjustment is perceived as being nothing more than the expression of the Republic's will. On this basis, the Fifth Constitutional Amendment and the previous decision of the Supreme Court in *Constantinou* can both be explained as an expression of the intention to participate in the EU system and as a voluntary limitation of powers.

1.3.3 Nonetheless, the extensive scope of the Fifth Constitutional Amendment, as explained in detail above, is so open-ended that it significantly constrains any room for disagreement. This is problematic because the Supreme Court has so far failed to develop a reservation formula that would set limits as to what is constitutionally acceptable. Moreover, this approach places Cyprus in the minority of Member States that have accepted the principle of primacy of EU law without serious reservations. Put differently, the Cypriot approach is purely national in nature and founded on what the Constitution provides in the aftermath of the amendment. There is no judicial elaboration as to the limitations that apply to the scope of the relevant constitutional amendment.

There has only been one notable attempt to discuss the limits of the principle of primacy of EU law and of the transfer of powers to the EU, the dissenting opinion of Judge Erotokritou in the 'bail in' case. The case concerned the imposition of a levy amounting to partial confiscation of all unsecured deposits, i.e. below 100,000 EUR, in the two systemic Cypriot banks. The dissenting judge underlined the significance of ensuring, through judicial review, that any European and national mechanism forming the foundation for the imposition of a bail-in, respects fundamental rights and the rule of law. The case and the dissenting opinion will be explored in greater detail, drawing parallels with the German Constitutional Court's *Honeywell* judgment.

1.3.4 The amended Art. 179(1) provides that '[w]ithout prej-udice to the provisions of Art. 1A, the Constitution shall be the supreme law of the Republic'. The Constitution has to give way in case of a conflict with EU law, and that would logically trigger a constitutional amendment. As seen with the EAW saga, the rectification of the incompatibility took years.

1.4 Democratic Control

1.4.1–1.4.2 In relation to applicable rules that govern the participation of the national parliament in the EU decision-making processes, in the case of Cyprus, no such rules exist. Moreover, no referendum has ever taken place in relation to the EU nor has there being any discussion about one.

1.5 The Reasons for, and the Role of, EU Amendments

1.5.1 The guiding background premise has been the traditional reluctance of the judiciary to approve constitutional amendments; on the other hand, the Supreme Court through its ruling in *Constantinou* in effect required the introduction of a constitutional amendment that would govern the relationship between EU law and the national constitutional order. The outcome was the introduction of the Fifth Constitutional Amendment that has an overly expansive scope and leaves little, if any, room for the subsequent establishment of specific boundaries for the relationship between EU law and Cypriot constitutional law. By way of an additional point of background infor-mation, the approach behind the amendment was modelled on the method of Art. 29(4)(3) of the Irish Constitution (now Art. 29(3)(10)).[37] The original idea was to ensure the primacy of EU law in one single article of the Constitution that would then function as the point of reference for any incompatibility of EU law with national constitutional law. That is now Art. 1A. Nonetheless, it must be noted that despite the fact that the introduction of an umbrella provision was based on the Irish model, the provisions of the Fifth Constitutional Amendment eventually took a completely different form in terms of methodology and approach. There is instead a

[37] Lycourgos 2010, pp. 104–106.

nexus of constitutional provisions that were amended in addition to the introduction of the single umbrella provision inserted in the Constitution (Arts. 11, 140, 169, 179).

1.5.2 The Cypriot example has two distinct phases in relation to EU-related constitutional amendments. The first phase, which lasted until 2006, was characterised by the conscious decision not to introduce a constitutional amendment in relation to EU law. The rationale related to the pre-existing caution towards constitutional amendments for reasons having to do with the doctrine of necessity, the protection of the international status of the Republic, political reasons and the complexity of the procedure for constitutional amendments. The second phase is characterised by the introduction of the Fifth Constitutional Amendment that has been extremely open and accommodating for EU law.

In relation to the issue of 'waning constitutionalism' raised in the Questionnaire, such argumentation has not appeared in the Cypriot context as a factor that could influence the decisions during either the first or the second phase. The rationale for both periods has been pragmatic and has reflected the approach that the Supreme Court had adopted at different stages. The shift in the judicial approach in the second phase was influenced by the clear clash between competing supremacies, namely the primacy of EU law and the supremacy of the Constitution. As a result, the judicial reasoning was founded on formal and substantive hierarchy and mirrored considerations relating to functionality and pragmatism.

1.5.3 The symbiosis of the national constitutional order with supranational legal orders that have dense constitutional characteristics is becoming more difficult as the areas of coexistence start to include fields traditionally associated with the state. The need to define and regulate the boundaries between the legal orders is becoming pressing, and the introduction of constitutional amendments represents the most preferable option for two reasons. First, the regulation of the relationship thus stems from the expression of the will of the state that is reflected in the Constitution. This is significant for symbolic and substantive reasons, as it justifies the transfer of powers from the national level to the supranational level by direct reference to the national Constitution. In addition, any amendment would be introduced on the basis of the usually enhanced procedures that require a higher threshold of democratic approval, thus attributing a much-needed element of legitimacy to the relationship between the national and the supranational legal orders. Secondly, the solution of introducing a constitutional amendment is the most functional way to delimit the boundaries, reinforce legal certainty and provide the opportunity to express any reservations that the state decides to apply as to those limits. Such considerations are specifically relevant in relation to the primacy of EU law, fundamental rights and the allocation of competences.

2 Constitutional Rights, the Rule of Law and EU Law

2.1 The Position of Constitutional Rights and the Rule of Law in the Constitution

2.1.1 The position of fundamental rights in the Cypriot constitutional system is central both in terms of their provision and effective protection. The 1960 Constitution contains an extensive bill of rights in Part II ('Fundamental Rights and Liberties'), which in terms of content is similar[38] to that of the European Convention on Human Rights (ECHR) and, as Kyriacou[39] and Pikis[40] rightly observe, the provisions of which in 'certain instances are wider in scope and substance compared to their counterparts found in the [Convention]'.[41] Moreover, the Constitution by a series of articles guarantees certain social and economic rights[42] to the individual which are to be exercised within the framework of the public interest and common good.[43] The relevant provisions are detailed and comprehensive, and the judiciary has been extremely active in ensuring the full protection of these rights.

It can be argued that the level and content of the judicial protection of fundamental rights has been developed in direct connection with the ECHR system, in which Cyprus participated as part of the colony regime even before independence in 1960. The ECHR has been used as a guiding factor for establishing the level of protection and it has become particularly relevant where there has been ambiguity either in the constitutional text[44] or in the facts of a specific case. Moreover, the Cypriot system has exceeded the standard that the European Court of Human Rights (ECtHR) requires in numerous cases, with the Supreme Court making direct reference to the need to adopt a higher standard of protection.[45]

In relation to general principles of law, this concept is present and active in the Cypriot system of public law, either as an independent source of law or as an auxiliary tool used for supplementing existing constitutional provisions. Such general principles can be directly derived from the common law that provides the early foundation for the Cypriot legal system (due process, *audi alteram partem*);

---

[38] Kombos and Pantazi 2012.

[39] Kyriacou 2010, p. 2.

[40] Pikis 2006, p. 43.

[41] Kyriacou 2010, p. 2.

[42] Tornaritis 1968, clarifies that Professor Bridel, who assisted in the drafting of the Constitution, recommended the incorporation of the liberty to work, trade and industry, liberty of contract and the right to strike.

[43] Tornaritis 1968, p. 2.

[44] For example, *Attorney General v. Afamis,* n. 25.

[45] *Charalambous and others v. Republic*, Joined cases 1480/2011, 11 June 2014; *Police v. Ekdotiki Eteria* [1982] 2 CLR 63; *David Scattergood v. Attorney General* [2005] 1 CLR 142 (see Sect. 2.3 below).

they are primarily procedural in nature yet with a substantive effect on the essence of the basic right to fair trial. Nonetheless, the influence of such principles has remained limited due to the fact that the Constitution exhaustively covers the rights to fair trial and personal liberty in a combined manner through Arts. 11, 12 and 30.

In terms of general principles not resulting directly from the Constitution, the most notable example is the principle of proportionality. Proportionality has been given an elevated status through the codification of the general principles of administrative law in Art. 52 of Law 158(I)/99. Nonetheless, proportionality already had a constitutional position as an unwritten principle of law and has been referred to by the Supreme Court in the landmark judgment *Ibrahim* as an essential criterion to be met in order for the constitutionally crucial doctrine of necessity to be applicable. The overall effect is that the principle of proportionality is not just a general principle of law with constitutional status, but it also constitutes an integral criterion for the assessment of the foundation of the Constitution post 1964, that is, the doctrine of necessity.

2.1.2 The Constitution in Art. 33 provides for the conditions under which restrictions can be imposed on rights:

> 1. Subject to the provisions of this Constitution relating to a state of emergency, the fundamental rights and liberties guaranteed by this Part shall not be subjected to any other limitations or restrictions than those in this Part provided.
>
> 2. The provisions of this Part relating to such limitations or restrictions shall be interpreted strictly and shall not be applied for any purpose other than those for which they have been prescribed.

Further considerations pertaining to Art. 33 will be explored.

2.1.3 The Cypriot Constitution makes no express reference to the concept of the rule of law, but this has not stopped the judiciary from positioning the concept at the epicentre of our constitutional law.

The clearest example of the general approach towards the rule of law can be found in the above-mentioned landmark judgment *Ibrahim* where the Supreme Court introduced the doctrine of necessity. The foundation for the decision was that after the withdrawal of the Turkish-Cypriots and the resignation of the two foreign judges, the administration of justice could not function, which thus directly affected the rights of the individual in a negative way. The consequence of this was to nullify the meaning of the rule of law that was defined as being inherently inter-linked with judicial supervision and effective judicial protection, fundamental rights and the principle of legality. This approach, which led to the introduction of the doctrine of necessity, has since permeated the Cypriot legal system.

In terms of justiciability, both parties to legal proceedings and the national courts frequently use the principle of the rule of law, but the principle is not independently justiciable. Rather, the invocation of the rule of law is combined with other legal principles that are content-specific in a manner that is constitutionally precise. The general perception as to the rule of law is that it represents the fundamental principle for the legal system and it forms part of all other constitutional principles that are to be construed with the principle of the rule of law in mind.

One such manifestation of the rule of law is access to courts, especially in relation to judicial review proceedings. Article 146 of the Constitution guarantees access to the jurisdiction of the Supreme Court as an administrative court in a liberal and generous way.[46] Specifically, Art. 146(2) states that '[s]uch a recourse may be made by a person whose any existing legitimate interest, which he has either as a person or by virtue of being a member of a Community, is adversely and directly affected by such decision or act or omission'.

Furthermore, the principle of the rule of law is present in the constitutional provisions that prohibit retroactivity (Art. 24(3) in relation to tax law and Art. 12(1) in relation to criminal law) and that guarantee legal certainty. Articles 3 and 104 require the publication of all laws as an essential requirement for their validity.

2.2 The Balancing of Fundamental Rights and Economic Freedoms in EU Law

2.2.1 In Cyprus, the balancing exercise pertaining to the protection of classic constitutional and/or fundamental rights must initially be considered with respect to the application of the doctrine of necessity. In *Alloupas v. National bank of Greece*,[47] it was held by the majority of the Supreme Court of Cyprus that constitutional rights may only be restricted on the *express* basis of the Constitution and by applying the 'strictest possible' criteria of necessity (does a state of necessity exist) and of proportionality (are such restric-tions proportionate to the necessity).[48] The principle of proportionality has been granted constitutional status as an 'unwritten principle of law', and it was referred to by the Supreme Court as an 'essential criterion' in the application of the doctrine of necessity. If the Supreme Court initially gave a rather wide interpretation to the principle of proportionality, starting with the *Ibrahim* case, it did so when the application of the doctrine of necessity 'did not concern the exercise of legislative powers by the executive, or the restriction of fundamental individual rights'.[49] The Court also gave a narrow interpretation to the principle of proportionality and refused to consider administrative acts of a final nature, decided by an administrative organ out of its own discretion (not deriving from a law) as

[46] See Kombos 2010b.

[47] [1983] 1 CLR 55.

[48] Emilianides 2013, p. 47.

[49] Ibid., pp. 42–4.

justified on the basis of the doctrine of necessity,[50] for the reason that administrative acts are not general in nature and are therefore more likely to be arbitrary. As a result, '[a]dministrative acts of a final nature could not themselves be justified on the grounds of the doctrine of necessity; however, administrative acts of a final nature which were based on a law, which was justified on the grounds of the doctrine of necessity, would also be justified'.[51] Thus, it appears that the protection of constitutionally safeguarded fundamental rights in Cyprus has remained largely outside of the scope of the doctrine of necessity.

The Constitution contains a detailed and extensive list of rights, which at times are more extensive than comparable rights under the ECHR, and that in the case of doubt, the interpretation favours the individual over the state. According to Emilianides, the protection of the rule of law is a 'cardinal principle' of the Constitution.[52] This, combined with the supremacy of the Constitution, means that 'the courts have the power to examine the constitutionality of both laws and action of the administration and that no law, regulation or administrative act may be inconsistent with the Constitution'.[53] This means that a trial court (i.e. any court other than the Supreme Court) has the power to declare unconstitutional any law which is contrary to the provisions safeguarding individual human rights as set out in the Constitution. This is the result of the mixed character that applies to the system of review of constitutionality in Cyprus after 1964 whereby the examination of claims of unconstitutionality is diffused and decentralised. This also entails that constitutionally safeguarded fundamental rights must be interpreted in favour of the individual protected rather than the state in case of doubt.[54]

As far as restrictions or limitations to constitutionally safeguarded fundamental rights are concerned, it is stated in Art. 33(1) of the Constitution that these can only be contained in express provisions of the Constitution (see Sect. 2.1.2). A careful review of Part II of the Constitution reveals that such restrictions or limitations can also be contained in legislation within the limits of the Constitution itself,[55] as introduced by the House of Representatives or 'deemed to be part of Cypriot law under Art. 188 of the Constitution'[56] or deriving from EU law,[57] subject to the

[50] See *Mesaritou v. The Cyprus Broadcasting Corporation* [1972] 3 CLR 100; *Theodorides v. Plousiou* [1976] 3 CLR 319.

[51] Emilianides 2013, p. 44.

[52] Ibid., p. 53. See Sect. 1.1.2 of this Report. See also Loizou (2001) (in Greek).

[53] Emilianides 2013, p. 53.

[54] *Fina (Cyprus) Ltd v. The Republic* [1962] 3 RSCC 26; see Emilianides 2013, p. 146.

[55] E.g. more recently *President of the Republic v. House of Representatives* [2000] 3 CLR 238 (in Greek).

[56] *Police v. Hondrou and Another* [1962] 3 RSCC 82.

[57] See Emilianides 2013, p. 146.

general principles *inter alia* of reasonableness and proportionality. Article 33(2) of the Constitution expressly provides that such restrictions or limitations must be interpreted strictly and cannot be applied 'for any purpose other than those for which they have been prescribed', thereby providing a general framework of necessity and/or proportionality to the restriction/limitation to constitutionally safeguarded fundamental rights. This provision of the Constitution must be read in conjunction with Art. 35 of the Constitution, which casts a vertical duty on the state and its various branches of government (within the limits of their respective competence) to ensure the efficient application of Part II of the Constitution vis-à-vis the beneficiaries of these fundamental rights.

Additionally, it should be noted that the fundamental rights safeguarded under the Constitution are minimum rights. Rights may be further protected or new rights may be established through legislation, in which case these are not protected as constitutional rights but as ordinary rights.[58] This last point may have direct implications for the protection afforded to rights deriving from EU law and their implementation in the national legal order.

While EU law (all provisions) should take precedence over conflicting constitutional provisions as a result of Art. 1A of the Constitution, the use of the EU Charter by the Supreme Court in its case law is far less developed than the (much older) use of the ECHR. This could perhaps also be explained by looking at the overall practice of the supremacy of EU law by the courts in Cyprus, especially by the Supreme Court. It could be said that despite the reference to Art. 1A in Art. 179 of the Constitution and because the Constitution in Cyprus still provides expressly for its own supremacy, considerations of EU law and the exercise of judicial review arising as a result of the application of EU law in Cyprus appear *prima facie* to be encompassed within the fabric of the Constitution. This may be the subject of some academic debate in Cyprus,[59] but in judicial and/or practical terms, the overall approach of the Supreme Court can be described as inconsistent and as sometimes ignoring EU law (or even the ECHR) to concentrate merely on the protection of fundamental rights in accordance with express constitutional provisions.[60]

---

[58] Emilianides 2013, p. 146.

[59] Emilianides argues that EU and EC law are considered an integral part of the Constitution, Emilianides 2013, p. 54; *contra* Kombos & Pantazi 2012, p. 309: 'the hierarchical rule resulting from Art. 179 does not apply to EU law'; see also Lycourgos 2010, p. 101. For a detailed analysis, see also Laulhé Shaelou 2010a, pp. 133–40 who concludes: 'The legislative objective of removing the potential conflict between EC/EU law and the Constitution appears *a priori* achieved; it will however no doubt face the judicial scrutiny of the Cypriot courts through cases on the enforcement of Community law rights in Cyprus', p. 139.

[60] Interview with Dr. Demetrios Hadjihambis, former President of the Supreme Court of Cyprus (June 2013–July 2014) and judge at the Supreme Court (1999–2013), 9 January 2015.

Some of the wide-ranging areas where the Ombudsman of Cyprus and equality bodies in Cyprus have pointed out that national law needs to better ensure fundamental freedoms and the principle of non-discrimination arising from EU law include e.g. the right of entry and residence for same-sex partners and/or the third country national spouse of an EU citizen, the free movement of workers, social assistance, and detention or expulsion orders of EU nationals.[61] The courts in particular would need to revise their role and adopt a more teleological or holistic approach, as legal actions brought before them normally fall within the (narrow) ambit of the judicial control of administrative acts under Art. 146 of the Constitution and do not entail any balancing exercise established within the fabric of the Constitution for the protection of constitutionally safeguarded fundamental rights.[62]

In general, the protection of constitutionally safeguarded fundamental rights in the Cypriot legal order, whether 'classic' fundamental rights, economic or social rights, has always been at the core of the case law of the Cypriot courts, independently of the supremacy of EU law. As such, the balancing of fundamental rights with economic rights can be said to amount to a 'routine' exercise for the Cypriot courts within the fabric of the Constitution, to which EU law 'merely' added one more – albeit fundamental in nature – dimension, thereby increasing the likelihood of constitutional issues arising. Whereas a full and comprehensive review of the balancing exercise between these rights within the fabric of the Constitution would be beyond the scope of this Report and has been explored elsewhere,[63] drawing general trends could prove useful. The balancing exercise usually involves a strict (but careful and delicate) construction of the restrictions/limitations to such rights on the basis of Arts. 33 and 35 of the Constitution and/or in accordance with the case law of the ECHR (in the case of a collision of classic rights).[64] It is also useful to mention that the collision between social rights '*per se*', especially within the framework of the freedom of movement that is so central to the case law of the CJEU, and the right to strike, have not arisen as such in the Cypriot legal order.[65] This could however be an area of potential conflict between the Cypriot and the EU legal orders given the attachment to social rights of the

[61] See in particular Trimikliniotis 2013 for a review of recent domestic case law related to these issues, pp. 121–140.

[62] Administrative recourses under Art. 146 fall under the exclusive revisional jurisdiction of the Supreme Court, both first instance and appellate, are strictly limited to the review of the legality of an administrative act, decision or omission, and exclude any review of the case on the merits. See Emilianides 2013, p. 197.

[63] For a detailed review of the collision between classic rights and/or socio-economic and cultural rights, including within these sub-categories of rights, see Kombos and Pantazi 2012, pp. 338–46. For a thorough consideration of the balancing exercise between economic freedoms and fundamental rights in the European public order with an emphasis on Cyprus, see Laulhé Shaelou 2011.

[64] Kombos and Pantazi 2012, p. 344.

[65] Kombos and Pantazi 2012, p. 343.

former[66] and to free movement of the latter.[67] It has been suggested that the overall balancing exercise currently taking place in the Cypriot legal order, whereby the Supreme Court 'advances its own perception' in the event that the standard of protection granted under the ECHR is lower, usually in the absence of any meaningful consideration of the case law of the CJEU, may have to change in the future, especially with respect to potential clashes between social rights and free movement. This could result in the 'lowering' or at least 'alteration' of the standard of protection offered to social rights in the Cypriot Constitution, with a special reference to the right to strike.[68] In the meantime and until such a conflict arises, what could be said is that the test to be satisfied for the protection of social rights 'within the framework of the public interest and common good' could end up in effect being higher than for other constitutionally protected fundamental rights. This would seem to be confirmed by the recent case law of the Supreme Court of Cyprus related to austerity measures put in place in response to the sovereign debt crisis.

For example, the case of *Georgos Charalambos and others v. Republic of Cyprus*[69] concerned a number of recourses brought before the Supreme Court by a number of civil servants against the Republic, the Ministry of Finance and the General Auditor, with respect to the law for the special levy on the pensions and gross salaries of officers and employees in the public sector as well as the pensions of retired persons (Law 112(I)/2011 as amended). The case was brought on the basis of Arts. 23, 24, 26, 28 and 146, but not Art. 9 of the Constitution (right to a decent existence and social security) which can be considered as requiring on a case-by-case basis a higher burden of proof to rebut the presumption of constitutionality afforded to legislation (on the basis of proportionality), including apparently in times of economic crisis. With respect to the combined principles of equal treatment and equality in taxation (Arts. 28 and 24 respectively), the Supreme Court confirmed its previous case law by stating that the principle of equality must be balanced with the economic situation and fiscal policy in place at the time, and that the state has the discretion in 'times of extreme economic crisis' to take measures targeting specific groups of the population 'without necessarily violating the principle of equal treatment'.[70] Adopting a comparative approach and after examining the legal framework put in place in Cyprus with respect to the special levy (including for the private sector), the Supreme Court subsequently ruled that there had been no breach

---

[66] In *Apostolides Georghios & Others v. the Republic of Cyprus through the Ministry of Labour and Social Insurance & Others* [1982] 3 CLR 928, the Supreme Court ruled that social rights are on an equal footing with political rights but that the economic situation and capacity of the country must be taken into account when assessing compliance of a measure with Art. 9 of the Constitution (right to a decent existence and social security); see Kombos and Pantazi 2012, pp. 314–315.

[67] Ibid. See also the analysis of the dissenting opinion of Judge Erotokritou in the case of *Myrto Christodoulou* in Sect. 2.7.3 of this Report.

[68] Kombos and Pantazi 2012, p. 345.

[69] Cases No. 1480-4/2011, 1591/2011 and 1625/2011, 11 June 2014 (majority decision) (in Greek).

[70] Translation by the author.

of the principle of equal treatment and that the measures put in place ('in coordination with the competent organs of the EU') could not be deemed 'extreme' and thus disproportionate (proportionality was raised with respect to the right to property), given the economic situation in which Cyprus found itself.

This judgment should be contrasted with the case of *Maria Koutselini-Ioannidou and others v. The Republic*,[71] with respect to the reduction of pensions of retired civil servants and public officers who have been re-employed in the public sector based on Law 88(I)/2011, which was deemed unconstitutional on the basis of Art. 23 of the Constitution, independently of the current economic climate and/or any obligations as may arise under EU membership and/or the ECHR. In this majority decision, the Supreme Court distinguished this case from the previous one on the basis that pensions are a property right which cannot be limited in the name of the public interest on the basis of Art. 23. In the second judgment in the case, however, Judge Michaelidou referred to the expression of the general concept of public interest, included in Art. 23 under the form of public benefit, and to the need to justify it.[72]

In a wider framework, it should be briefly noted that the right to free movement and residence on the territory of the Republic of Cyprus[73] arguably holds a strategic place in the Constitution, between the right of the accused and the 'no-exile' rule. It should therefore be regarded as a basic fundamental right in the Cypriot legal order and any restriction/limitation to this right should be interpreted strictly (the grounds are contained in the provision itself). To this consideration could be added the case law on shopping hours within the framework of Art. 25 of the Constitution (the right to work) where there has been an uneasy relationship between working conditions and open and fair competition in the name of the general public interest,[74] including post-EU accession.[75] It is undeniable, however, that there have been overall some gradual adjustments in the balancing of fundamental rights with economic free movement rights or associated/flanking policies, in the name of EU law and/or in favour of economic freedoms falling within the scope of EU law.[76] An example of this would be the (unanimous) decision in a reference to the Supreme Court[77] in relation to the law amending the law on the protection of beaches and transposing the Services Directive, analysed earlier in Sect. 2.1. As

[71] Joined Cases No. 740/2011-587/2012, 7 October 2014 (majority decision) (in Greek).

[72] In this respect, see speech by Judge Myron M. Nicolatos.

[73] Article 13 of the Constitution.

[74] See *Georgoulla Georgiou et al v. the Police* [1999] 2 CLR 616 (in Greek) and *Andronikos Vasiliadies Ltd et al v. the Police* (2001) 2 CLR 715 (in Greek).

[75] A power struggle involving the various branches of government of the Republic of Cyprus has been ongoing for the past few years, with no ultimate outcome yet, as to who has the power to regulate shopping days/hours and related working conditions, and on what constitutional basis/principle. Overall it would appear that the economic situation of the island prevails over any consideration of EU law.

[76] Dr. Hadjihambis, interview 9 January 2015.

[77] *President of the Republic v. House of Representatives, Reference 2/2013*, 9 May 2014 (in Greek).

seen, the national Law gave priority to the owners or operators of a seaside hotel or recreational business in relation to the tender procedure for leasing the relevant part of the beach. The lawyers of the House of Representatives justified this policy by the general public interest as an exception to the selection process, including under Art. 12(3) of the Directive (applicable 'where the number of authorisations available for an activity is limited because of scarcity of natural resources or technical capacity') and on the basis of Art. 25 of the Constitution. These arguments were rejected by the Supreme Court not only on the basis of the Directive's requirement that the licensing system should not be discriminatory and disproportionate, but also on the basis that the principles of free competition, as set out in EU law and in the Directive, should prevail.[78]

On a further point, the Court noted that there was no breach of the principle of legitimate expectations since the House of Representatives, in addition to not meeting the deadline for transposition of the Directive at the end of 2012, had through the amending law extended the existing situation until the end of October 2014, thereby giving ample time to all concerned to comply.[79]

2.3 Constitutional Rights, the European Arrest Warrant and EU Criminal Law

Introduction and constitutional amendments The European Arrest Warrant (EAW) Framework Decision (FD) was implemented in Cyprus by Law No. 133(I)/2004 on the European Arrest Warrant and the Surrender Procedures of Requested Persons, which has since been amended three times.[80] There were initial difficulties in some Member States with the very idea of surrendering their own nationals based on the principle of mutual recognition, including in Cyprus where 'expelling or extraditing' procedures were interpreted as being expressly limited to aliens under Art. 11(2)(f) of the Constitution.[81] This difficulty persisted following EU accession and the matter was brought before the full bench of the Supreme Court of Cyprus in November 2005.[82] The Court had to consider the

[78] Ibid., p. 12.

[79] Ibid., p. 14.

[80] Consolidated version available at http://www.cylaw.org/nomoi/enop/non-ind/2004_1_133/full.html (in Greek).

[81] See *Attorney General v. Afamis,* n. 25. An unofficial translation of Art. 11(2)(f) in force until the 2006 amendment is available in English at http://www.law.uj.edu.pl/~kpk/eaw/other/220_EAW.pdf, p. 170. See also case note by Tsadiras 2007, p. 1516.

[82] *Attorney General v. Constantinou* [2005] 1 CLR 1356, [2007] 3 CMLR 42; see Tsadiras 2007 and Laulhé Shaelou 2010a, pp. 134–137. See also http://www.supremecourt.gov.cy/Judicial/SC.nsf/All/1F76458C67091E86C2257348004BC6B6?OpenDocument and http://www.law.uj.edu.pl/~kpk/eaw/judicial_decisions/Cyprus_Constitutional_Court.pdf.

implementation of the FD in the national legal order and the compatibility of the implementing law with the Constitution.[83] The Court took the view that Art. 11 of the Constitution provided an exhaustive list of the reasons why a person could be arrested and it did not provide for the execution of an EAW.[84] It then reiterated its jurisprudence on the prohibition of the extradition of Cypriot nationals,[85] referred to the *Pupino* case[86] and to the lack of direct effect of the FD, and ruled as a result that it was left to its own discretion to interpret national law in this field in accordance with the FD. On this point, it decided that the implementing law was contrary to Art. 11 of the Constitution, as no provision in the implementing law could be interpreted 'in such a way so as to prevail and to be applied as regards the nationals of the Republic'.[87] This judicial decision triggered (indirectly) a legislative reaction and provided the necessary impetus to proceed with long-awaited amendments to the Constitution to reflect EU membership obligations, including with respect to Art. 11.[88] Following the 2006 amendment to the Constitution (the Fifth Amendment, see Sect. 1.2), the arrest and detention of a Cypriot national for the purpose of extradition to another EU Member State was made possible, provided that it related to offences committed after Cyprus became an EU Member State on 1 May 2004 (Art. 11(2)(f), sub-para. 1) and that such request was not motivated by grounds such as race, religion, ethnic origin or political opinion (sub-para. 3).[89]

---

[83] For the constitutional implications of this case in the Cypriot legal order, see Sect. 1.2.

[84] Laulhé Shaelou 2010a, p. 136.

[85] *Georgiou v. Director of Central Prisons* [1991] 1 CLR 814.

[86] Case C-105/03 *Pupino* [2005] ECR I-05285.

[87] *Constantinou*, para. 24. Translation by the author.

[88] See Sect. 1.2. See also Laulhé Shaelou 2010a, pp. 137–138, and Gorski & Hofmanski 2008.

[89] Sub-paragraph (f) of Art. 11(2) was substituted with the following:

> '(f) the arrest or detention of a person … or of an alien against whom action is being taken with a view to deportation or extradition or of a national of the Republic with a view to extraditing or surrendering him, subject to the following provisions:
>
> (i) the arrest or detention of a national of the Republic for the purpose of surrendering him under a European arrest warrant is possible solely in relation to events that occurred or acts done subsequent to the date of accession of the Republic to the European Union.
>
> (ii) the arrest or detention of a national of the Republic for the purpose of extraditing or surrendering him pursuant to an international agreement binding the Republic is possible solely in relation to events that occurred or acts done subsequent to the publication of the Fifth Amendment of the Constitution Law of 2006.
>
> (iii) the arrest or detention of any person for the purpose of extraditing or surrendering him pursuant to an international agreement is not possible if the competent body or authority under the law, has substantial grounds for believing that a request for extradition or surrender has been made for the purpose of prosecuting or punishing a person on grounds of his race, religion, ethnic or ethnotic origin, political opinion, or of any legal claims of collective or individual rights in accordance with international law.'

At the same time, Art. 7 of Law 133(I)/2004 was also amended to provide that a request for the issuing of an EAW for the purpose of criminal prosecution must be accompanied by the written approval of the Attorney General of the Republic of Cyprus (who is responsible for criminal proceedings in the territory of the Republic in accordance with Art. 113(2) of the Constitution).[90] Following these amendments, the legal framework of the EAW in Cyprus remained *prime facie* incompatible with the FD, to the extent that it set out additional requirements/limitations to the issuing and execution of an EAW, provided for additional protection of fundamental human rights not expressly provided in the FD and, as such, potentially affected the principle of mutual recognition and/or the rights of suspects and defendants.[91]

In 2013 Cyprus proceeded with a further amendment to its Constitution, allegedly to 'fully comply' with its obligations arising from the EAW FD.[92] The amendment was related to the pending extradition proceedings that were examined by the Supreme Court in *Dinos Michailides v. Attorney General.*[93] This case was an appeal and concerned a Cypriot citizen against whom a first EAW had been issued in 2013 by the Greek authorities who requested the surrender for purposes of criminal prosecution for money laundering. It should be noted that the prosecution related to events that took place between 1997 and 2001, and that Art. 11 of the Constitution as amended by the Fifth Constitutional Amendment allowed the extradition of Cypriot citizens only for events that took place after accession to the EU in 2004. Article 11(2) (f) was thus further amended in order to allow the extradition of Cypriot citizens in connection to events that took place at any time, even before accession to the EU.[94] All

---

[90] Amending law 112(I) of 2006, available at http://www.cylaw.org/nomoi/arith/2006_1_112.pdf (in Greek).

[91] See DG Internal Policies of the Union, Citizens' Rights and Constitutional Affairs (2009) 'Implementation of the European Arrest Warrant and joint investigation teams at EU and national level' available at http://www.eipa.eu/files/EUROPEANARRESTWARRANT.pdf 3, pp. 11–12, p. 14 and pp. 18–19; see also Kapardis 2008, pp. 12–23 and http://www.law.uj.edu.pl/~kpk/eaw/data/cyprus.html.

[92] Seventh Amendment to the Constitution Law 68(I)/2013, available in English at: http://www.olc.gov.cy/olc/olc.nsf/all/DA5878C1FB78D167C2257C16002284F7/$file/The%20Seventh%20Amendment%20of%20the%20Constitution%20Law%20of%202013.pdf?openelement.pdf.

[93] *Dinos Michailides v. Attorney General,* Case 221/13, 2 September 2013.

[94] The sub-paragraph (f) in Art. 11 was replaced as follows:

> '(f) … the arrest or detention of an alien against whom action is being taken with a view to deportation or extradition or the detention of a national of the Republic with a view to extraditing or surrendering him pursuant to a European arrest warrant or pursuant to an international treaty binding on the Republic, on condition that such treaty is applied by the other party thereto. However, the arrest or detention of any person for the purpose of extraditing or surrendering him is not possible if the competent body or authority under the law has substantial grounds for believing that a request for extradition or surrender has been made for the purpose of prosecuting or punishing a person on the grounds of his race, religion, nationality, ethnic origin, political opinion, or of any legal claims of collective or individual rights in accordance with international law.'

sub-paragraphs were deleted and time limitations were removed.[95] The guarantee of non-discrimination on grounds of race, religion and other grounds was clearly reiterated and now applies to all persons subject to extradition or surrender procedures, whether nationals of the Republic or not, and whether the subjects of a European or an international arrest warrant. This Seventh Amendment to the Constitution with respect to the surrender of Cypriot nationals was welcomed by the Supreme Court of Cyprus in its recent case law as necessary for the Republic to fully abide by its obligations under the FD.[96]

2.3.1 The Presumption of Innocence

2.3.1.1 The legal maxim of *nullum crimen nulla poena sine lege* is a fundamental principle of Cypriot criminal law embodied in Art. 12(1) of the Constitution, which provides that

> [n]o person shall be held guilty of any offence on account of any act or omission which did not constitute an offence under the law at the time when it was committed; and no person shall have a heavier punishment imposed on him for an offence other than that expressly provided for it by law at the time when it was committed.

It was on the basis of the principle of the non-retroactivity of criminal law deriving from this provision that the Republic had sought *inter alia* to limit the scope of application of the EAW in Cyprus to suspected offences committed post EU accession (in the Fifth Amendment). This concern, however, appeared unfounded for procedural law and was accordingly removed with the Seventh Amendment to the Constitution. Article 12(2) of the Constitution also sets out the rule against double penalty (*ne bis in idem*): 'a person who has been acquitted or convicted of an offence shall not be tried again for the same offence. No person shall be punished twice for the same act or omission except where death ensues from such act or omission'. This is a constitutional right that even precedes the birth of the Republic, without deviations, even in the name of public security.[97] There is also a guarantee in the Constitution against arbitrary punishment (Art. 12(3)) as well as against general confiscation of property (Art. 12(6)).[98]

The presumption of innocence also features in Art. 12(4) of the Constitution. It provides that 'every person charged with an offence shall be presumed innocent

---

[95] Cyprus had been criticised for having introduced such time restraints. See Christou 2012, p. 63 and fn. 31 in particular.

[96] See *Dinos Michailides v. Attorney General of the Republic*, Civil Appeal 221/13, 2/9/2013.

[97] Paraskeva 2015, p. 185. In the context of the EAW, see District Court of Larnaka, Case *No. 2/06*, based on Law 133(I)/2004 and concerning the execution of an EAW against Vakhtang Obolashvili, 4 May 2005, where the District Judge refused to execute the EAW against the requested person based on the principle of double jeopardy (developed below).

[98] For a general consideration of the rights of the accused, with respect in particular to Arts. 11 and 12 of the Constitution, see Emilianides 2013, pp. 157–159; see also Paraskeva 2015, pp. 176–220. On the rights of suspects of criminal offences, see also Stefanou 2011.

until proved guilty according to law'. This is a constitutional right without qualification, constitutes a human right and, in the context of procedural law, applies all throughout the process – before, during and until the final conviction of the accused. It is important to note that this right is afforded to all, whether nationals or aliens. It lies entirely in the hands of the judiciary to determine whether a criminal offence has been committed by a person, provided the prosecution can prove so beyond all reasonable doubt.[99] This means in particular that no public authority can speculate on the guilt of a person before he/she has been convicted by a competent court. Thus, it was held that administrative decisions attributing criminal acts to a person were in violation of the constitutional presumption of innocence and, as such, unconstitutional.[100] It should also be noted that the presumption of innocence in Cypriot constitutional law also implies that the accused has a right to silence and against self-incrimination.[101] Exercising these rights, which are ancillary to the presumption of innocence, does not mean admitting guilt.[102]

The absolute protection afforded to the presumption of innocence by the Constitution raises interesting questions in the context of the EAW and mutual recognition, with respect in particular to the authorities involved, the procedure and the nature of the arrest warrant. Following the Seventh Amendment to the Constitution, Art. 11(3) now provides that 'save when and as provided by law in case of a flagrant offence punishable with death or imprisonment', a person can only be arrested under the authority of a reasoned judicial warrant issued according to the formalities prescribed by the law or pursuant to an EAW (the latter reference to the EAW having been added by the Seventh Amendment). The police cannot therefore proceed with the arrest of a person without the issue of a judicial warrant/EAW and its communication to the relevant authorities of the Republic. The central authority for the issue and execution of EAWs in Cyprus is the Ministry of Justice and Public Order, i.e. an executive organ of the state, although other key actors such as the police force, the Law Office of the Republic and District Judges are also involved in the process.[103] The competence of the central authorities in other Member States was challenged before the courts in Cyprus in relation to the execution of EAWs, but in vain. The case of *Igor Ovakimyan v. Attorney General of the Republic* concerned the execution in Cyprus of an EAW issued by the Dutch Central Authority. The Supreme Court upheld the decision of the Limassol District Court to execute the EAW against the appellant and ruled that the Central Authority

---

[99] *Rex v. Mentesh* 14 CLR 233; *Police v. Chrysanthou* 15 CLR 50 and *Costis Panayi Kefalos v. The Queen* 19 CLR 121. For the reversal of the burden of proof in Cyprus law in specific instances, see Paraskeva 2015, pp. 197–198 and in particular fn. 790 and 792.

[100] *Kyriakides v. The Republic* [1997] 3 CLR 485 (in Greek). See Emilianides 2013, pp. 158–159.

[101] *President of the Republic v. House of Representatives* [1994] 3 CLR 1 (in Greek). See Emilianides 2013, p. 158; see also Paraskeva 2015, pp. 201–202.

[102] *Charalambous v. The Republic* [1985] 2 CLR 40; Emilianides 2013, p. 158.

[103] See http://www.police.gov.cy/police/police.nsf/All/367B2EB11E7D96B9C2257A1E002E2E17?OpenDocument.

can also be a public prosecutor or other judicial body as determined by the legal system of each state. In the Netherlands, as the Cypriot Supreme Court noted, despite being assigned to the Ministry of Justice, the public prosecution service belonged to the judiciary branch of government.[104] This was repeated in *Eva Karina Andersson v. Attorney General of the Republic* in the context of the execution of an EAW from Sweden.[105] It appears to be in line with the jurisprudence of the ECtHR on the nature of the 'court' as an independent organ from the executive power.[106] Thus, the essence of the matter seems to be that the EAW must remain *in effect* a 'judicial decision',[107] independent from the executive. This does not seem to be exactly the case in Cyprus[108] or at least was arguably not the case until 2014.

In Cyprus, once a request is transmitted to the Central Authority, it is communicated to the Attorney General who is also not a judicial authority, but an independent officer of the Republic (Arts. 112–114 of the Constitution). The latter is said to perform a 'double-check' to the extent that the police first 'presents the case' and subsequently a draft of the EAW for approval by the Attorney General. This administrative/technical process, prior to the judicial decision being taken, has been criticised in evaluation reports as being at the very least unnecessary and perhaps more seriously in violation of the principle of mutual recognition and/or the spirit of the FD, to the extent in particular that it could constitute an obstacle to a request reaching the District Court in Cyprus.[109] Furthermore, it should be noted that while the Attorney General performed its double check, the Central Authority would until 2014 scrutinise the EAW in terms of formalities but also substance, with the possibility to request further information or a re-issue of the EAW by the issuing state. It was only following this screening procedure that the Central Authority would proceed with issuing a certificate under Sect. 16(1) of the implementing law and transmit it to the judge who would decide under Sect. 16(2) on the issue of an arrest warrant under the implementing law. As ably noted by Christou, this certificate constituted no guarantee that the EAW would not be 'challenged before the courts', since the Central Authority is not a judicial authority either, thereby begging the question of the *real* judicial nature of the EAW and of the scope of the principle of mutual recognition in Cyprus.

The role of the Ministry and the Attorney General in the issue/execution of EAWs recently led for the first time to legal issues raised in the case of Mr. Louka in the context of an international arrest warrant from South Africa; the details will be provided in Sect. 3.6. This case entitles one to wonder whether considerations regarding extradition decisions based on political discretion could arise in the

---

[104] [2005] 1 CLR 1119.

[105] [2008] 1 CLR 1092. See Christou 2012, p. 64 and fn. 50.

[106] *Hutchison Reid v. the United Kingdom*, no. 50272/99, § 64, ECHR 2003-IV.

[107] See Art. 7(2) of the FD.

[108] See http://www.eipa.eu/files/EUROPEANARRESTWARRANT.pdf, p. 11.

[109] Christou 2012, pp. 64–65.

European context and what safeguards are available in the law to avoid potentially arbitrary results.[110]

It should be said from the outset that the legal framework surrounding international arrest warrants and EAWs certainly differs with respect to their spirit, scope, powers and processes.[111] With respect to the legal basis of an arrest warrant, the Supreme Court in *Scattergood* had clarified the judicial character of an arrest warrant issued under the law implementing the EAW FD (as opposed to an arrest warrant issued in other extradition procedures) and that the basis for such arrest warrant was the law implementing the FD (Sects. 3 and 18) and not domestic law.[112] The Court subsequently stated that a warrant issued on the basis of Art. 16 of the implementing law was a 'preliminary measure' which aimed at ensuring the arrest of the suspected offender, in order to then decide during the course of the procedure 'whether the execution of the EAW should be allowed'.[113] This was quite an ambiguous statement which appears to reveal that the execution of an EAW did not occur 'as if it were issued by the issuing state's own authorities',[114] as requested by the principle of mutual recognition. More recently, however, and within the context of the amendments to the law implementing the EAW FD in Cyprus,[115] the Supreme Court, referring to the case law of the ECJ,[116] clearly stated that there is an 'express obligation' to execute 'every' EAW in accordance with Art. 1(2) of the FD and this obligation is without exception outside of the framework provided in the FD (Arts. 3 and 4) and in the implementing law (Sects. 13 and 14) (see below).[117]

It therefore appeared that, at least until 2014, there were some weaknesses (i.e. extra scrutiny even where it may have favoured the defendant's rights) in the law implementing the EAW FD in Cyprus, with some of them also identified with respect to international arrest warrants. The House of Representatives passed two amending laws to the implementing law in 2014, one in early 2014 where

---

[110] For equivalent considerations arising (indirectly) from unsuccessful pleas by the lawyers of Dinos Michailides subject to an EAW issued by the Greek authorities, see *Dinos Michailides v. Attorney General of the Republic*, Civil Appeal 221/13, 2/9/2013.

[111] As noted by the Supreme Court itself in *Scattergood v. Attorney General* [2005] 1 CLR 142 (in Greek), the EAW procedure is a 'relative' of the extradition procedure under the relevant domestic law but as such, 'does not stop being different, based on another law enacted within the framework of the EU accession' (translation by the author).

[112] Ibid.

[113] Ibid.

[114] Christou 2012, p. 65.

[115] Amending Law 30(I)/2014 was published in the Official Gazette of the Republic on 7 March 2014 and Amending Law 183(I)/2014 on 12 December 2014.

[116] Case C-388/08 PPU *Laymann and Pustovarov* [2008] ECR I-08993, para. 51; Case C-261/09 *Mantello* [2010] ECR I-11477, para. 36.

[117] Civil Appeal No 184/2014, *Hadwen James v. Attorney General*, 17 July 2014; for a more flexible approach, see Civil Appeal No. 41/14, *Attorney General v. Mrukwa*, 5 March 2014; see also n. 127 below.

significant amendments were made to a number of provisions of the law,[118] and again in late 2014 where one additional amendment was made to the rights of the person subject to the EAW.[119] Through the first amending law, the power given to the Central Authority (CA) to scrutinise the EAW and issue a certificate of compliance under Art. 16 para. 1 was revoked, and the CA was merely left with the obligation to ensure the arrest of the person subject to the EAW; there is only mention of the power of the judge to proceed with the issue of a temporary arrest warrant in the case of an emergency and on the basis of an EAW *or before* the issue or the transmission of an EAW, following receipt of such a request through EUROPOL or otherwise (new para. 2). The detention time under the temporary arrest warrant was also extended from three to eight days (Art. 16(3)). Amending Law 30(I)/2014 also removed the reference to 'criminal proceedings' in Sect. 3 of the implementing law, thereby arguably enhancing judicial pre-trial and procedural powers.

The above changes appear to reconcile the implementing law with the spirit and provisions of the FD as well as the principle of mutual recognition. It remains, however, to be seen what the impact of the amendments to Sect. 16 of the implementing law will mean in terms of safeguards, including for the respect of the rights of suspects, the protection of the presumption of innocence and of other fundamental human rights/principles embodied in procedural guarantees. In addition to constitutional safeguards in each country, the protection of fundamental rights is also part of the principle of mutual recognition itself,[120] thereby arguably implying the exercise of a certain level of control by the competent authorities.[121] It should not mean, however, that the protection of fundamental rights can constitute an *autonomous* ground of refusal to execute an EAW. This was confirmed recently by the Supreme Court of Cyprus with respect to the EU Charter, in the case of *James Hadwen*,[122] with the Court noting that such arguments do not 'fit' within the 'specific procedure' of the execution of EAWs by District Courts (which the Court classified as *sui generis*).[123]

2.3.1.2 Until at least 2014, however, the authorities in Cyprus, and in particular the District Judges, would not 'automatically authorise extradition with minimum formality and no consideration of evidence' (cf. the Questionnaire). The courts

[118] Law 30(I)/2014, 7.3.2014.

[119] Law 183(I)/2014, 12.12.2014.

[120] For Cyprus, see Sect. 2(2) of the implementing law: 'The application of the provisions of the present Law cannot result in the violation of the obligation of respect of the fundamental rights and principles, in accordance with Art. 6 TEU. In any case, the requested person shall not be transferred to a country where he/she would be at serious risk of being subjected to the death penalty or subjected to torture or other inhuman or humiliating or treatment' (translation by the author).

[121] Christou et al. 2009, p. 113.

[122] See n. 117 above.

[123] Ibid.; see also *Dinos. Michailides v. Attorney General*, Civil Appeal No. 221/13, 2 September 2013.

proceeded with the review of pre-trial evidence to determine in particular the seriousness of the offence,[124] the time frame and the situation of the person, *inter alia* whether the person subject to the EAW was more 'at risk' if extradited to the issuing country rather than remaining under arrest and/or in detention in Cyprus. Overall, the courts proceeded on the assumption that there was 'reasonable suspicion' against the suspected person as evidenced by the EAW, which, however, had to be investigated and determined by the District Judge, with a view to arresting and/or detaining the person subject to the EAW. This is quite clearly expressed in the implementing law where it transpires that even after a suspected person is brought before the District Judge, extradition is still only a 'possibility' (Sect. 17 (1)) whereas his/her detention needs to be decided by the judge (Sect. 18(1)). Most of the time, however, an EAW is issued and/or executed,[125] with one commentator noting with respect to the role of the judge that judges need to 'be moved' by the parties, which is a characteristic of the common law tradition, as opposed to the civil law system where the role of the judge is more inquisitorial.[126] The Supreme Court of Cyprus has, however, recently expressed in rather strict terms the obligation on the District Courts to proceed with the execution of EAWs and appears to have framed the protection of fundamental rights (exclusively) within procedural guarantees as provided in the FD and the implementing law subject to a proportionality test, thereby potentially adopting a stricter reading than some District Judges on a case-by-case basis.[127]

---

[124] See e.g. Civil Appeal, *Panayiotis Philippou* (no. 2) [2009] 1 CLR 693.

[125] The latest public statistics available date back from 2010 when 34 EAWs were issued to Cyprus. The statistics of the Ministry of Justice do not specify how many EAWs were actually executed. The annual report only mentions that these EAWs were transmitted to the judicial authorities of the Republic for execution. It then states under the title 'transfer of sentenced persons' that 13 requests were received by the Ministry, out of which 11 culminated in extradition from or to Cyprus; see http://www.mjpo.gov.cy/mjpo/MJPO.nsf/All/88FC4FA80EAFB52AC22579BC003005DE/$file/etisia%202010%20-%20final.pdf, p. 37.

[126] Christou 2012, p. 66.

[127] This does or does not benefit the person subject to the EAW. In *James Hadwen* (see n. 117 above), the Supreme Court acting as an appeal court, upheld the findings of the trial court to the extent that it had allowed a request for adjournment in order to call an expert witness from Malta to testify that the offence for which he was arrested was time-barred but refused to grant a second adjournment, noting that the execution of an EAW must occur within a strict time frame. The fact that in the application of Sect. 15(2) of the implementing law, the trial court omitted to hear the appellant was not sufficient to render the decision of the District Court to execute the EAW invalid. In *Mrukwa* (see n. 117 above), the District Judge had refused to execute an EAW issued by the Polish authorities on the basis of delays in justice both in Poland and in Cyprus, and lack of justification, and referred to Sects. 2(2) and 4(1)(f) and/or (g) of the implementing law. In the appeal case, the Supreme Court upheld the decision of the trial court and confirmed that even though the implementing law does not provide for the refusal to execute an EAW on the basis of the timely administration of justice, account should be taken of Sect. 2(2) of the implementing law (and not of the Constitution, as stated by the District Court) which, in conjunction with Art. 6 TEU and the principle of mutual recognition, should ensure the protection of fundamental rights by the authorities of the issuing Member State.

2.3.2 *Nullum crimen, nulla poena sine lege*

2.3.2.1 The legal maxim of *nullum crimen nulla poena sine lege* was already discussed in Sect. 2.3.1.1 above in the context of constitutional rights.[128] It was also said that there is an express human right ground to reject requests for surrender of suspects in the implementing law, the scope of which, however, remains unclear. In line with the FD, the implementing law also includes a list of 32 offences in Sect. 12 (2) which do not require the double criminality principle to be satisfied, provided that the offences are punishable by a custodial sentence or detention order of a maximum period of at least three years in the law of the issuing state (verbatim transposition of Art. 2(2) of the FD). This list remains unamended to date and the section has been described as helping to serve 'substantial justice' by preventing suspects from escaping from justice on procedural grounds.[129] Despite controversies deriving from the abolition of double criminality, it has been seen as creating a 'better balance between private individuals and national interest in enforcing the law'.[130]

The above provision must be read in conjunction with Sect. 13 of the implementing law where the grounds for mandatory non-execution of an EAW are set out, including some not expressly provided in Art. 3 of the FD (amnesty, *ne bis in idem*, and lack of criminal responsibility due to age).[131] It is worth noting that Sect.13 of the implementing law was amended in 2014, but only with respect to the phrasing of sub-para. (d) which reflects Art. 11(2)(f) of the Constitution sub-para. 3, as amended. The two other grounds remain unaffected, namely that the Republic will refuse to execute the EAW in two situations. First, if a person subject to an EAW for the execution of a custodial sentence or detention order is a Cypriot citizen, the Republic will execute the sentence or detention order according to its own criminal laws. Secondly, if a person subject to an EAW for his/her prosecution is a Cypriot citizen, the Republic will not execute the request unless it is assured that after being heard, the person will be transferred to the Republic to serve his/her custodial sentence or execution order passed against him/her in the issuing Member State. These two additional grounds for the mandatory non-execution of an EAW appear to defeat the very purpose of the FD and of mutual recognition and sit rather uneasily with the amended version of Art. 11(2)(f) of the Constitution.

Mention should also be made of the optional grounds for non-execution of an EAW as set out in Art. 4 of the Framework Decision. The implementing law in Cyprus does not reproduce Art. 4(1) of the FD, which provides for the possibility to lift the requirement of double criminality for acts falling outside the list set in Art. 2(2) and within the ambit of Art. 2(4) of the FD. All other optional grounds have been implemented in the Cypriot law (Sect. 14). Given the human rights guarantees present in the implementing law, the perhaps intentional omission of Art. 4(1) FD may appear

[128] See also Christou et al. 2009, p. 114.

[129] Dr. Demetrios Hadjihambis, 9 January 2015.

[130] Ibid.

[131] Stefanou and Kapardis 2006, p. 264.

regrettable in terms of substantive justice and mutual recognition. It actually appears that even if an act falls within the ambit of Sect. 12(2) of the implementing law, for which the requirement of double criminality is lifted, the execution of the EAW can still fail on the basis of mandatory (or not) grounds for non-execution,[132] which provide specific procedural guarantees and/or, as a last resort, on the basis of the general clause for the protection of fundamental human rights in Sect. 2(2) of the implementing law.[133] In this respect, it should also be noted that in 2014, Sect. 14 of the implementing law was amended by Law 30(I)/2014 to the effect that sub-sections 2, 3 and 4 were added, thereby reinforcing the discretion of the judicial authorities to refuse the execution of an EAW in several additional instances involving the protection of human rights embodied in procedural guarantees.[134]

2.3.3 Fair Trial and *In Absentia* Judgments

2.3.3.1 Article 30(1) of the Constitution provides that '[n]o person shall be denied access to the court assigned to him by or under this Constitution'. The right of access to the courts is however not an absolute right and is subject to reasonable restrictions, such as time limitations.[135] Article 30(2) then provides that '[i]n the determination of his civil rights and obligations or of any criminal charge against him, every person is entitled to a fair and public hearing within a reasonable time by an independent, impartial and competent court established by law'. Again, this can be subject to restrictions.[136] Finally, Art. 30(3) combined with Art. 12(5) of the Constitution set out the minimum rights of litigants, including in criminal proceedings and in line with Art. 6(3) ECHR. Thus, every person has the right to (i) be informed of the reasons why he/she is required to appear before the court; (ii) to present his/her case before the court and to have sufficient time necessary for its preparation; (iii) to adduce or cause to be adduced his/her evidence and to examine witnesses according to law; (iv) to have a lawyer of his/her own choice and to have free legal assistance where the interests of justice so require and as provided by law; and (v) to have the free assistance of an interpreter if he/she cannot understand or

---

[132] Such grounds seem to be used within reason; see e.g. Civil Appeal, *Panayiotis Philippou* (no. 2) [2009] 1 CLR 693.

[133] In *Obolashvili*, the District Judge, after refusing to execute an EAW on the grounds of the principle of double jeopardy (Sect. 13(b) of the implementing law), also clearly stated that in any case, a person would not be surrendered if his/her human rights were violated as protected under Sect. 2(2) of the same law. In this case, the length of time since the alleged offence was found by the District Judge to be unacceptable and sufficient in itself to refuse the execution of the EAW. See also Christou 2012, p. 68. Trial court decisions should however be contrasted with judgments delivered by the Supreme Court in its appeal capacity (see Sect. 2.3.1 and n. 97 above).

[134] For a pre-2014 review of procedural guarantees, see Christou 2012, pp. 71–77.

[135] See Emilianides 2013, p. 171.

[136] Ibid., p. 172.

speak the language used in court. These minimum requirements are deemed to constitute 'fundamental elements of a fair trial' and any deviation therefrom would be in violation of the latter principle and invalidate the proceedings.[137]

Article 12(5)(c) of the Constitution provides in particular that every person charged with an offence has the right to 'to defend himself in person or through a lawyer …'. If it is possible in civil proceedings to have a judgment *in absentia* provided all minimum rights to a fair trial have been allegedly duly respected,[138] this does not appear to be the case in criminal proceedings.[139] For serious offences in particular, the presence of the accused at the trial is required, given the nature of the burden of proof in criminal proceedings and the right to self-representation and participation in the proceedings guaranteed in the Constitution.[140] As a matter of public order, the presence of the lawyer of the person charged does not discharge the authorities from their obligation to ensure that the accused is present at the trial, at least at first instance, unless that person has fled the country or has waived the relevant rights.[141]

Despite the exceptional nature of judgments *in absentia* in the Cypriot legal order, legislation was enacted in 2014 in Cyprus to implement the relevant provisions of the EAW FD, as amended by the FD 2009/299/JHA of 26 February 2009, reproducing verbatim the amendments, thereby enhancing the procedural rights of

---

[137] Ibid., pp. 173–174.

[138] See *Apostolides v. Orams*, Case No. 9968/04, 9 November 2004, where Mr. Apostolides obtained a judgment by default of appearance in the Nicosia District Court against Mr. and Mrs. Orams, British citizens who had purchased his property in the area not under the effective control of the Republic of Cyprus. On 19 April 2005, a second judgment was delivered by the District Court refusing to set aside the earlier judgment on the ground that there was no valid defence to the claim (the court set aside appearance) – a judgment later upheld by the Supreme Court (*Apostolides v. Orams* [2006] 1 CLR 1402). Those judgments were then registered in, and declared enforceable by, the Queen's Bench Division of the High Court of England pursuant to the Brussels Regulation (Orders made by Master Eyre, 21 October 2005) and successfully challenged by the Orams before the High Court Judge pursuant to Art. 43 of the Brussels Regulation (*Orams v. Apostolides* (QB) [2007] 1 WLR 241). Mr. Apostolides appealed under Art. 44 of the Brussels Regulation before the Court of Appeal of England and Wales, which decided to stay the proceedings and refer five questions pertaining also to the right of the defence, service of documents and public order as grounds for refusal of enforcement of judgments to the ECJ (Case C-420/07 *Apostolides* [2009] ECR I-03571). For a detailed analysis of the judgment of the ECJ in this case, see S. Laulhé Shaelou 2011, pp. 342–356.

[139] See Report by the European Committee on Crime Problems (CDPC), Council of Europe, writing about judgments *in absentia* in Cyprus that 'it is not possible except in the case of specified very minor offences for which the accused requests to be permitted to be represented only by his counsel (section 45 of the Criminal Procedure Code) or if summons is proved to have been served on him and he fails to appear in which case the Court may hear the case in his absence (section 89 of the Criminal Procedure Code)', available at http://www.coe.int/t/dghl/standardsetting/pc-oc/PCOC_documents/Documents%202013/PC-OC%20(2013)%201%20Summary%20and%20Compilation%20of%20Replies%20Quest%20judgements%20in%20absentia%20and%20the%20possibility%20of%20retrial.pdf.

[140] See also Sect. 63 of the Criminal Procedure Code, Chapter 155 of the laws of Cyprus.

[141] Paraskeva 2015, p. 212.

persons and fostering the application of the principle of mutual recognition to decisions rendered in the absence of the person concerned at the trial. The courts are now under an obligation (as opposed to this being within their discretion before) to fill in Annex A reproduced from the amending FD. The new legal framework has been perceived positively by the Cypriot courts as giving them additional discretionary grounds to refuse the execution of an EAW (even if no judgments seem to have been issued *in absentia* so far).[142]

2.3.4 The Right to a Fair Trial – Practical Challenges Regarding a Trial Abroad

2.3.4.1–2.3.4.2 As previously noted, judges in Cyprus try to ensure that EAWs are executed.[143] Beyond the legal framework as developed above, no further information is available on the assistance which Cyprus extends to its own nationals in extradition procedures. Generally and in terms of issuing EAWs, there have been cases where persons requested under an EAW issued by the Cypriot authorities and executed in another Member State have been subsequently cleared of charges by the courts in Cyprus.[144] There have also been cases where EU nationals extradited to Cyprus under an EAW have been found guilty by the Cypriot courts and transferred back to their country to serve their sentence.[145] Cyprus, however, remains a place for fugitives to hide in the areas not under the effective control of its government, where the application of EU law is suspended, thereby avoiding EAWs issued by Cypriot or other Member States' authorities.[146] There are, however, some (rare) examples of surrender of a requested persons under an EAW in connection with the illegal purchase of property in the occupied areas of the Republic of Cyprus, which falls under the category of 'fraud',[147] forming part of the 32 offences for which the requirement of double criminality has been lifted. On this basis, the UK surrendered a requested person under an EAW to the Cypriot authorities in accordance with the principle of mutual recognition and despite not having an equivalent offence under UK law.[148]

---

[142] See e.g. *John Constandinides v. Attorney General*, Civil Appeal No. 347/2014, 5 March 2015 (in Greek).

[143] See Christou et al. 2009, p. 113.

[144] See also http://gmadvocates.com/cases/cypriot-businessman-brought-cyprus-under-european-arrest-warrant-found-be-innocent-charges.

[145] http://www.fairtrials.org/cases/michael-binnington-and-luke-atkinson/.

[146] http://www.bbc.com/news/uk-19485421. For a detailed legal analysis of the application of EU law in Cyprus, including in relation to the areas not under the effective control of the government, see Laulhé Shaelou 2010a.

[147] See http://www.mfa.gov.cy/mfa/embassies/embassy_stockholm.nsf/ecsw19_en/ecsw19_en?OpenDocument.

[148] See http://www.chroniclelive.co.uk/news/local-news/former-north-east-nightclub-owner-1363996; see also Christou 2012, pp. 61–62.

2.3.5 The Right to Effective Judicial Protection

2.3.5.1–2.3.5.4 There are mechanisms available in the Cypriot legal order that guarantee access to justice for individuals, such as the principle that time does not start running until full knowledge of the facts has been obtained. In administrative cases, if the Supreme Court has to decide on a matter of facts, it hears evidence first, including from other jurisdictions if necessary. The principle of mutual recognition is based on the mutual recognition of foreign law/judgments; this principle existed in Cyprus before it was applied in an EU context to civil and criminal matters, as Cyprus is a mixed legal system.[149] As such, the conception of the role of the courts in Cyprus has not really changed and remains, in the context of mutual recognition, mainly concerned with a review of coercive actions by the executive and the justification by the state for its actions.[150] In a wider framework, the courts in Cyprus may be criticised for privileging formalities over substance. The *Apostolides v. Orams* case is probably an example of extreme formalism through a literal interpretation of the meaning of losing a case 'by default' (lack of appearance) rather than on the merits, thereby taking the right to appear to the extreme.[151]

2.4 The EU Data Retention Directive

2.4.1 The implementation of the Data Retention Directive raised serious constitutional problems in Cyprus and resulted in the Sixth Constitutional Amendment (Law 51 (I)/2010 of 4 June 2010) after a decision of the Supreme Court in *Alexandrou* (see below). The effect was the amendment of Art. 17(2) of the Constitution that provided for the limitations available for Art. 17(1). Article 17(1) states that '[e]very person has the right to respect for, and to the secrecy of, his correspondence and other communication if such other communication is made through means not prohibited by law'. The new provision of Art. 17(2) allows interference with the aforementioned right through data retention on the basis of a judicial order that relates to the investigation of serious crimes carrying a prison sentence of five years or more. That amendment remains in full force today despite the decision of the CJEU in *Digital Rights Ireland and Seitlinger and Others*.[152]

Originally, the Republic implemented the Directive with the Law 183(I)/2007 (as amended) that introduced a system for data retention along the lines the Directive requires. However, in terms of scope, the Law applied for any crime that is defined in Sect. 2(1) as 'a felony' either by the Criminal Code or any other

[149] See Hatzimihail 2013.

[150] Interview with Dr. Demetrios Hadjihambis, 9 January 2015.

[151] Ibid.

[152] Joined cases C-293/12 and 594/12 *Digital Rights Ireland and Seitlinger and Others* [2014] ECLI:EU:C:2014:238.

legislation and/or which carries a maximum prison sentence of five years. Therefore, the Cypriot approach opted for the widest possible definition of serious crime, in order to resolve long-lasting problems relating to the law of evidence and to the empowerment of the police to effectively combat crime in general.

The constitutionality of Law 183(I)/2007 was examined by the Supreme Court in the case of *Alexandrou*[153] that concerned the criminal investigation and prosecution of an individual. The Supreme Court assessed whether to grant leave for *certiorari* in relation to an *ex parte* order of a first instance court that permitted the use of the data retention system. The reasoning of the Supreme Court needs to be examined carefully because the decision in *Alexandrou* is often wrongly cited as an example of national reaction to the Directive's approach.

In reality, the Court disassociated the implementation of the Directive from Law 183(I)/2007 despite the fact that the preamble of the legislation expressly stated implementation of the Directive as its intention. The consequence of that disassociation was that the relevant Law was a national measure that had no connection with EU law, and thus could not benefit from the protective scope of Art. 1A of the Constitution. This reasoning of the Supreme Court was formed by relying on the ECJ ruling in *Ireland v. Parliament and Council*,[154] from which it deduced that since the Directive was adopted on the correct legal basis (Art. 95 EC that provides for harmonising measures for the common market), then as a corollary the Directive has *as its only purpose* exactly that. Therefore, the Supreme Court construed the ECJ ruling as limiting the scope of application of the Directive only to matters relating to the legal basis upon which the adoption of the Directive was based. Criminal law and the effective combating of crime were outside the scope of the Directive and therefore the relevant national legislation was disconnected from the Directive. Moreover, it must be noted that the Supreme Court did not examine the provisions of the Directive *per se*, as that was held to be unnecessary since the ECJ had already examined the purpose of the Directive. In addition, the Supreme Court did not consider whether it was necessary to submit a preliminary reference. The outcome of the preceding reasoning was to approach the relevant law as purely domestic in content and, as such, as unconstitutional and in conflict with Art. 17 (1) of the Constitution.

The judgment paved the way for the Sixth Constitutional Amendment. It must be noted that the constitutional amendment cannot on its own regulate the area in full and hence a legislative act was required in order to specify the scope and manner of application of what the amendment permitted. The only legislation in force that practically enables access to electronic data remains Law 183(I)/2007 that has as its stated aim the implementation of the Directive. Therefore, the retention of data became a domestic issue and policy engraved in the Constitution, but its application is governed by legislation intended to implement the Directive. Moreover, that legislation was held by the Supreme Court to be going beyond the proper scope of

---

[153] *Alexandrou* [2010] 1 CLR 17.

[154] Case C-301/06 *Ireland v. Parliament and Council* [2009] ECR I-00593.

the Directive that was identified as relating only to market harmonisation. This creates a constitutional paradox since the matter of data retention in its criminal law context seems to have been regulated in Cyprus as a matter of national law and not EU law. This poses the question whether in the absence of the Directive such a course of action would have been followed, and the answer can only be negative.

Before the entry into force of the Constitutional Amendment, a case came before the Supreme Court that touched upon similar matters. In *Demetris Siamishis*,[155] the Supreme Court had to examine the constitutionality of the execution of a data retention order that chronologically took place prior the introduction of the Sixth Amendment. The case concerned an appeal from a criminal conviction, and since the appeal could only take into account the law as it stood at the time of the conviction, that conviction was held by the Supreme Court to be unstable as it had taken into account evidence obtained via infringement of the right to privacy. The Court emphasised the connection between the Directive and Law 183(I)/2007, which was considered to be an act implementing the Directive and as such enjoyed the protective status under Art. 1A of the Constitution. It therefore becomes puzzling to compare the preceding statement with the rationale of the decision in *Alexandrou,* and there is clearly inconsistency as to whether Art. 1A could apply to Law 183(I)/2007. If *Demetris Siamishis* is good law, then there was no need for amending the Constitution. If *Alexandrou* is good law, then there should not be any substantially different approach in *Demetris Siamishis*.

The next important decision that followed the Constitutional Amendment was that in *Christos Matsia.*[156] The details of the case are crucial since the case was decided after the aforementioned amendment, but the relevant orders instructing the telecommunications company to make the data retained available to the police were issued prior to the amendment. The Supreme Court in a much lengthier judgment approached the issue of the relation of Law 183(I)/2007 and the proper implementation of the Directive, and reached the same conclusion as in *Alexandrou*. It was held that the Law exceeded what was required for the implementation of the Directive and was therefore beyond the scope of Art. 1A of the Constitution and, by implication, beyond the relevant supremacy clause that would have shielded Law 183(I)/2007 from a finding of unconstitutionality. The new element in the reasoning of the Supreme Court was that the Court expressly stated that '[t]he Law in question exceeds the necessary and proportionate of what the obligations of the Republic entail under EU law'.[157] That conclusion was solely justified by full citation of paras. 80–85 of the CJEU's decision in *Ireland v. Parliament and Council.*

The new element in *Christos Matsia* was the analysis of the importance of the right to privacy and the detailed citation of its development through the case law, with specific reference to the jurisprudence of the ECtHR. However, at no point was there a comparison of the standards applied under pre-existing national

[155] [2011] 2 CLR 308.

[156] [2011] 1 CLR 152.

[157] Paragraph 170 of the Judgment (translation by the author).

jurisprudence and under the ECHR with the EU standard, hence no criticism of the Directive was in any way attempted. The key point is that the right to privacy provided the benchmark, and that right did not form part of the argumentation that the ECJ had adopted in *Ireland v. Parliament and Council*. This was a clear example of a situation in which a preliminary reference should have been submitted to the CJEU with the same content as the subsequent references in *Digital Rights Ireland and Seitlinger and Others.*

After the entry into force of the Sixth Constitutional Amendment, the Supreme Court consistently held that the data retention system was constitutionally permissible as a matter of national law. From that case law, reference can be made to two judgments that were chronologically subsequent to the ECJ judgment in *Digital Rights Ireland and Seitlinger and Others.* In the case of *Attorney General v. Isaia*[158] and in the case of *Sikifantou,*[159] the important issue was the impact of the ECJ decision in *Digital Rights Ireland and Seitlinger and Others* on the system of data retention that Law 183(I)/2007 introduced. Surprisingly, the Supreme Court in both cases stated that 'the impact of the CJEU's ruling is apparent' since 'Law 183 (I)/2007, according to its preamble, was adopted for the purpose of implementing the Directive on Data Retention'. Nonetheless, the 'apparent' is problematic given the earlier finding in *Alexandrou;* however, in the case of *Attorney General v. Isaia,* the Court, by a majority, relied on exactly that statement.

In that case the majority of the Supreme Court held that the annulment of the Directive does not impact on the case before it because Law 183(I)/2007 remains in force as a national measure. The majority decision was extremely brief on the matter and made no mention of the Directive or the ECJ judgment that annulled it. The Court insisted on the existence of a clear distinction between the Directive and Law 183(I)/2007, thus following the rationale and approach of the earlier case law on the matter. It is submitted that such a distinction is formalistic and distorts the legislative intent that was clearly stated in the preamble of Law 183(I)/2007.

The minority judgment (Nathanael and Nicolatos JJ) adopted a rather different approach on the matter. The emphasis was placed on the ECJ decision in *Digital Rights Ireland and Seitlinger and Others* and on the argumentation that the ECJ applied especially in relation to the principle of proportionality. The conclusion reached stated that Law 183(I)/2007 was founded on the Directive, and that becomes evident from the preamble of the Law. As a result of the annulment of the Directive, the 'legitimising foundation' of the Law disappears and takes with it the totality of the system that enables the police to have access to the retained data. Therefore, the issue arises whether the minority considers Law 183(I)/2007 as being invalid and, if yes, on what basis, given the existence of the Sixth Constitutional Amendment.

To summarise, the approach of the Supreme Court in the area of data retention, either as a matter of EU law or as a matter of national constitutional law, is

---

[158] Case 402/2012, 07 July 2014.

[159] Case 213/2014, 18 December 2014.

inconsistent and inherently problematic. The Supreme Court has in effect necessitated a Constitutional Amendment that altered the balance of the content of the right to privacy. The consequence is that the implementation of the Directive has become a matter of national law, irrespective of the stated intention in the preamble of the relevant Law. Therefore, the subsequent annulment of the Directive by the CJEU becomes irrelevant, whereas the whole issue arose out of the need to implement the Directive. This is clearly conceptually cyclical, structurally unsound and constitutionally heretical.

2.5 Unpublished or Secret Legislation

2.5.1 Articles 3 and 104 of the Constitution require the publication of all laws as an essential requirement for their validity. There is no case law nor academic comment on this point. The principle of due publication is implicitly also embodied in the principle of good administration.

2.6 Rights and General Principles of Law in the Context of Market Regulation: Property Rights, Legal Certainty, Non-retroactivity and Proportionality

2.6.1 As a background to this important part of the Report for Cyprus, the reader should be reminded of the fact that Art. 41 of the 2003 Act of Accession provided that the European Commission had the power to 'adopt measures to facilitate the transition' of the new Member States to the regime of the Common Agricultural Policy.[160] The European Commission therefore adopted Regulation (EC) No 1972/2003[161] (for agricultural products) and Regulation (EC) 60/2004[162] (for the sugar market) on this basis, mainly in order to avoid the risk of speculation. Both Regulations required the new Member States to levy charges on holders of surplus stocks on 1 May 2004 for products in free circulation. With respect to the sugar market more specifically,[163] Art. 6(1) of Regulation No 60/2004 required the European Commission to determine by 31 October 2004 at the latest, for each

[160] See Laulhé Shaelou 2010b, pp. 496–497.

[161] Commission Regulation (EC) No 1972/2003 of 10 November 2003 on transitional measures to be adopted in respect of trade in agricultural products on account of the accession of the Czech Republic, Estonia, Cyprus, Latvia, Lithuania, Hungary, Malta, Poland, Slovenia and Slovakia, [2004] OJ 2003 L 293/3.

[162] Commission Regulation (EC) No 60/2004 of 14 January 2004 laying down transitional measures in the sugar sector by reason of the accession of the Czech Republic, Estonia, Cyprus, Latvia, Lithuania, Hungary, Malta, Poland, Slovenia and Slovakia, [2004] OJ L 9/8.

[163] For litigation regarding other agricultural products, see Laulhé Shaelou 2010b pp. 498–500.

Member State, the quantity of sugar as such or in processed products exceeding 'the quantity considered as being normal carry-over stock at 1 May 2004', which needed to be eliminated from the market 'at the expense of the new Member States'. Article 6(2) also provided that Member States had to eliminate such quantities in excess by 30 April 2005, as determined by the Commission. For this purpose, Art. 6(3) of the Regulation required the new Member States to dispose on 1 May 2004 of a system for the identification of traded or produced surplus quantities and to use the system to compel the operators concerned to eliminate quantities at their own expense. The burden of proof was on the operators and, if not satisfied by 30 April 2005, the new Member States were entitled to charge an amount to the operators concerned. With Commission Regulation (EC) No 832/2005,[164] the European Commission fixed the surplus quantities to be eliminated for each new Member State, taking into consideration activities in the sugar sector of each new Member State before accession (period 1 May 2003–30 April 2004 compared to the average of quantities in the same period for the three previous years). The figure for Cyprus was 40,213 tonnes. The Commission subsequently extended the deadlines with Commission Regulation (EC) No 651/2005.[165]

At the national level, Law 40(1)/2005 was passed to implement the Commission Regulations on the transitional measures in the sector of agricultural goods. The Ministry of Commerce, Industry and Tourism, appointed as the competent authority, had informed the operators of Regulation 60/2004 prior to accession and, upon accession, had requested the relevant information from the operators. In 2005, it set out the surplus quantity for each operator and, in 2006, it proceeded with issuing penalties against the operators concerned on the basis of Art. 5(1) of Law 40(1)/2005.[166] Two administrative actions were therefore taken by the Ministry of Commerce on the basis of Law 40(1)/2005: (i) a decision dated 2 August 2005, requesting the addressees to eliminate the surplus quantities allocated to them by 30 November 2005; and (ii) a decision dated 21 August 2006, imposing a penalty on the operators who did not comply (or only partly complied) with the first decision. As a result, 33 recourses were introduced before the Supreme Court of Cyprus against the 2005 decision, as well as 18 recourses against the 2006 decision, totalling 51 actions which were joined and brought before the Full Chamber of the Supreme Court. In fact, there were actually 52 actions in total, but one of them was judged on the merits on 16 July 2007 by a single judge chamber.[167] Judge Hadjihambis ruled in this case

[164] Commission Regulation (EC) No 832/2005 of 31 May 2005 on the determination of surplus quantities of sugar, isoglucose and fructose for the Czech Republic, Estonia, Cyprus, Latvia, Lithuania, Hungary, Malta, Poland, Slovenia and Slovakia, [2005] OJ L 138/3.

[165] Commission Regulation (EC) No 651/2005 of 28 April 2005 amending Regulation (EC) No 60/2004 laying down transitional measures in the sugar sector by reason of the accession of the Czech Republic, Estonia, Cyprus, Latvia, Lithuania, Hungary, Malta, Poland, Slovenia and Slovakia, [2005] OJ L 108/3.

[166] Laulhé Shaelou 2010b, pp. 496–497.

[167] *Morphis Morphy & Associates Ltd v. RoC through Ministry of Commerce*, Case No. 121/2007, 16 July 2007.

that the system put in place for calculating the surplus quantities fell within the scope of Commission Regulation No 60/2004, due to the margin of discretion left to the new Member States to determine the method for such calculation.[168] The case was appealed[169] but the Supreme Court decided that this appeal would not be heard until a decision had been issued in the 51 other actions.

During the process of judicial review of administrative actions under Art.146 of the Constitution, an act must be deemed both administrative and executory in order to be reviewed. An act is deemed executory if it is 'determinative in itself of the rights and obligations of a person under the authority of the administration', and the Supreme Court examines whether an act is executory *ex proprio motu*.[170] On 13 July 2011, the Supreme Court (Full Chamber) considered the 33 joined actions challenging the 2005 decision[171] and ruled that the 2005 decision was not executory in view of the 2006 decision which imposed the penalties. It therefore rejected the 33 actions based on preliminary objections. On 21 March 2013, the Supreme Court (Full Chamber) reconvened to consider the 18 recourses for judicial review of the 2006 decision. The Court found (preliminary objections) that the 2005 and 2006 decisions constituted a series of two administrative actions and could be reviewed by the Court in accordance with the *Chrikar* jurisprudence. It then considered the following grounds for review: (i) retroactivity of taxation prohibited by Art. 24 of the Constitution; (ii) lack of reasonable and due inquiry; (iii) lack of due reasoning; and (iv) lack of competence. The Court ruled that the consideration of the retroactivity of the charge, at the constitutional level, was not 'necessary' in order to establish the *ratio* of the case and gave no further explanation as to why this was so. The Court then found several reasons why there was a lack of due inquiry on the part of the Republic of Cyprus. For instance, it noted that there was no system specified by law as of 1 May 2004, but on 15 April 2005 (Art. 6 Law 40(I)/105 provided for the retroactive ratification of acts taken during this period). It noted the absence of a legal system duly notifying natural and legal persons of their rights and obligations. Since the surplus quantities had not been established with certainty, the Court found that there was no need to refer to the ECJ and distinguished the facts of the present case from the ones arising in the *Balbiino* case referred to the ECJ by the Tallinn Administrative Court (Estonia) in the 'sugar saga'.[172] The Court further ruled that there was a lack of justification in the methods of assessment and identification of surpluses and, finally, that there was lack of competence, since the Minister himself had not authorised the actions.

---

[168] Laulhé Shaelou 2010b, p. 499.

[169] The Appeal, scheduled for 12 September 2014 for procedural considerations, was withdrawn. The action was initially based on its compatibility with EU law, the violation of constitutional rights – no retroactivity of taxation, right to trade and non-discrimination, and finally on a review of administrative actions.

[170] Emilianides 2013, p. 197.

[171] *Chrikar Trading* and others [2011] 3 CLR 541.

[172] Case C-560/07 *Balbiino* [2009] ECR I-04447. For a review of the relevant litigation in the new Member States, see Albi 2009 and Lazowski 2010.

The Court's decision in the above case was based on the principles of sound administration as established in Law 158(I)/1999 on the General Principles of Administrative Law. As seen in Sect. 2.1, this law is a source of constitutional law as it refers to matters of public law. Some principles like retroactivity and non-discrimination are protected both under the Constitution and this law. But since an Art. 146 recourse is limited by nature to considerations of administrative law and does not extend to a review of constitutionality, it would appear that only the constitutional principles expressly mentioned among the general principles of administrative law are *implicit* in a review of administrative actions under Art. 146 (namely the protection of legitimate expectations and the principle of proportionality). Even so, it would appear that they will only be considered by the Court when *necessary* for the establishment of the *ratio* of the case. This is also true of rights protected expressly under the Constitution, but the Court will not raise constitutional issues out of its own motion.[173]

Thus, contrary to constitutional courts in other new Member States such as Hungary, Estonia and the Czech Republic,[174] the Supreme Court in Cyprus did not consider any constitutional issues raised in the sugar cases. It restrained itself to a mere control of administrative actions. There is no reference to the EU legal framework either, even if the supremacy of EU law appears to be implicit. To the extent that this decision of the Supreme Court relieves operators from penalties, it could be said to participate in the protection of individual (economic) rights. It is also a clear signal to the public administration in Cyprus that despite EU accession, legal certainty in administrative procedures must prevail and no lowering of national standards is permitted by the Court.[175] It is argued that this finding could be of utmost significance, especially in the context of the financial crisis (on concerns about the protection of property rights in a dissenting opinion in the 'bail-in' case, see Sect. 2.7.3).

In the meantime, Cyprus requested the annulment of Regulation 651/2005 before the General Court of the EU because it argued that it changed its legal situation under Regulation 60/2004.[176] The General Court found on the contrary that the amendments with respect to Cyprus were purely procedural and that the act (as amended) had become final vis-à-vis Cyprus since it had not been challenged within the deadline.[177] The action was therefore found inadmissible. However, this was based on the findings of the General Court that there was no need to be a Member State to challenge generally applicable acts under (then) Art. 230 EC, and that it was sufficient to be a legal person.[178] The General Court had concluded that there was no violation of the principle of effective judicial protection towards

---

[173] Interview with Dr. Demetrios Hadjihambis, 20 August 2014.

[174] See Albi 2009, Lazowski 2010 and Laulhé Shaelou 2010b.

[175] Interview with Dr. Demetrios Hadjihambis, 20 August 2014.

[176] Joined Cases T-300/05 and T-316/05 *Republic of Cyprus v. Commission* [2009] ECR II-00192.

[177] Ibid., paras. 258–260.

[178] Ibid., paras. 241, 245.

Cyprus in this case.[179] The ECJ however overruled the specific finding of the General Court on the *locus standi* of new Member States in the Polish case seeking the annulment of Regulation 1972/2003, finding that the General Court had erred in law.[180] Cyprus did not appeal the decision of the General Court although its arguments with respect to Regulation 651/2005 had not been heard, contrary to Poland for whom Regulation 735/2004 was found to make substantial changes to Regulation 1972/2003 and whose action was deemed admissible, thereby raising the question of effective judicial protection vis-à-vis Cyprus.

2.7 The ESM Treaty, Austerity Programmes and the Democratic, Rule-of-Law-Based State

2.7.1–2.7.2 The constitutionality of the Treaty Establishing the European Stability Mechanism (ESM Treaty) has not been directly raised in Cyprus despite the fact that the Supreme Court had to examine the legality of the 'bail-in' that was imposed on Cyprus. Specifically, issues relating to the structure of the financial stability mechanism and its actual funding were not discussed in connection with budget autonomy and responsibility. Moreover, no constitutional amendment was introduced in relation to those matters or Eurobonds and the Banking Union.

2.7.3 Some of the case law regarding the impact of austerity measures on constitutional rights was provided in Sect. 2.2.

A further central case regarding the judicial protection of property rights and judicial review concerned the 'bail-in' measures in 2013. As is explained in Sect. 3.5, the bail-in decision resulted from a political agreement at the Eurogroup level and had the effect of imposing a levy amounting to partial confiscation of all unsecured deposits, that is below 100,000 EUR, in the two systemic Cypriot banks.

The legality of the measures adopted to impose the 'bail-in' were contested in *Myrto Christodoulou*,[181] or what is referred to in the rest of the Report as the 'bail in' case. The majority decision, taking an unsatisfactory position, classified the matter as one belonging to the sphere of private law, and therefore the proper course of action was to initiate actions for damage for breach of contract and tort law. Therefore, the issue was not one of administrative law, as it concerned the relationship between depositors and the banks, and the recourse filed under Art. 146 of the Constitution was dismissed. In terms of the civil actions, the criterion to be applied was whether the loss suffered would have been greater if the 'bail-in' had not taken place. This criterion was mentioned eight times in the judgment of the majority. The majority judgment did not examine the EU aspect of the matter nor consider the possibility of sending a preliminary reference.

---

179 Ibid., paras. 242–247.

180 Case C–335/09 P *Poland v. Commission* [2012] ECLI:EU:C:2012:385.

181 *Myrto Christodoulou* [2013] 3 CLR 427.

In contrast to that formalistic approach, the dissenting judgment by Judge Erotokritou takes a different and much more preferable approach that is perhaps the most complete attempt in Cyprus to discuss the nature of the principle of primacy of EU law and its relationship with national constitutional law. Judge Erotokritou stated that the matter is one that relates to human rights, as it affects the right to property as protected under Art. 17 of the EU Charter and under Protocol 1 ECHR, as well as under Art. 23 of the Constitution. The adopted approach is so important that it necessitates fuller citations:

> Recent events in Europe due to the financial crisis and the measures taken, give the impression that not only international law, but also the European and national law seems to be rewritten. It is therefore imperative in order to safeguard the rights of the parties arising from the TEU, to give the chance to national administrative courts to control not only the legality of the contested acts, but also the compatibility of the various national laws which led to the contested measures with EU law.

In this part, the dissenting judgment raises the point that the situation that is emerging is one that deviates from pre-existing EU law and creates a new set of factors that are different from those upon which the relationship between national law and EU law has been based so far. Therefore, the 'bail-in issue' is rightly approached as an issue exceeding the consensus that pre-existed, thus necessitating the scrutiny of the compatibility of the new EU/international law measures with the rights arising from EU law. Judge Erotokritou continued:

> Where conflict is found and there is no ambiguity, Union law is to be applied, as it takes precedence and is directly applicable. Where conflict is found, but the requisite clarity as to the content and validity of the provisions of Union law is not present, then the national court has the power under Art. 267 TFEU to apply with a preliminary question to the CJEU calling either for the interpretation of certain provisions of EU law, e.g. free movement of capital (Art. 63 TEU), or for a ruling on the validity of specific legal instruments of the EU institutions. With this assistance, the national court may now proceed to examine the compatibility of national law with EU law.

In this part of the approach, Judge Erotokritou focused on the use of the preliminary reference procedure as a useful tool for exercising the national judicial power of scrutiny. In addition, Judge Erotokritou stated:

> National sovereignty undoubtedly gives way to the supremacy of European law and rightly so I would say. But it seems that the further erosion of that national sovereignty and the parallel erosion of fundamental rights, often through informal procedures should at some stage be scrutinised by the CJEU, albeit indirectly through Article 267, as to whether it is compatible with the primary law of the European Union.

This is perhaps the centre of gravity of the approach of Judge Erotokritou. The judge adopts a pragmatic approach that accepts the limitation of national sovereignty as a logical consequence of the need to apply the principle of primacy of EU law. This indirectly refers to the nature of the EU system as being founded on the principle of conferred powers that the Member States have voluntarily transferred to the Union. It is respectfully submitted that if this point would have been specifically included in the dissenting opinion, then it would have acquired a more holistic theoretical and substantial character in relation to the way that the national constitutional system sees the Union. This would therefore have formed an opportunity for starting to express the inherent reservations as regards the principle of primacy of EU law and for starting to set the limits to the acceptance of the principle.

The next argument is also very interesting, as it identifies the problem that is created by any further unilateral alteration of the equilibrium that relates to the transfer of sovereignty to the EU and to the corresponding application of the principle of primacy of EU law. This becomes especially relevant if the impact of the alteration is directed towards the protection of fundamental rights and has as a result a unilateral and substantial shift in competences. However, this point could have been further explained as having the meaning that any expansion of EU competences at the expense of national sovereignty in a way that structurally affects the constitutional identity cannot be accepted by the national legal order and even by the ECJ.

One cannot avoid making the comparison of the dissenting decision with the decision and the reasoning of the *Bundesverfassungsgericht* in the *Honeywell* case.[182] There it was held that the *ultra vires* review by the Federal Constitutional Court, namely the striking down of an EU act, can only be considered by the national court if a breach of competences on the part of the European bodies is manifestly in breach of competences and the impugned act led to a structurally significant shift in the structure of competences that is to the detriment of the Member States. A reference to this judgment would have given an essential element of justification to the argument that Judge Erotokritou was making. This would have been useful also because the Judge impliedly followed the reasoning of the German Court by requiring the CJEU to scrutinise the potential erosion of competences, thus placing the responsibility on the CJEU and not solely on the national court. This reflects exactly the inherent idea that the relationship between national constitutional law and EU law is one that both parties have an obligation to safeguard in order for the relationship to remain one of partnership. Judge Erotokritou continued to reinforce exactly the preceding point by stating that:

> In the EU legal system, the supremacy of the rule of law and of legal protection, which form a fundamental principle of the European Union and which are inextricably intertwined with the Republic, can not be eliminated through the creation of exemptions from judicial administrative control, each time for various reasons national governments are in trouble and take decisions which violate basic human rights that are derived from the legal order of the European Union and generally from the European *acquis communautaire.* The legal restrictions imposed by the Constitution on the exercise of state power must be maintained even in critical and difficult conditions such as those that exist today, in order to ensure the supremacy of the rule of law and of the principle of legality.

To summarise, the approach is the best and only example of real discussion about the nature of the relationship between national constitutional law and the principle of primacy of EU law in Cyprus. The approach by Judge Erotokritou

---

[182] BVerfG, Order of 06 July 2010 - 2 BvR 2661/06 - Rn. (1-116).

contains many important structural and substantive points that reflect the theoretical perspective about the principle of primacy of EU law and which has two dimensions: that of the CJEU and that of the national Constitution. Moreover, Judge Erotokritou places both parties under an obligation to safeguard the delicate equilibrium in order to prevent any unilateral alterations that could create a clash. In doing so, Judge Erotokritou removes the possibility of tensions arising by requiring the national court to first submit a preliminary reference. This is the same approach inherent in *Honeywell*. The identification of the delicate issue of fundamental rights and the indirect reference to competences through the connection with the erosion of national sovereignty is also in line with the rich jurisprudence of other national constitutional courts.

Nonetheless, the approach of Judge Erotokritou also does not go far enough and does not fully elaborate on all the crucial points that it raised. The lack of any reference to the jurisprudence of other national constitutional courts, including *Honeywell*, is one such step short of full elaboration.

The last point to be made is that the dissenting opinion was unfortunately not endorsed by the majority. Nonetheless, it is submitted that the fact that views expressed were not endorsed by the majority does not pre-empt the subsequent adoption of the reasoning of Judge Erotokritou as the formula that the Supreme Court can apply to the primacy of EU law. The dissenting judgment exists and can always be used to supplement the already incomplete approach of the Supreme Court on this issue, regardless of the different views of the majority on one specific matter, i.e. bail-in.

2.8 *Judicial Review of EU Measures: Access to Justice and the Standard of Review*

2.8.1–2.8.6 The characteristics of judicial review in the Cypriot legal order have already been addressed elsewhere in this Report.[183] Overall, standing requirements have been said to be construed broadly by the Supreme Court, thereby 'guaranteeing the procedural access to effective judicial protection'.[184] As a manifestation of the doctrine of separation of powers, the Supreme Court in Cyprus seems to be responsible for keeping the balance between access to judicial review and the good administration of justice.[185] This duty appears to extend also to indirect judicial review in the context of preliminary references to the CJEU.

[183] See e.g. Sects. 2.1.3, 2.2 and 2.6 above. No statistical data regarding annulment and relevant grounds is available.

[184] Kombos 2010b, pp. 329 and 350.

[185] Ibid., p. 338.

It should be noted in this respect that the Courts Law of 1960, as amended,[186] used to provide for a right of appeal against decisions of lower courts to refer or not to refer a matter to the CJEU, limited initially (in 2007) to instances where the court ruled on the basis of an application made by one of the parties to the case, and subsequently extended (in 2008) to cases where the courts would decide to refer on their own motion. The authors of the present Report respectively provided at the time an extensive critical analysis of the right to refer or not to refer a matter to the CJEU.[187] Suffice to note here that following the *Cartesio* case,[188] the Law since 2009 provides that no such appeal is possible.

Following the removal of the right to appeal decisions of lower courts to refer or not to refer to the CJEU, it can be said that lower courts are quite free to use the preliminary reference mechanism, including in matters of interpretation and validity of EU legal acts. However, the first preliminary reference to the CJEU from a court other than the Supreme Court only came in 2013 and did not concern matters of validity of EU legal acts.[189] In the meantime, the lower courts have gradually developed their legal reasoning in terms of dealing with requests from applicants to refer questions of interpretation of EU law to the CJEU, but still too often reject such requests with little justification, resulting in a very low number of preliminary references to the CJEU from such courts (three in total).[190] As far as the Supreme Court is concerned, only four preliminary references have been made to date.[191] These four references appear to indicate a steady trend towards the progressive awareness and 'mastering' of the preliminary reference mechanism by the Court.[192] Suffice to note here that none of these references appears to raise issues of validity of EU legal acts.

Regarding concerns about a gap in judicial review, in the context of the financial crisis measures, it might be worth briefly recalling the concern in the dissenting opinion of Judge Erotokritou (Sect. 2.7.3) that in the intertwined EU legal order 'the rule of law and legal protection can not be eliminated through the creation of exemptions from judicial administrative control, each time for various reasons national governments are in trouble and take decisions which violate basic human rights'.

---

[186] Law 14 of 1960, Sect. 25, new sub-sect. 2A, as amended in 2007, 2008 and 2009.

[187] Laulhé Shaelou 2010b; Kombos 2010b. For a comprehensive, unpublished study see Lycourgos 2014.

[188] Case C-210/06 *Cartesio* [2008] ECR I-09641.

[189] *Sotiris (Akis) Papasavvas v. O Philelftheros Dimosia Eteria ltd and others*, Nicosia District Court, Case No. 9493/10, 27 March 2013 (in Greek).

[190] Court of Justice of the European Union, Annual report 2013, Luxembourg 2014, pp. 118.

[191] Ibid.

[192] Especially *Cypra Ltd v. the Republic*, Administrative Appeal 78/2009, 5 June 2013 and *Alpha Bank Cyprus Ltd v. Si Senh Dau and others*, Joined Civil Appeals E23/2013-E29/2013, 13 September 2013 (in Greek). See Laulhé Shaelou 2010b.

2.9 *Other Constitutional Rights and Principles*

2.9.1 There have been no further notable developments in Cyprus.

2.10 *Common Constitutional Traditions*

2.10.1–2.10.2 The influence and impact of the common constitutional traditions on the definition and interpretation of concepts of EU law has been minimal. From the Cypriot perspective, the matter has not been examined by the Supreme Court, but it can be argued that the opportunity to do so was missed in the 'bail-in' case and in relation to social rights that form a distinct and important part of the national Constitution. Reference can be made to the rather unique passage in Art. 9 of the Constitution that states '[e]very person has the right to a decent existence and to social security. A law shall provide for the protection of the workers, assistance to the poor and for a system of social insurance.'

Nonetheless, the content and scope of the preceding provision is rather idiosyncratic and specifically relevant to the Cypriot context, even if a parallel can perhaps be found in the German Basic Law and the fundamental principle of the 'social state'. It would however be difficult to establish the universality of the principle to the required extent that would qualify it as forming part of the common constitutional traditions. The same could apply in relation to various other national constitutional principles to be found in other jurisdictions. The issue can also be assessed through the perspective and the experience of the ECHR on margin of appreciation and European common ground. The key factor is the progression of time and the maturing of a legal principle that is reflected in the growing acceptance and adoption by the majority of the participating legal orders. In practical terms, the highlighting of the centrality of a legal system in the national constitutional order can be useful especially in the context of the preliminary reference procedure.

2.11 *Article 53 of the Charter and the Issue of Stricter Constitutional Standards*

2.11.1 The Cypriot constitutional system places considerable emphasis on the protection of fundamental rights and on the continuation of a fruitful relationship between the national Constitution and the ECHR. This relationship has been very close and can be characterised as an example of harmonious coexistence. The EU dimension of the matter creates *de facto* and *de jure* a legal triangle that governs the applicable standard of protection, but in the Cypriot context the issue has never been discussed fully. The prevailing approach, as can be seen in relation to the Data Retention Directive in Sect. 2.4, tends to isolate the EU aspect at least to the point where it resolves any clash with the national standards of protection in favour of the EU standard. Methodologically this is achieved by 'nationalising' the issue and by subsequently modifying the national standard; this is an unfortunate and problematic approach and outcome. Some cases where the Cypriot Constitution and the Supreme Court provide a higher standard of protection than the ECHR were noted in Sects. 1.1.2 and 2.1. Additionally, it will be recalled from Sect. 2.7.3 that Judge Erotokritou in a dissenting opinion has expressed concern about the 'erosion of fundamental rights' 'often through informal procedures'.

At the general level, the constitutional triangle of protection must be 'isosceles'. That would reflect the equality of the legal orders, which is a fundamental prerequisite for the symbiosis of legal orders. This argument is reinforced by two considerations. First, the respect for the constitutional identity of each system and secondly, because of the forthcoming accession of the EU to the ECHR system. As a result, the upwards modification of the EU standard that would favour the protection afforded to a fundamental right must be encouraged, as it will be constructive for both the right in question and for the relationship with national courts. The concept of deference is therefore to be reinforced, and the CJEU has shown such willingness in the *Omega* case.[193]

2.12 Democratic Debate on Constitutional Rights and Values

2.12.1–2.12.3 In relation to the democratic element as expressed through the participation in open discussions about EU measures bound to have a substantial impact on national constitutional values, it can be safely argued that in Cyprus no such deliberations took place at any stage in relation to the EAW or the Data Retention Directive. Moreover, when problems arose in those areas, the Supreme Court indirectly facilitated the opening of a democratic dialogue by requiring the introduction of constitutional amendments. This had the effect of creating a new opportunity for the legislature to discuss in full such matters before proceeding with the constitutional amendments, but the character of that discussion has remained the responsibility of the legislature and the executive. Normally in such situations the legislature invites professional bodies and experts to express their opinions, but such discussion is not conducted at the national level and the public remains largely disassociated. The matter is indeed important given the standing restrictions in relation to an action for annulment of an EU act and it also touches upon the legitimacy of the EU system. However, the fact that Member States through their elective representatives participate in the adoption and implementation of such EU acts cannot be ignored. The responsibility remains at the national level, and the creation of a specific procedure could be beneficial in terms of legitimacy, but it is

[193] Case C-36/02 *Omega* [2004] ECR I-09609. For analysis, see Kombos 2006.

questionable whether it could be effective and efficient. One such procedural route could be the assessment of legality prior to the entry into force of the EU act, at both the national and EU level. This, however, has to be assessed in relation to the privileged standing status of Member States and to the efficiency of the EU system. Moreover, issues of national procedural autonomy also arise and there is the potential of national constitutional courts engaging in the review of validity of EU acts in the making that would trigger the preliminary reference obligation for national courts of last resort. The other suggested option, recognising the fact that unconstitutionality has been identified in accordance with the domestic system of control of constitutionality as a defence for the Member State in an infringement proceeding, is problematic. This would occur at a later stage of the entry into force of the EU measure and would create differing levels of compliance for Member States, thus affecting the effectiveness of EU law.

2.13 Experts' Analysis on the Protection of Constitutional Rights in EU Law

2.13.1–2.13.2 The symbiosis of the different standards of protection is proving problematic, but it is submitted that this has been the situation for decades, as the experience with the *Solange* jurisprudence[194] clearly indicates. The matter is nonetheless bound to come to the forefront of the discussion with the accession of the EU to the ECHR system, and it is perhaps crucial to assess the method and rules of accession especially after the recent approach of the CJEU in *Opinion 2/2013*.[195] This author acted as co-agent for Cyprus in those proceedings, and it can be argued that the concerns of the CJEU about the relationship between the two systems and the two Courts were evident in both the questionnaire sent to the intervening parties and in the questions that the CJEU raised during the oral stage of the proceedings.

To summarise, the concerns about the different standards of protection are legitimate but are not new; they form part of the history of the constitutional coexistence.

2.13.3 As regards the quality of the reasoning of the CJEU in cases concerning constitutional sensitivities, it is submitted that unfortunately the Cypriot Supreme Court has so far not raised such concerns or issues for that matter. The limited number of preliminary references submitted by Cypriot courts have concerned specific issues that did not relate to deep constitutional concerns.

In terms of the broader issue, it can be argued that the key is in the formulation of the preliminary reference by the national courts. The detailed statement of the national perception and of the relevant applicable jurisprudence can hopefully steer the approach of the CJEU towards a more detailed reasoning. Such examples, albeit

---

[194] *Internationale Handelsgesellschaft mbH v Einfurh- und Vorratstelle für Getreide und Futtermittel* [1974] 2 CMLR 540; *Wünsche Handelsgesellschaft* (Solange II) [1987] 3 CMLR 225.

[195] Opinion 2/13 *Opinion pursuant to Art. 218(11) TFEU* [2014] ECLI:EU:C:2014:2454.

with varying success, can be found in the preliminary references in *Digital Rights Ireland and Seitlinger and Others* and in *Outright Monetary Transactions (OMT)*.[196] Moreover, the introduction of dissenting judgments would be beneficial for the clarity and completeness of the stated judicial reasoning, but there are strong informal signs that the CJEU is firmly against any such reform.

2.13.4 In the Cypriot context there is an urgent need to re-establish the boundaries between national constitutional law and EU law because the Fifth Constitutional Amendment and the approach of the Supreme Court have created a tight and restricted topos for airing national concerns about the shaping and upholding of constitutional rights and principles.

3 Constitutional Issues in Global Governance

3.1–3.2 Constitutional Rules on International Organisations and the Ratification and Application of Treaties

The ratification of treaties in Cyprus[197] and the transfer of powers to international organisations need to be considered within the framework of the status of the Republic of Cyprus in public international law and the rigid nature of its Constitution, as already analysed in detail in Sect. 1.1. One of the peculiar implications for the Republic of Cyprus deriving from its unique constitutional setting relates to its membership in international organisations. It should be noted that almost from the date of its creation up to its accession to the EU (1961–2004), the Republic of Cyprus was a member of the non-aligned movement. Cyprus is also the only EU Member State that is not a member of NATO or of the Partnership for Peace Programme.[198] The relationship the Republic maintains with international organisations must of course be examined in the light of the *de facto* division of its territory and in view of the several attempts (including currently ongoing) to find a solution to the Cyprus problem.

The Council of Ministers has the power to conclude any international agreement by virtue of Arts. 50 and 54 of the Constitution. There is a difference between international agreements concluded with a foreign state or an international organisation falling under the scope of Art. 169(1) of the Constitution and relating to 'commercial matters, economic co-operation and *motus vivendi*', which are concluded under a decision of the Council of Ministers, and any other treaty,

---

[196] See respectively Joined cases C-293/12 and 594/12, n. 152; Case C-62/14 *Gauweiler and Others* [2015] ECLI:EU:C:2015:400.

[197] For a legal analysis of the reception of international legal agreements in the Cypriot national legal order, see Laulhé Shaelou 2010b, pp. 471–484; see also Laulhé Shaelou 2010a, pp. 130–140.

[198] Emilianides reports that 'a decision of the House of Representatives that the Republic should apply for membership in the Partnership for Peace programme was vetoed by the President of the Republic Demetris Christofias on 2 March 2011', Emilianides 2013, p. 20.

convention or international agreement falling under Art. 169(2) of the Constitution which requires such international agreements to be 'negotiated and signed under a decision of the Council of Ministers' but will 'only be operative and binding on the Republic when approved by a law made by the House of Representatives whereupon it shall be concluded'. In accordance with Art. 169(3) of the Constitution, all such treaties, conventions and agreements have, 'as from their publication in the official Gazette of the Republic, superior force to any municipal law on condition that such treaties, conventions and agreements are applied by the other party thereto'.[199] Article 170(1) of the Constitution further provides that the Republic of Cyprus 'shall, by agreement on appropriate terms, accord most-favoured-nation treatment to the Kingdom of Greece, the Republic of Turkey and the United Kingdom of Great Britain and Northern Ireland for all agreements whatever their nature might be'. The Treaty of Guarantee also provides in its Art. I that the

> Republic of Cyprus undertakes to ensure the maintenance of its independence, territorial integrity and security, as well as respect for its Constitution and undertakes not to participate, in whole or in part, in any political or economic union with any State whatsoever. It accordingly declares prohibited any activity likely to promote, directly or indirectly, either union with any other State or partition of the Island.

These provisions of the constitutional framework of the Republic of Cyprus were at the centre of legal debates prior to Cyprus joining the EU. A group of international legal experts concluded that none of these provisions were an obstacle to Cyprus' EU membership.[200]

3.3–3.5 Democratic Control, Judicial Review and the Social Welfare Dimension

As for democratic control by the House of Representatives, it was already noted that most of the time democratic deliberations are non-existent or limited. The Constitution of Cyprus is, however, based on the principle of representative democracy.[201] Democratic debates within the House of Representatives take place on a regular basis but not systematically (referendums can take place upon a decision of the House of Representatives following a proposal from the Council of Ministers as per the Referendum Law No 286/1989, but are kept for issues of special importance and of public interest).[202] It was noted for example in the context of the run-up towards Cyprus' EU accession that there was very little or no

[199] The role of the Supreme Court with respect in particular to the ECHR has already been developed in this Report.

[200] Emilianides 2013, p. 212. For a pre-accession consideration of other debates surrounding the impact of Cyprus' EU membership on the Constitution, including with respect to conflict of powers and transfer of powers, see Laulhé Shaelou 2010a, pp. 133–134.

[201] For a detailed description and analysis of the system of government in Cyprus including political parties and their role in the House of Representatives as interpreted recently by the Supreme Court, see Emilianides 2013, pp. 65–75.

[202] For a review of the Referendum Law, see Emilianides 2013, pp. 75–76.

democratic debate taking place in the Parliament, as Cyprus's strategy was mainly based on external considerations and concerns.[203]

More recently, however, mention should be made of the more active role currently played by the House of Representatives in the context of the EU/IMF macro-economic adjustment programme for Cyprus[204] and of its pivotal role during the negotiations leading to the programme.[205]

The lack of judicial activism in respect of the same matter has been noted elsewhere in this Report.[206]

3.6 Constitutional Rights and Values in Selected Areas of Global Governance

3.6.1 The constitutional amendment regarding extradition under international/ European arrangements was discussed in the introduction to Sect. 2.3.

The question of what safeguards are available to avoid potentially arbitrary results in the context of an international arrest warrant arose in the case against Mr. Louka, requested by South Africa, signatory to the European Convention on Extradition since 2003, in *George Louka v. Minister of Justice and Public Order*.[207] In the first decision, the Supreme Court had to review the (alleged) administrative decision of the Minister to sign the international arrest warrant issued against Mr. Louka. The lower court had considered the discretionary powers of the Minister to sign the said warrant as an '*acte de gouvernement*', which meant that it fell beyond the scope of the Court's powers of review of administrative acts under Art. 146 of the Constitution. The recourse before the Supreme Court was therefore rejected. In the second decision, the Supreme Court ruled in final instance on the request for the issue of an order in the form of *habeas corpus*, as part of the prerogative orders under Art. 155(4) of the Constitution whereby the Court has the exclusive jurisdiction to review the action of a lower court, in order to determine the lawfulness of

[203] Laulhé Shaelou 2010a, p. 42.

[204] With respect for example to the legal framework regarding non-performing loans and the protection of the dwelling house.

[205] See Sect. 2.7.3 and Laulhé Shaelou 2013.

[206] See Sect. 2.7.3 for case law related to the bail-in and Sect. 2.2 for the austerity measures put in place in Cyprus as a result of the financial crisis. On 16 March 2013, a first political agreement was reached between the Eurogroup, IMF and the Cypriot authorities which included a one-off stability levy for all resident and non-resident depositors, both insured and uninsured. This political agreement was rejected by the House of Representatives on 19 March 2013. On 25 March 2013, a second political agreement was reached between the Eurogroup and the Cypriot authorities, supported by all euro area Member States and the international lenders on the policy Programme and the loan package associated with it (10bn EUR in total). The political agreement included *inter alia* bail-in measures for unsecured deposits in the two main Cypriot commercial banks and a resolution programme. The Memorandum of Understanding was signed between the Cypriot authorities, IMF and the European Commission on 26 April 2013. On 30 April 2013, the Programme was endorsed by the House of Representatives.

[207] Case 5965/2013, 16 October 2013 and Case 124/2013, 8 January 2014.

the authority to detain a person–in this case Mr. Louka.[208] Not surprisingly, the Court decided that in the case of international arrest warrants to be executed under the relevant law in Cyprus,[209] the *ultimate* decision remains with the Minister who can exercise his discretion to sign the warrant. The Court characterised this discretionary power as 'political' and 'executive' in nature, intimately linked to the country's international obligations, thereby falling beyond the scope of judicial control which it found had been effectively exhausted in this case, including with respect to the protection of fundamental human rights and in terms of access to justice. Finally, the Court noted that both the courts and the Minister examine the same criteria and therefore the scope of the examination ought to be different, taking a 'political dimension' in the case of the examination by the latter. It is hardly of any comfort to know that the judicial decision on the extradition of a person may ultimately be subject to political considerations independently of the judicial process accompanying the execution of the warrant. Given the role of the Ministry and the Attorney General in the issue/execution of arrest warrants, one is entitled to wonder what safeguards are available in the law to avoid potentially arbitrary results.

In general, in view of the characteristics of the Constitution as developed in this Report, many of them unique, and the lack of prospects for constitutional improvements pending a solution to the Cyprus problem,[210] it is debatable to what extent Cyprus is equipped to face a process of globalised constitutional governance.

References

Albi A. (2005) EU Enlargement and the Constitutions of Central and Eastern Europe. Cambridge University Press, Cambridge.

Albi A. (2009) Ironies in human rights protection in the EU: pre-accession conditionality and post-accession conundrums. ELJ 15:46–69.

Besselink L. (2006) The Dutch Constitution, the European Constitution and the Referendum in the Netherlands. In: Albi A., Ziller J. (eds.) The European Constitution and National Constitutions: Ratification and Beyond. Kluwer, The Hague, pp. 149–156.

---

[208] For prerogative orders, see Emilianides 2013, p. 124.

[209] For the applicable legal framework, see http://www.coe.int/t/dghl/standardsetting/pc-oc/Country_information1_en_files/CYPRUS%20%20national%20procedures%20for%20extradition.pdf.

[210] For an attempt to submit a group of international agreements to a referendum in Cyprus (under the auspices of the UN and not within the framework of the Constitution of the Republic of Cyprus), mention should be made of the so-called Annan Plan put to a referendum in 2004 on both sides of the divide, allegedly promoting a comprehensive settlement to the Cyprus problem and creating a new constitutional framework for the country. See http://www.hri.org/docs/annan/. This Plan was rejected by the Greek Cypriot community and endorsed by the Turkish Cypriot community. For a legal analysis of the Plan from the point of view of EU law, see Laulhé Shaelou 2010a, Chap. 6.

Birkinshaw P., Kombos C. (2009) The UK Approach to the Emergence of European Constitutionalism – Repositioning the Debate: Departure from Constitutional Ontology and the Introduction of the Typological Discussion. In: Arnold R. (ed.) The Emergence of European Constitutional Law. Bruylant, Brussels, pp. 35–75.

Christou T., Kousoupi E., Xanthaki H. (2009) Mutual recognition in criminal matters in Cyprus. European Journal of Law Reform 11(1):111 et seq.

Christou T. (2012) The European Arrest Warrant and human rights in the context of the Republic of Cyprus. Cyprus Human Rights Law Review 1(1):57 et seq.

De Smith S.A. (1964) The Commonwealth and its Constitutions. Penguin Books, London.

Emilianides A. (2006) Beyond the Constitution of Cyprus. Sakkoulas, Thessaloniki.

Emilianides A. (2013) Cyprus Constitutional Law. Wolters Kluwer, The Hague.

Evriviades M. (1975) The Legal Dimension of the Cyprus Conflict. Texas International Law Journal 10:227 et seq.

Gorski A., Hofmanski P. (eds.) (2008) The European Arrest Warrant and its implementation in the Member States of the EU. Wydawnictwo C.H. Beck, Warsaw.

Hatzimihail N. (2013) Cyprus as a Mixed Legal System. Journal of Civil Law Studies 6 (1):37–96.

Kapardis A. (2008) The European Arrest Warrant in Cyprus and constitutional concerns. In Gorski A., Hofmanski P. (eds.) (2008) The European Arrest Warrant and its implementation in the Member States of the EU. Wydawnictwo C.H. Beck, Warsaw.

Kombos C. (2006) Fundamental Rights and Fundamental Freedoms: A Symbiosis on the basis of Subsidiarity. EPL 12 (3):433 et seq.

Kombos C. (2010a) The Esoteric Dimension of Constitutional Pluralism. In: Birkinshaw P., Varney M. (eds.) The End of the 1992 Legal Order. Kluwer, Alphen Aan Den Rijn, pp. 291–323.

Kombos C. (2010b) The Supreme Court's of Cyprus and the CJEU's Approach to Standing for Judicial Review and to the Preliminary Reference Procedure. EPL 16(3):327–355.

Kombos C. (2015a) The Doctrine of Necessity in Constitutional Law. Sakkoulas, Athens.

Kombos C. (2015b) The Impact of EU Law on Cypriot Public Law. Sakkoulas, Athens.

Kombos C., Arestis G., Kyriakou N. (2015) Human Rights in Cyprus. In: Merten D., Papier H. J. (eds.) Handbook of fundamental rights in Germany and Europe. C.F. Müller Verlag, Heidelberg.

Kombos C., Pantazi Lambrou A. (2012) Cyprus. In: Laffranque J. (ed.) The Protection of Fundamental Rights Post-Lisbon, Reports of the XXV FIDE Congress Tallinn 2012, Vol. 1, Tartu University Press, Tallinn, pp. 303–354.

Kyriakou N. (2010) National Judges and Supranational Laws on the Effective Application of the EC Law and the ECHR: The Case of Cyprus. Available at SSRN: http://ssrn.com/abstract=1623560.

Laulhé Shaelou S. (2010a) The EU and Cyprus: principles and strategies of full integration. SEUR vol. 3. Martinus Nijhoff, Leiden.

Laulhé Shaelou S. (2010b) 'Back to reality': the implications of EU membership in the constitutional legal order of Cyprus. In: Lazowski A. (ed.) Brave new world: application of EU law in the new member states. T.M.C. Asser Press, The Hague.

Laulhé Shaelou S. (2011) Market freedoms, fundamental rights and the European public order. YEL 30(1):298–357.

Laulhé Shaelou S. (2013) The EU in crisis. Myths and Realities. Paper presented at the seminar 'Cyprus in the eyes of the storm: legal implications of the economic and financial crisis'. UCLan Cyprus, 27 June 2013.

Lazowski A. (ed.) (2010) Brave new world: application of EU law in the new member states. T.M.C. Asser Press, The Hague.

Legrand P. (2002) Public law, Europeanisation, and convergence: can comparatists contribute? In: Beaumont P., Lyons C., Walker N. (eds.) Convergence and Divergence in European Public Law. Hart Publishing, Oxford, pp. 225 et seq.

Loizou A. (2001) The Constitution of the Republic of Cyprus. Nicosia.

Lycourgos C. (2010) Cyprus Public Law as Affected by Accession to the EU. In: Kombos C. (ed.) Studies in European Public Law. Sakkoulas, Athens, pp. 101–115.

Lycourgos C. (2014). Preliminary reference to the Court of Justice of the European Union – Law and practice in Cyprus ten years after accession to the EU (March 2014, unpublished study) (on file with the author).

Nicolaou I. (2000) The Control of the Constitutionality of the Laws and the Separation of Powers of the State Institutions of Cyprus. Sakkoulas, Athens.

Paraskeva C. (2015) Cypriot Constitutional Law: Fundamental Rights and Freedoms. Nomiki Bibliothiki, Athens.

Pikis G. (2006) Constitutionalism – Human Rights – Separation of Powers. Martinus Nijhoff, Leiden.

Polyviou P. (2013) Cyprus on the Edge: a Study in Constitutional Survival. Nicosia.

Polyviou P. (2015a) Cyprus: A Study in the Theory, Structure and Method of the Legal System of the Republic of Cyprus. Nicosia.

Polyviou P. (2015b) Ibrahim: The Doctrine of Necessity and the Republic of Cyprus. Nicosia.

Stefanou E. (2011) Rights of suspects in Cyprus. Speech delivered at the meeting of the European Criminal Bar Association, 24 September 2011. http://www.kscp.com.cy/documents/SUSPECTS_RIGHTS_24092011.pdf.

Stefanou E., Kapardis A. (2006) The first two years of fiddling around with the implementation of the EAW in Cyprus. Cyprus and European Law Review 2:258 et seq.

Soulioti S. (2006) Fettered Independence: Cyprus 1878–1964 vol.1: The Narrative. Minnesota Mediterranean and East European Monographs, Minneapolis.

Tornaritis C. (1968) The Social and Economic Rights Under the Law of the Republic of Cyprus. In: Mélanges Marcel Bridel: recueil de travaux. Imprimeries Réunies, Lausanne, pp. 533–556.

Tornaritis C. (1980) Cyprus and its Constitutional and Other Problems. Nicosia.

Tsadiras A. (2007) Case note. CML Rev. 44:1515 et seq.

Trimikliniotis N. (2013) Cyprus National Report 2012–2013. Network on free movement of workers. http://works.bepress.com/nicos_trimikliniotis/41/.

3

The Future Mandate of the Constitution of Slovenia: A Potent Tradition Under Strain

Samo Bardutzky

Abstract The 1991 Constitution of Slovenia belongs to the category of strong constitutions, with a detailed list of rights. The report informs that the concept of the rule of law mostly draws on German commentaries on the constitutional *Rechtsstaat*, and its main elements are expressly entrenched in constitutional provisions. Particularly notable are the detailed limits on the power of the state in prosecuting crimes and detailed guarantees for judicial protection, which are identified as more extensive than those in the ECHR and the EU Charter. The constitutional amendments for EU and international co-operation contain a clause on the respect for human rights, democracy and the rule of law. The report extensively documents areas where the above, potent constitutional tradition has come under strain in the context of EU law. The examples range from the Data Retention Directive – the implementation of which was rushed under the threat of EU fines – to concerns by scholars with regard to *Viking Line* and *Laval* that the Constitution limits the limitations on fundamental rights, and that economic freedoms ought not to trump fundamental rights despite the status that the former have been accorded by the ECJ. A particularly acute awareness emerges with regard to the changing role of courts in European Arrest Warrant cases, with warnings by lawyers about the danger of instrumentalising judges, and transforming judges into 'ticking box' automatons neglecting their duty of safeguarding fundamental rights. The constitutional protection of the right to water has also been debated with reference to an EU directive. More broadly, the report expresses concern that because of the different approach to judicial review of EU measures, the heavy

The author is Assistant Professor of Constitutional Law at the University of Ljubljana, Slovenia; at the time of writing Research Associate, University of Kent, United Kingdom. e-mail: S.Bardutzky@pf.uni-lj.si.

The author is indebted to Anneli Albi, Mojca Plesničar, Andraž Zidar, Peter Pavlin and Maria Gomes for their careful reading of the draft text and valuable comments, and very grateful to Marjan Kos for his thorough and enthusiastic research assistance.

S. Bardutzky (✉)
University of Ljubljana, Ljubljana, Slovenia
e-mail: S.Bardutzky@pf.uni-lj.si

books with commentary on the Constitution are no longer carried by civil servants to meetings to identify constraints on the exercise of public power placed by the Constitutional Court.

Keywords The Constitution of Slovenia • Constitutional amendments regarding EU and international co-operation • The Slovenian Constitutional Court Constitutional review statistics and grounds • German influences on the rule of law and the constitutional *Rechtsstaat* • Limitation of rights • Referendums on accession and on euro crisis measures • European Arrest Warrant, judicial review and defence rights • The changing role of courts • Data Retention Directive and the threat of EU fines • Article 53 EU Charter and the question of a higher standard of protection • The constitutional right to water

1 Constitutional Amendments Regarding EU Membership

1.1 Constitutional Culture

1.1.1 The adoption of the Constitution of the Republic of Slovenia in 1991[1] followed two tectonic changes. The first was the transition from a non-democratic political system with socialist consensus economics and where the pivotal role in society was played by the Communist party, to a multi-party democracy, market economy and society based on respect for human rights and fundamental freedoms.[2] The second change was the declaration of independence from the Socialist Federal Republic of Yugoslavia of which Slovenia was a constituent part.[3]

Stemming from the decision of the Slovenian people to establish independence and democracy, the Constitution belongs to the category of strong constitutions. It possesses a dominant legal character, not only through the establishment of a

[1] *Ustava Republike Slovenije* in Slovene. The original text is published in the Official Journal of the Republic of Slovenia (*Uradni list Republike Slovenije*, hereinafter UL) 33/91-I, with subsequent amendments in UL 42/97, 66/2000, 24/03, 69/04, 68/06 in 47/13. I have drawn on the English translation available from the website of the Constitutional Court, http://www.us-rs.si/en/about-the-court/legal-basis/constitution/.

[2] 1989 Amendments XIII–XXXIV to the 1974 Constitution of the Socialist Republic of Slovenia introduced several elements of economic liberalisation, while the 1990 Amendments XCI–XCV provided for a basis for the first democratic election to the tricameral Assembly of the Republic, which took place in April 1990.

[3] The Basic Constitutional Charter on the Sovereignty and Independence of the Republic of Slovenia (UL 1/91-I), proclaiming Slovenia to be an independent state on 25 June 1991 (4 months before the adoption of the Constitution), continues to be considered a 'valid constitutional act' of Slovenian constitutional law by the Constitutional Court (CCRS Rm-1/09, Opinion of 18 March 2010, UL 25/2010).

special Constitutional Court charged with safeguarding the Constitution and vested with the power to annul legislation (Chap. VIII),[4] but also through the subjection of the courts (Art. 125) and the public administration (Art. 120(2)) to the Constitution. Furthermore, human rights and fundamental freedoms are exercised *directly* on the basis of the Constitution (Art. 15(3), emphasis added). This is complemented by the detailed, almost technical phrasing of some of the constitutional guarantees (e.g. Art. 20(2)).

However, some of the solutions adopted in the 1991 Constitution also draw on the tradition of the pre-1991 constitutional system. The superior position of the representative assembly in relation to the other branches of government serves as a simple example. To what extent the aspiration of the Constitution to regulate or at least broadly define the country's economic and social system can be understood as a legacy of the pre-1991 system is a more complex issue, capable of influencing the understanding of the nature and content of the Slovenian constitutional identity.[5] The gradual *legal* transition from the old to the new constitutional system (the old 1974 constitution was amended in 1989 and 1990 before the adoption of a new constitutional text) is an additional argument against viewing the Constitution as a revolutionary constitution.[6] In that sense, it is somewhat helpful to invoke Rosenfeld's 'pacted transition model of constitution-making',[7] but only to appreciate the limits of the categorisation proposed in the questionnaire and its relevance for the Slovenian case.[8]

1.1.2 The Constitution is concerned with both the organisation of the state and limiting public power, and both elements of the rationale are important. Regarding the latter, the provisions on human rights and fundamental freedoms, along with some of the central principles of the Constitution, such as the separation of powers, are of pivotal importance. This can be said for lawmaking, where constitutional standards are enforced through the case law of the Constitutional Court, as well as with regard to decision making in the judiciary and the public administration. At the same time, the fact that the democratic system in Slovenia is relatively young means that the constitutional provisions establishing the system of government are frequently invoked in public discussions triggered by events in the everyday political life of the country. The financial crisis has to a significant extent also led to a political crisis resulting in unstable governments, snap elections and referendums. In many cases these events have been unprecedented in the history of the nation, sparking the constitutional imagination of the general and professional public.

We can add to the discussion on the rationale of the Constitution that it also purports to lay down the fundamental features of the socio-economic system

---

[4] Plesničar and Modic 2007.

[5] The 'third rationale' of the Constitution (Ch. III) is outlined below in Sect. 1.1.2.

[6] See above n. 2.

[7] Rosenfeld 2009, pp. 197–201.

[8] Rosenfeld's categorisation would also struggle to provide an adequate framework within which the Slovenian path to constitutionalism at the end of the XX century can be understood.

(Chap. III: Economic and Social Relations). This extends beyond protecting economic and social human rights (some of the third generation human rights, e.g. the right to social security including old-age pension, health care and education, are also entrenched in Chap. II 'Bill of Rights'). The provisions of Chap. III further protect collective industrial action,[9] natural and cultural heritage, free economic initiative within the boundaries of the public interest, etc. Some of the provisions in the chapter enjoy the status of a justiciable human right (e.g. right to a healthy living environment, Art. 72).[10] Other provisions (e.g. on housing, Art. 78) have a programmatic character.[11]

1.2 The Amendment of the Constitution in Relation to the European Union

1.2.1 The first EU-related constitutional reform was the 1997 amendment of Art. 68, the provision on acquisition of land by foreigners. The 'Europe Agreement', an association agreement between the members of the then European Communities and Slovenia, envisaged a liberalisation of land acquisition by foreigners.[12] The agreement was found partly unconstitutional by the Constitutional Court, which triggered an amendment process.[13] With the constitutional reform, land acquisition was liberalised and subjected to conditions laid down by a statute or an international agreement.[14]

The central EU-related constitutional reform took place in 2003, which saw yet another amendment of Art. 68, an amendment of Art. 47 (the absolute prohibition on extradition of a national citizen was relativised) and the introduction of the 'Europe clause' (Art. 3.a).[15] The latter allows for transfer of the exercise of part of Slovenia's sovereign rights to international organisations by virtue of ratification of an international treaty (para. 1; see Sect. 1.3.1). It also provides for a referendum that can be called prior to the ratification of such a treaty (para. 2; see Sect. 1.4.2). Article 3.a also refers to the law of the international organisations mentioned in

---

[9] See also Sect. 2.2.1.

[10] Čebulj 2011, p. 1027.

[11] Kresal 2011, p. 1080.

[12] Europe Agreement establishing an association between the European Communities and their Member States, acting within the framework of the European Union, of the one part, and the Republic of Slovenia, of the other part, [1999] OJ L 51/3.

[13] CCRS Rm-1/97 (OdlUS VI, 86).

[14] Constitutional Act amending Art. 68 of the Constitution of the Republic of Slovenia, UL 42/97. See also Ribičič 2003, pp. 31–34.

[15] Constitutional Act amending Chapter 1 and Arts. 47 and 68 of the Constitution of the Republic of Slovenia, UL 24/03.

Para. 1 (Para. 3; see Sect. 1.3.1) and entrenches the rights of Parliament in the new situation arising post-accession (Para. IV; see Sect. 1.4.1).

In 2013, a 'fiscal rule' was introduced in Art. 148 in order to comply with the obligations undertaken by Slovenia under the Treaty on Stability, Coordination and Governance.[16] The rule requires that the revenues and expenditures of the state budget must in principle be balanced in the medium term, without borrowing (or revenues must exceed expenditures). Article 148 foresees that a statute, adopted by the same majority as required for a constitutional amendment, will lay down the way in which the fiscal rule works in more detail.[17]

1.2.2 A proposal to initiate the procedure for amending the Constitution can be lodged by twenty deputies of the National Assembly, the Government or at least thirty thousand voters. The National Assembly votes upon such proposals. If a proposal is supported by two-thirds of the deputies present, the procedure to amend the Constitution is initiated (Art. 168 Constitution).

A successful vote is followed by a procedure in the Constitutional Commission, a body of the National Assembly. The Commission is composed of deputies from the political parties, proportionally to the size of each party's parliamentary group in the National Assembly. The Commission, however, also convenes an *ad hoc* expert group, typically composed of law professors.

If the idea for the amendment of the Constitution enjoys sufficient support in the Constitutional Commission, the latter drafts the amendment for the National Assembly. Importantly, the drafting is thus withdrawn from the influence of the subject that initially triggered the procedure (e.g. the Government). The National Assembly (in plenary session) may not change the text (Arts. 172–181 Rules of Procedure of the National Assembly; hereinafter PoDZ-1).[18]

The proposal must be adopted by a two-thirds majority of all deputies. An amendment can still be subjected to a constitutional referendum if one-third of the deputies so require (Arts. 169–170 Constitution). This is a relatively onerous requirement, and no such referendum has yet been held.[19]

1.2.3 The prevalent view was that the accession to the EU required a constitutional amendment. The principal reasons were threefold. The first reason was that transfer

---

[16] Constitutional Act amending Art. 148 of the Constitution of the Republic of Slovenia (UZ148), UL 47/13.

[17] I.e. the mode and timeframe of exercising the rule, criteria to determine whether exceptional circumstances prevent it, etc. This statute was to be adopted within 6 months of the constitutional reform (Sect. II UZ148). The draft Fiscal Rule Act (ZFisP-1) was still in parliamentary procedure in June 2015 (EPA 0227-VII).

[18] Rules of Procedure of the National Assembly, UL 92/07, 105/10, 80/13.

[19] Kaučič ascribes this difficultly attainable quorum of deputies to a drafting error. Kaučič 2011b, p. 1545.

of a part of sovereignty to another entity under an international treaty would be unconstitutional without express authorisation in the text of the Constitution. Secondly, without a collision rule between EU law and national constitutional law, the Constitutional Court could find itself in a position where it would have to declare EU law unconstitutional. Thirdly, given the symbolic and constitutive value of sovereignty, accession to the EU required a high level of transparency in constitutional lawmaking.[20]

Despite the fact that Art. 3.a was adopted in order to provide a constitutional basis for the entry of Slovenia into the EU, the text of the article does not expressly refer to it. It instead refers to an international organisation. Matej Avbelj traces this approach to constitutional drafting back to the 'international law' approach to the understanding of the EU, which does not sufficiently distinguish the EU from the sphere of international law and international organisations.[21]

At the time of drafting, a more concretised text was also on the table, explicitly referring to the EU. It seems that the abstract, 'minimalist' approach was chosen for the following reasons. First, a broad phrasing can accommodate the different outcomes of the evolution of the legal nature of the EU and the related terminology (Community/Union). Secondly, the Slovenian membership was not completely certain at the time of drafting. Thirdly, the abstract phrasing of the constitutional provisions, capable of accommodating a wide range of legal and factual situations, was considered to be part of the Slovenian constitutional tradition. Moreover, it seems that there was an important time factor that in the end curtailed discussions in the Constitutional Commission of the National Assembly.[22]

The abstract approach to the wording of the 'Europe clause' was advocated by the Government that initiated the amendment procedure. An increasing number of experts advised against the approach taken by the Government, and this opposing view also became prevalent in the expert group of the Constitutional Commission. However, the expert group failed in its attempt to replace the abstract approach with a compromise 'combined' approach in the final stages of the procedure in the Constitutional Commission. Under the combined approach, there would have been a clause that explicitly authorised the transfer of the exercise of part of sovereignty to the EU, but also another clause which would have abstractly allowed for the exercise of sovereignty to be partly transferred to an international organisation or international tribunal.[23]

1.2.4 There have been no further amendment proposals in relation to the EU that have not materialised in practice.

---

[20] Cerar 2003b, pp. 6–7.

[21] Avbelj 2012b, p. 6.

[22] Cerar 2003a, pp. 1463–1474; see also Sect. 1.4.2.

[23] Cerar 2003a, pp. 1464–1465.

1.3 Conceptualising Sovereignty and the Limits to the Transfer of Powers

1.3.1 Transfer of the exercise of a part of Slovenia's sovereign rights to 'international organisations' and the conditions therefor are envisaged in Art. 3.a(1):

> Pursuant to a treaty ratified by the National Assembly by a two-thirds majority vote of all deputies, Slovenia may transfer the exercise of part of its sovereign rights to international organisations which are based on respect for human rights and fundamental freedoms, democracy, and the principles of the rule of law and may enter into a defensive alliance with states which are based on respect for these values.

Hence, according to the text of the Constitution, only the *exercise* of sovereignty and not sovereignty itself can be transferred. Behind this wording is arguably the idea that transfer is not eternal in the sense that Slovenia could at some point in the future resume exercising its sovereignty. However, this phrasing and its explanation have been met with scepticism.[24] Notably, the majority required for the ratification of an Art. 3.a treaty is the same as the majority required for a constitutional amendment.

In line with the abstract 'international organisation' approach of Art. 3.a, the text of para. 3 provides that

> [l]egal acts and decisions adopted within international organisations to which Slovenia has transferred the exercise of part of its sovereign rights shall be applied in Slovenia in accordance with the legal regulation of these organisations.

This accommodates the supremacy and direct effect of EU law in the Slovenian constitutional order.

1.3.2 The key decision in the case law of the Slovenian Constitutional Court on sovereignty is its 2003 decision on the 'Vatican Agreement'.[25] Adopted after Art. 3.a had already been inserted into the Constitution (albeit not on this basis), it emphasises that neither the internal nor the external element of sovereignty are absolute, the latter because of public international law. Sovereignty prevents the state from transferring sovereign powers to other states or institutions; Art. 3.a is the only exception (allowing for transfer *of the exercise* of sovereign powers).[26]

The position in the *Vatican Agreement* decision served as the basis for the recent *State Holding & Bank Stability Referendum* decision of the Constitutional Court, with which it prevented the holding of a legislative referendum on two anti-crisis measures.[27] Avbelj has commented that in this decision, the Court demonstrated its awareness that Slovenia will have to take into consideration the existence of a host

[24] Cerar 2003a, pp. 1471–1474.

[25] Agreement between the Republic of Slovenia and the Holy See on legal issues, UL 13/2004.

[26] CCRS Rm-1/02, UL 118/2003, paras. 22– 24.

[27] CCRS U-II-1/12, U-II-2/12, UL 102/2012.

of transnational actors and learn to react to their impulses if it is to retain its 'legal and political' sovereignty.[28]

The National Assembly opposed the referendum by claiming that failure to enact the Act on the Measures to Strengthen Bank Stability (ZUKSB)[29] would push Slovenia into a bail-out situation. European and IMF financial assistance would lead to an encroachment upon sovereignty contrary to Art. 3.a. The Constitutional Court rejected this view and held that the sovereignty of Slovenia entails the prerogative to conclude international agreements. A financial assistance agreement with the IMF would not *per se* amount to an impermissible encroachment on sovereignty, rather it is the substance of the international agreement that would need to be examined.

1.3.3 The text of the Constitution itself sets a limit to transfer of the exercise of sovereign rights. Such transfer may only be to an international organisation that is based on (1) respect for human rights and fundamental freedoms, (2) democracy and (3) the principles of the rule of law (*pravna država*[30] in Slovenian). This provision was modelled after Art. 23(1) of the German *Grundgesetz* and can be understood as introducing a kind of *causa* for accession to the EU.[31] The selection of the three substantive limits by the constitutional legislature (human rights, democracy, *pravna država*) was careful and reflects the general perception of what the essential constitutional principles are. Each of these three principles is unattainable unless all three are respected, while at the same time they set limits to one other.[32]

The limits to transfer cannot be understood as empowering the Constitutional Court to reject the application of individual EU legal norms that would be found incompatible with the Constitution. The limits would probably only be invoked should the EU at some point 'in its fundaments' digress from these constitutional principles. In such a scenario, the limits could provide a legal basis for the Slovenian authorities to reject the application of EU legal acts and refuse to execute decisions of the EU.[33] Nevertheless, the text prescribing the limits to transfer can serve to infuse the Slovenian court with some self-confidence when it needs to take a stance with regard to the effects of EU law.[34]

1.3.4 The Constitution does not explicitly declare itself supreme, but it does, however, command that all 'statutes, regulations, and other general acts' must be in conformity with it (Art. 153(1)), in reference to domestic legal norms. The Constitution also envisages control of the conformity of treaties with the

[28] Avbelj 2013c, p. 6. See also the opinion of Judge Petrič infra n. 150.

[29] UL 105/12.

[30] See Sect. 2.1.3.

[31] Testen 2011, p. 91.

[32] Cerar 2011, pp. 78–79.

[33] Ibid.

[34] Testen 2011, p. 91.

Constitution (discussed below in Sect. 3.4.1). Theoretically then, a review of the constitutionality of a new treaty of EU primary law is not excluded.[35] When it comes to EU secondary law, the Constitutional Court, citing *Foto-Frost,* has declared its respect for the exclusive jurisdiction of the Court of Justice (ECJ) over questions of validity.[36] At the same time, the Court has not relinquished its jurisdiction over domestic legal acts implementing EU law.[37] As we have recently seen in U-I-295/13 (see Sect. 2.6.1), it seems that the Constitutional Court will exercise this jurisdiction in dialogue with the ECJ. However, the Court has so far refused to choose between the unconditional supremacy of EU law over the Constitution on the one hand and the possibility that EU law would in exceptional circumstances have to give way to the Slovenian Constitution. The Court again refused to rule on this issue in the *State Holding & Bank Stability Referendum* case (see Sect. 1.3.2). Notably, in this case the Court found that it did not face a dilemma due to the 'gravitas of the respect for EU law as a value of constitutional law', based on Art. 3. a Constitution.[38]

1.4 Democratic Control

1.4.1 The essential guarantee of the participation of the National Assembly in EU affairs is entrenched in the Constitution, establishing a 'Danish model' of the relationship between Parliament and Government in EU affairs.[39] According to Art. 3.a(4):

> In procedures for the adoption of legal acts and decisions in international organisations to which Slovenia has transferred the exercise of part of its sovereign rights, the Government shall promptly inform the National Assembly of proposals for such acts and decisions as well as of its own activities. The National Assembly may adopt positions thereon, which the Government shall take into consideration in its activities. The relationship between the National Assembly and the Government arising from this paragraph shall be regulated in detail by a statute adopted by a two-thirds majority vote of deputies present.

However, should the Government disregard its duties to inform and to take the positions of the National Assembly into consideration, only a political sanction could be imposed.[40] A more detailed system of parliamentary participation is laid down in a statute adopted with a qualified majority of two-thirds of deputies present.[41]

---

[35] See also Nerad 2012, p. 387.

[36] CCRS U-I-113/04, Order of 8 July 2004, UL 83/04, para. 7; Oven 2014, p. 25.

[37] For example in CCRS U-I-65/13, Order of 26 Sept 2013, para. 7.

[38] CCRS U-II-1/12, U-II-2/12, UL 102/2012, para. 53.

[39] Avbelj 2012a, p. 346.

[40] Grad 2007, p. 112.

[41] UL 34/04, 43/10, 107/10. See also Grad 2007, p. 111.

In the Act on Cooperation between the National Assembly and the Government in EU Affairs (ZVSDZVZEU), the National Assembly has recognised that it is the Government that represents Slovenia and furthers its positions in the processes in the institutions of the Union. The Government is independent and accountable in EU affairs, but within the boundaries set by the Constitution, the statute regulating the Government and the ZSDZVZEU (Art. 2). This dominant position of the Government is balanced by the rights of the National Assembly safeguarded in the ZSDZVZEU. The National Assembly, through its standing committees, participates in the formulation of the positions of Slovenia in those EU affairs that would – given their substance – otherwise fall within the competence of the National Assembly (Art. 4). The Government's duty to extensively inform is with regard to Art. 4 EU affairs (Arts. 8–9). The Act instructs the National Assembly to discuss any proposed changes to the founding Treaties and adopt a position. A position on the political direction that Slovenia will take in the EU institutions is also to be adopted in a plenary debate once a year (Art. 5).

The ZSDZVZEU only safeguards the rights of the National Assembly and does not foresee any role for Slovenia's weak and unusually composed second chamber of Parliament, the National Council. The latter challenged the ZSDZVZEU before the Constitutional Court, claiming that the Act is incompatible with the Lisbon Treaty (sic). The Court established that the distribution of powers among organs of the state in relation to EU affairs is by and large a matter for national law. Given that the National Council is not mentioned in Art. 3.a, the Court found that the ZSDZVZEU was in conformity with the Constitution.[42]

1.4.2 There has only been one EU-related referendum, held on 23 March 2003. The electorate was asked to vote not only on Slovenian membership in the EU, but also in the North Atlantic Treaty Organization (NATO).[43] Unlike several other Member States that joined the EU in the 2004 enlargement but had been members of NATO for some time, Slovenians faced two major decisions on the (geo)political course that their country was about to take at exactly the same time. Joining the EU enjoyed significantly broader support than joining NATO.[44]

As was mentioned above (Sect. 1.2.3), time was an important factor in the referendum story. The referendum was called by the National Assembly on 30 January 2003, and the date of the ballot was set. The referendum was called as a *consultative* referendum, i.e. a referendum without legally binding results for the organs of the state.[45] Less than a month later, on 27 February 2003, the

---

[42] CCRS U-I-17/11, UL 87/2012.

[43] See Sect. 3.1.1 regarding membership in NATO.

[44] 89.64% of the votes cast were in support of EU membership, in comparison to 66.08% in favour of joining NATO. The turnout was approximately 60%. See National Electoral Commission, Report on the referendum on the accession of Slovenia to the EU, 1 April 2003, http://www.dvk-rs.si/files/files/porocilo-o-referendumu-EU.pdf.

[45] Ordinance calling a consultative referendum on the accession of the Republic of Slovenia to the European Union, UL 13/03.

constitutional amendment inserting Art. 3.a into the text of the Constitution was adopted, and para. 2 of the new Art. 3.a laid down the rules for referendums on transfers of powers:

> Before ratifying a treaty referred to in the preceding paragraph, the National Assembly may call a referendum. A proposal is passed in the referendum if a majority of voters who have cast valid votes vote in favour of the same. The National Assembly is bound by the result of such referendum. If such referendum has been held, a referendum regarding the statute on the ratification of the treaty concerned may not be called.

The constitutional act also provided that the EU and NATO referendums shall be considered to fall under Art. 3.a.[46] The popular vote was thus linked to the EU amendments, albeit in a peculiar manner.

The haste with which the referendum was coupled with the constitutional reform seems to have been behind the questionable decision for an 'abstract approach' to the phrasing of Art. 3.a. Applying Art. 3.a to the March 2003 referendums first and foremost meant that the result was legally binding on the National Assembly. As far as future referendums are concerned, it is important to note that an Art 3.a referendum is not obligatory. Whether such referendum will be called or not lies within the discretion of the National Assembly.

Igor Kaučič has warned that, strictly speaking, the object of an Art. 3.a referendum is not the treaty in question nor the statute ratifying the treaty, but an individual question that is of crucial or central importance to the treaty.[47] In 2003, the voters voted on whether they were in favour of Slovenia becoming a member of the European Union. This approach put into question the 'usefulness' of an Art. 3.a referendum for future reforms of the European Union, where it might be more difficult to identify the central question of the treaty. The relevance of a referendum where the electorate decides on a narrow point addressed by the treaty in question is likewise questionable. This inevitably raises the question whether the Art 3.a referendum was at all conceived as a functional tool of direct democracy in the processes of supranational integration or rather as an *una tantum* event based on an abstractly worded constitutional basis.

1.5 The Reasons for, and the Role of, EU Amendments

1.5.1 The 2003 reform The decision for a constitutional reform was based predominantly on the scholarly opinion that without such reform, accession to the EU would be unconstitutional. However, it seems that the influence of scholars was much more limited when it came to the shaping of the amendments. It seems that in the desire to provide additional, 'constitutional' legitimacy and weight to the

---

[46] Sect. II, Constitutional Act amending Chapter 1 and Arts. 47 and 68 of the Constitution of the Republic of Slovenia, UL 24/03.

[47] Kaučič 2011a, p. 85.

referendum, politicians were ready to settle for a suboptimal phrasing of Art. 3.a, sacrificing a lengthier and more profound debate. This settling and sacrifice seem to have been unnecessary in relation to the process of joining the EU. The 89.64% vote in favour of joining the Union reflects the wide support that European integration enjoyed among the electorate. As far as the European Union was concerned, engaging in legal engineering instead of a substantial debate seems to have been uncalled for. It has to be taken into account, however, that the parallel process of joining NATO was much more controversial and might have lead the political elite to rig the rules of the game somewhat.[48] In that sense, choosing an abstract, 'minimalist' approach to the constitutional reform and intentionally avoiding any explicit reference to the EU or NATO might have served the additional purpose of 'pooling' the legitimacy of both integration processes in order to ensure a smooth entry into both organisations. It seems that the whole process would have been more democratically and intellectually honest if the Constitution had, in the words of Confucius, 'called things by their proper name'.

This is not, however, to dismiss the explanations for the choice of the 'abstract' model provided by Slovenian scholars. In particular, the argument was put forth that the abstract model is compatible with the standard practice of constitutional drafting, which often opts for laconic phrases, combining them with a rule that prescribes that a statute is required to regulate the matter further.[49] From my personal experience in observing and participating in the drafting of constitutional amendments (albeit not the EU-related ones), the prominent constitutionalists indeed seem to have a certain sense of what kind of wording is appropriate in the text of the Constitution. This indefinable aesthetics of constitution-making is probably a result of practice or custom and connected to the otherwise frequently cited belief that constitutional amendments are to be written 'with a trembling hand', i.e. with great caution and reserve. The laconic, 'aesthetic' approach might well partly be behind the division of the matter of the fiscal rule between constitutional and statutory text, discussed in Sect. 1.2.1.[50]

Regarding some of the other matters covered by EU amendments in other Member States, a possible explanation for why Slovenia has not enacted similar clauses is that the Constitution in its original text was to a certain extent already one of 'open statehood'. It is worth noting, for example, that the original text of the Constitution (1991) foresaw the possibility for a statute to grant electoral votes to foreigners, and the legislature indeed did so even before Slovenia joined the EU.[51]

---

[48] Traynor, I. (2003, March 22). Slovenia split in run-up to Nato referendum. The Guardian. http://www.theguardian.com/world/2003/mar/22/iantraynor.

[49] E.g. Art. 12.

[50] The other possible reason would be strategic: by 'throwing a bone', i.e. introducing the constitutional reform, the country probably assuaged the financial markets and bought time before more invasive measures were taken with the adoption of the fiscal rule statute.

[51] The active right of permanently resident foreigners to vote in the indirect elections to the National Council, the upper chamber of Parliament, was recognised in 1992. Article 2 National Council Act; however, the right to vote in local elections dates back to 2002, before accession.

The 2013 reform of Art. 148 The introduction of the fiscal rule was not uncontested. First, opinions diverged on whether the treaty required Slovenia to change the constitutional text.[52] Secondly, Slovenian constitutional scholars felt that there was no room for a strong expression of ideology or one particular economic doctrine in the constitution. Constitutionalisation represents a long-term commitment that would require considerable effort to be overturned in the future, when the economic reality or policy may change.[53] Additionally, the reasonableness of pursuing the European project by imposing a top-down constitutional reform on the Member States was questioned.[54] It has also been pointed out that tension between debt limitations and the concept of the social state is inevitable, with calls made for the priority of the latter as a fundamental value of the Constitution.[55]

1.5.2 Not applicable.

1.5.3 The national constitution remains a powerful tool in the hands of the citizenry of a Member State whenever concerns arise that the power to make decisions on issues that affect them might shift from the democratic organs of the Member State to more distant centres, or simply wither away, with the hands of the elected politicians tied, as was the case with the Fiscal Compact (see above Sects. 1.2.1 and 1.5.1). The eurozone crisis has shown how quickly the Member States positioned the newly established rules and mechanisms (European Stability Mechanism; the Banking Union) in the grey postnational zone of *Ersatzunionsrecht* rather than within EU law.[56] A strong case can be made for the requirement that such treaties must be submitted to a regime similar to the Art. 3.a regime (heightened ratification threshold, and substantive requirements for respect for human rights, *pravna država* and democracy). However, given the wording of Art. 3.a., it is likely that they would fall outside its scope of application. In a potential future constitutional reform, especially one that would introduce a clause calling Europe by its proper name (see above Sect. 1.5.1), I would support combining the latter with a more broadly applicable provision. Such a clause would be capable of submitting a range of different mechanisms of global and regional governance to the requirement of respect for the fundamental values of the Constitution.

---

[52] On this debate, see Ahtik et al. 2014, p. 530.

[53] Bugarič 2012, p. 3; Vuksanović 2011, pp. 41– 42.

[54] Nahtigal 2012, p. 22.

[55] Nahtigal 2012, p. 22; Strban 2012, p. 3.

[56] Federal Constitutional Court of Germany, 2 BvR 1390/12, Judgment of 12 September 2012, para. 153; Bardutzky and Fahey 2014, p. 343.

2 Constitutional Rights, the Rule of Law and EU Law

2.1 The Position of Constitutional Rights and the Rule of Law in the Constitution

2.1.1 The Constitution, as one of its basic principles, establishes the duty of the state to protect human rights on its territory (Art. 5). It further provides for a comprehensive catalogue of human rights (Chap. II).

The initial provisions of the Chapter guarantee equality in the exercise of human rights (Art. 14(1)) and provide for structural rules on the exercise and limitation of human rights and fundamental freedoms (Art. 15(1–3)). Importantly, the non-enumeration clause (Art. 15(5)) opens the catalogue: no human right or fundamental freedom entrenched in a legal act that is in force in Slovenia may be restricted on the grounds that it is not recognised by the Constitution (see Sect. 3.2.2).

The Constitution guarantees judicial protection of human rights and fundamental freedoms and restitution of the consequences of human rights violations (Art. 15(4)). An individual alleging a human rights violation by an individual legal act (court judgment, administrative decision, etc.) can access the Constitutional Court via a constitutional complaint (modelled after the German *Verfassungsbeschwerde*) after other remedies have been exhausted (Art. 160).

The Constitution expressly prohibits the retroactive effect of statutes, regulations and other general acts, and lays down the only exception from this rule (Art. 155).[57] Legal certainty, protection of legitimate expectations and, perhaps most notably, proportionality are considered elements of the principle of *pravna država*, entrenched in Art. 2 Constitution (see Sect. 2.1.3).

Pravna država is not considered a human right, so one cannot base a constitutional complaint to the Constitutional Court on an allegation that it has been violated. Nevertheless, Art. 2 can and does serve as a yardstick in the procedure for the review of constitutionality of legislation (and other general acts). This procedure can be abstract, triggered by a number of privileged and semi-privileged applicants, concrete (a preliminary ruling-like mechanism initiated by the *iudex a quo*) and, under certain conditions, also accessible to individuals aggrieved by the norm in question.

2.1.2 The Constitution distinguishes between defining the manner in which a human right is exercised (Art. 15(2)), on the one hand, and limiting a human right (Art. 15(3)) on the other.

A statute can define how a human right is to be *exercised* 'whenever the Constitution so provides or where this is necessary due to the particular nature of an individual right or freedom'. For example: '[e]very citizen has the right, *in*

---

[57] 'Only a statute may provide for retroactive effect of some of its provisions, if this is required in the public interest and under the condition that no acquired rights are infringed.' (Art. 155(2)).

accordance with statute, to participate either directly or through elected representatives in the management of public affairs' (Art. 44 Constitution, emphasis added).[58]

On the other hand, human rights and fundamental freedoms can only be *limited* by the rights of others and in the cases that are provided by the Constitution. First, as for limitations based on the rights of others, the text of the Constitution does not explicitly state that such right must be a constitutional or human right; however, a limitation imposed on a human right is not likely to pass the proportionality test if it is grounded in a right of lower rank (e.g. statutory, contractual).[59] Secondly, there can be a statutory reservation that limits a human right. For example, the right to free movement (which is to be distinguished from the right to personal freedom) can be limited by statute only when this is necessary to ensure the conduct of criminal procedure, to prevent the spread of a contagious disease, to protect public order or if this is required for the defence of the state (Art. 32). In addition, the Constitutional Court has recognised that human rights can be limited on a third ground: the public interest.[60]

It is difficult to distinguish between a statutory provision that regulates the exercise of a human right (a para. II case) and a limitation of a human right (a para. III case). The distinction is nevertheless important: a lower threshold will be applied to cases where the legislature has regulated the exercise of a human right: it will suffice to show that the legislative solutions are not arbitrary, irrational, etc. However, whenever there is a limitation on a human right, the legislation will be submitted to a proportionality test.[61]

2.1.3 The Constitution (Art. 2) declares Slovenia to be a *pravna država*, a concept that can be considered equivalent to the German *Rechtsstaat.* The Slovenian term almost literally translates into (or from) the German equivalent; it is customarily translated into English as 'state governed by the rule of law'. Scholarship considers *pravna država*, democracy (Art. 1) and the social (welfare) state (*socialna država*; Art. 2) to be fundamental general constitutional principles.[62]

The discussion of the contents of this principle in the only commentary of the Constitution mostly draws on German commentaries of the *Grundgesetz* (Maunz/Duerig).[63] The majority of what is traditionally considered to be safeguarded by the principle of *Rechtsstaat* is entrenched *expressis verbis* in several provisions of the Slovenian Constitution: the principle of separation of powers (Art. 3), limitations on restrictions of human rights (Art. 15, see Sect. 2.1.2), the binding of the executive to statutory legislation (Art. 120(2)), the hierarchy of legal acts (Art. 153), the

[58] CCRS U-I-47/94, OdlUS IV, 4, para. 2; Avbelj 2011, p. 732.

[59] Testen 2002a, p. 198.

[60] Ibid., p. 200.

[61] Ibid., p. 196.

[62] Šturm 2002, p. 53. Brkan and Nendl 2012 accord *pravna država* a pivotal role in the constitutional order.

[63] Šturm 2002, p. 54.

prohibition of retroactive effect (Art. 155), the obligation to publish legal norms (Art. 154), the right to appeal and judicial review (Art. 25), the right to a constitutional complaint (Art. 160, see supra) and a system of procedural guarantees across the different procedures conducted by organs of public power (Arts. 17–31).

There are, however, three essential elements of *pravna država* not expressly codified in the text of the Constitution, but which have instead been recognised as such by the Constitutional Court:

- the principle of proportionality;[64]
- the principle of the protection of trust in the law, which requires that legal regulation be stable and foreseeable, and sets a limit on the *de facto* retroactive effect of legal norms;[65]
- the principle of clarity and coherence of legal norms, which aims at determining legal relationships to a sufficient level of exactness to exclude the arbitrariness of the organs of public power.[66] Norms need to be clear and precise so that it is possible to determine the meaning of the norms using the methods of legal interpretation.[67] This principle also precludes the formulation of a norm in such a loose manner that the definition of the content of the norm would *de facto* lay in the hands of the authority enforcing the norm.[68]

In the context of this report, this becomes important when read together with the provisions of the Constitution that require that certain norms can only be adopted in the form of a statute (*zakon*). In addition to the rules mentioned above (only a statute can regulate the exercise of a human right and statutory reservations, etc.), the form of a statute is generally required whenever rights or duties are conferred on 'citizens and other persons' (Art. 87), in order to define criminal offences (*nulla poena nullum crimen sine lege praevia* – Art. 28) and in order for the state to 'impose taxes, customs duties, and other charges' (Art. 147).

The provision set out in Art. 87 accords the role of the 'essential legal acts' in the Slovenian legal system to statutes.[69] Peter Pavlin has remarked that this is not merely true on the normative level; the statutes play this very role in the reality of the legal system as well. Sub-statutory, i.e. executive or other general legal acts can only regulate certain details regarding the exercise of a certain right or duty, and cannot hollow out or substitute its contents. 'Rights' in the sense of Art. 87 are not

---

[64] The principle of proportionality is also crucially linked to Art. 15(3), the provision on limitations on human rights and fundamental freedoms (see above Sect. 2.1.2). First, limitations on human rights and fundamental freedoms have to pass a proportionality test. Secondly, limitations are themselves limited, this also means that there are cases where the proportionality test cannot be used to justify a limitation (I am grateful to Andraž Zidar for this remark).

[65] See e.g. CCRS U-I-47/94, UL 13/95.

[66] See e.g. CCRS U-I-282/94, OdlUS IV, 108.

[67] CCRS U-I-32/00, UL 73/03.

[68] CCRS U-I-287/95, UL 68/96.

[69] CCRS U-I-40/96, OdlUS VI, 46.

only human or constitutional rights, but all rights.[70] It should be added that the impact of the use of the *zakon* as a legal form goes beyond the democratic legitimacy bestowed through the deliberations and vote in the directly elected National Assembly. Before a *zakon* comes into force, it is also exposed to potential further verification through a possible veto in the National Council and a legislative referendum that can be demanded by 40,000 voters. After a *zakon* has entered into force, however, it enjoys a privileged position in the legal system: courts of law are only bound by the Constitution and statutes (Art. 125 Constitution). They can refuse to apply a sub-statutory act that is not in conformity with the Constitution or the statutes (*exceptio illegalis*).

Pravna država and the derived or related principles are widely applied in the review of constitutionality and are the basis of extensive Constitutional Court case law.

In addition to the field of constitutional law, *pravna država* plays an important political role. The recent economic crisis (2009–ongoing) has caused a strong sentiment in society that the legal system was unable both to prevent and later to penalise the actions that damaged the economic system (politically sanctioned toxic loans issued by state-owned banks in order to finance managerial takeovers, acts of corruption and cartel agreements in large public tenders, etc.). Consequently, the public has criticised what it perceives as 'inefficiency' or even a 'lack' of rule of law, and expects that the legal system, in simplified terms, will ensure that the innocent walk, but even more that the guilty end up serving time. Given this atmosphere, it is not surprising that the winning party in the 2014 parliamentary election had stated that *pravna država* was its primary value and objective. The increased use of this notion in political discourse has probably already led to its diverging, multi-layered meanings. In the future, the challenge may lie in retaining the relevance and awareness of the core ideas of *pravna država* that are essential for the protection of the individual from excessive use of public power.

2.2 The Balancing of Fundamental Rights and Economic Freedoms in EU Law

2.2.1 There is no available evidence that the courts have transformed the optic or adjusted the balancing approach in a way that would favour economic freedoms over human rights. However, this could simply be due to the relatively limited engagement with EU law in Slovenian courts.[71]

In a contribution by Katarina Kresal Šoltes, a labour law scholar, the national constitution was explicitly positioned as relevant for the *Viking* and *Laval*

[70] Pavlin 2011, pp. 1154–1155.

[71] See Sect. 2.8.1.

controversy. The importance of the right (autonomy) of collective industrial negotiation was underlined, and it was emphasised that despite the status that the economic freedoms have been accorded in ECJ case law, they cannot trump fundamental rights, especially the right to collective industrial action that is entrenched in a range of international documents.[72] Kresal Šoltes also claims a (national) constitutional status for the right to autonomous collective negotiation, derived from the provisions of Art. 76 Constitution,[73] and warns that the Constitution limits the limitations on human rights and fundamental freedoms (Art. 15(3), see Sect. 2.12). Kresal Šoltes has called for an interpretation of the 'free market and competition rules of EC law' that would – regardless of the *Viking* and *Laval* case law – refrain from limiting the right to collective industrial negotiation beyond the extent permitted under the constitutional traditions of the Member States.[74] Worth noting is also the perspective of Damjan Kukovec, who discusses the *Viking* and *Laval* controversy by openly describing himself as a legal scholar from a periphery Member State (i.e. Slovenia). In his view, the typical framing of the *Viking* and *Laval* discussion, i.e. freedom of movement *versus* right to collective industrial action, overlooks the centre-periphery dynamics of European integration.[75]

2.3 *Constitutional Rights, the European Arrest Warrant and EU Criminal Law*

Introductory remark There are several clauses of the Slovenian Constitution that set limits on the power of the state in investigating and prosecuting crimes. Compared to international human rights documents, these provisions can be considered quite detailed: even some time limits are laid down by the Constitution itself. By way of illustration, a narrow selection of directly relevant articles – Art. 19 (Protection of Personal Liberty), Art. 20 (Orders for and Duration of Detention), Art. 23 (Right to Judicial Protection), Art. 25 (Right to Legal Remedies), Art. 27 (Presumption of Innocence), Art. 28 ((Principle of Legality in Criminal Law) and Art. 29 (Legal Guarantees in Criminal Proceedings) – contain almost 600 words (in their English translation). The text of these provisions has been partly provided in the footnotes in Sect. 2.3.

[72] Kresal Šoltes 2009.

[73] 'The freedom to establish, operate, and join trade unions shall be guaranteed.'

[74] Kresal Šoltes 2009, p. 485.

[75] Kukovec 2014.

2.3.1 The Presumption of Innocence

2.3.1.1 The European Arrest Warrant (EAW) has not been contested based on the presumption of innocence.[76] This can possibly be traced back to the phrasing of the relevant constitutional provision.[77] In light of the Constitutional Court's case law, it is doubtful whether Art. 27 could be perceived as an argument against a measure such as the EAW. The Court does not consider the presumption of innocence to be an obstacle to the judicial detention of a criminal defendant ordered on the basis of the probability that the person in question might *repeat* the criminal act (Art. 201(1)(3) ZKP). The presumption of innocence is related to criminal guilt (*nullum poena sine culpa*)[78] and the key consequences derived from this presumption are closely linked to the establishment of criminal guilt: the *onus probandi* is on the state rather than on the defendant. Moreover, the risk of failing to prove the case is borne by the state, as the defendant is protected by the principle of *in dubio pro reo.*[79]

2.3.1.2 A person who is to be surrendered to another Member State on the basis of an EAW has to first be brought before an investigating judge. The scope of the judicial review before surrender, in a nutshell, is the following: the judge will instruct the person with regard to his or her rights, the contents of the warrant and the possibility of consenting to surrender (Arts. 19–22 ZSDČEUKZ-1). If the person does not consent to surrender, the judge will hear the testimony of the person to determine whether there are statutory reasons for refusal to surrender (Art. 23).[80]

The only information on refusals of EAWs by the courts is available from a study by the Institute of Criminology, which looked at all 58 warrants received in the first three years (2004–2007) after the entry into force of the European Arrest

[76] The author is grateful to Mojca Plesničar for confirming that this argument did not appear in the qualitative study that was based on a number of interviews with practitioners and policy-makers. See Šugman Stubbs and Plesničar 2009, pp. 501–522.

[77] Article 27 Constitution: 'Any person charged with criminal conduct shall be presumed innocent until found guilty by a final judgment.' Zupančič positions the Slovenian constitutional provision between the broader guarantee of the French Declaration on the Rights of Man and of the Citizen of 1789 on the one hand and the narrower phrasing of Art. 6 ECHR, lamenting that the thus phrased provision is 'no longer a broad ethical postulate, but is rather limited to the context of criminal law'. Zupančič 2002, p. 302.

[78] Bele 2011, p. 412.

[79] CCRS U-I-18-93, UL 25/96, para. 67. We must note the institutional consequences of this understanding of the presumption of innocence. By unloading the burden and the risk of *probation* onto the 'state', it distinguishes the state in principal terms from the independent judiciary (Zupančič 2002, p. 303). This, in turn, requires that there is a prosecutor, an attorney of the state, who will pursue the state's case in an adversary manner.

[80] See also Šugman Stubbs 2008. It is in practice commonly considered the duty of the person to be surrendered to invoke grounds for refusal rather than this being an *ex officio* task of the court. Šugman Stubbs and Plesničar 2009, pp. 506–507.

Warrant Act (hereinafter ZENPP).[81] Five of these warrants were rejected: three cases involved Slovenian citizens where the offence was committed on Slovenian territory, one was rejected due to amnesty/pardon and one warrant was rejected because the requesting authority failed to provide assurances.[82] It seems that at least in the first years of the operation of the system, there were no refusals to execute an EAW based on concerns related to the presumption of innocence.

2.3.2 *Nullum crimen, nulla poena sine lege*

2.3.2.1 The principle of *nullum crimen sine lege praevia* is expressly entrenched in Art. 28 Constitution as the 'principle of legality in criminal law'.[83] This article lays down a further formal requirement by referring to a statute (*zakon*); indeed, the provision set out in Art. 28 has been linked to Art. 87 Constitution by commentators (see above Sect. 2.1.3 on Art. 87).[84] Also, the Constitutional Court has found that the requirement that a statute defining a criminal offence be clear and precise (*nullum crimen nulla poena sine lege certa*) derives from the text of Art. 28.[85]

Mojca M. Plesničar and Katja Šugman Stubbs have warned that the significant differences between the Member States' penal laws and the definitions of individual offences in the different systems can lead to a number of difficulties and to violation of the principle of legality as the fundamental principle of criminal law. The Slovenian lawyers who participated in the process of implementing mutual recognition, interviewed by Plesničar and Šugman Stubbs, assessed that the EU's plunge into mutual recognition in the field of criminal law was too hasty, but at the same time they felt that it was too late for a renegotiation through which the review of double criminality could be reinstated. As an alternative, it was suggested that each Member State could compile a list of offences (criminalised under its own penal law) that belong to the categories set out in Art. 2 of the EAW Framework Decision[86] (EAWFD). In addition to this 'positive list', Member States could enact a 'negative list' which would enumerate the offences under penal law that definitely

---

[81] UL 37/04. ZENPP was substituted by the Cooperation in Criminal Matters with the Member States of the European Union Act in 2008 (ZSKZDČEU; UL 102/07). A new act (ZSKZDČEU-1) was adopted in 2013.

[82] Šugman Stubbs and Gorkič 2008, Sect. 11.4.2.e.

[83] '(1) No one may be punished for an act which had not been declared a criminal offence under statute or for which a penalty had not been prescribed at the time the act was performed. (2) Acts that are criminal shall be established and the resulting penalties pronounced according to the statute that was in force at the time the act was performed, except where a more recent statute adopted is more lenient towards the offender.'

[84] Zupančič 2002, p. 312 citing the dissenting opinion of Judge Zupančič, joined by Judges Šturm and Šinkovec, to the CCRS decision Up-40/94 (OdlUS IV, 136).

[85] CCRS U-I-247/96, UL 70/98, para. 11; Zupančič 2002, p. 313.

[86] Council Framework Decision of 13 June 2002 on the European arrest warrant and the surrender procedures between Member States (2002/584/JHA), [2002] OJ L 190/1.

do not fall within the EAWFD categories. This latter solution, however, was found to be more difficult to implement in practice.[87]

2.3.3 Fair Trial and *In Absentia* Judgments

2.3.3.1 In the Slovenian context, the issue of the right to a fair trial and the EAW was raised by the failed challenge of Zoran Matešič, whose surrender was requested by an Italian court, against the ZENPP before the Constitutional Court.[88] The constitutional concerns were also presented by Mr. Matešič's attorney in a periodical for legal professionals, and thus became more visible to academics and practitioners.[89]

The case did not raise issues relating to *in absentia* trials, but rather addressed the right to a fair trial more generally. First, the challenge invoked the Art. 23(1) right to judicial protection, which not only guarantees everyone a formal appearance before a court, but also that the competent court will substantively review the matter at hand.[90] However, by limiting the court to a review of purely formal non-execution grounds, the EAW procedures prevent the judiciary from providing any substantive judicial protection. Similarly, this can be seen as a violation of the Art. 25 right to a legal remedy:[91] the Higher Courts that review the orders issued by the first instance panels do not exercise any substantive second instance control. Thirdly, the criminal procedural guarantees set out in Art. 29 Constitution, entrenching everyone's right to a fair trial and more precisely the right of a person 'to present all evidence to his benefit' are ignored.[92] The requested person *de facto* has no possibility to present evidence and if he did, it would be to no avail: even if

---

[87] Šugman Stubbs and Plesničar 2009, p. 207; Šugman Stubbs and Gorkič 2009a, p. 262; Šugman Stubbs and Plesničar 2009, p. 505.

[88] CCRS U-I-14/06, order of 22 June 2006, not reported. Šugman Stubbs and Plesničar 2009, pp. 516–517.

[89] Kovačič Mlinar 2006a, p. 13.

[90] Article 23 (Right to Judicial Protection):

'(1) Everyone has the right to have any decision regarding his rights, duties, and any charges brought against him made without undue delay by an independent, impartial court constituted by statute.

(2) Only a judge duly appointed pursuant to rules previously established by statute and by judicial regulations may judge such an individual.'

[91] 'Everyone shall be guaranteed the right to appeal or to any other legal remedy against the decisions of courts and other state authorities, local community authorities, and bearers of public authority by which his rights, duties, or legal interests are determined.'

[92] Article 29 (Legal Guarantees in Criminal Proceedings): 'Anyone charged with a criminal offence must, in addition to absolute equality, be guaranteed the following rights:
the right to have adequate time and facilities to prepare his defence;
the right to be present at his trial and to conduct his own defence or to be defended by a legal representative;
the right to present all evidence to his benefit;
the right not to incriminate himself or his relatives or those close to him, or to admit guilt.'

the person were able to present convincing evidence that would disprove probable cause or refute the claims made against him or her in the requesting state, this would not have any impact whatsoever on the outcome of the judicial proceeding in the Slovenian court.[93]

The challenge against the ZENPP was submitted to the Constitutional Court while the EAW procedure was still pending before the first instance court, together with a motion for interim relief. However, the Constitutional Court refused to grant interim relief. As a result, immediately after the second instance criminal court had confirmed the decision to surrender Mr. Matešič, he was surrendered to Italy by the police. Having been surrendered, he lost legal standing in the procedure before the Constitutional Court, and his challenge was dismissed on procedural grounds. The decision was ascribed to the Constitutional Court lacking the courage to take an active position on the protection of human rights in the context of EU law.[94]

2.3.4 The Right to a Fair Trial – Practical Challenges Regarding a Trial Abroad

2.3.4.1 Šugman Stubbs and Plesničar interviewed a Slovenian defence attorney who often represents persons requested under an EAW. The following is their summary of the lawyer's experience with requested persons, who are usually

> completely ignorant of the proceedings on EAW and expect that the hearing will give them a chance to prove their innocence. When faced with what seems to be merely an identification process they feel lost and bewildered. They are assigned a defence lawyer but usually are unable to communicate with him/her directly because of the language barriers between them. To requested persons, the entire process seems depersonalised and confusing, since they are usually unfamiliar with the system of surrender based on EAW, with the system in the executing State and very frequently with the system in the issuing country.[95]

To my knowledge, there is no assistance available to persons surrendered on the basis of an EAW after surrender.[96] In discussing the burdens upon surrendered persons, three points should be made.

First, the burden of transportation to another country and undergoing a criminal trial there should in any case be made conditional upon a suitable standard of proof.

---

[93] Kovačič Mlinar 2006a p. 13.

[94] Kovačič Mlinar 2006b, p. 15; Erbežnik 2008, II–VII.

[95] Šugman Stubbs and Plesničar 2009, pp. 520–521.

[96] Article 11(2) EAWFD was from the beginning implemented in such a way that a person who is subject to an EAW has to be represented by a criminal defence attorney from the moment the person is brought before the investigating judge up to the actual surrender, with the attorney appointed *ex officio* if the person does not appoint one himself (Art. 15(4) ZENPP, Art. 16(1) ZSKZDČEU, Art. 17(1) ZSKZDČEU-1). Hence, while the legislature has recognised the need for legal counsel and representation in EAW procedures, it has confined this assistance to the territory under its jurisdiction.

According to the Slovenian Constitution, a *judge* may only order the *detention* of a person who can be *reasonably suspected* of having committed a crime (Art. 20 Constitution; emphasis added).[97] I see no compelling reason to adopt a lower standard for judges to detain and surrender persons under an EAW.

Secondly, in cases such as *Symeou*, where the person was surrendered on the basis of an EAW to face inhuman detention conditions, true concern for human rights protection in Europe does not limit itself to fear for the wellbeing of the fellow nationals of one's own Member State upon potential surrender to another Member State.[98] A finding that persons who are detained in a certain Member State suffer undue hardship should lead us not only to contest the system of judicial co-operation but the systemic violations of human rights in that Member State as well.

Thirdly, the potential for better ensuring the effective protection of the human rights of surrendered persons lies in involving a wide array of actors and institutions, from NGOs and defence lawyers to institutions on the national and European level, including ombudspersons. Traditionally, consular authorities are one of the initial points of assistance and information for a non-national facing a foreign repressive system. Despite the protection of this right being provided for in EU law (Art. 7 Directive 2013/48/EU[99]), this unfortunately remains to a great extent dependent on the facilities and capabilities of the Member State. Slovenia, for example, has never had representations in all of the EU Member States, and has recently even closed some of its existing representations due to cuts in public spending. While this has happened in a number of countries, we cannot escape the fact that it is comparatively much more burdensome for smaller countries to

[97] Article 20 (Orders for and Duration of Detention):

'(1) A person reasonably suspected of having committed a criminal offence may be detained only on the basis of a court order when this is absolutely necessary for the course of criminal proceedings or for reasons of public safety. (2) Upon detention, but no later than twenty-four hours thereafter, the person detained must be handed the written court order with a statement of reasons. The person detained has the right to appeal against the court order … .'

It should be noted that the Constitution safeguards personal liberty also in a more general (in scope) yet nevertheless detailed provision of Art. 19 (Protection of Personal Liberty):

'(1) Everyone has the right to personal liberty.

(2) No one may be deprived of his liberty except in such cases and pursuant to such procedures as are provided by law.

(3) Anyone deprived of his liberty must be immediately informed in his mother tongue, or in a language which he understands, of the reasons for being deprived of his liberty. Within the shortest possible time thereafter, he must also be informed in writing of why he has been deprived of his liberty. He must be instructed immediately that he is not obliged to make any statement, that he has the right to immediate legal representation of his own free choice and that the competent authority must, on his request, notify his relatives or those close to him of the deprivation of his liberty.'

[98] I am grateful to Monica Claes for this remark.

[99] Directive 2013/48/EU of the European Parliament and of the Council of 22 October 2013 on the right of access to a lawyer in criminal proceedings and in European arrest warrant proceedings, and on the right to have a third party informed upon deprivation of liberty and to communicate with third persons and with consular authorities while deprived of liberty, [2013] OJ L 294/1.

maintain a diplomatic and consular presence abroad. This becomes compounded, as smaller countries tend to first close their representations in other small countries.[100]

2.3.4.2 To my knowledge, data on subsequent acquittals is not collected. A case could, however, be made for the collection and processing of a similar data set, as even some Slovenian judges feel that having knowledge of the outcome of the procedure that follows after a person has been surrendered would gradually deepen mutual trust between the judiciaries.[101]

2.3.5 The Right to Effective Judicial Protection: The Principle of Mutual Recognition in EU Criminal Law and Abolition of the Exequatur in Civil and Commercial Matters

2.3.5.1 See Sect. 2.3.3.1.

2.3.5.2 In his critique of mutual recognition in EU criminal law, Anže Erbežnik has warned that while *Cassis de Dijon*-style mutual recognition under the former first pillar has served to enhance European citizens' freedoms in the common market, transplanting this principle to criminal law without the prior substantial harmonisation of defence rights has mostly benefitted state authorities.[102] The experts interviewed by Šugman Stubbs and Plesničar similarly found that former first-pillar EU law typically does not involve such subtle balances between the rights of the state and the rights of individuals.[103] This is aggravated by the fact that in the former third pillar, this principle was introduced as an intergovernmental project, in absence of a democratic debate.[104]

2.3.5.3 Scholarship has warned that the 'uncritical application of the principle of mutual recognition bears the danger of transforming the judge into a kind of a "ticking box" automaton checking only pre-established criteria and neglecting his/her duty of a critical assessment and safeguarding fundamental (constitutional) rights to the defendant'. This argument is grounded in the principle of separation of powers.[105] Zvonko Fišer has found the ZENPP to instrumentalise the judge.[106] In similar vein, the interpretation of the provision abolishing the dual criminality check for the 32 categories of offences, which was favoured by the European Commission and according to which the judge in the executing state is barred from

[100] Unfortunately, this observation goes hand in hand with Albi's concern that there are no proactive NGOs that would monitor such cases in smaller Member States. Albi 2015, p. 171.

[101] Šugman Stubbs and Plesničar 2009, p. 520.

[102] Erbežnik 2014a, pp. 138–139; citing Möstl 2010; Mitsilegas 2006.

[103] Šugman Stubbs and Plesničar 2009.

[104] Erbežnik 2014a, pp. 138–139.

[105] Erbežnik 2014a, p. 131.

[106] Fišer 2008, Sect. 3.4. Fišer currently serves as State Prosecutor General.

checking *prima facie* whether the legal qualification put forward by the requesting state is correct or even sensible, has been considered as insulting to the judicial function.[107] More generally, reducing the scope of judicial review has been considered to also reduce 'the awareness that it is for the judiciary to observe and to enforce procedural safeguards as guaranteed by national constitutional orders, thus preserving the delicate balance between the individual and the state … [certainly,] the balance has shifted'.[108]

2.3.5.4 In my view, it is a fundamental premise of the exercise of public power that interference with the rights and freedoms of the individual must be in proportion with the legitimate interests pursued. The image of a judge whose intellectual activity has been reduced to ticking boxes and who has been purged of the constitutional constraints that should be present at all times is incompatible with this fundamental premise (and with the guarantees of Art. 20 Constitution, see Sect. 2.3.4.1). Stories such as that of Neeme Laurits,[109] for whom the execution of what proved to be a groundless EAW led to grave consequences for his private and family life, have to make us consider the guarantees provided by Art. 8 of the European Convention on Human Rights (ECHR) and analogous national constitutional provisions.

As an illustration of how the right of family life (Arts. 53, 54 and 56 Constitution) can soften the effect of the penal system in a situation where a person is to be separated from his environment and sent abroad, consider the *Vizgirda* decision of the Slovenian Constitutional Court. The case is not connected to the issues of mutual recognition and does not apply EU law. However, the complainant, a Lithuanian citizen, had been convicted in a Slovenian court and was to be expelled from the national territory.[110] The Supreme Court had rejected Mr. Vizgirda's request for an extraordinary suspension of the expulsion sentence, in which he had pleaded that he had fathered a child – a Slovenian citizen, living in Slovenia. The Constitutional Court found that the penalty of expulsion served a legitimate goal of public safety. Nevertheless, in Mr. Vizgirda's case, it was not proportionate in light of the constitutional right to family life and the rights of the child. Relying on ECHR case law, the Constitutional Court stressed that the deeper the integration of the person concerned in the country in question, the higher the level of protection from expulsion must be. The state was under a duty to consider a range of circumstances before it adopted a final decision.[111]

The *Vizgirda* decision undoubtedly arose in a very different legal setting, which has to be taken into account when comparing it to EAW cases. Nevertheless, it demonstrates how constitutional judges are prepared to protect an individual's right to family life even in the face of compelling public interest. That, I would suggest,

---

[107] Šugman Stubbs and Gorkič 2008, Sect. 9.1.2.

[108] Šugman Stubbs and Gorkič 2009b, p. 242.

[109] Albi 2015, p. 171.

[110] Expulsion of a foreign national as a criminal sentence was abolished in 2008.

[111] CCRS Up-690/10, UL 42/2012.

should be a serious argument when analysing the law and policy behind cases such as that of Mr. Laurits.

2.3.6 Constitutional Rights Regarding Other Aspects of EU Criminal Law

In Slovenia, the state prosecutor (*državni tožilec*) is perceived as one of the parties in criminal proceedings. This role is not quasi-judicial, as is the case in some other Member States.[112] Erbežnik has warned that it is unsettling for a state such as Slovenia to sanction a direct execution per its judges of a decision taken by a state prosecutor in another Member State. The perception of the role of a prosecutor in a state is often historically rooted as an element of the state's legal culture and identity. Erbežnik fears that a possible spillover effect of the system of mutual recognition might be the obliteration of the differences in the perception of the role of the prosecutor in different Member States, and an overall trend towards the judicialisation of the prosecutor's role, with the prosecutor being armed with various powers over criminal suspects.[113]

Language seems to be an issue in the operation of systems based on mutual recognition. Smaller Member States can experience practical difficulties in arranging for the adequate translation of EAW requests, especially those issued by other small Member States, i.e. written in the less commonly spoken languages of the Union.[114] In 2014, a police officer of the Ljubljana Schengen Compensatory Measures Unit wrote a very interesting short note defending the legal stance of the Police. The Police had refused to detain a Romanian citizen who was subjected to an EAW until a Romanian translator was found.[115]

2.4 The EU Data Retention Directive

2.4.1 A constitutional challenge against the Electronic Communications Act (ZEKom-1),[116] the legislation implementing the Data Retention Directive,[117] was

[112] The Office of the State Prosecutor General is a constitutional institution (Arts. 135–136).

[113] Erbežnik 2010, p. 213; Erbežnik 2014a, pp. 141–143.

[114] EAW requests are also accepted by Slovenian authorities if they are issued or translated into English (Art. 6(6) ZSKZDČEU-1). The concerns raised by this rule among the Slovenian practitioners, in a country highly sensitive of its linguistic identity, were recorded by Šugman Stubbs and Plesničar 2009, p. 520. As the official languages of Slovenia are defined by the Constitution (Art. 11), the use of other languages in legal proceedings could present a constitutional issue.

[115] Jurič 2014, pp. 8–10.

[116] UL 109/12.

[117] Directive 2006/24/EC of the European Parliament and of the Council of 15 March 2006 on the retention of data generated or processed in connection with the provision of publicly available

filed by the Information Commissioner in 2013.[118] The claim of the Commissioner was that the retention of data on such a massive scale is a disproportionate limitation on freedom of movement (Art. 32 Constitution), the right to privacy (Art. 35), the right to privacy of correspondence and other means of communication (Art. 37) and the right to protection of personal data (Art. 38). The Commissioner also put forward a claim that the implementation of the directive was flawed, as the Slovenian legislature defined a broader set of legitimate objectives than provided in the text of the Directive.

The Information Commissioner underlined that data retention under ZEKom-1 effectively violated the freedom of movement as it enabled location tracking and, as such, was capable of providing a complete record of an individual's movements. In that sense it was comparable to a hypothetical general obligation to carry location tracking chips. Similarly, there were concerns regarding freedom of speech, as the control of communications on such a scale can be expected to lead to self-censorship by individuals communicating with one another. With billions of calls and messages recorded and only several hundred requests made to the processors every year, as few as 0.012% of the personal data retained is ever used in pursuit of the objectives for which data retention was introduced.

The Commissioner also warned of a function creep. In the course of inspecting communication providers, it was established that the providers were receiving requests unrelated to criminal investigations, but rather in connection to, for example, civil litigation or labour disputes.[119]

In September 2013, the Constitutional Court decided to stay the proceedings and wait for the outcome of the cases C-293/12 and C-594/12 in the ECJ.[120] The decision to stay and wait was based on the finding that the Commissioner's claim was in effect that the Directive violated Arts. 7 and 8 of the Charter of Fundamental Rights.[121] Hence, the Constitutional Court noted that 'the decision on the validity of the Directive is of key relevance to the review of constitutionality of national legislation'.[122] The Court did not refer any questions for a preliminary ruling, as

---

electronic communications services or of public communications networks and amending Directive 2002/58/EC, [2006] OJ L 105/54.

[118] The Information Commissioner is an independent authority charged with the protection of personal data and access to documents. The Commissioner reviews decisions to deny access to public documents and refusals to disclose personal data. (Act on the Information Commissioner, UL 113/05 and 51/07). The Commissioner has standing before the Constitutional Court, when in a procedure conducted by the Commissioner, a question of the constitutionality of the legislation that the Commissioner has to apply is raised. (Art. 23.a ZUstS).

[119] The request of the Information Commissioner is available (in Slovene) at https://www.ip-rs.si/fileadmin/user_upload/Pdf/ocene_ustavnosti/ZEKom_-_Zahteva_za_oceno_ustavnosti__data_retention_.pdf.

[120] The Court found that the ECJ decision in Case C-301/06 *Ireland v. Council* was 'with regard to the issue of legal basis *only*' (emphasis added). CCRS U-I-65/13, Order of 26 Sept 2013, para. 9.

[121] U-I-65/13, para. 5.

[122] Ibid., para. 8.

similar proceedings were already in progress.[123] In the resumed proceedings (after the ECJ judgment), the Court established that even after the annulment of the Directive, data retention remained a matter for EU law: Directive 2002/58/EC[124] allows the Member States to adopt legislative measures encroaching on the confidentiality of data in transit, including data retention, when this is necessary, appropriate and adequate in a democratic society to serve a number of legitimate aims. The Constitutional Court found these requirements to correspond, in substance, to the requirement of proportionality that must be fulfilled in order for a limitation on a human right to be legal under Slovenian constitutional law. The Court annulled the contested provisions and ordered the processors to immediately destroy all retained data. While the Information Commissioner invoked several human rights provisions of the Constitution, the review by the Court was based on Art. 38(1), which focuses on the personal data aspect of the issue:

> The protection of personal data shall be guaranteed. The use of personal data contrary to the purpose for which it was collected is prohibited.[125]

It is clear from this case that the annulment of a 'source' directive is not sufficient to remove the legal norms that implement it from the Slovenian legal system. It is, however, questionable whether the precious resources of the Constitutional Court are well allocated with the Court taking over this 'purification' function, which could be left to the legislature. A solution (that would admittedly probably require some dialogue among the branches of government) could be found where the Court would only resume the proceedings (in the interest of protecting the individuals aggrieved by the implementing measure) if the legislative and executive branches were dragging their feet after an ECJ annulment. This is far from saying that the Court should not engage with EU law that violates human rights; in fact, it is almost the opposite. Rather than waiting for the ECJ to deliver a judgment and then going through the mental exercise of checking the conformity of the implementing measure with the Constitution, feeding on the arguments of the ECJ, the Court should do the mental exercise at an earlier stage and incorporate the results of the mental exercise into a reference for a preliminary ruling.

---

[123] Bardutzky 2014b.

[124] Directive 2002/58/EC of the European Parliament and of the Council of 12 July 2002 concerning the processing of personal data and the protection of privacy in the electronic communications sector (Directive on privacy and electronic communications), [2002] OJ L 201/37.

[125] The focus on Art. 38(1) is interesting in its own right, as the provisions of Art. 37 (Protection of the Privacy of Correspondence and Other Means of Communication) offer stricter guarantees: '(1) The privacy of correspondence and other means of communication shall be guaranteed.

(2) Only a statute may prescribe that on the basis of a court order the protection of the privacy of correspondence and other means of communication and the inviolability of personal privacy be suspended for a set time where such is necessary for the institution or course of criminal proceedings or for reasons of national security.'

2.5 Unpublished or Secret Legislation

2.5.1 It is almost completely unimaginable that unpublished or secret legislation could ever be compatible with the Slovenian constitutional order. The very concept evokes nightmarish flashbacks of the Communist Party controlled regime that was removed in 1990–1991 – *inter alia* by adopting the new Constitution. There were two types of secret legislation in the former Yugoslavia. First, in addition to the Official Gazette, there was also a secret official gazette that was made available to only between 22 and 40 authorised recipients. The federal secret official gazette was established in 1980, and in the following year, all six constituent republics started issuing their own secret official gazettes. The scope of secret legislation was broad and comparable to the scope of 'public' legislation. In addition to numerous executive and sub-statutory acts, as many as 55 *statutes* (i.e. acts of the legislature of general application) were published in the federal secret official gazette; often, economic and financial regulation was published in this way. Secondly, before and after the introduction of the secret official gazette, there were legal norms in use that were too classified even for 'secret publication'. These norms primarily dealt with state security. Based on this experience, the opinion was formed that secret legal norms are not legal norms at all; they merely pose as such and can never be part of the legal order.[126] According to the Constitutional Court, the 'mere existence of secret norms that contained authorisations for the political police was tantamount to a gross violation of human rights and fundamental freedoms'.[127]

The Constitution states that all general and abstract legal acts (*predpis*) have to be published before they can enter into force. Legal acts of the state are to be published in the Official Gazette; legal acts of the local communities are to be published in gazettes chosen by the communities (Art. 154). The Constitutional Court has built its Art. 154 case law mostly upon developing a material conception of the *predpis*. The form of a legal act is less relevant for the question whether the act needs to be published; the essential questions are whether the text contains any general and abstract legal norms, whether it regulates a right or a duty and whether it creates external legal effects.[128]

[126] Šturm 1998, pp. 285–287; Testen 2002b, p. 1033.

[127] CCRS U-I-25/95, UL 5/98, para. 84. The case echoed in Sadurski's account as follows: 'No doubt the evocation of this recent history, from before the collapse of Yugoslavia, added a powerful persuasive force to the court's hostility towards the use of such secretive means, even for the perfectly justifiable ends of fighting crime, particularly organised crime.' Sadurski 2005, p 147.

[128] Šturm 2011, pp. 1363 et seq. In 1998, the Constitutional Court was seized with a challenge against a secret agreement between the defence ministries (or rather the military intelligence services) of Slovenia and Israel. The Court dismissed the challenge on procedural grounds given that there was no legal act whatsoever that the Court could review; however, *obiter dicta*, the Court made it clear that without complying with a proper procedure of ratification and publication, an agreement between two states cannot become part of the Slovenian legal order. CCRS U-I-128/98, Order of 23 September 1998, OdlUS VII, 173. See also Sect. 3.1.

2.6 Rights and General Principles of Law in the Context of Market Regulation: Property Rights, Legal Certainty, Non-retroactivity and Proportionality

2.6.1 The first request for a preliminary ruling from the Constitutional Court expresses doubt as to the legality of the Commission's 'Banking Communication'.[129] At the time of writing, the case was pending before the ECJ.[130] A challenge was brought against the provisions of the Banking Act (ZBan-1)[131] that were the legal basis for a bail-in operation, executed via decisions of the Bank of Slovenia and that affected the holders of bonds of five different Slovenian banks.

In response, the Government and the National Assembly argued that the contested provisions were adopted in order for Slovenia to comply with the requirements put forward by the European Commission in the Banking Communication. The only way that the Commission would find that the state aid given to the banks was legal was if Slovenia complied with the Banking Communication in advance.[132] In effect, the enactment of the problematic provisions of the Banking Act was allegedly a 'transposition' of this, at least by name, soft law measure. The Constitutional Court has therefore first asked whether the Banking Communication, 'taking into account the legal effects that are *de facto* created' and given the exclusive competence of the European Union in state aid law, is to be interpreted as being binding for the Member States.

The Court has also asked for a preliminary ruling as to the validity of the Communication, to first determine whether it was within the boundaries of the Commission's competences. However, even if this should be the case, the Constitutional Court has its concerns with regard to the principle of protection of legitimate expectations and the right to private property.

According to the Court, legitimate expectations might be disrupted for the persons who held instruments of equity and debt that had been issued before the Banking Communication was issued. At the time of investing their assets, the affected persons did not know that in the future, state aid to banks would be made conditional upon negative changes to the instruments in their hands. With the exception of insolvency proceedings, there was no legal regime in existence that could lead to the deterioration or obliteration of their entitlements at the time when they chose to invest in the affected instruments. At the same time, the Court has recognised that there is an element of public interest in not limiting the temporal

---

[129] Communication from the Commission on the application, from 1 August 2013, of State aid rules to support measures in favour of banks in the context of the financial crisis ('Banking Communication'), [2013] OJ C 216/1; CCRS U-I-295/13, Order of 6 November 2014.

[130] Case C-526/14 *Kotnik and Others* [2006] ECLI:EU:C:2016:570.

[131] UL 99/10 etc., the provisions contested in U-I-295/13 were inserted by the ZBan-1L amendments (UL 96/13).

[132] CCRS U-I-295/13, Order of 6 November 2014, para. 10.

scope of the Banking Communication. To do so would increase the strain on public finances and harm competition.[133]

There is no doubt that the measures required by the Banking Commission encroach upon the right to private property of the persons affected. The question thus is whether the encroachment is permissible under EU law.[134] The Court doubts that the encroachment is proportionate, as it does not necessarily make it possible for the concrete circumstances in the individual Member States which could determine the proportionality of the encroachments to be taken into account.

The Constitutional Court has evoked ECHR case law on appropriate compensation for encroachments upon private property and questioned the proportionality of the erasure of the affected entitlements that is based only on an evaluation of the liquidation value of the bank, whereas the actual liquidation will never take place.

The Court is concerned that the persons affected by the Banking Communication measures will be excessively burdened with the costs of restructuring the bank. This is especially the case under the contested regime, as not all categories of stakeholders in the banks participate in the losses; on the contrary, depositors and senior bond holders only reap the benefits of the state aid that will subsequently be given to the bank in question. At the same time, the Court recognises that the Communication pertains to the stakeholders whose position has been more exposed to risk from the beginning.[135]

2.7 *The ESM Treaty, Austerity Programmes and the Democratic, Rule-of-Law-Based State*

2.7.1 The European Stability Mechanism (ESM) – or the participation of Slovenia therein – has not been challenged before the Constitutional Court. Given the substantial commitment undertaken by Slovenia upon participating in the ESM (the entire capital subscription amounts to almost one-third of the annual state budget),[136] it is notable that the political debate was almost non-existent. The record of the discussion at the plenary session of the National Assembly in which the ratification statute was adopted is no longer than 1,121 words. The representatives of the largest governing party and the largest opposition party took the floor. For the former, the ESM Treaty was 'in the utmost interest of Slovenia', while according to

[133] Ibid., para. 44.

[134] Ibid., para. 48.

[135] Ibid., paras. 50–51.

[136] Slovenia's share in the total authorised capital stock of the ESM is 0.42%, which amounts to 2.993 million EUR (ESM Treaty – consolidated version following Lithuania's accession to the ESM, Annex I). The State expenditure for 2015 is 9.485 million EUR (Budget of the Republic of Slovenia, UL 102/13, 14/15).

the latter, 'any measure that strengthens the common currency is more than welcome'.[137]

2.7.2 While the ESM has not been contested in Slovenia, there was a constitutional challenge to one of its predecessors, the European Financial Stability Facility (EFSF). A group of 37 deputies of the National Assembly challenged the ZPZFSEu, the statute that provided the legal basis for the participation of Slovenia in the EFSF, before the Constitutional Court.[138] The deputies claimed that the ZPZFSEu, in determining only the total sum and duration of Slovenia's guarantees for the EFSF's funding instruments, violated Art. 149 Constitution.[139] The deputies asserted that the Constitution demands a special statute for each state guarantee, which lays down all the elements of the guarantee. Failure to provide such statute also amounts to a violation of the principle of separation of powers, as the role of the National Assembly is limited to being informed of any guarantees given.[140]

The Constitutional Court rejected all of the deputies' claims and found that the ZPZFSEu does not envisage a series of guarantees. It is the legal basis for one large scale guarantee, with withdrawals to be made gradually, over a longer period of time, and in proportion to what is required.[141] In laying down the grounds for its ruling, the Court formulated some important positions. First, long term economic effects and their consequences for financial stability cannot be evaluated by looking at an individual measure, but rather require constant observation and continuous assessment. This, however, is not a task for the courts. It is for the Government and the Parliament to undertake and, in doing so, they are to enjoy a wide margin of appreciation. Hence, the judicial review of such questions has to be reserved.[142]

Secondly, even before the fiscal rule was introduced in the Constitution (see Sect. 1.2.1), the Court had found that Art. 149 Constitution cannot be interpreted as allowing the National Assembly to provide a *carte blanche* to the Government in matters of borrowing: the obligations undertaken must be, if not determined, at least determinable. This is regardless of the fact that Art. 149 does not set any material conditions or limitations for state borrowing or guarantees. The determinability of (future) obligations is required by the principle of *pravna država* and, not less

---

[137] Record of the plenary session of the National Assembly of 19 April 2012. However, Ahtik et al. 2014, p. 529 report on the calls of parliamentarians to be more fully involved in the Economic and Monetary Union governance.

[138] Act Regulating the Guarantees of the Republic of Slovenia for Ensuring Financial Stability in the Euro Area (UL 59/10, 79/11).

[139] Art. 149: 'State borrowings and state guarantees for loans are permitted only on the basis of a statute.' See Bardutzky 2011, p. 1338.

[140] CCRS U-I-178/10, UL 12/2011, para. 1.

[141] Ibid., para. 29.

[142] Ibid., para. 9.

importantly, the principle of the social (welfare) state (*socialna država*) that commands that

> the State, in any given moment and also for future generations, which are to bear the burden of the debt incurred in the present, must provide the social minimum, that amounts not merely to the minimum required to survive, but ensures the possibilities to foster social relationships and to participate in social, cultural and political life.[143]

It is quite striking that the Court not only looked beyond the constitutional provisions that would conventionally be considered most narrowly related to the issue at hand, but it also invoked none other than the principle of *socialna država*. The latter traditionally stands for demands for solidarity within society and recognises the value of wide access to public services. It can potentially present a strong obstacle to a spectrum of different designs for Europe's economic constitution. In the hands of the Slovenian Constitutional Court, visibly influenced by the discourse prevalent in the German Federal Constitutional Court, it was deployed in order to establish an 'unwritten debt cap'. Meta Ahtik, Maja Brkan and Živa Nendl have thus justifiably wondered whether the Court has not taken 'a step too far in limiting the state's margin of manoeuvre for guaranteeing the respect for the value that the Court appears to hold at the heart of its reasoning'.[144] Whether the Court's concern for the welfare state (of future generations) will consequently be employed in the future to further the ordoliberal ideals of prudent public spending, remains to be seen.

2.7.3 Perhaps the most commonly mentioned reason for the Slovenian economic crisis is the large influx of cheap capital between 2004 in 2008.[145] This was cut short by the global financial crisis when lenders refused to extend loans which businesses were unable to repay, thus exposing the fact that the borrowing was excessive. The banking sector itself was not inflated (as was for example the case in Cyprus),[146] but it was detrimental that the majority of it was state owned, as the losses of the banks immediately impacted state finances.[147] State ownership of the banks and the resulting political influence over lending decisions led the banks to finance managerial takeovers of state-owned businesses in the real sector. This contributed to the sum of toxic loans in the banks' balances. In general, Slovenia stands out somewhat from the other post-socialist Member States of the European Union, as its process of privatisation of state-owned companies has been exceptionally slow and is in fact not yet finished.[148] As a consequence, foreign direct investment in the country remains low.

---

[143] Ibid., para. 25.

[144] Ahtik et al. 2014, p. 535.

[145] See for example Križanič 2012.

[146] (2013, November 30). Slovenia's financial crisis: Stressed out. The Economist. http://www.economist.com/news/finance-and-economics/21590956-fight-avoid-sixth-euro-zone-bail-out-reaches-climax-stressed-out.

[147] Jazbec 2014.

[148] For an overview of the privatisation process in Slovenia until 2005, see Mencinger 2006

Slovenia has so far avoided having to ask for financial support and entering an externally imposed austerity programme. However, as there were severe difficulties with the state's public finances in recent years, Slovenia found itself in a situation where the bailout scenario appeared to be an inevitable reality.[149] In my view, the general public was prevalently opposed to the possibility of a bail-out and, consequently, to any austerity programme designed by the EU and the IMF. This might be attributable to the fact that at the time Slovenia was facing this scenario, the public was already aware of the experiences of other countries that had gone down that road before, especially Greece.[150] A scenario of external financial support was by and large considered undesirable by Slovenian lawyers and economists;[151] however, this view was not unanimous. Avbelj discussed the possibility of the troika as a 'catalyst for democracy'. In his argument, the insolvency of a state is a reflection of its dysfunctional democratic process. The most persuasive out of a range of possible reasons for this dysfunction is that the system has been captured by smaller interest groups that prevent it from cleansing itself of bad rulers. If this were the case, the right to vote would become no more than illusory; once the state is totally captured, the only solution is an intervention from outside. This option harbours the potential to liberate the state from its captors, thus reinstating factual democracy. In reality, it is unlikely that the troika would wield sufficient power to truly prevent the interest groups from releasing their grip on the state.[152]

---

[149] Slovenia remains in an excessive deficit procedure (Regulation 473/2013) that has been ongoing since 2009, and is considered to be experiencing excessive macroeconomic imbalances in the sense of Regulation 1176/2011.

[150] That the image of Greece and its experience was present even in the discussions of the judges of the Constitutional Court is revealed in the concurring opinion of Judge Petrič (a professor of international law) in U-II-1/12, U-II-2/12 (the decision is discussed above in Sect. 1.3.4): 'The position of Greece in relation to those, who *de facto* (albeit in the form of negotiations) determine the conditions of assistance and subsequently oversee the implementation of that agreement (including the parliaments of the other EU/Eurozone Member States), from a substantive point of view amounts to a limitation of Greece's sovereignty, even if the country – from a formal point of view of international law – remains a sovereign state.', para. 4.

[151] As an example, the opinion of Bogomir Kovač, Professor of Economics at the University of Ljubljana, that the reforms of economic governance have turned the EU into a tyranny, with the troika as the essence of European democracy rather than a deviation from it (Kovač, B. (2014, January 24) 1, 2, 3. Mladina.). See also Trampuš, J. (2013, October 10). Klicanje trojke (Calling the troika). Mladina, for a selection of views of politicians and other public figures on the consequences of possible entry into an austerity programme for Slovenia.

[152] Avbelj 2013a, b.

2.8 *Judicial Review of EU Measures: Access to Justice and the Standard of Review*

2.8.1 Slovenian courts have not been very active in requesting preliminary rulings from the ECJ (nine requests altogether since the 2004 accession).[153] The eight requests filed by the Supreme Court, the Administrative Court and the High Court of Maribor were all with regard to the interpretation of EU law.[154] Only the request filed by the Constitutional Court (currently pending) regards the conformity of an EU soft law measure with superior EU law and legal principles (see Sect. 2.6.1).

2.8.2–2.8.3 The tables below indicate the intensity of judicial review before the Constitutional Court between 2009 and 2013. The data presented is with regard to the two most important types of procedure: the review of abstract legal norms, including parliamentary legislation, executive and local regulations, etc. (the 'U-I' docket), and constitutional complaints against individual legal acts (the 'Up' docket; see Sect. 2.1.1). In general terms, the Constitutional Court controls the regulatory activity of the legislative and executive branches and of the local governments in U-I cases. In Up cases, it oversees the compliance of the judiciary with human rights requirements.

In the observed period, between 7 and 15% of challenges against the different abstract legal norms were successful, as described in Table 1.[155]

With regard to constitutional complaints, it must first be noted that the Constitutional Court is seized every year with more than one thousand complaints, but only a tiny percent advance to the merit stage.[156] Of the less than one hundred cases heard on the merits, a huge majority are successful. However, it is clear that many unfounded cases are dealt with in the admissibility stage. Therefore, in order to provide an accurate picture of the Constitutional Court's review of other

[153] Zagorc and Bardutzky 2010, p. 444.

[154] The database of preliminary rulings requested by Slovenian courts other than the Constitutional Court is maintained by the Supreme Court and available at http://www.sodisce.si/znanje/sodna_praksa/baza_seu/.

[155] The numbers in the table encompass all challenges regardless of the type of act that was challenged (parliamentary legislation, executive regulation, local act) and the type of applicant (state institution, private citizen or court by way of *incidenter* proceedings). Under 'successful challenges', I have counted all the cases where a norm was annulled or a situation of nonconformity with superior law was merely established. Under 'unsuccessful challenges', I have counted all cases where the Court has ruled that the measure is not contrary to superior law and the cases where a private citizen's claim was rejected, which occurs when a claim is either manifestly unfounded or does not address an important issue (Art. 26(2) ZUstS). Challenges are dismissed on procedural grounds mostly when the private citizen that filed a claim is not considered to be affected by the contested measure (*pravni interes*; Art. 24 ZUstS), but also when other procedural requirements are not fulfilled.

[156] Legislation enables the Court to weed out the complaints that neither bear grave consequences for the complainant nor lead to the resolution of an important question (Arts. 55–56 ZUstS).

Table 1 Outcome of the review of legislation and other abstract legal norms

Year	2013	2012	2011	2010	2009
Successful challenges	26	31	49	25	32
	7.16 %	8.86 %	14.45 %	9.77 %	9.61 %
Unsuccessful challenges	77	50	76	42	68
	21.21 %	14.29 %	22.42 %	16.41 %	20.42 %
Challenges dismissed on procedural grounds	260	269	214	189	233
	71.63 %	76.86 %	63.13 %	73.83 %	69.97 %
Total	363	350	339	256	333

Source Annual Report of the Constitutional Court (2013)
The figures are from the Annual Report of the Constitutional Court (2013), p. 77, http://www.us-rs.si/media/rsus_porocilo_o_delu_2013_web.pdf

Table 2 Success of constitutional complaints in 2009–2013

Year	2013	2012	2011	2010	2009
All cases received	1031	1203	1358	1582	1495
Cases admitted	23	47	26	74	58
Percentage of cases admitted (%)	2.2	3.9	1.9	4.9	3.9
All cases where final decision was made	22	44	26	58	63
Complaint granted	18	41	21	57	37
Complaint rejected	4	3	8	1	26
Percentage of successful cases out of all cases where final decision was made (%)	81.82	93.18	80.77	98.28	58.73

Source Annual Report of the Constitutional Court (2013)
The figures are from the Annual Report of the Constitutional Court (2013), p. 79

Slovenian courts, the numbers have to be read together; these are provided in Table 2.

2.8.4 See Sect. 1.3.4.

2.8.5 In my opinion, the perception of whether there is a gap in judicial review will depend to a great extent on the outcome of the recent, first request for a preliminary ruling made by the Constitutional Court (see Sect. 2.6.1) and especially on the course of the judicial dialogue.

2.8.6 The situation where different sets of rules would apply to a 'purely domestic' criminal case on the one hand and a case with an element of EU law on the other has been described using Ronald Dworkin's concept of 'checkerboard laws': 'laws that treat similar [cases] differently on arbitrary grounds'.[157] In light of the position of the scholarship that 'the Constitution of the Republic of Slovenia which, even in the circumstances of the full Slovenian EU membership, precludes any decrease in

[157] Erbežnik 2010, p. 216; Dworkin 1986, p. 179.

the already existing constitutional standards of human rights protection',[158] it seems inevitable that this issue will be addressed in Slovenian constitutional law. The gruesome example of the 'anticanon' *Dred Scott* case teaches us that historically, the existence of checkerboard laws has led to the absolute harmonisation of constitutional rights on the federal/supranational level.[159] A possible alternative to the process of harmonisation is to institute a 'maximum standard' mechanism, as proposed by Ciril Ribičič: the law that provides the higher standard of human rights protection is applied.[160]

It should be noted that the equality clause in the Slovenian Constitution (Art. 14(1)) expressly guarantees *equal human rights and fundamental freedoms* to everyone regardless of their personal circumstances. If the EU human rights 'checkerboard laws' were to face a constitutional challenge based on Art. 14(1), the Constitutional Court would probably administer a strict proportionality test.[161] It is likely that the Court would recognise mutual recognition among the Member States of the EU as a legitimate goal; however, the result of the balancing phase of the test is less predictable. If in weighing equality against mutual recognition the Court were to favour the former, this would mean adopting a maximum standard approach. If, on the other hand, the Court were to let mutual recognition prevail, it is hard to imagine that it would not accompany this move with a *Solange* type caveat. This, in turn, could contribute to a move for absolute harmonisation on the EU level.

2.9 *Other Constitutional Rights and Principles*

Implementation and minimum standards Boštjan Zalar has reported on how the implementation of the Asylum Procedures Directive,[162] which defines minimum standards for the procedure in which refugee status is recognised and withdrawn, has led to the lowering of procedural standards in Slovenian refugee law.[163] What is especially problematic is that these standards were established by the case law of the Slovenian Constitutional Court. Zalar has observed that, nevertheless, 'the Constitution itself and the existing case law of the Constitutional Court … are not considered strong enough factors to force the executive and legislative branch of government towards the preservation of fundamental standards of human rights in the transposition of the [Directive]'.[164]

---

[158] Avbelj and Peršolja 2012, pp. 395–396. In a similar vein, see Novak 2004, p. 113.

[159] *Dred Scott v. Sandford*, 60 U.S. 393 (1857); Erbežnik 2012, p. 9; Halberstam 2015.

[160] Ribičič 2006, n. 7. See Halberstam 2015 for scepticism toward the 'higher standards' approach.

[161] CCRS U-I-425/06, UL, especially paras. 7 and 14.

[162] Directive 2013/32/EU of the European Parliament and of the Council of 26 June 2013 on common procedures for granting and withdrawing international protection, [2013] OJ L 180/60.

[163] Council Directive 2005/85/EC on minimum standards on procedures in Member States for granting and withdrawing refugee status, [2005] OJ L 326/13.

[164] Zalar 2008, p. 202.

Choice of legal form for implementation Implementation of EU law has not brought about a significant change in the legal form in which legal norms are adopted. The constitutional rule under which the rights and duties of citizens and other persons may be determined by the National Assembly only by statute (Art. 87 Constitution, see Sect. 2.1.3; for the reflection of this provision in the rules on the ratification of treaties see Sect. 3.1.1) functions as a bulwark against a large-scale erosion of this kind.[165] The rights and duties of individuals, however, are not the only type of legal norms for which the preferred form in the Slovenian legal system under normal circumstances would be a statute. When it comes to the assignment of different tasks to the various administrative organs, for example, the instructions found in the text of the Constitution (Art. 3 – separation of powers and Art. 120 – organisation and work in the state administration) are perhaps less direct than in Art. 87. Nevertheless, the Constitution also demands the use of a statute in a number of situations based on these clauses. In these types of cases, I believe it might happen that EU legislation, especially when the implementation deadline is approaching, would be implemented in the Slovenian legal system with the use of a sub-statutory instrument; however, later, the situation would be remedied in legislation.[166]

2.10 Common Constitutional Traditions

2.10.1 Traditions, by definition, originate in the past that is (or has been) passed on to the present. At first sight, the different historical characteristics of the Member States' constitutions (even beyond the strong/evolutionary divide, see Sect. 1.1.1), could lead us to a finding that there is little commonality in the Member States' traditions. In addition, a 'statistical' analysis of constitutional texts could easily turn into a cynical operation through which a minimum common denominator is to be identified, possibly leading to a reduction in the scope of European human rights law. At the same time, there is in my opinion nevertheless a message that is common to European constitutionalism as a whole: the rejection of the various totalitarian regimes that have abused public power and trampled on the integrity and dignity of the individual. In that sense, the constitutional traditions common to the

---

[165] I am grateful to Peter Pavlin for an informative discussion on this matter.

[166] I have been able to find one such example. In 2011, the Governmental decree on the implementation of legal acts of the European Union on the stepping up of cross-border cooperation, particularly in combating terrorism and cross-border crime (UL 18/11), in order to implement Council Resolutions 2008/615/JHA and 2008/616/JHA of 23 June 2008, assigned the execution of the relevant legal norms to the Ministry of Internal Affairs and designated the different units of the Police as national contact points. In 2013, the National Assembly adopted the new Police Tasks and Powers Act (UL 15/13). The Act, in Art. 161, assigned (again) the execution of the same norms to the Ministry and gave an authorisation to the Government to designate the national contact points pursuant to the Council Resolutions.

Member States are legal expressions of the 'never again' cries that have followed periods of suffering and injustice in Europe.[167] However, the text of Art. 6(3) TEU assigns a future-oriented purpose to the essentially retrospective concept of constitutional tradition. If it is to become a workable tool for the European courts, an approach will have to be identified that can apply historical lessons not only to the problems of which we are presently aware (e.g. data retention), but also to a host of yet unforeseeable challenges.

2.10.2 As discussed in Sect. 1.3.1, the principles of supremacy and direct effect of EU law have not been accommodated in Slovenian constitutional law explicitly, but with a rather more abstract provision according to which the legal acts of Art. 3.a. organisations (i.e. the EU) 'shall be applied in Slovenia in accordance with the *legal regulation*' of such organisations.[168] The term 'legal regulation of such organisations' is most commonly interpreted as a device that accommodates supremacy and direct effect as structural principles of EU law within the Slovenian constitutional order. However, supremacy and direct effect are not the only principles of this rank. Zalar has recalled that respect for the common constitutional traditions, via Art. 6(3) TEU, also needs to be considered part of this 'legal regulation'.[169] Indeed, the traditions inform the general principles governing the body of EU law. Were we to accept Zalar's reading of Art. 3.a, this would mean that pursuant to this article, EU law would have to be applied in Slovenia in accordance with respect for the common constitutional traditions. In effect, the Slovenian Constitution would bind EU law, insofar as it is applied in Slovenia, to the Member States' constitutions. A demand that fundamental rights, as they result from the common constitutional traditions, be respected by EU law, would then be based not only in the TEU, but also in the Constitution.

2.11 *Article 53 of the Charter and the Issue of Stricter Constitutional Standards*

2.11.1 In the domestic context, Constitutional Court Judge Ribičič has vocally opposed the practice of reducing the standard of human rights protection from the higher Slovenian constitutional level to the lower level of the ECHR. His reasoning is that the mission of the Council of Europe system of human rights protection, including the Convention and the Strasbourg Court, is to progressively ensure as high as possible minimum standards. To allow the states to drop from established standards would put an end to the positive development of human rights standards

---

[167] Cf. Jambrek 2012, p. 32.

[168] See above Sect. 1.3.1. Emphasis added.

[169] Zalar 2005; Ahtik et al. 2014, p. 771. It is unlikely that this was the intention of the drafters who adhered to what I have referred to as the indefinable aesthetics of constitution making (Sect. 1.5.1); however, the more laconic the wording, the wider the field of interpretation.

in Europe, amounting to abuse of the Convention as prohibited by Arts. 17 and 18 ECHR.[170] Ribičič's position – in my opinion – accurately illustrates the perception of the ECHR as an absolute 'floor' among Slovenian lawyers.[171]

2.12 Democratic Debate on Constitutional Rights and Values

2.12.1 The Government took the usual steps to include the views of the public in the process of drafting the ZEKom-1, the implementing statute for the Data Retention Directive (see Sect. 2.4.1). It invited written comments and held two public consultation sessions. Throughout the dialogue with the public, fifty different entities (state authorities, businesses, individuals) submitted comments (however, the ZEKom-1 regulates the entire area of electronic communications, and therefore the consultation and the public discussion covered several issues beyond data retention).[172] Concerns were repeatedly expressed regarding the provisions on data retention: whether data retention is truly necessary and whether the data retained indeed is useful in criminal investigations. The Government 'warned' the public that the Commission had lodged an action against Germany for non-implementation of the Directive, imposing a daily penalty of 315,036.54 EUR until implementation.[173] In this sense, the implementation of the Data Retention Directive in Slovenia is an example of infringement proceedings for non-implementation echoing in domestic lawmaking procedures.

2.12.2–2.12.3 In Art. 260 TFEU proceedings, a Member State should be allowed to raise a 'constitutional defence' if it has failed to implement a directive because the implementation encountered serious constitutional obstacles articulated in the course of procedures established at the national level for the review of constitutionality, such as a procedure before the constitutional court or an analogous procedure in parliament.[174]

[170] CCRS U-I-272/98, UL 48/2003, Concurring opinion of Judge Ribičič, para. 8.

[171] See also Erbežnik 2014b and the discussion in Sect. 2.8.6. I would also like to acknowledge Mojca Plesničar's comment that all the practitioners and policy-makers interviewed in the framework of the study on the EAW (see Sect. 2.3) expressed fears that the standard of human rights protection was being reduced, towards a minimum common denominator.

[172] Predlog ZEKom-1, Sect. I.2.3.d.

[173] Ibid., Sects. III. and XIII.

[174] Bardutzky 2014a; see also Douglas-Scott 2002, pp. 411–413.

2.13 *Experts' Analysis on the Protection of Constitutional Rights in EU Law*

2.13.1–2.13.3 I believe that to a certain extent Slovenia has faced a reduction in the standard of protection of fundamental rights as one of the consequences of European Union membership. Even though it was later successfully challenged before the ECJ, I believe that data retention can serve as an example. If this had been a purely domestic legislative project, it would have probably met insurmountable constitutional and democratic obstacles. But as it originated in the EU, it became part of the law in a very different atmosphere (see Sect. 2.12.1).

The reduction in standards is likely to be accepted among the citizenry as a trade-off for the benefits of integration. It is not to be dismissed that Slovenians, perhaps in contrast to other post-socialist Member States, have only recently begun to take advantage of the freedom of movement as a consequence of the economic crisis. This has made the benefits of membership very visible, especially among the young, educated and unemployed. In addition to the economic benefits of integration, I believe that governance on the European level is perceived as an additional check on national politics, with the latter enjoying relatively low respect among Slovenians.

While this may explain the forgiving attitude of the citizenry with regard to the reduction in standards, it does not supply an 'across the board' justification, at least not from the point of view of a constitutional lawyer. Whenever a supranational measure sits uncomfortably with domestic constitutional standards, the tension cannot simply be decided in favour of the former by saying the magic words 'effectiveness and unity'; a certain type of weighing is in order to ascertain whether the attainment of effectiveness and unity is needed sufficiently urgently as to justify the setting aside of constitutional standards.

Primarily, this is a matter for the courts. The recent 'new era' (to borrow the words of Giuseppe Martinico)[175] of preliminary references from constitutional courts to the ECJ is a promise of a more proactive attitude. Constitutional courts should not shy away from eloquently sharing their concerns and positions with the ECJ, substantiating them with national constitutional (case) law whenever they question the validity of EU secondary law, measured against the yardstick of fundamental rights. The ECJ should respect fundamental rights as informed by the constitutional traditions common to the Member States by building these arguments into the fundaments of its reasoning.[176]

[175] Martinico 2010, p. 221.

[176] As a small comparative side note, the US Supreme Court is known to let constitutional issues 'percolate' upward through the judicial system before it grants *certiorari* to one of the cases dealing with a particular issue and finally resolves the issue. In other words, before the Justices take a stand on a matter, they wish to have before them an array of the different possible solutions provided by the lower courts (and scholarly commentary!). Although in a much less hierarchical setting, this logic might make sense in the courts of the European Union as well. In situations

This is not to idealise the conciliatory effects of judicial dialogue. Even in a situation where national constitutional courts are proactive and 'in the mood for dialogue' (to borrow more of Martinico's vocabulary),[177] and the ECJ is responsive, it cannot be excluded that the standards are simply different. In mutual trust scenarios (such as *Melloni*), Daniel Halberstam's 'safety valve' proposal should be considered seriously.[178] It remains open whether a similar solution can be found beyond scenarios involving mutual trust.

2.13.4 While in the scholarly quest for democracy and constitutionalism in the European Union attention on the Member State level is most often paid to national parliaments and (constitutional) courts, this focus of attention leaves out a crucial element: the administration. I acknowledge my personal bias in this matter, having previously served in a government department in a Member State; indeed my observations are based on my personal experience. Civil servants are important gatekeepers of the legal system and have enormous potential to prevent the adoption of unconstitutional norms. They draft legislation, including implementing legislation. At the same time, they exert influence on lawmaking at the European level, either directly or by way of expertise provided to the ministers.[179] Again, based on my personal experience, the national constitution is far from a solemn monument to dwindling sovereignty; it is rather a workable tool, a source of arguments and a constant yardstick. We did not carry the heavy commentary of the Constitution to meetings in other departments to celebrate the country's sovereignty; we did it because in our work, we felt constrained by the constitutional court case law and scholarly opinion.

This account is of course part prescriptive and part descriptive. The claim here is not that all bureaucrats are staunch defenders of constitutionalist values. Whether the words 'the Constitutional Court will never allow it' gets the person who utters them in a meeting in a government department attention or gets him waved off by his interlocutors depends on a number of factors. The first factor is education, including continuous professional development. The second is the position and role of the professional civil service in the system of government. Third, the constitutional judiciary can (and has to) play a crucial role here by developing consistent

where a number of constitutional courts are seized of challenges to EU (implementing) legislation, procedural solutions could be established and a principle could be formulated according to which the ECJ would ensure that national constitutional courts' concerns are articulated, so that the ECJ can adequately respond to them. Perry 1991, pp. 230–234.

[177] Martinico 2010, p. 221.

[178] Halberstam 2015.

[179] Notably, Plesničar and Šugman Stubbs 2009, p. 212 recorded the discontent of Slovenian civil servants regarding the implementation of the EAW. The limited capacities of the (small Member State's) public administration mean that the persons in charge of the legislative drafting in the ministries are not the ones negotiating the instruments in EU lawmaking procedures; the small number of staff at the permanent representation to the EU prevents a sufficient specialisation among them; often, the transfer of information between the negotiators and the implementers is inadequate.

and well-argued case law. Pythic holdings may be useful for disguising disagreement on the bench, but they are unlikely to strengthen the constitutionalist discourse among government lawyers.[180] A transparent and consistent stance on the scope of the court's deference to the legislative branch is also likely to strengthen the legitimacy of the court's judgments by dispelling the impression among the readers of the case law that the court is acting on prevalently political motives.

3 Constitutional Issues in Global Governance

3.1 Constitutional Rules on International Organisations and the Ratification of Treaties

3.1.1 Ratification of treaties The Constitution distinguishes between international treaties that are to be ratified by the National Assembly and all other international treaties. Only the international treaties that are ratified by the National Assembly enjoy an elevated position in the hierarchy of legal acts: they are superior to all other legal acts except the Constitution, including statutes. International treaties that are not ratified by the National Assembly are only superior to sub-statutory legal acts.

The text of the Constitution does not delimit the two categories of international treaties further nor designate the body responsible for the ratification of 'sub-statutory' treaties. The legislature, by virtue of the Foreign Affairs Act (FAA),[181] has vested the power of ratification of 'sub-statutory' treaties in the Government. The FAA further provides that the Government shall only ratify an international treaty if the incorporation of the treaty does not require statutory reform. Also, the Government only ratifies international treaties which:

- regulate questions that would, pursuant to the domestic legal order, fall within the Government's sphere of competences;
- are concluded in order to execute acts of international organisations that bind Slovenia, previously concluded international treaties and decisions of international cooperation in defence or internal affairs matters;
- regulate diplomatic and consular relations.

All other treaties need to be ratified by the National Assembly (Art. 75 FAA). The division of competences between the executive and legislative branches in the ratification of international treaties hence follows the dividing line drawn between the branches in domestic lawmaking. As was discussed above in Sect. 2.1.3, the Constitution demands that rights and duties be conferred by a statute, which accords

[180] In the context of the ECJ, a similar argument was recently presented in Bobek 2013, p. 207.

[181] UL 113/03, 20/06, 76/08, 108/09, 80/10.

a relatively strong position to the National Assembly in terms of the breadth of its competences.

The ratification and publication of treaties is considered of constitutional importance; the Constitutional Court considers secret international agreements to be contrary to the fundaments of the Slovenian constitutional system.[182]

Transfer of powers Article 3.a Constitution does not refer to the European Union, but generically to 'international organisations' and provides a legal basis for transfer of the exercise of sovereign powers (see Sects. 1.2.1 and 1.3.1). To this day, this limb of Art. 3.a has only been used in relation to the European Union; however, this is not to say that it would be inapplicable to possible accession to international organisations in the future.

Article 3.a was also adopted in order to provide a legal basis for the accession of the Republic of Slovenia to the North Atlantic Treaty Organization (NATO). With that purpose, the text of the provision, in its second limb, also includes an authorisation for the state to 'enter a defensive alliance with [other] states', provided that such alliance is based on the respect for human rights and fundamental freedoms, democracy and the rule of law. In Slovenian constitutional law, membership in defence alliances thus represents a special category of Slovenian participation in mechanisms of global governance.

3.1.2 There has been no reform of this kind.

3.1.3 A few years before the EU-related reform of the Constitution, Ivan Kristan wrote in favour of expanding Art. 8 Constitution. While Kristan also proposed Art. 8 as the *locus* for the legal basis for accession to the EU, he would additionally *in concreto* anchor Slovenia's membership in some of the important international organisations (United Nations, NATO, Organization for Security and Co-operation in Europe) in Art. 8.[183]

3.1.4 See Sect. 1.5.3.

3.2 The Position of International Law in National Law

3.2.1 As mentioned above in Sect. 3.1.1, Slovenian constitutional law recognises two categories of international treaties with different positions in the hierarchy of legal norms. Statutes (and all other lower norms) also have to be in conformity with the 'generally valid principles of international law' (Art. 153(2)).

The Constitution also provides for the direct applicability of international treaties that have been ratified and published (Art. 8). Legal commentary adds that not all international treaties (or all provisions of a treaty) are suitable for direct

[182] See above n. 128.

[183] Kristan 2001, p. 4.

applicability; only those with a self-executing character can be applied directly.[184] The Constitution is silent on the form of ratification; as per Art. 169(1) PoDZ-1, treaties are ratified by statute (*zakon*).

3.2.2 It would seem that the dualism-monism dichotomy is of little use when attempting to conceptualise the position of the sources of international law in the Slovenian legal (constitutional) system. The way the Constitutional Court has worded its position on the purpose of Art. 8, namely that it 'defines, in principal terms, the relationship between the international legal order and the Slovenian legal order'[185] has been interpreted as stemming from a position of dualism, namely recognising that these are two separate legal spheres.[186] However, Urška Umek has also underlined the important elements of monism in the Slovenian system: first, treaties are incorporated into the legal system by simple adoption; secondly, treaties thus incorporated can be directly applicable.[187]

At the same time, Art. 8 cannot be read in isolation from the non-enumeration clause (Art. 15(5)) mentioned above (see Sect. 2.1.1). The position of the Constitutional Court is that by virtue of Art. 15(5), human rights and fundamental freedoms enshrined in international treaties that are in force in Slovenia are accorded 'constitutional rank'.[188] The tangible consequence of this position is that the Constitutional Court has in its history already issued a decision, which in its operative part established that the complainant's ECHR right had been violated.[189] Upon finding that the text of the Constitution did not explicitly provide for the human right in question while the ECHR did, the Constitutional Court adopted the provision of the ECHR as *premissa maior* in the concrete case. It explained that the non-enumeration clause in Art. 15(5) Constitution is (*inter alia*) a response to the requirement of Art. 13 ECHR, the latter calling on States Parties to provide for effective remedies for violations of Convention rights.

Sketching the case of direct application of the ECHR by the Constitutional Court ultimately serves to illustrate the relative ineptitude of the concepts of dualism and monism when it comes to explaining the everyday interplay of the different instruments of human rights protection in action. There is enough support in the text of the Constitution for us to understand the Slovenian constitutional system as one open to international law. Seeing domestic and international law as two separate systems cannot be understood as an impediment to the perception of international law as a functional tool in the hands of the citizen and the judge. This openness

[184] Umek 2011, p. 133.

[185] CCRS U-I-274/02, OdlUS XI, 204, para. 4.

[186] See also CCRS Rm-1/09, para. 18. The Court used the phrase 'separate legal system' and immediately stressed the importance of international law for the interpretation of domestic law where the substance of domestic law originates from international law obligations.

[187] Umek 2011, p. 135.

[188] Up-43/96, OdlUS IX, 141.

[189] CCRS Up-555/03, Up-827/04, Ur. list 78/2006.

reaches its highest level in the case of international human rights law, with the recognition of the constitutional rank of the rights recognised by its instruments.

3.3 Democratic Control

3.3.1 In the case of international treaties that have to be ratified by the National Assembly, the National Assembly is involved not merely in the procedure of ratification, but also earlier, in the phase that precedes the negotiations.[190]

The internal aspect of the procedure to conclude an international treaty commences with the formulation of an official initiative to conclude a certain treaty. The initiative is sponsored by the Ministry of Foreign Affairs or another department of the Government and must already state the reasons in favour of conclusion of such a treaty and the draft positions of the future state delegation negotiating the treaty. It must nominate the members of the state delegation. If possible, a draft text of the treaty is to be attached together with a statement of the essential elements of the treaty. The initiative must provide an assessment of the financial impact of the treaty, of conformity of the treaty with valid law and whether the potential conclusion of the treaty will require legislative reform.

In any case, the Government must approve the initiative before negotiations can start. If an international treaty requires ratification in the National Assembly, the initiative is also sent to the Assembly's Committee of Foreign Policy for confirmation (Art. 70 FAA). The state delegation is bound by the positions in the approved initiative; should the negotiations diverge from the foreseen course, new positions need to be approved by the parliamentary committee (Art. 71 FAA).

The legislative branch and the directly elected representatives of the people are thus not only present, but are also given a veto power over a draft from the very beginning. Indirectly, the National Assembly will also be able to exert its influence over all the elements of the international treaty that are already included in the text of the initiative and thus co-decide the frame of the negotiations.

The National Assembly then plays the central role again when it comes to ratification of the treaty, i.e. the adoption of the ratification statute. The ratification statute will contain little more than the text of the international treaty. As further amendments to the text of the international treaty are inadmissible in this phase (Art. 169(4) PoDZ-1), the National Assembly expedites this quasi-legislative

[190] The response to question 3.3.1 refers to the National Assembly, the lower chamber of the Slovenian Parliament. The National Council as the upper chamber does not have any competences under the FAA. In practice, the National Council can still exercise the general powers that it has within the legislative function (Art. 97 Constitution) also with regard to ratification statutes. Thus the International Relations and European Affairs Committee of the National Council regularly scrutinises the international treaties ratified in the National Assembly and issues consultative opinions. At least in theory, the National Council could use its power of suspensive veto to prevent the ratification of a treaty approved by the National Assembly.

procedure by following the procedural rules applicable to the emergency procedure (Art. 169(3) PoDZ-1). The emergency procedure is otherwise applied when for reasons of security, defence or due to a natural disaster, etc., the adoption of a statute cannot wait (Arts 143-144 PoDZ-1).

The National Assembly can adopt declarations to 'express general positions on issues of internal and external policies ... '. (Art. 110 PoDZ-1). Such declarations do not produce legal effects. The National Assembly has made use of this possibility infrequently, but it has used it, notably, to formulate the starting points of Slovenia's general strategy in international relations.[191] With regard to global governance, the 1999 Declaration on the Foreign Policy of Slovenia, for example, listed the international organisations that Slovenia was planning to join at the time and the values and objectives that Slovenia would advocate in global politics.[192] The instrument of declaration harbours potential for the increase of parliamentary participation in global governance affairs, especially in areas that are beyond the reach of the Parliament's power to ratify international treaties, e.g. the participation of Slovenia's representatives in international organisations. The process of adopting a declaration is an opportunity for the participation not only of the parliamentary opposition but also of civil society in the formulation of priorities, objectives and values that are to be pursued in foreign policy. Despite the fact that the text of the declaration is *de facto* drafted in the executive branch, the parliamentary procedure offers an appropriate platform that can attract an exchange of views across society.[193] Whether the potential of the declaration to pursue these goals is developed to the full extent of course depends on the interest and capability of the parliamentarians to take an active role in global governance affairs.

3.3.2 The 2013 revision of the Constitution changed a number of defining features of the system of direct democracy in Slovenia.[194] The reform was introduced after

---

[191] Declaration on the Foreign Policy of Slovenia (DeZPRS), UL 108/99. The National Assembly has issued declarations e.g. to formulate its position on the role of Slovenia in global climate change policies (Declaration on the Active Role of Slovenia in the Shaping of a New Global Climate Change Policy), UL 95/09) or to define Slovenia's position towards the countries of the Western Balkans (Western Balkans Declaration, UL 58/10).

[192] For example: 'In the area of global and regional international economic relations, the Republic of Slovenia will stand for solutions that will ensure full employment, higher quality of life and conditions for economic and social progress and development.' DeZPRS, Introduction.

[193] The 2014 coalition agreement between the political parties forming the government foresees a new declaration on foreign policy to be adopted by the National Assembly in 2015 'by broadest possible consensus, following negotiations within the coalition and the parliament, a public debate and with consideration to other strategic documents of the state ...'. Coalition Agreement for the Parliamentary Term 2014–2018, p. 52, http://www.vlada.si/fileadmin/dokumenti/si/dokumenti/2014_Koalicijski_sporazum_parafiran.pdf.

[194] Constitutional Act amending Arts. 90, 97 and 99 of the Constitution of the Republic of Slovenia, UL 47/13. No revision was made to Art. 3.a (discussed above) nor to Art. 170 discussed above in Sect. 1.2.2. Albeit adopted in the same session of the National Assembly (24 May 2013), this is nevertheless formally a separate constitutional revision from the amendments to Art. 148 introducing the fiscal rule (discussed above in Sects. 1.2.1 and 1.5.1).

the 2010–2012 'referendum wave' with a number of controversial decisions.[195] The central element of the reform was the removal of the right of the National Council and the parliamentary minority to demand that a referendum be called (Art. 90(1)). Even after the reform, 40,000 voters can require the National Assembly to call a referendum as a matter of right. However, the previously extraordinarily strong role of the legislative referendum was also curtailed by limiting referendums *ratione materiae,* i.e. a referendum is no longer possible if the statute regulates certain questions. The list includes statutes ratifying international treaties.[196]

The proposal for the revision of the Constitution filed by a group of National Assembly deputies did not include ratification statutes in the list of limitations on legislative referendums.[197] This additional limitation was added to the draft text following a suggestion by the expert group to the Constitutional Commission (see above Sect. 1.2.2), i.e. by constitutional lawyers rather than politicians. The expert group pointed out that the possibility to challenge the ratification of an international treaty is unusual in the comparative perspective, where treaties are rarely ratified by statute but rather by another type of parliamentary legal act (e.g. decree).[198] For the expert group, it was the 'specific nature of the way international treaties are concluded' that called for referendums on ratification statutes to be banned.[199] The expert group did not elaborate further how this specific nature collides with the possibility of a referendum. With the adoption of the Constitutional Act, there is now no opportunity in Slovenian constitutional law to challenge a decision of the National Assembly to ratify an international treaty by popular vote with a legally binding result. What remains is the general possibility for the National Assembly to call *sua sponte* for a non-binding, consultative referendum (Arts. 26–29 Referendum and Popular Initiative Act).[200]

---

[195] Referendums were used not only in attempts to block economic reforms (see Skledar 2013) but also to prevent the coming into force of a family law reform that featured significant moves towards sexual orientation equality (Ribičič and Kaučič 2014, p. 904).

[196] Article 90(2) Constitution. In addition to ratification statutes, a legislative referendum is not allowed for

- statutes enacting emergency measures to ensure the defence of the state or security or that remedy damage caused by natural disasters;
- statutes on taxes and other compulsory contributions and on the statute for the execution of the state budget;
- statutes adopted to remedy an unconstitutional situation.

[197] Proposal of Katarina Hočevar et al. to initiate the procedure to amend the Constitution (13 September 2012, EPA 620-VI).

[198] See also above n. 190 with regard to the consequences of choosing statute as the form in which the Parliament ratifies treaties.

[199] Report of the Constitutional Commission of the National Assembly on the Proposal for the initiation of the procedure for an amendment of the Constitution of the Republic of Slovenia – UZ 90, 97, 99 (15 January 2013, EPA 620-IV), p. 13. See *contra* Vuksanović 2013, p. 13.

[200] As the expert group stressed, certain international treaties (Art. 3.a) could still be subjected to a referendum (the Art. 3.a referendum was discussed above in Sect. 1.4.2).

Generally speaking, the referendum-related constitutional revision of 2013 was necessary to put a stop to the erosion of the power of representative democracy and the disproportionate rise of direct democracy, which was happening at the expense of constitutional democracy.[201] However, this observation may not apply to the limitation imposed on referendums on ratification statutes. The laconic case for the elimination of referendums on ratification statutes makes it quite difficult to provide a clear-cut analysis of this reform. Two objections can be raised against the argumentation put forward by the expert group. First, in its case against the ratification statute referendum, it did not engage to a sufficient extent with the details of the ratification procedure in Slovenian foreign affairs law, especially not with the attention paid in diplomatic practice to the internal procedures of ratification.[202] Secondly, while displaying consideration for the rules of international lawmaking, it failed to take into account the growing role of global governance, its impact on the everyday life of citizens and the erosion of constitutionalism to which it can lead.

Holding a referendum on a ratification statute may not be the optimal solution for the inclusion of direct democracy in domestic processes of participation in international lawmaking. It is very much a zero-sum game, capable of taking the negotiators as well as legislators by surprise at the very last moment when the expectations of international partners are the highest. The problem that we can observe is that the process of constitutional reform at this important moment was restrained from looking beyond the established categories and types of referendums. We could also speculate that the debates on the important domestic question of limiting referendums overshadowed the global governance dimension of the issue. Should the discussion be reopened, it would need to be liberated from exclusively using the language of Slovenian constitutional law while at the same time retaining the values of the Slovenian Constitution. This is the first precondition if we want to see the constituent power conjure up, on the national level, a robust system of decision making in foreign policy that strikes a workable balance between the pace dictated by the processes of globalisation on the one hand, and the requirements of constitutionalism and democracy on the other.

3.4 *Judicial Review*

3.4.1 The Constitution (Art. 160(2)) establishes a special procedure before the Constitutional Court where the Court issues a legally binding opinion on the constitutionality of a treaty. This procedure is somewhat different from the review of constitutionality of statutes and other norms. There are comparatively few subjects with legal standing: the President of the Republic, the Government, or one-third of the deputies of the National Assembly. In contrast to the procedures for

---

[201] Compare Ribičič and Kaučič 2014, p. 901.

[202] See below Sect. 3.4.1 and especially n. 209.

the review of domestic norms (see Art. 24 ZUstS), there is no standing for the individual citizen. However, this is the only procedure for review of constitutionality that the President can initiate. This is likely related to the President's functions in the field of foreign affairs (Arts. 102 and 107 Constitution).

In contrast to the generally *a posteriori* procedures before the Constitutional Court, the opinion on an international treaty is issued *a priori,* 'in the process of ratifying an international treaty'. According to Nerad, this is to prevent the state, by ratification, from committing to international law obligations at odds with the Constitution, which would happen if there were self-executing legal norms in the treaty or if the treaty contained an obligation for the state to adopt an unconstitutional legal act.[203]

There have so far been five proceedings of review of an international treaty before the Slovenian Constitutional Court. Three of them were brought by the Government and two by the parliamentary minority.[204] It is notable that the Constitutional Court has used 'interpretative decisions' three times in procedures of treaty review.[205] These are decisions where the Court uses the operative part of its decision to declare how to interpret a contested provision in order for it to stay within the confines of the Constitution. The Court – at least within *a priori* procedures, much less so in *a posteriori* cases – has not shunned away from full review on the merits and has in that sense confirmed the position of Mirjam Škrk (herself formerly a judge of the Court) that

> [w]hile the executive and legislative branches, also when it comes to *a priori* review, may expect a 'kind' attitude from the Constitutional Court, since the executive branch has already externally displayed the interest of the state to conclude the treaty under review, one should nevertheless not lose sight of the fact that the internal ratification of the international treaty is in the exclusive domain of the sovereignty of every state and subject to the decision of independent political (or judicial) organs that hold the respective competences.[206]

A priori review of the constitutionality of international treaties does not create a tension with the principle of *pacta sunt servanda.* This is mainly because in diplomatic practice, for Slovenia, the signing (or acceptance) of an international treaty does not yet represent consent to be bound.[207] For a treaty to enter into force,

---

[203] Nerad 2011, p. 1441.

[204] Drenik 2013, pp. 77–78. There have also been attempts to contest a statute ratifying an international treaty. For example the Constitutional Court in Opinion Rm-1/09 reviewed the Croatia-Slovenia Arbitration Agreement, and later, after the Agreement had been ratified, in its Decision U-I-180/10, the ratification statute.

[205] CCRS Rm-1/97 (the European Accession Agreement), CCRS Rm-1/02 (the Agreement with the Holy See), CCRS Rm-1/09. Škrk 2006, p. 83.

[206] Škrk 2006, p. 95.

[207] Jager Agius 2013, p. 13. Signature is an expression of the state's intent to bind itself and not to act contrary to the purpose of the treaty. Should the treaty include a provision stating that the parties will be bound by it by force of signature, Slovenia has to sign the treaty with a 'subject to ratification' reservation. For Škrk, the Slovenian legal system does not recognise signature as a possible way of concluding an international treaty. Škrk 2006, p. 77.

it needs to be ratified, and diplomatic practice distinguishes internal ratification (procedure in the National Assembly or the Government) and international ratification (exchange of ratification instruments between the states parties to the treaty).[208] In that sense, the Art. 160(2) procedure falls squarely within the internal phase of ratification; the President will only issue a ratification instrument once the ratification statute has been published in the Official Gazette.[209]

3.5 *The Social Welfare Dimension of the Constitution*

3.5.1–3.5.2 Slovenia has not been subject to a programme of financial assistance. The constitutional implications of such a scenario were discussed hypothetically in the Constitutional Court's *State Holding & Bank Stability Referendum* decision (see Sect. 1.3.2).

3.6 *Constitutional Rights and Values in Selected Areas of Global Governance*

The right to water In the past two years, demands have been voiced for the introduction of constitutional protection for the right to water. After the 2013 initiative of the National Council, proposals were formulated by groups of National Assembly deputies. A proposal submitted in 2014 failed, as the parliamentary term came to an end. At the time of preparing this report, a new proposal had been tabled.[210]

The proposal refers to the experience of Greece, Portugal, Italy, Spain and France, where privatisation of the water supply system has led to an increase in the prices charged to the end users and to a decrease in the quality of water. In several

[208] Jager Agius 2013, p. 16.

[209] Drenik 2013, pp. 64–65 (Table 1). With regard to the discussion above in Sect. 3.3.2, the same logic also applies to the legislative referendum (that is no longer admissible since 2013). The referendum would in any case be held *after* the adoption of the statute in the National Assembly and *before* the statute is promulgated by the President of the Republic (Art. 9 Referendum and Popular Initiative Act). In other words, it is impossible that the ratification statute would be struck down *after* the ratification instruments have been exchanged, thus violating Slovenia's international obligations. In this sense, the *a posteriori* legislative referendum is different from *a posteriori* judicial review of constitutionality. The former will always be held before the promulgation of the statute by the President and its publication in *Uradni list.* The latter can be filed at any time after the statute has entered into force and hence long after the ratification instruments have been exchanged and the treaty has entered into force.

[210] (2015, February 17). *Znova predlog o ustavni zaščiti pitne vode* (Again a proposal for constitutional protection of potable water). Delo. http://www.delo.si/novice/okolje/znova-predlog-o-ustavni-zasciti-pitne-vode.html.

cases, privatisation of the water supply was demanded by the 'troika' as part of the conditionality for the country to receive financial support. It mentions Bolivia as an example of a country where privatisation of the water supply was one of the conditions put forward by the World Bank in order to extend a loan. The purpose of the initiative is thus to prevent changes in water regulation: the proposal mentions that Directive 2014/23/EU[211] initially planned to liberalise the system of concessions for water. To that end, two paragraphs would be added to Art. 70 of the Constitution:

> Everyone has the right to potable water.
>
> Water sources that supply potable water and household water to the population shall be exploited in the form of a non-profit public service.[212]

Transatlantic Trade and Investment Partnership (TTIP) The TTIP has been met with criticism in Slovenia predominantly from environmentalist NGOs and trade unions. A number of them have jointly demanded from the government ministers that Slovenia reject the introduction of the investor-state dispute settlement (ISDS) mechanisms in the TTIP. This protest rejects any scenario according to which states would be exposed to legal claims against their public policies in arbitration tribunals.[213] The concerns seems to have spread comparatively widely among the population, as Slovenia is among the countries where the number of signatures in support of the 'Stop TTIP' initiative has reached the 'country quorum' (Art. 7, Regulation 211/2011/EU).[214,215]

It seems that the concerns with regard to the TTIP are slowly making their way into the institutions of the state. The National Council, in early 2015, hosted an NGO-convened conference with the telling title of 'TTIP – are corporations to kidnap our future?'[216] In the Government commissioned study on the effects of the TTIP on the Slovenian economy, scholars warn of the unpredictable outcomes of the ISDS mechanisms and recommend maintaining the jurisdiction of national and

[211] Directive 2014/23/EU of the European Parliament and of the Council of 26 February 2014 on the award of concession contracts, [2014] OJ L 94/1. The 2014 proposal for constitutional reform mentioned that the pressure from the environmental NGO Right2Water which collected 1.5 million signatures demanding that water services be excluded from liberalisation (http://www.right2water.eu/news/vote-right-water-european-parliament-approaches) led Commissioner Michel Barnier to announce that the water services would be excluded from the scope of Directive 2014/23/EU. See Art. 12 ('Specific exclusions in the field of water') Directive 2014/23/EU.

[212] Order of the National Council of 15 May 2013, No. 802-01/13-6; Proposal of Brane Golubovič et al. to initiate a procedure to amend the Constitution (20 March 2014, EPA 1861–VI).

[213] http://www.umanotera.org/wp-content/uploads/2015/02/Javni-poziv-za-izklju%C4%8Ditev-mehanizma-ISDS.pdf.

[214] Regulation (EU) No. 211/2011 of the European Parliament and of the Council of 16 February 2011 on the citizens' initiative, [2011] OJ L 65/1.

[215] https://stop-ttip.org/signatures-member-states/.

[216] http://www.umanotera.org/wp-content/uploads/2015/02/POSVET-vabilo-TTIP.pdf.

European courts over TTIP disputes.[217] Finally, the relevant committees of the National Assembly have adopted a position on the TTIP, the Comprehensive Trade and Economic Agreement with Canada and the WTO Trade in Services Agreement. The committees have called on the Government to negotiate for the exclusion of ISDS mechanisms from the agreements, to ensure that the agreements will not compromise the level of EU standards in environment, health and labour and social rights, and to defend the position that the Comprehensive Economic and Trade Agreement (CETA) and TTIP are mixed agreements.[218]

References

Ahtik M., Brkan M., Nendl Ž. (2014) In: Neergaard U., Jacqueson C., Danielsen J.H. (eds.) The Economic and Monetary Union: Constitutional and Institutional Aspects of the Economic Governance within the EU, The XXVI FIDE Congress in Copenhagen, 2014 Congress Publications Vol. 1. DJØF Publishing, Copenhagen, pp. 515–545.

Albi, A. (2015) Erosion of Constitutional Rights in EU Law: A Call for 'Substantive Co-operative Constitutionalism', Part 1. Vienna Journal of International Constitutional Law (ICL Journal) 9:151–185, http://ssrn.com/author=1246144.

Avbelj M. (2011) 44. člen (Article 44). In: Šturm L. (ed.) Komentar Ustave Republike Slovenije: dopolnitev – A (Commentary of the Constitution of the Republic of Slovenia – Supplement A). Fakulteta za podiplomske državne in evropske študije, Kranj, pp. 730–735.

Avbelj M. (2012a) Slovensko ustavno pravo v odnosu do prava EU (Slovenian constitutional law in relation to EU law). In: Kaučič I. (ed.) Dvajset let Ustave Republike Slovenije: pomen ustavnosti in ustavna demokracija (Twenty years of the Constitution of the Republic of Slovenia: the relevance of constitutionality and constitutional democracy). Pravna fakulteta Univerze v Ljubljani and Ustavno sodišče Republike Slovenije, Ljubljana, pp. 341–351.

Avbelj M. (2012b) Ustavni pluralizem v EU in Sloveniji (Constitutional pluralism in the EU and in Slovenia). Pravna praksa 31(6):6–9.

Avbelj M. (2013a) Trojka kot katalizator demokracije (The Troika as a democracy catalyst), 11.10.2013, http://www.insolvinfo.si/DnevneVsebine/Kolumna.aspx?Id=105711.

Avbelj M. (2013b) Trojka kot instrument regresije (The troika as an instrument of regression), 25.10.2013, http://www.insolvinfo.si/DnevneVsebine/Kolumna.aspx?Id=106676.

Avbelj M. (2013c) Konec ali začetek slovenskega ustavnega prava (The beginning or the end of Slovenian constitutional law). Pravna praksa 32 (1):6 et seq.

Avbelj M., Persolja N. (2012) Slovenia. In: Laffranque J. (ed.) The Area of Freedom Security and Justice, Including Information Society Issues, Reports of the XXV FIDE Congress Tallinn 2012, Vol. 3. Tartu University Press, Tallinn, pp. 555–574.

Bardutzky S. (2011) 149. člen (Article 149). In: Šturm L. (ed.) Komentar Ustave Republike Slovenije: dopolnitev – A (Commentary of the Constitution of the Republic of Slovenia – Supplement A). Fakulteta za podiplomske državne in evropske študije, Kranj, pp. 1338–1343.

Bardutzky S. (2014a) Constitution as argument in infringement/enforcement proceedings: The case study of fines for delays in implementing the Data Retention Directive. Paper presented at the 'Assessing the EU's responsiveness to constitutional rights: Data Retention, Arrest

[217] Damijan et al. 2014. http://www.vlada.si/fileadmin/dokumenti/si/projekti/2015/TTIP/TTIP_Analiza__1_.pdf.

[218] National Assembly, Resolutions of the Joint Session of the EU Affairs Committee (22nd Session) and the Economic Committee (5th Session), 12 February 2015.

Warrants and beyond' Work-in-Progress Seminar, University of Kent, Canterbury, 28–29 August 2014.

Bardutzky S. (2014b) The Timing of Dialogue: Slovenian Constitutional Court and the Data Retention Directive. http://verfassungsblog.de/timing-dialogue-slovenian-constitutional-court-data-retention-directive/.

Bardutzky S., Fahey E. (2014) Who Got to Adjudicate the EU's Financial Crisis and Why? Judicial Review of the Legal Instruments of the Eurozone. In: Adams M., Fabbrini F., Larouche P. (eds.) The Constitutionalization of European Budgetary Constraints. Hart Publishing, Oxford, pp. 341–358.

Bele I. (2011) 27. člen (Article 27). In: Šturm L. (ed.) Komentar Ustave Republike Slovenije: dopolnitev – A (Commentary of the Constitution of the Republic of Slovenia – Supplement A). Fakulteta za podiplomske državne in evropske študije, Kranj, pp. 412–414.

Bobek M. (2013) Of Feasibility and Silent Elephants: The Legitimacy of the Court of Justice through the Eyes of National Courts. In: Adams M., de Waele H., Meeusen J., Straetmans G. (eds.) Judging Europe's Judges: The Legitimacy of the Case Law of the European Court of Justice. Hart, Oxford, pp. 197–234.

Brkan M., Nendl Ž. (2012) Slovenia. In: Laffranque J. (ed.) The Protection of Fundamental Rights Post-Lisbon, Reports of the XXV FIDE Congress Tallinn 2012, Vol. 1. Tartu University Press, Tallinn, pp. 775–800.

Bugarič B. (2012) Reševanje evra in začetek konca EU? (The saving of the euro and the beginning of the end of the EU?). Pravna praksa 31 (issue 5):3.

Čebulj J. (2011) 72. člen (Article 72). In: Šturm L. (ed.) Komentar Ustave Republike Slovenije: dopolnitev – A (Commentary of the Constitution of the Republic of Slovenia – Supplement A). Fakulteta za podiplomske državne in evropske študije, Kranj, pp. 1026–1031.

Cerar M. (2003a) Ustavna podlaga za prenos suverenosti in za vstop v obrambne zveze (Constitutional basis for a transfer of sovereignty and accession to defence alliances). Podjetje in delo 29:1463–1474.

Cerar M. (2003b) O nujnosti sprejetja novega 3.a člen Ustave (Of the necessity of adoption of the new Article 3.a of the Constitution). Evro PP 1(1):6–7.

Cerar M. (2011) Komentar k drugemu odstavku 3.a člena (Commentary of the first paragraph of Article 3.a). In: Šturm L (ed.) Komentar Ustave Republike Slovenije: dopolnitev – A (Commentary of the Constitution of the Republic of Slovenia – Supplement A). Fakulteta za podiplomske državne in evropske študije, Kranj, pp. 73–84.

Damijan J., Kostevc Č., Redek T. (2014) Vpliv Transatlantic Trade and Investment Partnership (TTIP) na slovensko gospodarstvo (The impact of the Transatlantic Trade and Investment Partnership (TTIP) on the Slovenian economy). Center poslovne odličnosti Ekonomske fakultete, Ljubljana. http://www.vlada.si/fileadmin/dokumenti/si/projekti/2015/TTIP/TTIP_Analiza__1_.pdf.

Douglas-Scott S. (2002) Constitutional Law of the European Union. Longman, Harlow.

Drenik S. (2013) Mednarodne pogodbe v pravnem redu Republike Slovenije (International law treaties in the legal order of the Republic of Slovenia). In: Polak Petrič A., Jager Agius I., Zidar A. (eds.) Pravo mednarodnih pogodb. Fakulteta za družbene vede, Založba FDV and Ministrstvo za zunanje zadeve Republike Slovenije, Ljubljana, pp. 33–104.

Dworkin R. (1986). Law's Empire. Belknap Press, Cambridge.

Erbežnik A. (2008) Ustavno sodišče RS ter evropski nalog za prijetje in predajo ali 'kdo se boji Virginije Woolf' (The Constitutional Court of the Republic of Slovenia and the European Arrest Warrant or 'who's afraid of Virginia Woolf?'). Pravna praksa 27(1):II–VII.

Erbežnik A. (2010) Načelo vzajemnega priznavanja v okviru EU kot slaba utilitaristična rešitev (The principle of mutual recognition in the EU as a bad utilitarian solution). Dignitas 47/48:205–224.

Erbežnik A. (2012) The principle of mutual recognition as a utilitarian solution, and the way forward. EuCLR 2(1):3–19.

Erbežnik A. (2014a) Mutual Recognition in EU Criminal Law and Its Effects on the Role of a National Judge. In: Peršak N. (ed.) Legitimacy and Trust in Criminal Law, Policy and Justice

Norms, Procedures, Outcomes. Ashgate Publishing Limited, Farnham, pp. 131–152.

Erbežnik A. (2014b) Skupni standardi EU na področju kazenskega prava v primerjavi z nacionalnimi (ustavnopravnimi) standardi – Solange Reloaded (Common EU standards in criminal law in comparison to national (constitutional) standards – Solange Reloaded). Pravna praksa 33(26):II–VI.

Fišer Z. (2008) Izročitev, predaja in njuna uvedba v slovensko kazensko pravo (Introducing extradition and surrender into Slovenian criminal law). In: Šugman Stubbs K. et al. (eds.) Evropski nalog za prijetje in predajo: primerjalnopravni in nacionalni vidiki – Poročilo (The European Arrest Warrant: comparative and national perspectives – Report). Inštitut za kriminologijo pri Pravni fakulteti v Ljubljani, Ljubljana, pp. 19–59.

Grad F. (2007) Nova razmerja med parlamentom in vlado (New relations between the parliament and the government). Javna uprava 43(1):101–113.

Halberstam D. (2015) 'It's the Autonomy, Stupid!' A Modest Defense of Opinion 2/13 on EU Accession to the ECHR, and the Way Forward. German Law Journal 16:105–146.

Jager Agius I. (2013) Postopek sklepanja mednarodnih pogodb in drugih mednarodnih aktov – priročnik (The procedure of concluding treaties and other international acts – a *vademecum*). In: Polak Petrič A., Jager Agius I., Zidar A. (eds.) Pravo mednarodnih pogodb (The law of treaties). Fakulteta za družbene vede, Založba FDV and Ministrstvo za zunanje zadeve Republike Slovenije, Ljubljana, pp. 3–28.

Jambrek P. (2012) Iskanje neusahljivega vira slovenske državnosti ter njegove ustavne identitete (The quest for the inexhaustible source of Slovenian statehood and its constitutional identity). In: Kaučič I. (ed.) Dvajset let Ustave Republike Slovenije: pomen ustavnosti in ustavna demokracija (Twenty years of the Constitution of the Republic of Slovenia: the relevance of constitutionality and constitutional democracy). Pravna fakulteta Univerze v Ljubljani and Ustavno sodišče Republike Slovenije, Ljubljana, pp. 23–33.

Jazbec B. (2014) Financial crises and the current situation in Slovenia. Address by Mr. Boštjan Jazbec, Governor of the Bank of Slovenia, at the Annual Conference of the Bank Association of Slovenia, Ljubljana, 18 November 2014. http://www.bis.org/review/r150205e.htm.

Jurič T. (2014) Evropski nalog za prijetje in predajo – kritična presoja zakonitosti ravnanja sodišča in Policije (The European Arrest Warrant – a critical assessment of the legality of actions of the courts and of the police). Pravna praksa 35(28):8–10.

Kaučič I. (2011a) Komentar k drugemu odstavku 3.a člena (Commentary on the second paragraph of Article 3.a). In: Šturm L. (ed.) Komentar Ustave Republike Slovenije: dopolnitev – A (Commentary of the Constitution of the Republic of Slovenia – Supplement A). Fakulteta za podiplomske državne in evropske študije, Kranj, pp. 84–88.

Kaučič I. (2011b) 170. člen (Article 170). In: Šturm L. (ed.) Komentar Ustave Republike Slovenije: dopolnitev – A (Commentary of the Constitution of the Republic of Slovenia – Supplement A). Fakulteta za podiplomske državne in evropske študije, Kranj, pp. 1543–1548.

Kovačič Mlinar B. (2006a) Je ZENPP v neskladju z ustavo? (Is ZENPP unconstitutional?). Pravna praksa 25:(4):13–14.

Kovačič Mlinar B. (2006b) Pomanjkanje poguma pri odločitvi o pobudi za oceno ustavnosti ZENPP (A lack of courage in the decision regarding the initiative to review the constitutionality of ZENPP). Pravna praksa 25:(37):15–16.

Kresal B. (2011) 78. člen (Article 78). In: Šturm L. (ed.) Komentar Ustave Republike Slovenije: dopolnitev – A (Commentary of the Constitution of the Republic of Slovenia – Supplement A). Fakulteta za podiplomske državne in evropske študije, Kranj, pp. 1080–1085.

Kresal Šoltes K. (2009) Primera Laval in Viking z vidika slovenske pravne ureditve avtonomije kolektivnega pogajanja (Laval and Viking case law from the perspective of the Slovenian law of autonomy of collective negotiations). Delavci in delodajalci 9:465–489.

Kristan I. (2001) Dimenzije 'evropskega člena' (Dimensions of the 'European clause'). Pravna praksa 20(31):4–5.

Križanič F. (2012) Fiskalna restrikcija v času recesije (Fiscal restriction in the time of the recession). Gospodarska gibanja 2012(447). http://www.eipf.si/publikacije/gospodarska-gibanja/2012/gospodarska-gibanja-447/fiskalna-restrikcija-v-casu-recesije/.

Kukovec D. (2014) Law and the Periphery. ELJ 21:406–428.

Martinico G. (2010) Preliminary References and Constitutional Courts: Are You in the Mood for Dialogue? In: Fontanelli F., Martinico G., Carrozza P. (eds.) Shaping Rule of Law through Dialogue: International and Supranational Experiences. Europa Law Publishing, Groningen, pp. 221– 253.

Mencinger J. (2006) Privatization in Slovenia. Slovenian Law Review 3:65–81.

Mitsilegas V. (2006) The constitutional implications of mutual recognition in criminal matters in the EU. CML Rev. 43:1277–1311.

Möstl M. (2010) Preconditions and Limits of Mutual Recognition. CML Rev. 47:405–436.

Nahtigal M. (2012) Evropski fiskalni pakt – preveč tog in omejevalen (The European Fiscal Compact – too rigid and limiting). Pravna praksa 31(12):II–VII.

Nerad S. (2011) 160. člen (Article 160). In: Šturm L. (ed.) Komentar Ustave Republike Slovenije: dopolnitev – A (Commentary of the Constitution of the Republic of Slovenia – Supplement A). Fakulteta za podiplomske državne in evropske študije, Kranj, pp. 1414–1462.

Nerad S. (2012) Recepcija prava Evropske unije v nacionalno ustavno pravo (Reception of EU law into national constitutional law). In: Kaučič I. (ed.) Dvajset let Ustave Republike Slovenije: pomen ustavnosti in ustavna demokracija (Twenty years of the Constitution of the Republic of Slovenia: the relevance of constitutionality and constitutional democracy). Pravna fakulteta Univerze v Ljubljani and Ustavno sodišče Republike Slovenije, Ljubljana, pp. 379–392.

Novak M. (2004) Slovenska ustavna identiteta v primežu evropskega prava – preliminarna razmišljanja (Slovenian constitutional identity in the vice of European law – preliminary thoughts). Revus 2(2): 95–115.

Oven B. (2014) Ustavno sodišče med sekundarnim pravom EU in ustavo Republike Slovenije: diplomsko delo (Constitutional Court between secondary EU law and the constitution of the Republic of Slovenia: thesis). Pravna fakulteta Univerze v Ljubljani, Ljubljana.

Pavlin P. (2011) 87. člen (Article 87). In: Šturm L. (ed.) Komentar Ustave Republike Slovenije: dopolnitev – A (Commentary of the Constitution of the Republic of Slovenia – Supplement A). Fakulteta za podiplomske državne in evropske študije, Kranj, pp. 1151–1163.

Perry H.W. (1991). Deciding to decide: Agenda setting in the United States Supreme Court. Harvard University Press, Cambridge.

Plesničar M.M., Modic M. (2007) The Constitutional Court of the Republic of Slovenia. Slovenian Law Review 4 (Dec. 2007):287–307.

Plesničar M.M., Šugman Stubbs K. (2009) Implementacija in percepcija načela vzajemnega priznavanja v slovenskem kazenskem pravu (Implementation and perception of the principle of mutual recognition in Slovenian criminal law). Zbornik znanstvenih razprav 69:203–228.

Ribičič C. (2003) Mozaik ustavnih sprememb: od slovenske ustavnosti k evropski (The mosaic of constitutional reform: from Slovenian towards European constitutionality). GV Založba, Ljubljana.

Ribičič C. (2006) Položaj slovenske ustave po vključitvi v EU (The position of the Slovenian constitution after the accession to the EU). Pravna praksa 25(29/30):II–VI.

Ribičič C., Kaučič I. (2014) Constitutional Limits of Legislative Referendum: The Case of Slovenia. Lex Localis – Journal of Local Self-Government 12:899–928.

Rosenfeld M. (2009). The Identity of the Constitutional Subject: Selfhood, Citizenship, Culture and Community. Routledge, London.

Sadurski W. (2005) Rights Before Courts: A Study of Constitutional Courts in Postcommunist States of Central and Eastern Europe. Springer, Dordrecht.

Skledar Š. (2013) Changes proposed to referendum rules, 7. 4. 2013, https://www.eurofound.europa.eu/publications/article/2013/changes-proposed-to-referendum-rules.

Škrk M. (2006) Ustavnosodna presoja mednarodnih pogodb (Constitutional review of treaties). Revus 4(6):73–96.

Strban G. (2012) Ustavna zapoved socialne države ni pravno nezavezujoča norma (The Constitutional commandment of social state is not legally non-binding). Pravna praksa 31 (22):3.

Šturm L. (1998) Omejitev oblasti: ustavna izhodišča javnega prava (The limits on power: constitutional foundations of public law). Nova revija, Ljubljana.

Šturm L. (2002) 2. člen (Article 2). In: Šturm L. (ed.) Komentar Ustave Republike Slovenije (Commentary of the Constitution of the Republic of Slovenia). Fakulteta za podiplomske državne in evropske študije, Ljubljana, pp. 52–98.

Šturm L. (2011) 154. člen (Article 154). In: Šturm L. (ed.) Komentar Ustave Republike Slovenije: dopolnitev – A (Commentary of the Constitution of the Republic of Slovenia – Supplement A). Fakulteta za podiplomske državne in evropske študije, Kranj, pp. 1363–1370.

Šugman Stubbs K. (2008) Obseg sodne kontrole ENPP (The scope of judicial review of the European Arrest Warrant). In: Šugman Stubbs K. et al. (eds.) Evropski nalog za prijetje in predajo: primerjalnopravni in nacionalni vidiki – Poročilo (European Arrest Warrant: comparative and national perspectives – Report). Inštitut za kriminologijo pri Pravni fakulteti v Ljubljani, Ljubljana, pp. 136–141.

Šugman Stubbs K., Gorkič P. (2008) Empirična analiza postopkov v zadevah odločanja o ENPP (Empirical analysis of procedures in European Arrest Warrant cases). In: Šugman Stubbs K. et al. (eds.) Evropski nalog za prijetje in predajo: primerjalnopravni in nacionalni vidiki – Poročilo (European Arrest Warrant: comparative and national perspectives – Report). Inštitut za kriminologijo pri Pravni fakulteti v Ljubljani, Ljubljana, pp. 155–186.

Šugman Stubbs K., Gorkič P. (2009a) Abuse of the EAW System. In: Keijzer N., van Sliedregt E. (eds.) The European Arrest Warrant in Practice. TMC Asser Press, The Hague, pp. 245–264.

Šugman Stubbs K., Gorkič P. (2009b) Denial of Guilt. In: Keijzer N., van Sliedregt E. (eds.) The European Arrest Warrant in Practice. TMC Asser Press, The Hague, pp. 229–243.

Šugman Stubbs K., Plesničar M.M. (2009) Mutual recognition in the context of Slovenian criminal law. In: Vernimment-Van Tiggelen G., Surano L., Weyembergh A. (eds.) The future of mutual recognition in criminal matters in the European Union. Ed. de l'Université de Bruxelles, Brussels, pp. 501–522.

Testen F. (2002a) 15. člen (Article 15). In: Šturm L. (ed.) Komentar Ustave Republike Slovenije (Commentary of the Constitution of the Republic of Slovenia). Fakulteta za podiplomske državne in evropske študije, Ljubljana, pp. 192–204.

Testen F. (2002b) 154. člen (Article 154). In: Šturm L. (ed.) Komentar Ustave Republike Slovenije (Commentary of the Constitution of the Republic of Slovenia). Fakulteta za podiplomske državne in evropske študije, Ljubljana, pp. 1024–1049.

Testen F. (2011) Komentar k tretjemu odstavku 3. a člena (Commentary on Article 3. a, Paragraph III). In: Šturm L. (ed.) Komentar Ustave Republike Slovenije – dopolnitev A (Commentary of the Constitution of the Republic of Slovenia – Supplement A). Fakulteta za podiplomske državne in evropske študije, Ljubljana, pp. 89–95.

Umek U. (2011) 8. člen (Article 8). In: Šturm L (ed.) Komentar Ustave Republike Slovenije: dopolnitev – A (Commentary of the Constitution of the Republic of Slovenia – Supplement A). Fakulteta za podiplomske državne in evropske študije, Kranj, pp. 131–145.

Vuksanović I. (2011) Ustava in ekonomska politika (Constitution and economic policy). Pravna praksa 30(41/42):18–20.

Vuksanović I. (2013) Ustavne omejitve referenduma (Constitutional limitations of the referendum). Pravna praksa 32(2):13–14.

Zagorc S., Bardutzky S. (2010) Application of EU law in Slovenia: teething troubles of the blue-eyed boy. In: Lazowski A. (ed.) Application of EU Law in the New Member States: Brave New World. T.M.C. Asser Press, The Hague, pp. 421–451.

Zalar B. (2005) Prve izkušnje sodišča in sodnikovi pogledi na uporabo prava Evropske unije (First experiences of the court and the views of a judge on the application of European Union law). Pravna praksa 24(6): I–VIII.

Zalar B. (2008) Constitutionalisation of the implementing act of the procedures directive: the Slovenian perspective. European Journal of Migration and Law 10:187–217.

Zupančič B.M. (2002) 28. člen (Article 28). In: Šturm L. (ed.) Komentar Ustave Republike Slovenije (Commentary of the Constitution of the Republic of Slovenia). Fakulteta za podiplomske državne in evropske študije, Ljubljana, pp. 306–314.

4

The Constitution of Italy: Axiological Continuity Between the Domestic and International Levels of Governance?

Giuseppe Martinico, Barbara Guastaferro and Oreste Pollicino

Abstract The Italian Constitution (1948) belongs to the group of constitutions described as 'constitutions born from the Resistance', forged to reject totalitarian experiences. According to the report, the concept of the '*Stato di diritto*' is similar to

---

Giuseppe Martinico is Associate Professor in Comparative Public Law at the Scuola Superiore Sant'Anna, Pisa. e-mail: martinico@sssup.it.

Barbara Guastaferro is Tenured Assistant Professor of Constitutional Law, University of Naples 'Federico II'; at the time of writing Research Fellow in Law, Durham Law School. e-mail: barbara.guastaferro@unina.it.

Oreste Pollicino is Full Professor in Comparative Constitutional Law at Bocconi University, Milan. e-mail: oreste.pollicino@unibocconi.it.

Giuseppe Martinico wrote Sects. 1.1.1, 1.2.1–1.2.3, 1.3.1, 1.3.4, 1.5.3, 2.8.4, 2.10.1, 2.10.2, 2.11.1, 2.13.1, 2.13.2, 2.13.3, 2.13.4, 3.1.1–3.1.2, 3.1.3, 3.1.4, 3.2.1, 3.2.2, 3.3.1 and 3.4.1. Barbara Guastaferro wrote Sects. 1.4.2, 2.1.3, 2.2.1, 2.3.1.1, 2.3.1.2, 2.3.2.1, 2.3.3.1, 2.3.4.1, 2.3.4.2, 2.3.5.1, 2.3.5.2, 2.3.5.3, 2.3.5.4, 2.5.1, 2.6.1, 2.8.6, 2.9.1, 2.12.1, 2.12.2 and 2.12.3. Oreste Pollicino wrote Sects. 1.1.2, 1.2.4, 1.4.1, 1.5.1, 1.5.2, 2.1.1, 2.1.2, 2.4.1, 2.4.2, 2.7.1, 2.7.2, 2.7.3, 2.8.1, 2.8.2, 2.8.3, 2.8.5, 3.3.2, 3.5.1, 3.5.2 and 3.6.1. The authors would like to thank Amedeo Barletta, Gaetano De Amicis, Giacomo Delledonne, Cristina Fasone, Massimo Fichera, Filippo Fontanelli, Adriano Maffeo, Ignazio Patrone and Leonardo Pierdominici for their help and comments. Despite the terminology employed in the Lisbon Treaty we shall use 'ECJ' instead of 'CJEU' to refer to the Court of Justice. The terms 'Community law', 'EC law' and 'EU law' will be treated as interchangeable. Unless otherwise stated, all the decisions of the Italian Constitutional Court have been taken from its official website (www.cortecostituzionale.it).

G. Martinico (✉)
Scuola Superiore Sant'Anna, Pisa, Italy
e-mail: martinico@sssup.it

B. Guastaferro
University of Naples 'Federico II', Naples, Italy
e-mail: barbara.guastaferro@unina.it

B. Guastaferro
Durham Law School, Durham, England

O. Pollicino
Bocconi University, Milan, Italy
e-mail: oreste.pollicino@unibocconi.it

the *Rechtsstaat*, with two key dimensions: (a) constitutional provisions on access to courts and judicial review; and (b) the legality principle, which subordinates administrative acts to parliamentary statutes. Under the latter, the introduction of criminal offences and imposition of obligations and taxation is permissible only on the basis of a parliamentary statute. The need to protect these tenets in the context of implementing the European Arrest Warrant system gave ground to extensive concerns on the part of governmental committees and legal scholars, leading to the introduction of fundamental rights safeguards, which, however, were criticised by the European Commission. Other areas where constitutional values have come under strain include the protection of social rights and the powers of the regions. More broadly, the report explores how to ensure axiological continuity between the principles and values that govern the life of a given polity within its boundaries and those that should characterise the international community. The report also observes that the autonomous language of transnational 'constitutionalism' does not readily correspond to what constitutional lawyers mean by the same word. In Italian scholarship, a number of scholars have come to speak about 'weak' or 'post-modern' constitutionalism, typical of the era of globalisation. Constitutional amendments regarding the EU are limited; further amendments have been considered, including a reference to 'supreme principles of the Italian legal order and of the inviolable human rights'.

Keywords The Constitution of Italy · Amendment of the Constitution in relation to EU and international co-operation · The Italian Constitutional Court
'*Stato di diritto*'/*Rechtsstaat* · The rule of law, the legality principle, access to courts and judicial protection · European Arrest Warrant and fundamental rights safeguards · Defence rights and *nulla poena sine lege* · Data Retention Directive
Changing language of constitutionalism at the transnational level
Fundamental rights · General principles of law and the principle of proportionality
Supremacy and *controlimiti* · Fundamental rights protection in the international fight against terrorism

1 Constitutional Amendments Regarding EU Membership

1.1 Constitutional Culture

1.1.1 The Italian Constitution belongs to the group of constitutions that Mortati has called 'constitutions born from the Resistance',[1] as they were forged with the clear intent to deny and overcome the whole of the 'values' (or anti-values) that had characterised the Fascist (or elsewhere, totalitarian) era. By 'constitutions born from the Resistance', Mortati also referred to other documents, for instance, the French

[1] Mortati 1973, p. 222.

(IV Republic) and German constitutions. As Carrozza[2] has recently noted, today we could include the Portuguese, Spanish and Greek constitutions that were promulgated during the 1970s within this group.

Openness is precisely one of the most evident features that characterises these texts, and it is possible to find the roots of this phenomenon even earlier, looking back at what, in the thirties, Mirkine-Guetzévitch called the 'internationalization of modern constitutions'.[3] In other words, openness seems to belong within the core of the '*nouvelles tendances du droit constitutionnel*'. It is possible to find this element in many constitutions born from the Resistance, which have been the product of a political compromise among very different democratic forces that had, as their only common point, the rejection of the totalitarian experiences, and that are characterised by a strong programmatic character, inspired by the sincere denial of the features of the previous regime and by the need for an entirely different society. Some of these constitutions (including the Italian Constitution) claimed the need for new societal models and were very rich in declarations of principle, reflecting a wish to produce a break with the past. In some cases, these so-called announced revolutions[4] have remained solely on paper, as one of the most influential members of the Italian Constituent Assembly, Calamandrei, bitterly acknowledged with regard to many provisions of the Italian Constitution a few years after it came into force.[5] This programmatic character implied the need for a real turning point in the ways of conceiving not only the values and premises of the social life within the national boundaries, but, frequently, they also induced the founding fathers of these constitutions born from the Resistance to hazard the codification of the values that should inspire the life and contribution of their nations to the international arena and community (external openness). Usually, it is said that the Italian Constitution is the result of a political compromise ('*compromesso*') among the three most important forces that acted as the engine of the constituent phase: the liberal, the Christian democratic and the socialist-communist (left-wing) traditions. They gathered together in the National Liberation Committee (CLN), and the 'glue' of this compromise was their shared anti-fascism. Indeed, the Italian case is very interesting for the study of constitutional openness that can be understood as a product of the anti-fascism[6] that had a crucial role in unifying the leading forces of the CLN. Unlike the German case, the Italian constituent experience is less known abroad and, at the same time, it is probably a more genuine case of a constituent phase because of the lesser impact of foreign influences, at least in the writing of the constitution. This does not mean that there was no foreign influence on the Italian constituent process, but scholars have shown that the Italian Constituent Assembly

---

[2] Carrozza 2007, p. 180.

[3] Mirkine-Guetzévitch 1931, p. 48.

[4] Calamandrei 1966, p. 421.

[5] Calamandrei 1965, p. 553.

[6] Luciani 1991, p. 191. See also Delledonne 2009.

was really free to write a new constitution that was an 'autogenous product' of the Assembly.[7]

The Italian Constitution came into force on 1 January 1948. All of the main members of the Constituent Assembly, although so different in their cultural and political backgrounds, were united around the memory of the past.

As we will see, all of the constitutional provisions that govern the foreign relations of the Italian Republic result from this idea, starting with Art. 11, which is devoted to the pacifist principle.

1.1.2 The Constitution is composed of 139 articles, with its main parts organised as follows: the first 12 articles are devoted to Fundamental Principles. Thereafter, Part I concerns the 'Rights and Duties of Citizens', while Part II is devoted to the 'Organisation of Republic' (Arts. 55–139). Part I (Arts. 13–54) contains the following subsections: 'Civil Relations'; 'Ethical and Social Rights and Duties'; 'Economic Rights and Duties', and 'Political Rights and Duties'. Part II is divided into six 'Titles': the Houses and the Legislative Process; the President of the Republic; the Government; the 'Judicial Branch', covering both the 'Organization of the Judiciary' and the 'Rules on Jurisdiction'; and 'Regions, Provinces, Municipalities' (amended in 2001). Part II also contains a section entitled 'Constitutional Guarantees', which concerns the structure, composition and functioning of the Constitutional Court (Arts. 134–137) and includes the relevant provisions concerning 'Amendments to the Constitution and Constitutional Laws' (Arts. 138–139). According to the case law of the Italian Constitutional Court (ItCC) the formula 'Republican form' included in Art. 139 (devoted, as we will see, to the impossibility to amend the 'Republican form') corresponds to the supreme principles included in the very first articles of the Italian Constitution.[8] The logic is the following: any change concerning these principles would result in a revolution in the technical sense of the word. These fundamental principles thus represent the 'centre of gravity' of our Constitution.

1.2 The Amendment of the Constitution in Relation to the European Union

1.2.1 At first and for a long time, the ItCC used Art. 11 in order to cover the necessary limitations of sovereignty required by the European integration process (see Sect. 3.1.1 for the full wording of the article). This was the case until 2001 when the first important amendment concerning European integration was introduced with codification of the duty to exercise legislative power in compliance with Community law. Other amendments were introduced in 2012 to constitutionalise the so-called 'golden rule'. For details see Sect. 1.2.3.

[7] Bruno 1980, p. 59.

[8] ItCC, Decision No. 1146/1988.

1.2.2 The constitutional amendment procedure is governed by Art. 138 of the Italian Constitution:

> Laws amending the Constitution and other constitutional laws shall be adopted by each House after two successive debates at intervals of not less than three months, and shall be approved by an absolute majority of the members of each House in the second voting. Said laws are submitted to a popular referendum when, within three months of their publication, such request is made by one-fifth of the members of a House or five hundred thousand voters or five Regional Councils. The law submitted to referendum shall not be promulgated if not approved by a majority of valid votes. A referendum shall not be held if the law has been approved in the second voting by each of the Houses by a majority of two-thirds of the members.[9]

No other options are available and thus this was the procedure followed to change, *inter alia*, Art. 117. It is interesting to note that more recently, according to the reform proposed by the Renzi Government, it has been suggested that Art.117(1) should be terminologically amended by replacing 'Community law' with 'EU law', following the terminology adopted after the coming into force of the Lisbon Treaty.

1.2.3 The new Art. 117(1) currently reads, '[l]egislative powers shall be vested in the State and the Regions in compliance with the Constitution and with the constraints deriving from Community and international obligations'. A more recent amendment was introduced to change the text of Art. 81 of the Constitution to introduce an express mention of the 'balanced budget' principle through Constitutional Law No. 1/2012. Articles 97, 117 and, above all, the first paragraph of Art. 119[10] were also amended.

Looking at the judicial parameter, we will see that Art. 117(1) has provoked interesting innovations in the ItCC's case law. Soon after the reform, the interpretation of this norm created a division among scholars.[11] According to some, Art. 117(1) simply codified the pre-existing situation: it granted a sort of *a posteriori* assent to European primacy[12] as had been developed by the Court of the Justice (ECJ) and accepted across the European Union. Other scholars, on the other hand, emphasised

---

[9] The translations of the Italian Constitution reported in this chapter, with some limited exceptions, have been taken from the following sites: https://www.senato.it/documenti/repository/istituzione/costituzione_inglese.pdf and http://www.servat.unibe.ch/icl/it00000.html

[10] Article 81 Italian Constitution: 'General government entities, in accordance with European Union law, shall ensure the balance of their budgets and the sustainability of the public debt'. The Italian Constitution goes on to limit the scope of action of Regions and Local Authorities in the field of matters of regional and local finance, by introducing new constraints on the local authorities. Art. 119 Italian Constitution: 'Municipalities, provinces, metropolitan cities and regions shall have revenue and expenditure autonomy, subject to the obligation to balance their budgets, and shall contribute to ensuring compliance with the economic and financial constraints imposed under European Union law. ...'. For a general discussion of these reforms, see Groppi, 2012.

[11] For an overview, see Chieppa 2007.

[12] Pinelli 2001, p. 194.

the importance of the constitutional status given to primacy of EU law, and asserted that Art. 117 paved the way for acceptance of the Italian monist thesis.[13]

1.2.4 It is interesting to note that there have been other attempts to revise the Constitution: for instance we can recall three *ad hoc* parliamentary committees (in 1983–1985 the so-called 'Bozzi Bicameral Committee'; 1992–1994 the so-called 'De Mita-Jotti Bicameral Committee'; and 1997–1998 the so-called 'D'Alema Bicameral Committee') that worked with no immediate outcome.[14] The D'Alema Committee (named after former Prime Minister Massimo D'Alema, who chaired the committee in 1997–1998) had a certain impact on the reforms adopted in 1999 and 2001 (especially with regard to the reform of Italian regionalism). The D'Alema Committee prepared a text which proposed the inclusion of Title VI, entirely devoted to participation of the Italian Republic in the European Union and composed of three articles (Arts. 114–116) in the Constitution. In particular, the proposed Art. 114 would have codified respect of the 'supreme principles of the Italian legal order and of the inviolable human rights' as a condition for participation in the 'European unification' (sic!) process, in order to promote and encourage 'an order based on the principles of democracy and subsidiarity'. The same provision stated that the limitations of sovereignty should be covered by a law passed by an absolute majority of the members of each House, and then added:

> The law is subject to a popular referendum when, within three months of its publication, such request is made by one third of the members of a House or eight hundred thousand electors or five regional councils. The law submitted to referendum shall not be promulgated if not approved by a majority of valid votes.

The proposed Art. 115 regulated the involvement of the Parliamentary Houses in EU affairs and the duty of the Government to inform them. Article 116 was devoted to participation of the regions in the EU integration process.[15] The wording of Art. 114 as proposed by the D'Alema Committee was recently used in some proposed amendments to Art. 11 that aimed at introducing a specific reference to the EU and the possibility of a referendum, should there be any further limitations of sovereignty, and at codifying the duty to respect the fundamental principles and inviolable rights recognised by the Italian legal order.[16] Italian scholars have emphasised the insufficiency of Art. 11 to regulate the EU integration process and have advocated for a possible reform of its wording.[17]

---

[13] Paterniti 2004, p. 2101; Pajno 2003, p. 814.

[14] Fusaro 2005.

[15] See the Italian version at: http://www.camera.it/parlam/bicam/rifcost/dossier/aindice.htm.

[16] See Fasone 2010.

[17] Cassese 1975, p. 583. For this debate, see Fasone 2010.

As we will see, the conservative approach to our constitutional text, the complicated procedure for constitutional amendments and the fact that Art. 11 is included in the very first part of the Constitution are the main reasons for the failure of these attempts (so far at least).

The recent package of measures proposed by the Renzi Government has focused, among other things, on the necessity to constitutionalise the role of the parliamentary chambers in EU affairs.[18]

1.3 Conceptualising Sovereignty and the Limits to the Transfer of Powers

1.3.1 The ItCC originally established that Art. 11 of the Italian Constitution was the basis for accepting Community law as supranational law with primacy and direct effect. This acceptance, however, did not come about immediately. On the contrary, it was the result of a long series of judgments. One of the reasons for this can be attributed to the absence of an explicit European clause in the Italian Constitution. In fact, Art. 11 was originally conceived to deal with Italian membership in organisations like the United Nations rather than to justify the consequence of supranationalism (a phenomenon that was unknown at the time the Italian Constitution came into force). This changed in 2001 with the constitutional reform of Title V of the Italian Constitution, with the introduction of Art. 117(1). Because of the dualist tradition, to which we will come back, international treaties acquire the same force as the domestic statutes adopted for their entry into force in the domestic legal system. This explains why, since the beginning, EU law has been considered as a primary source in the Italian legal system.

1.3.2–1.3.4 If we take a look at the history of the ItCC's case law regarding EU law, it is possible to notice a progressive departure from the pure dualist view first adopted by the Court. Over the years, this purity has been overcome and the ItCC, when referring to the domestic order and to the EC order, began to talk about two 'autonomous and separated, although coordinated'[19] legal systems. At the same time, the ECJ, in often adopting a benign and tolerant attitude, has demonstrated that it appreciates the efforts made by the national courts. Some scholars have labelled this partial convergence with the term *(limited) flexibilization of supremacies.*[20] Despite this rapprochement, the expansion of the European Communities' competences has often given rise to some degree of tension between

---

[18] See proposal A.S. 1429-A, Art. 55 It. Const ('functions of the Chambers'). See also proposal regarding Art. 70 Italian Constitution, which makes the law establishing forms and deadlines for the compliance with the obligations stemming from EU membership a constitutionally necessary law.

[19] ItCC, Decision No. 170/1984, *Granital* [1984] CMLR 756.

[20] Ferreres Comella 2005, pp. 80–89.

the domestic judiciary and the EC courts, each time that the allocation of competence on borderline issues has been at stake. First of all, the ECJ has progressively obtained the trust of ordinary national judges, who also play a fundamental role in the constitutional review proceedings at domestic level. Such influence has resulted in the deterioration of the relationship between ordinary judges and the ItCC: when ordinary judges want to obtain an explanation regarding the relationship between EC law and the national constitution, they do not refer to the ItCC, but rather to the ECJ. This is a consequence of the self-exiled status of the ItCC, which has normally preferred not to address questions concerning the relationship between legal orders. Suffice it here to recall that for instance in 2002, the ItCC decided only ten cases (of a total of 500) that were related to the EC legal order.[21] In case No. 14/1964[22] the ItCC interpreted the relationship between national and EC acts in light of the chronological criterion *lex posterior derogat priori* (since the enabling domestic act ratifying the Treaties was an ordinary legislative act); later on, in case No. 183/1973[23] the ItCC changed its position and claimed that the constitutional basis for EC law primacy can be found in Art. 11 of the Italian Constitution. As we know, this provision was originally conceived to justify Italy's membership in the United Nations, rather than in the EU. EU membership, in fact, imposes limitations of sovereignty for goals that clearly go beyond 'peace and justice between nations'. Thus the ItCC was forced to 'manipulate' the original meaning of Art. 11 in order to allow for these limitations.[24] The ItCC had kept the task of monitoring respect for primacy of EC law (as a control of indirect violation of Art. 11 occurring when national provisions are found to be in conflict with EC law), but the consistency of EC law with the Italian Constitution could not be reviewed by the ItCC, given that it can rule on the validity of Italian norms only. Confirmation of the progressive flexibilization of the Court's original position can be found in the words used in *Granital*,[25] in which the Court found it necessary to 'clarify further the way in which the relationship between the two legal systems works'[26] and recognised that 'conclusions reached in previous decisions must therefore be rewritten'[27].

An important specific feature of the approach of the ItCC to EU law is the counter-limits doctrine, devised by the ItCC in 1973, soon after the well-known *Internationale Handelsgesellschaft*[28] case before the ECJ. In that judgment, the ECJ pointed out the primacy of EU law over national law, including national constitutional principles. In this respect the Italian position – along with that of Germany

---

[21] Cartabia and Celotto 2002, p. 4477.

[22] ItCC, Decision No. 14/1964.

[23] ItCC, Decision No. 183/1973, *Frontini*, [1974] 2 CMLR 372.

[24] Since 2001, an explicit reference to the European Community legal order is contained in Art. 117, as noted above.

[25] ItCC, Decision No. 170/1984, *Granital*, n. 19. On this issue, see Cartabia 1995.

[26] ItCC, Decision No. 170/1984, *Granital*, n. 19.

[27] Ibid.

[28] Case 11/70 *Internationale Handelsgesellschaft* [1970] ECR 1125.

– is relevant for a complete understanding of the reasons for the 'resistance'. Constitutional courts have claimed to maintain their own role (the role of the guardians of the national constitutional identity) without exceptions. They have denied the acceptance of dangerous monist visions in order to preserve the constitutional identity of their legal orders. On the contrary, they have raised some ultimate barriers against the penetration of EU law in order to define the fundamental principles of the legal orders of which they are the guardians. Hypothetically, if an EU provision were to conflict with the fundamental principles of the national legal order, the constitutional court could strike down the national statute executing the EC Treaty, thus causing a 'rupture' between the national and supranational legal orders. Constitutional courts in fact normally have jurisdiction over national legislation (including the legal source of execution of treaties) but not over EC provisions: the latter are beyond their jurisdiction because, as they argue, they belong to another legal order. If one proceeds from this approach, one can understand why the constitutional courts have traditionally refused the possibility to strike down EU law provisions, since the acceptance of this option would imply adhesion to the monist theory of the ECJ. It is by a legal fiction that it is possible to defend the hard core of constitutional legal orders by preserving the formal autonomy of the national and supranational orders and the jurisdiction of the ECJ. The identification of these barriers to European integration represents the essence of the counter-limits doctrine ('*dottrina dei controlimiti*'), devised by the ItCC in the *Frontini* judgment[29] (but see also the *Granital* judgment[30]). The consequence of a possible declaration of invalidity could spell Italy's withdrawal from the EU. According to Cartabia, in these two cases the counter-limits test was conceived of as a way to carry out an exceptional control of respect of the conditions for constitutionality of the Italian accession to the EU.[31] Following this reconstruction, the counter-limits originally worked as conditions for evaluating the legitimacy of the limitations of sovereignty accepted by the Italian accession to the European venture. Later on (with the *Fragd* judgment[32]), the nature of the counter-limits doctrine changed and was transformed from an exceptional control into a 'simple' control of the compatibility of EU law with the Constitution which could not threaten Italy's membership of the EU. Because of the 'transformation' of this doctrine, the counter-limits have worked as a limitation to European primacy: that is why, according to the same scholarship, starting from the *Fragd* judgment, the ItCC has implicitly admitted that a possible conflict with the Constitution would not cause the invalidity of the statute adopted for execution of the EC Treaty, but just the non-applicability of the EC rule.[33]

[29] ItCC, Decision No. 183/1973, *Frontini*, n. 23.

[30] ItCC, Decision No. 170/1984, *Granital*, n. 19.

[31] Cartabia 1995, p. 110.

[32] ItCC, Decision No. 232/1989. In English: *Fragd*, [1990] 27 CML Rev. 93.

[33] See Cartabia and Weiler 2000, pp. 171–172.

Concerning the possibility to overcome such limitations of sovereignty by referendum, it is necessary to recall what the ItCC pointed out in *Frontini* decision:

> The doubt that the limitations of sovereignty consequent upon the signature of the Rome Treaty and the entry of Italy into the EEC could require the use of the procedure of constitutional amendment for approval of the ratification and implementation Bill has its exact equivalent in the analogous doubt already expressed in 1951 on the occasion of the approval of the Treaty instituting the European Coal and Steel Community: a doubt correctly resolved by the Italian Parliament deciding that the ratification and implementation of that Treaty could be made by means of an ordinary statute. In truth, as this Court has already stated in COSTA v. ENEL, Article 11 means that, when its pre-conditions are met, it is possible to sign treaties which involve limitation of sovereignty and to agree to make them executory by an ordinary statute. The provision would finish emptied of its specific normative content if it were held that for every limitation of sovereignty covered by Article 11 recourse had to be had to a constitutional statute. It is clear that it has not only a substantive but also a procedural value, in the sense that it permits such limitations of sovereignty, on the conditions and for the ends therein set out, releasing Parliament from the necessity of making use of its power of constitutional amendment.[34]

Nevertheless, more recently, with particular regard to the Treaty establishing a Constitution for Europe, Marta Cartabia has advocated the necessity to 'cover' the reform of the EU Treaties by means of a constitutional law.[35] Finally, according to the case law of the ItCC, the formula 'Republican form' used in Art. 139 of the Italian Constitution corresponds to the supreme principles included in the first part of the Italian Constitution. This means that in case of correspondence between the content of the counter-limits doctrine and that of the Republican form, no referendum may be used to surpass these limits.

1.4 Democratic Control

1.4.1 Specific measures for the involvement of the Parliament (and regional assemblies) in EU affairs have been codified in law No. 11/2005 (the so-called '*Legge Buttiglione*'), devoted to participation of Italy in EU decision-making with regard to the involvement of the State and regions in the preparatory phase of the EU decision-making process. This statute has been replaced by law No. 234-2012, which provides for measures concerning, among other things, the direct involvement of the national Parliament in the subsidiarity check of EU draft legislation and the obligation of information of the Government vis-à-vis the Parliament.[36] Further mechanisms have been implemented in the new Rules of Procedure of the Chambers. As written elsewhere in this report, in the package of measures proposed by the Renzi Government there is also a specific provision (Art. 55) aimed at constitutionalising the role of the national chambers in EU affairs.

---

[34] ItCC, Decision No. 182/73. See also Fasone 2010.

[35] Cartabia 2004.

[36] Committee of Regions, 2013.

1.4.2 The ratification of EU Treaties does not require a referendum. The only EU-related referendum in Italy was held in 1989, but it was 'consultative', as it asked whether the Italian population was in favour of the transformation of the European Communities into a European Union with a Government accountable to the European Parliament, and with a European Parliament entitled to draft a Constitution for Europe. The outcome was highly positive, with 88.03% of the population in favour and only 11.97% of the population against. Nevertheless, the referendum was conceived to have symbolic value rather than any legal implication, also since in the Italian legal order referendums are only allowed either to abrogate parliamentary laws (as per Art. 75 of the Constitution) or to confirm a parliamentary constitutional law aimed at revising the Constitution (as per Art. 138 of the Constitution). In this respect, a specific constitutional law was adopted (Law No. 2 of 3 April 1989) in order to have such a 'consultative referendum' on the future of the European Union.

1.5 The Reasons for, and the Role of, EU Amendments

1.5.1–1.5.2 As noted above, the EU–amendments have been limited in their content and have codified some of the content of the ItCC's case law. This can be explained in light of our 'conservative' approach to the constitutional text due to two technical reasons: the complicated procedure of Art. 138 and what Calamandrei calls the 'far sighted'[37] nature of many constitutional provisions. In other words, our Constitution is rich in programmatic provisions containing generic guidelines that have guaranteed the 'adaptability' of our constitutional text. The detailed provisions dealing with the new challenges of the EU integration process have been introduced by means of primary legislation.

1.5.3 At the time of its adoption, the Italian Constitution was considered a long and detailed constitution. The updating of the constitutional pact has been guaranteed by the interpretative function carried out by the relevant constitutional actors, but also by a sort of cascade system of norms designed by the constitution. In other words, in Italy, many of the issues that have been called 'constitutional' in this questionnaire have been treated, over the years, by means of primary sources that have developed the guidelines included in the Constitution (either statutes of Parliament or the internal Rules of Procedure of the Chambers). This choice has a price, of course. First of all, if the legislator is negligent many provisions may never be implemented and that is why it would be better to constitutionalise some of these matters. As stated above, it is interesting to note that the last version of the package of measures proposed by the Renzi Government contains several welcomed proposals to this effect.

[37] Calamandrei 1955a.

2 Constitutional Rights, the Rule of Law and EU Law

2.1 The Position of Constitutional Rights and the Rule of Law in the Constitution

2.1.1 As noted above, fundamental rights are codified in Part I of the Constitution and divided into three sub-groups of provisions which more or less correspond to civil, political and social rights. In terms of the position of principles, some principles are codified in our Constitution (e.g. the principle of equality) or can be traced back to some constitutional provisions (the proportionality test is frequently associated with reasonableness[38] in the case law of our Constitutional Court and employed in cases concerning discrimination). There are also some general principles that cannot be considered as 'constitutional', such as the principle of separation of powers.[39] Some of these provisions remain just on paper or have very limited justiciability. Social rights are a classic example of this.

2.1.2 Some constitutional provisions provide for the possibility of limiting fundamental rights 'in exceptional circumstances and under such conditions of necessity and urgency as shall conclusively be defined by the law'. Such restrictions are contained, for instance, in Art. 13 (personal liberty), Art. 14 (inviolability of dwelling), Art. 15 (freedom of correspondence) and Art. 16 (freedom of movement).

2.1.3 Although the core concepts of the rule of law belong to the Italian constitutional order, the Italian Constitution does not explicitly mention a constitutional category equivalent or similar to the rule of law. Nevertheless, at least two conceptualisations of the same principle can be inferred from the text of the Constitution and have been developed by scholarly literature, which usually refers to the concept of rule of law by the term '*Stato di diritto*' (similar to *Rechtsstaat; État de droit*). On the one hand, there is the *subjective* facet of the rule of law, related to access to courts and to the right of defence, enshrined in Title I of the first part of the Constitution, which is dedicated to civil rights. Article 24 states:

> All persons are entitled to take judicial action to protect their individual rights and legitimate interests. The right of defence is inviolable at every stage and level of the proceedings. The indigent are assured, by appropriate measures, the means for legal action and defence in all levels of jurisdiction. The law determines the conditions and the means for the redress of judicial errors.

The right to judicial review is also constitutionally entrenched by Art. 25, according to which '[n]o one may be withheld from the jurisdiction previously

[38] Scaccia 2007.

[39] Modugno 1966; De Marco 1996; Pizzorusso 1981.

ascertained by law', thus ensuring that the tribunal established by law is independent and impartial. On the other hand, the second conceptualisation of the rule of law is related to the so-called '*principio di legalità*' (legality principle), which in the hierarchy of norms subordinates administrative acts to parliamentary statutes (*legge*), as the latter are an expression of the *volonté générale* according to the Rousseauian tradition. In light of this legality principle, the imposition of personal obligations, administrative charges and taxation are only permissible on the basis of a parliamentary statute (see Art. 23). When applied to criminal law, the principle of legality is connected to the principle of non-retroactivity and entails the principle that no one may be punished except by virtue of a law that is in force before an offence is committed (*nulla poena sine lege*).[40] Also another core element of the rule of law, i.e. the rule that only published laws can be valid, is covered by the concept of *Stato di diritto.*

2.2 *The Balancing of Fundamental Rights and Economic Freedoms in EU Law*

2.2.1 It is almost impossible to have a univocal answer for the Italian context. Even if at first glance we might state that the balancing of fundamental rights with economic free movement rights has not raised significant constitutional issues, it is worth noting that many scholars have complained about lower standards for social rights at the EU level, when compared with the standard set out by many constitutions (including the Italian Constitution) which protect social-democratic values and the rights of workers.[41] The fear that the balancing of the Court of Justice may affect national judges has been raised in the scholarly literature.[42] The main criticism related to rulings such as *Viking*,[43] *Laval*[44] and *Rüffert*[45] is that the right to strike is not considered as a human right, thus lowering the standard of protection of Art. 40 of the Italian Constitution, which qualifies it as a fundamental constitutional right.[46] Indeed, in the ECJ case law, the right to strike can be balanced against internal market fundamental freedoms on equal footing (in the sense that it is considered a legitimate interest that must be protected but its possible infringement of an internal market fundamental freedom must be proportionate).

---

40 For a general overview on the two concepts, see Bin 2004 and Sorrentino 2007.

41 Gambino 2014, p. 35.

42 Giubboni 2009; Caruso 2009.

43 Case C-438/05 *The International Transport Workers' Federation and The Finnish Seamen's Union* [2007] ECR I-10779.

44 Case C-341/05 *Laval un Partneri* [2007] ECR I-11767.

45 Case C-346/06 *Rüffert* [2008] ECR I-01989.

46 Gambino 2014, p. 39.

Moreover, it can also be pointed out that the focus of the ECJ is on the formal facet of the principle of equality (protecting non-discrimination), while the Italian constitutional tradition strongly protects 'substantive' rather than merely 'formal' equality. In this interpretation, there is a positive obligation upon the State to remove all obstacles to equality by providing economic assistance to people who are poor or discriminated against in order to provide them equal treatment. While it is possible to say that the Italian Constitutional Court has not expressly adjusted its balancing to match the ECJ's approach, in the field of so-called reverse discrimination, its case law on the principle of equality has been affected by the jurisprudence of the Luxembourg Court.[47] In order to deal with cases of reverse discrimination the Italian Constitutional Court has progressively extended its scrutiny in light of Art. 3 (principle of equality).[48] More recently, the issue of reverse discrimination has created 'problems of coordination' between the national and supranational levels. In a decision of the ECJ that was recently strongly criticised by Peers,[49] a woman brought a claim for state compensation based on Directive 2012/29/EU 'establishing minimum standards on the rights, support and protection of victims of crime',[50] after having obtained the conviction of her attacker for sexual assault. Since the offender did not have the money to pay the compensation ordered by the national court, the victim tried to obtain compensation from the Italian state, but the ECJ ruled that the Directive in question was not applicable to purely domestic cases.

2.3 *Constitutional Rights, the European Arrest Warrant and EU Criminal Law*

2.3.1 The Presumption of Innocence

2.3.1.1 The presumption of innocence is a fundamental principle in the Italian constitutional order. It is implicit in Art. 13 which is devoted to personal liberty. Article 13 first states that 'personal liberty is inviolable and that no form of

[47] Case C-35-36/82 *Morson and Jhanjan* [1982] ECR 03723; Case C-229/83 *Leclerc* [1985] ECR 00305; Case 355/85 *Cognet* [1986] ECR 03231; Case C-90/86 *Zoni*, [1988] ECR 04285; Case C-33/88 *Allué I* [1989] ECR 01591; Joined cases C-259/91, C-331/91 and C-332/91 *Allué II* [1993] ECR I-04309.

[48] ItCC, Decisions No. 249/1995, No. 61/1996 and No. 443/1997. On reverse discrimination in the case law of both the ECJ and the ItCC, see Spitaleri 2011 and Dani 2011.

[49] Case C-122/13 *C* [2014] ECLI:EU:C:2014:59. See the comment by Peers 2014.

[50] Directive 2012/29/EU of the European Parliament and of the Council of 25 October 2012 establishing minimum standards on the rights, support and protection of victims of crime, and replacing Council Framework Decision 2001/220/JHA, [2012] OJ L 315/58.

detention, inspection nor any other restriction on personal freedom is permitted, except by a reasoned warrant issued by a judicial authority, and only in the cases and the manner provided for by law'. Article 13 then continues:

> In exceptional cases of necessity and urgency, strictly defined by the law, law-enforcement authorities may adopt temporary measures that must be communicated to the judicial authorities within forty-eight hours. Should the judicial authorities not confirm such measures within the next forty-eight hours, they are revoked and become invalid.

In order to respect the presumption of innocence, Art. 13(5) specifies: 'The law establishes the maximum period of preventive detention'. In order to protect the presumption of innocence at the same level as in our constitutional order, Italy has introduced an additional ground of refusal when implementing the European Arrest Warrant Framework Decision[51] (EAW Framework Decision). Indeed, according to Art. 18(e) of Law No. 69/2005 implementing the EAW Framework Decision, surrender of the individual shall be refused if the legal system of the Member State issuing the European Arrest Warrant (EAW) does not stipulate maximum limits to the duration of preventive detention. Nevertheless, the Supreme Court has construed this article in a way that has sometimes undermined the level of protection of the presumption of innocence in our constitutional system, in order to provide for a consistent interpretation of domestic law with EU law. The Supreme Court has often been satisfied with the procedural rules of other Member States (even when these have enshrined lower standards of protection) which for example envisage a system of subsequent intermediate periods, which may be extended under jurisdictional scrutiny. In other words, the Supreme Court has adopted a substantive rather than a formalistic approach to the interpretation of the notion of 'maximum limits' contemplated in Italian law, so as to allow for the extradition of accused persons to countries which have a 'similar' or 'equivalent' level of protection of the individual, but not necessarily the same.[52] It is interesting to note that this position of the Supreme Court (which in the specific case allowed the surrender of an individual upon a request made by Germany) marks a shift in the case law of the same Court. It is worth noting that the Supreme Court had previously refused to surrender a citizen to Belgium because of the absence of maximum limits to the duration of precautionary detention like those in the Italian legal order.[53]

---

[51] Council Framework Decision of 13 June 2002 on the European arrest warrant and the surrender procedures between Member States (2002/584/JHA), [2002] OJ L 190/1.

[52] Corte di Cassazione, Sezioni Unite, *Ramoci Villaznim* Decision No. 4614 of 30 January 2007. Also the Decision No. 17810 of 24 April 2007 (Sezione sesta penale, caso *Zanotti)* has been criticised for surrendering the individual to Poland, although in that country there were no maximum limits for preventive detention as envisaged by the Italian legal order.

[53] Corte di Cassazione, Sez. VI, *Cusini*, Decision No. 16542 of 8 May 2006. On the changing orientation of the Supreme Court of Cassation, see Cavallini 2007.

2.3.1.2 The procedure for surrender of the individual is enshrined in Law No. 69 of 2005 implementing the Framework Decision (from Art. 5 to Art. 27).[54] The *Corte d'Appello* of the district where the citizen resides is the competent authority for execution of the EAW. While it must be acknowledged that the Italian courts usually execute and very rarely refuse EAW requests, Law No. 69 of 2005 envisages appropriate guarantees for the accused, which include, for example, the possibility to appeal to the Supreme Court of Cassation for a second trial in case of disagreement with the outcome of the first trial before the Court of Appeal.[55] Moreover, the accused individual has the right to have both a public defender and an interpreter, and to be judged at a public hearing.[56]

2.3.2 *Nullum crimen, nulla poena sine lege*

2.3.2.1 The principle *nulla poena sine lege* is enshrined in Art. 25 of the Italian Constitution, according to which '[n]o one may be punished except on the basis of a law in force prior to the time when the offence was committed'. In this respect, criminal legislation must satisfy the conditions of precision, clarity and predictability, allowing each person to know whether an act constitutes an offence. In this respect, the abolition of double criminality for 32 categories of crimes as provided by the EAW framework decision might be in breach of the principle of legality in criminal matters. While the issue has never reached the Constitutional Court, it has raised a significant debate in scholarly literature.[57]

On the one hand, some scholars have noted that the principle *nulla poena sine lege* is deeply jeopardised by the EAW requirement according to which the State of execution shall provide its assistance in punishing an act which may not be qualified as a crime in the domestic legal order: the focus here is on the breach of the principle according to which only parliamentary statutory law may restrict personal freedom.[58] On the other hand, there is a second line of criticism which builds on the assumption that the dual criminality rule not only protects the principle of legality but also the principle of sovereignty.[59] In this respect, abolition of the double

---

[54] The text of the Law is available at http://www.camera.it/parlam/leggi/05069l.htm.

[55] More generally, it is the Constitution itself, in Art. 111, which states that 'Appeals to the Court of Cassation in cases of violations of the law are always allowed against sentences and against measures affecting personal freedom pronounced by ordinary and special courts. This rule can only be waived in cases of sentences by military tribunals in time of war'.

[56] An accurate overview of the procedure is available on the website of the Italian National Association of Judges: http://www.associazionemagistrati.it/doc/1518/il-mandato-di-arresto-europeo.htm.

[57] For a general overview, see Calvano 2007.

[58] Cf. Bartone 2003; Caianello and Vassalli 2002; Gualtieri 2004; Manacorda 2004 and 2007 amongst others.

[59] Pisa 1973.

criminality rule may also configure a sort of 'superiority' of the criminal law of the country issuing the EAW upon the country executing it.[60]

In fact, the problematic aspect of the EAW Framework Decision lies in legal certainty. Indeed, the Framework Decision enumerates the types of crimes for which the rule of double criminality is abolished, but it does not specify the behaviours connected to those crimes, leaving definition of the constitutive elements of the crime to the Member States. Under the same label of corruption, organised crime or drug trafficking, Member States' law may define very different behaviours. In this respect, individuals who are in a foreign country that has a legal and juridical culture different from that of their home country may experience a 'journey into the unknown'.[61]

For some of the categories of offences listed in Art. 2 of the Framework Decision it is not possible to identify corresponding or common models of incrimination. Some acts may be criminalised in some national legal systems but not in others. This significantly jeopardises the principle of legality in its pivotal function: that of guiding the behaviour of individuals in the light of certain and predictable rules.[62] In order to avoid this *vulnus* to the constitutionally protected principle of legality, some proposals were put forward to revisit the Italian criminal law framework in order to create a perfect correspondence between the list provided for in Art. 2 of the Framework Decision and Italian material criminal law, to ensure legal certainty without infringing the principle of mutual recognition in the criminal sphere.[63]

2.3.3 Fair Trial and *In Absentia* Judgments

2.3.3.1 The principle of fair trial is enshrined in Art. 111 of the Italian Constitution, which is composed of a first part related to due process more broadly, and a second part specifically dedicated to criminal trials. According to Art. 111:

> Jurisdiction is implemented through due process regulated by law. All court trials are conducted with adversary proceedings and the parties are entitled to equal conditions before an impartial judge in third party position. The law provides for the reasonable duration of trials. In criminal law trials, the law provides that the alleged offender shall be promptly informed confidentially of the nature and reasons for the charges that are brought and shall have adequate time and conditions to prepare a defence. The defendant shall have the right to cross-examine or to have cross-examined before a judge the persons making accusations and to summon and examine persons for the defence in the same conditions as the prosecution, as well as the right to produce all other evidence in favour of the defence.

---

[60] Barazzetta 2004; Picotti 2005; Selvaggi and Villoni 2002.

[61] Mitsilegas 2006.

[62] On the difficulties for individuals to be aware of the definition and scope of crimes in foreign countries, see Del Tufo 2005 and Di Martino 2006, pp. 133–135.

[63] Iuzzolino 2002; Barazzetta 2004.

While Art. 111 of the Constitution, as amended in 1999, seems to provide sufficient protection of the principle according to which the defendant shall be duly informed of the process and shall participate therein, the Strasbourg Court has on several occasions condemned Italy for *in absentia* judgments that do not comply with the procedural guarantees provided for in Art. 6 of the European Convention on Human Rights (ECHR).[64] The Italian criminal code has very recently been revised by Law No. 67 of 28 April 2014, in order to conform to the ECHR standards that allow prosecution of an alleged offender only where there is certainty of the knowledge of the process and where there is unequivocal evidence of the willingness of the alleged offender to waive the right to participate into the process. The reform significantly changes Italian traditional criminal law which looked at *in absentia* judgments as a right of the defendant, rather than as a possible infringement upon his/her rights.[65] In this respect, judges will have to collect more evidence about the effective willingness to be absent on the part of the defendant before condemning him/her with an *in absentia* judgment.

In addition, the Italian Constitutional Court has annulled a provision of the Italian criminal code related to *in absentia* judgments in that it violated Art. 6 of the ECHR which enshrines the right of the accused to participate in his or her trial and to be informed promptly.[66] More specifically, the annulled provision was Art. 175 (2) of the Code of Criminal Procedure, which did not allow the release of the accused person within the time limit for appealing against an *in absentia* judgment, where a similar appeal had previously been proposed by the public defender's office. This judgment is very important in that it marks a shift in the position of the Constitutional Court, which had earlier held that trials against individuals who had ignored allegations against them and had not been properly informed did not violate Art. 111 of the Italian Constitution, and that the ECHR did not grant guarantees greater than those provided for in this Article.[67] Moreover, it must be stressed that in this judgment, the Constitutional Court, in balancing constitutional values, attributed greater importance to the right of the defendant than to the principle of due process and of the reasonable duration of the process. By way of contrast, the Supreme Court of Cassation stated in a similar case that the reopening of the process with the possibility for the 'uninformed' alleged offender to make an appeal could jeopardise the smoothness and reasonable length of the process protected by Art. 111 of the Constitution.[68]

---

[64] ECtHR, *Colozza v. Italy*, 12 February 1985, Series A no. 89; *Somogyi v. Italy*, no. 67972/01, ECHR 2004-IV; *Sejdovic v. Italy* [GC], no. 56581/00, ECHR 2006-II.

[65] Quattrocolo 2014.

[66] ItCC, Decision No. 317/2009.

[67] ItCC, Order No. 89/2008 and Decision No. 117/2007.

[68] Cassazione penale, Sezioni Unite, Judgment No. 6026 of 31 January 2008.

2.3.4 The Right to a Fair Trial – Practical Challenges Regarding a Trial Abroad

2.3.4.1 The Italian Constitution, in Art. 111, states that in all criminal trials 'the defendant is entitled to the assistance of an interpreter in the case that he or she does not speak or understand the language in which the court proceedings are conducted'. Nevertheless, in the opinion of many defence lawyers, extradited citizens or residents are unfortunately not provided with quality translation and legal aid or travel expenses. Introduction of a publicly funded state or non-governmental body to provide such assistance would be highly recommended. Some proposals have been made by defence attorneys in order to guarantee appropriate protection of the constitutional rights of residents who are involved in trials abroad. The focus of such proposals largely built on the 2012 Justice Report 'European Arrest Warrant – Ensuring an Effective Defence' and stressed the necessity of immediate legal assistance both in the issuing and in the executing Member State, and a high level of specialisation on the part of defence attorneys in order to ensure an effective defence. Moreover, the report suggests a proportionality test on the part of the judge, so as to ensure that the infringement of fundamental rights is proportionate in the light of the seriousness of the crime (especially in the light of the discrepancies between Member States' sanctions, which would at least require a comparative analysis of the relevant national legal frameworks).[69]

2.3.4.2 Unfortunately, there are no statistical data available to indicate how many extradited individuals have subsequently been found innocent. This is because the Ministry of Justice does not collect data on how many individuals are found innocent even in the course of domestic trials.[70] Nevertheless, information on the website of the Minister of the Economy and Finance indicates that approximately 50,000 people have been victims of injustice. This data is available since Italian law requires the state to provide such persons with monetary compensation, which is counted as an item of expenditure.[71] While we do not have statistics on extradited individuals or on individuals surrendered subsequent to an EAW request who have subsequently been found innocent, two cases have been covered in the media, both of which related to a mistaken identity. A Spanish doctor, José Vincent Pier Ripoll, was extradited from Spain to Italy and was held in jail for 8 months due to a miscarriage of justice by judges who accused him of being an international drug trafficker. He received 85,000 EUR in compensation.[72] In 2009, an Italian gardener

---

[69] Barletta et al. 2013.

[70] The only statistics available are at: http://www.giustizia.it/giustizia/it/mg_1_14.wp?frame10_item=4&all=true.

[71] The so called R.I.D. (*Riparazione per ingiusta detenzione*), for which Italy paid 575,698,145 EUR from 1991 to 2013. The data are available at: http://www.errorigiudiziari.com/errori-giudiziari-statistiche-numeri-dati/.

[72] http://www.errorigiudiziari.com/?vittime=jose-ripoll-scambiato-per-narco-in-carcere-per-8-mesi-da-innocente.

was jailed for 50 days pursuant to a European Arrest Warrant from Germany in which he was accused of aggravated theft in Austria and Germany, where the gardener had never lived or even travelled.[73] In another case (*Arapi*) which was also reported in the news, the defendant was convicted of murder in his absence in Italy, although he was not aware of the trial. After surrender to the Italian authorities was ordered by a UK court, the EAW request was dropped and he received compensation in the amount of 18,000 GBP.[74]

2.3.5 The Right of Effective Judicial Protection and the Principle of Mutual Recognition in EU Criminal Law

2.3.5.1 While the application of the principle of mutual recognition in civil and commercial matters has not raised significant constitutional issues in Italy, its application in criminal law has been quite tormented. In the scholarly literature, the transposition of mutual recognition to the criminal sphere was not only considered as an attack on national sovereignty, but also as 'the first serious threat of disablement of the constitutional guarantees to the right of liberty'.[75] Following the same line of reasoning, a significant political debate concerned about a possible infringement upon fundamental constitutional rights, accompanied both the adoption and the implementation of the European Arrest Warrant Framework Decision.[76]

While it did not succeed in jeopardising the adoption of the Framework Decision during the 2001 Laeken Summit or in reducing the list of crimes provided for in Art. 2 of the Decision to only six crimes strictly related to terrorism, the Italian Government managed, together with Austria, to delay the adoption of the decision. It also requested a declaration to be recorded at the moment of the decision. In this political declaration (devoid of any legal value) the Government stressed the need to change the Italian criminal system (with respect to the constitutional principles and in particular respect for fundamental rights) to be able to adapt to what is established in the Framework Decision.[77] The Government also asked for a *parere pro veritate* from two prominent lawyers, Vincenzo Caianiello and Giuliano Vassalli, both of them former Ministers of Justice and former Chairs of the Italian Constitutional Court. Both of them found that the introduction of the mutual recognition rule in criminal law was incompatible with many of the principles enshrined in the Italian Constitution. Caianiello and Vassalli in particular lamented

---

[73] http://www.errorigiudiziari.com/?vittime=finisce-in-carcere-per-50-giorni-per-uno-scambio-di-identita.

[74] http://www.fairtrials.org/press/italian-shock-decision-to-drop-european-arrest-warrant-against-edmond-arapi/.

[75] Pinelli 2012, p. 2399.

[76] Salazar 2002.

[77] Barletta 2006.

about: (a) a violation of the principle of the rule of law, in its facet of the 'principle of legality', which should ensure that crimes are foreseen in a predictable and specific way, by national statutory laws, enacted by the Parliament, rather than generically listed in the EAW Framework Decision enacted by EU institutions; (b) a violation of the constitutional principle of personal freedom as envisaged by Arts. 13, 104 and 111 of the Constitution. According to the Italian Constitution, any measure restricting personal freedom, such as for example measures for the enactment and enforcement of custody orders, shall be provided by statutory laws, in that those laws are subject to a strict scrutiny of respect for constitutional fundamental rights carried out by the Constitutional Court; (c) a violation of the rules on extradition contemplated in Arts. 10 and 26 of the Italian Constitution, aimed at protecting the fundamental rights of individuals.[78]

These constitutional concerns have all been translated into a law on implementation of the EAW Framework Decision which does not completely comply with EU law, as pointed out by the European Commission several times. Just to give an example, in order to guarantee effective judicial protection to individuals, Law No. 69 of 2005 significantly increases the grounds for refusal to deny the execution of an EAW, compared to those set out in the EAW Framework Decision. It can be argued that constitutional guarantees related to effective judicial protection have not been undermined by the introduction of the mutual recognition rule in criminal law, in the light of the fact that the Italian constitutional order has preserved some flexibility in implementing the Framework Decision.[79]

2.3.5.2 In our view, mutual recognition, when compared with harmonisation, still represents the method that best suits a pluralistic legal order, allowing for respect for the different legal traditions of the Member States in the European legal space. Nevertheless, transposition of mutual recognition from internal market matters to criminal law is problematic. While the case for mutual recognition in criminal matters was largely based on the success of the principle in the area of the internal market,[80] the so-called 'single market analogy'[81] raises the following contested issues. First of all, the freedom of movement of 'judicial decisions' may not be compared to the movement of persons, products and services: if mutual recognition requires that practices and standards of other Member States be deemed legitimate in an extra-territorial way,[82] criminal law has traditionally been considered as a national affair strictly related to national sovereignty. Secondly, while internal

[78] Caianiello and Vassalli 2002, pp. 462–467; Casetti 2005.

[79] On the implementation of the EAW Framework Decision in Italy, see Fichera 2011 and Barletta 2011.

[80] Flore 2009, p. 269.

[81] Lavenex 2007.

[82] Mitsilegas 2009, p. 118.

market fundamental freedoms considerably expand the sphere of individual rights, the free movement of judicial decisions in criminal matters does not provide an immediate benefit to the individual, but is reflected in a direct benefit for the Member State.[83] Indeed, it is the judicial decision of a sovereign Member State which can be executed and recognised in other Member States. By way of contrast, such decisions are often imposed on individuals. Nevertheless, there is an 'indirect' benefit upon citizens which comes from more security. In sum, mutual recognition represents a good instrument for guaranteeing efficiency and the security of citizens, only insofar as it does not entail an infringement of fundamental rights related to effective judicial protection. To this end, in order to ensure mutual trust among judicial authorities, the most significant discrepancies between Member States on the core elements of the rule of law should be reduced.

Some authors have given serious consideration to the possibility of combining mutual recognition with minimum approximation of offences and penalties. They usually refer to the debate during the negotiations of the EAW Framework Decision, when the choice between 'pure' or 'absolute' mutual recognition (including only formal grounds for non-execution and/or relating to only a few serious offences) and 'relative' mutual recognition was discussed. It has also been suggested that the list of types of crimes be reduced to a few core offences, for which common criteria for definition and punishment may be found more easily.[84] In addition, the EU institutions have underestimated the role of mutual trust. The initial assumption that mutual trust would be generated automatically proved wrong. There are also signs of a shift from a 'mutual trust' to an 'effectiveness' paradigm.[85]

2.3.5.3 In Italy, some criticisms of the possible change in the role of courts (from providing judicial protection against unwarranted measures by the authorities, to having become actors of loyal co-operation, efficiency and trust) were raised with regard to the Supreme Court of Cassation. This Court, indeed, in some judgments, favoured the logics of co-operation and efficiency inherent in the EAW framework at the expense of the more guarantistic procedures contemplated by domestic law.[86] Guarantism is the political doctrine developed in the nineteenth century, which aimed at protecting constitutional guarantees for individual liberty and collective freedoms against potential arbitrariness by the public authorities. In the 1960s to 1990s, guarantees in the penal process to avoid arbitrariness in political or judicial power, especially in the context of emergency legislation, became a central element of the concept.[87] Just to give two examples, the Supreme Court stated that an arrest warrant has to be executed when the requesting Member State respects the right to a fair trial, even if the degree of such protection is lower than the level ensured by the

[83] Klip 2012, p. 22; Lavenex 2007, pp. 764–765; Mostl 2010, p. 409.

[84] Fichera 2011, p. 80.

[85] Herlin-Karnell 2013, pp. 79–91.

[86] For a survey, see Barletta 2011.

[87] The key scholars behind this concept are Luigi Ferrajoli and Norberto Bobbio; for a key book, see Ferrajoli 2009.

Italian Constitution in Art. 111.[88] Moreover, the Supreme Court of Cassation provided a restrictive interpretation of the 'safeguard clause' contemplated in Art. 2 of Law No. 69/2005 implementing the EAW Framework Decision, according to which the application of the Framework Decision shall fully respect fundamental rights as provided by international treaties and the Italian Constitution, and according to which the violation of those constitutional guarantees by the Member State issuing the EAW may result in a refusal to surrender the individual. More specifically, when the 'safeguard clause' was invoked, the Supreme Court refused to apply it, by retaining that the absence of alternative measures to detention, aimed at the re-socialisation of the detainees, did not amount to a breach of a common constitutional principle of the Member States.[89]

In our opinion, the fact that the Supreme Court limited the field of application of the safeguard clause provided by Art. 2 of Law No. 69/2005 to the domestic constitutional principles that are also mentioned in Art. 6 TEU, cannot be criticised as such. The reasoning behind this case law is not the sacrifice of constitutional guarantees to serve the goals of efficiency in the area of freedom, security and justice. More simply, the Court of Cassation has tried to mitigate the discrepancies between the EAW Framework Decision and the Italian implementing law, while providing an interpretation of Italian law that is consistent with EU law.[90]

2.3.5.4 In Italy, there have been no explicit calls to reintroduce some form of judicial review in the country of residence of the individual affected. In any case, this is inherent in the law implementing the EAW Framework Decision, which is not completely consistent with the Framework Decision, in that it provides greater protection of constitutional rights. Just to give an example, according to the Italian implementing law, the surrender of the accused individual should be subject to the existence of serious evidence of guilt. The EAW Framework Decision does not include this condition. Indeed, it could be regarded as contrary to the decision itself, to the extent that such a determination results in an undue overlap of assessments carried out by an Italian judge with respect to judgments that fall within the exclusive jurisdiction of the judicial authority of the Member State issuing the EAW. This is clearly inconsistent with the very essence of the principle of mutual recognition.[91] Shifting to the behaviour of the courts, it can be said that

> Italian Courts execute the EAW as far as the requesting State offers adequate judicial remedies to the lack of discussion and cross-examination, such as the possibility to appeal (Corte Cass., Sez, VI, *Tavano*, n. 7812/2008; Sez. VI, *Finotto*, n. 7813/2008), to ask for revision of the Judgement (Corte Cass., Sez. VI, *Bolun*, n. 5909/2007, regarding Hungary, and Sez. VI, *Salkanovic*, n. 3927/2008, regarding France) or to start a new phase of the proceedings (Corte Cass., Sez. F, *D'Onorio*, n. 33327/2007, concerning Belgium).[92]

[88] See Corte di Cassazione, Sez. VI, *Melina*, Decision No. 17632/2007 of 3 May 2007.

[89] Corte di Cassazione, Sez. VI, *Hantig*, Decision No. 46296/2008 of 10 December 2008.

[90] See also Corte di Cassazione, SS. UU., *Ramoci*, Decision No. 4614/2007 of 30 January 2007.

[91] Selvaggi and De Amicis 2005, p. 1814.

[92] Porchia and Puoti 2013, pp. 441–442.

2.4 The EU Data Retention Directive

2.4.1–2.4.2 The implementation of the Data Retention Directive[93] has not raised constitutional issues in our country, although the decisions coming from the other countries have been addressed to a certain degree in the Italian literature,[94] and many have welcomed the decision of the ECJ.[95] The implementation occurred with some delay by Legislative Decree No. 109/2008. However, before the entry into force of this legislative decree, the Privacy Code already contained Art. 132 on Traffic Data Retention for Other Purposes. After the decision of the ECJ, some colleagues[96] pointed out the necessity to disapply (due to conflict with Art. 7 and 8 of the Charter of Fundamental Rights,) or to declare unconstitutional Art. 132 of Legislative Decree No. 2003/196 (a.k.a. 'Data Protection Code')[97] in light of Art. 117.

It has been noted that until the entry into force of the Law implementing Directive 2006/24, Italy was among the countries with the provision for the longest retention periods for data traffic, on the basis of Art. 6 of Decree Law No. 144/2005 (converted into Law No. 155/2005) on urgent measures to combat international terrorism, which modified the wording of Art. 132 of the Privacy Code. This latter provision requires that providers retain telephone traffic data for 24 months from the date of the communication to detect and suppress criminal offences, and that electronic communications traffic data, except for the contents of communications, is to be retained by the provider for twelve months from the date of the communication for the same purpose. Article 132(1bis) also allows for data retention of unsuccessful calls for thirty days. As for the modalities of transfer, under Art. 132 (3), data may be acquired from the provider by means of a reasoned order issued by a public prosecutor or at the request of defence counsel, the person under investigation, the injured party or any other private party.[98]

This provision was introduced into our legal system before the entry into force of the Directive.

2.5 Unpublished or Secret Legislation

2.5.1 The duty of public entities to publish documents is an important indicator of the true democratic character of a given legal system. In this respect, unpublished

---

93 Directive 2006/24/EC of the European Parliament and of the Council of 15 March 2006 on the retention of data generated or processed in connection with the provision of publicly available electronic communications services or of public communications networks and amending Directive 2002/58/EC, [2006] OJ L 105/54.

94 For example, see Passaglia 2010.

95 Including Ferro 2014 and Pastena 2014.

96 See Vecchio 2014 amongst others.

97 For an overview of this code, see: http://www.garanteprivacy.it/home_en/italian-legislation.

98 Porchia and Puoti 2013, p. 447.

legislation cannot be deemed to be valid in Italy since publication is considered to be a constitutive element of parliamentary statutes, which are not considered to exist or to be valid until they are published in the '*Gazzetta Ufficiale*' of the Italian Republic. Having said that, the Italian legal order recognises the existence of state secrets, which, as defined by law,[99] include all acts, documents, facts and activities the disclosure of which may undermine the integrity, independence and defence of the State, its relations with other States, or the functioning of State institutions and bodies of constitutional relevance.[100] The Constitutional Court has ruled that the state secrets privilege is not incompatible with the Constitution, insofar as it is designed to protect national security as per Art. 126 of the Constitution.[101] The Penal Code provides that disclosure of information classified as a state secret is punishable by imprisonment of at least five years. More recently, the Constitutional Court stated that the selection of acts, documents and information to be classified as a state secret is a highly discretionary political activity that cannot be subject to judicial review.[102]

2.6 Rights and General Principles of Law in the Context of Market Regulation: Property Rights, Legal Certainty, Non-retroactivity and Proportionality

2.6.1 No specific issues with regard to the standard of protection of property rights, legal certainty, legitimate expectations, non-retroactivity or proportionality have arisen in Italy in relation to EU measures, although in the early days the concern about rights protection in the internal market was the main reason behind the creation of the counter-limits doctrine by the ItCC. Some of these issues have been tackled in relation to the European Convention on Human Rights, which has, for example, increased the standard of protection of property rights by providing for appropriate compensation after expropriation (more specifically, the ItCC invalidated a national parliamentary statute for violation of Art. 1 of Protocol 1 ECHR).

However, an indication that the above principles may play a more prominent role and be subject to a stricter standard of protection in Italy in comparison with the EU system of judicial review may be implied from a study by Gari and Tridimas. Their research shows that Italy's low success in challenging EU measures may be linked to the fact that Italy has based most of its arguments on violations of general principles, with the following general principles of EC law having been invoked by Italy unsuccessfully: proportionality; statement of reasons; non-discrimination and equal treatment; legitimate expectations and legal certainty; and right to a fair

---

99 Law No. 124 of 3 Aug. 2007, and Law No. 133 of 7 August 2012.

100 For a general overview see Mastroianni and Arena 2011, pp. 121–123.

101 See ItCC, Order No. 49/1977, Decision No. 82/1977 and Decision No. 86/1977.

102 ItCC, Decision No. 106/2009.

hearing. The authors have noted that Italy's low success rate (with 8.7% of successful cases) stands in contrast to Spain's higher success rate, which they attribute to arguments that are based on more technical grounds.[103]

2.7 *The ESM Treaty, Austerity Programmes and the Democratic, Rule-of-Law-Based State*

2.7.1–2.7.3 The constitutionality of the Treaty Establishing the European Stability Mechanism (ESM Treaty) has not been questioned in our country, and even the parliamentary debate was very poor. As Pierdominici has pointed out, in both Chambers and in the relevant Parliamentary Committees, the procedure for authorisation by law of the Fiscal Compact was combined with other procedures related to the Treaty amendment in Art. 136(3) TFEU and the ESM Treaty.[104]

Some authors have tried to argue that the Fiscal Compact is invalid, but in light of its presumed conflict with the EU Treaties.[105] There has been no constitutional litigation on the validity of these measures and this 'seems to be explained first of all by the way the system of constitutional adjudication is designed'.[106] In other words, because of the absence of something like the *Verfassungsbeschwerde* or the possibility for parliamentary minorities to bring a case before the ItCC, the *Corte Costituzionale* has not had the chance to be involved in this issue. As we will see later in Sect. 3.5 concerning the impact on the welfare state dimension, the ItCC has delivered some decisions in this field.

2.8 *Judicial Review of EU Measures: Access to Justice and the Standard of Review*

2.8.1 Between 1952 and 2013, 1,227 references were sent by Italian judges to the ECJ: 2 from the *Corte Costituzionale*, 119 from the Court of Cassation, 101 from the State Council and 1,005 from other courts or tribunals.[107] According to the study by Tridimas and Gari 'the intra-judicial conversation which takes place via the preliminary ruling procedure pertains in its overwhelming majority to the interpretation of Community law and the compatibility of national action with it rather than the constitutionality of Community action'.[108] As we will see, this

[103] Tridimas and Gari 2010, pp. 171, 172 et seq. and 152.

[104] Pierdominici 2014.

[105] For instance Guarino 2014.

[106] Fasone 2014.

[107] Court of Justice of the European Union 2015, p. 108.

[108] Tridimas and Gari 2010, p. 139.

conclusion seems confirmed in light of our data. According to the annual report of the ECJ of 2013,[109] between 2006 and 2013 there were 365[110] preliminary references from Italian courts. Our search in the ECJ online database identified 306 cases. The overwhelming majority of these preliminary references concerned the interpretation of acts of EU law. In many cases the national judges *de facto* asked the ECJ to decide on the compatibility of a national norm with an EU law norm to be interpreted. There was also one case, *Kamberaj*,[111] where the referring judge tried to obtain an argument to question the established case law of the Constitutional Court (concerning the direct effect of the ECHR, see below for further details) from the ECJ. In only 12 cases did the referring judge question the validity of an EU act, which is consistent with the findings of Tridimas and Gari, according to whom: 'The ECJ issued few preliminary rulings on the validity of Community measures with a minimum of six in 2001 and a maximum of 12 in 2004'.[112] In a nutshell, the ECJ had to deal with the presumed invalidity of EU acts in the following cases: *Fastweb*[113] (public sector); *Torresi*[114] (freedom to provide services); *SFIR*[115] (sugar industry); *Manzi*[116](transport and environment); *Nunziatina*[117] (State aid); *Azienda Agricola Disarò Antonio and Others*[118] (milk products sector); *Gowan Comércio Internacional e Serviços*[119] (agriculture); *Bavaria and Bavaria Italia*[120] (registration of geographical indications); *Nuova Agricast*[121] (State aid); *Carp*[122] (construction products); *Confcooperative Friuli Venezia Giulia and Others*[123] (agriculture) and, finally, *RAI*[124] (State aid). In not one of these cases did the ECJ declare the invalidity of the EU law measure.

2.8.2 A univocal answer to whether there is a lower standard of judicial review by the EU courts than in Italy probably does not exist. In other words, the situation created by a different standard of protection depends on the specific case. Italian scholars are of course aware of some deficiencies in the EU legal system. It is likely

---

[109] Court of Justice of the European Union 2015, p. 106.

[110] References by year: 34 (2006); 43 (2007); 39 (2008); 29 (2009); 49 (2010); 44 (2011); 65 (2012); 62 (2013).

[111] Case C-571/10 *Kamberaj* [2012] ECLI:EU:C:2012:233.

[112] Tridimas and Gari 2010, p. 140.

[113] Case C-19/13 *Fastweb* [2014] ECLI:EU:C:2014:2194.

[114] Case C-58/13 *Torresi* [2014] ECLI:EU:C:2014:2088.

[115] Case C-187/12 *SFIR e a.* [2013] ECLI:EU:C:2013:737.

[116] Case C-537/11 *Manzi e Compagnia Naviera Orchestra* [2014] ECLI:EU:C:2014:19.

[117] Case C-138/09 *Todaro Nunziatina & C.* [2010] ECR I-04561.

[118] Case C-34/08 *Azienda Agricola Disarò Antonio and Others* [2009] ECR I-04023.

[119] Case C-77/09 *Gowan Comércio Internacional e Serviços* [2010] ECR I-13533.

[120] Case C-343/07 *Bavaria and Bavaria Italia* [2009] ECR I-05491.

[121] Case C-390/06 *Nuova Agricast* [2008] ECR I-02577.

[122] Case C-80/06 *Carp* [2007] ECR I-04473.

[123] Case C-23/07 *Confcooperative Friuli Venezia Giulia and Others* [2008] ECR I-04277.

[124] Case C-305/07 *RAI* [2008] ECR I-00055.

that the future accession of the EU to the ECHR will contribute towards solving these, and some weaknesses related to the original, purely economic nature of the EU integration process will be challenged (for instance the problematic issue of the application of insufficient review when dealing with the Commission's determinations in competition proceedings).[125] Scholars have also pointed to the important factor of 'incoherence' in the case law of the ECJ due to an oscillating use of proportionality, depending on whether the measure under review was taken by an EU institution or by a Member State. In the first scenario, the ECJ rarely declares the illegality of the measures, and generally acts as a third party arbiter at best. In contrast, with regard to the Member States, the Court adopts a stricter stance, and often derives additional duties from the interests of integration, declaring a violation of the duty of loyal co-operation set by the Treaties.[126] However, cases like those treated in the *Kadi* saga[127] should be taken into account before condemning the EU legal system *in toto* from this point of view.

2.8.3 The ItCC has a limited jurisdiction, since it may adjudicate cases concerning the constitutional legitimacy of laws and enactments having the force of law issued by the State and Regions. This excludes other administrative or regulatory acts. The only acts of the Government that may be subject to the jurisdiction of the Court are its decree laws and legislative decrees (governed respectively by Arts. 77 and 76 of the Italian Constitution). The former are acts issued in case of necessity and urgency and adopted under its own responsibility by the Government. They are provided with the force of law. The latter are the product of the exercise of the delegation of the legislative function on the basis of some principles and criteria established in an enabling act of the Parliament. Article 77 of the Italian Constitution provides that decree laws lose effect from the beginning if they are not transposed into law by Parliament within sixty days of publication. In 1996 the ItCC declared decree laws that reiterated the contents of other decree laws that had not been converted into law by Parliament to be unconstitutional.[128] After a long period in which the Constitutional Court seemed to not scrutinise the prerequisite of necessity and urgency of decree laws, the ItCC has more recently begun to declare decree laws unconstitutional for a manifest lack of necessity and urgency.[129]

As for regulations (which are from a formal point of view administrative acts), the consistency between these measures and the law is guaranteed by the administrative judges who are empowered to annul them in these cases. In theory, the

---

[125] Bernatt 2014.

[126] Harbo 2010, p. 172, 'Proportionality in the narrow sense – *stricto sensu* – is, according to the claim, applied whenever the court finds it suitable in order to promote the desired outcome. Accordingly, the proportionality analysis conducted by the court is not objective in the sense that it is value-neutral. On the contrary, the analysis is informed by a very strong substantial bias, namely that of promoting European integration'. In Italian, see Galetta 2005.

[127] Avbelj, Fontanelli and Martinico 2014.

[128] ItCC, Decision No. 360/1996.

[129] ItCC, Decision No. 171/2007.

notion of 'violation of law' in this case also covers cases of violation of the Constitution, but if the regulation in question has been adopted on the basis of a law, the administrative judge will probably prefer to refer a question of constitutionality to the ItCC.

No statistical data on constitutional and judicial review by Italian courts was available at the time of writing (August 2014).

2.8.4 We discussed the issue of the extent to which the Constitutional Court and Supreme Court review measures that implement EU legislation when dealing with questions 1.3.2 and 1.3.3. After *Internationale Handelsgesellschaft*, the ItCC was the first court to react to the doctrine of absolute primacy by raising the walls of the counter-limits and threatening to exercise an indirect review of EU legislation. As we know, the counter-limits doctrine in Italy was primarily prompted by fundamental rights protection.

2.8.5 We do not think that an unequivocal answer to the question of potential gaps in judicial review exists. It depends on the specific field and on the structure of the balancing in the specific case. Of course, because of the origin of its legal order (law of the common market), the ECJ still sometimes establishes a lower standard, but in other cases the standard employed by the Luxembourg Court might appear higher. This is inherent in the logic of a system in which each level contributes to improving the protection of the multilevel fundamental rights in the other, and is part of the normal dialectic between the levels. On accession of the EU to the ECHR, see Sects. 2.13.1–2.13.2.

2.8.6 In Italy, there is an important judgment of the Constitutional Court that tackles the issue of equal treatment of individuals falling within the scope of EU law and those falling within the scope of the domestic protection of constitutional rights. Notoriously, Law No. 69/2005 implementing the EAW Framework Decision has significantly expanded the grounds of refusal that an Italian Court of Appeal can invoke to deny the execution of a European Arrest Warrant, and it has also rendered mandatory a ground that is deemed to be optional in the EAW Framework Decision. Article 18 of Law No. 65/2009 lists the grounds of refusal and states in letter r) that the surrender of Italian citizens sentenced to custody, or security measures involving deprivation of liberty can be refused but must be subordinated to the execution of the detention order or of the sentence in Italy. The Italian Constitutional Court, with its judgment No. 227 of 2010, found this provision discriminatory in that it did not apply to non-Italian citizens. The limitation provided by Art. 18 was indeed declared incompatible with the equality principle enshrined in Art. 3 of the Italian Constitution, with Arts. 11 and 117 of the Italian Constitution and with the principle of non-discrimination codified in Art. 18 TFEU. Indeed, with regard to the EU principle of non-discrimination, the Court underscored that using the criterion of nationality to determine the applicability of this ground of refusal was disproportionate and, ultimately, contrary to the *ratio* of Art. 4(6) of the EAW Framework Decision.

2.9 Other Constitutional Rights and Principles

2.9.1 There are no other significant issues that have arisen in Italy with regard to constitutional rights or the rule of law, apart from those arising from the questionnaire.

2.10 Common Constitutional Traditions

2.10.1 Undoubtedly the Charter of Fundamental Rights of the EU represents a good starting point for identifying the rights that form part of the common constitutional traditions. However, we must consider that, according to certain literature, general principles (as inspired by common constitutional traditions) have a scope of application or a content which might be broader than that of the Charter. A good example of this inexact correspondence is represented by the principle of good administration as pointed out by Hofmann and Mihaescu.[130]

This imperfect correspondence between common constitutional traditions and the Charter would also explain why the ECJ might still refer to them in the future, even when fundamental rights are codified by the Charter. In other words, reference to general principles would be a way to use general principles as a Trojan horse to enlarge the scope of EU law by circumventing Art. 51 of the Charter. A confirmation of this reading might be found in the approach followed by the ECJ in some cases where it has adopted the general principles as a starting point for its reasoning, and has recalled only subsequently that the given principle is also codified by the Charter. In this way, it might appear to recognise a mere codificatory value of the Charter.[131] The written nature of the Charter will of course open the door to a sort of integrative function for the unwritten common constitutional traditions, especially in the future.

2.10.2 The natural instrument for rendering the common constitutional traditions more relevant would be the preliminary ruling mechanism; this would be particularly true if the constitutional courts that have so far refused to send a preliminary reference to the ECJ were to change their practice. However, Member States might have an important role in this field even if they rely on other procedural instruments, for instance if they try to justify apparent violations of EU law in light of the national identity argument. Although 'national'[132] (or, according to another terminology 'constitutional'[133]) identity and common constitutional traditions are two different concepts, the former might serve as a source of inspiration for the latter.

[130] Hofmann and Mihaescu 2013.

[131] On this debate, see Safjan 2012.

[132] Guastaferro 2012.

[133] Saiz Arnaiz and Alcoberro Llivina 2013.

2.11 Article 53 of the Charter and the Issue of Stricter Constitutional Standards

2.11.1 There have been no issues in terms of the standard of protection comparable to *Melloni*[134] in our country (except for EAW issues as set out in previous sections). More problematic is the answer with regard to the ECHR. Our Constitutional Court has sometimes departed from the interpretation given to a particular right of the ECHR by the Strasbourg Court. When doing so, the ItCC has taken into account the case law of the European Court of Human Rights (ECtHR) in order to find a solution to the case, but then has decided not to follow the conclusion reached by the ECtHR, and has justified this decision either in light of the particular national context or in light of the different structure and type of balancing. In other words, like other courts have done elsewhere,[135] the ItCC has distinguished the type of balancing struck by an international court from the balancing by the Constitutional Court. For instance in *Maggio*,[136] the ECtHR considered a retroactive legislative act of 'authentic interpretation' to be in breach of Art. 6 of the ECHR. In confirming the constitutionality of the same act, the ItCC recalled:

> In contrast to the European Court, this Court carries out a systemic and not an isolated assessment of the values affected by the provisions reviewed from time to time, and is therefore required to carry out that balancing operation, which falls to this Court alone.[137]

In Decision No. 223/2014, the Court added that

> in the field of fundamental rights, the respect of international obligations can never cause a decrease of protection in comparison with the protection guaranteed by domestic law … on the other hand, Art. 53 of the ECHR expressly states that the interpretation of the provisions of the Convention may not limit or impair human rights and fundamental freedoms which may be ensured under the laws of any High Contracting Party (or under any other agreement to which it is a party): confirming, thus, that the guarantee scheme of the Convention aims to strengthen the protection offered at national level, and never impose limitations, as would claim the a quo judge.[138]

2.12 Democratic Debate on Constitutional Rights

2.12.1 While the adoption of the EU Data Retention Directive did not raise significant political debate, the adoption of the EAW Framework Decision was quite

[134] Case C-399/11 *Melloni* [2013] ECLI:EU:C:2013:107.

[135] UKSC, *R v. Horncastle and Others* [2009] UKSC 14, para. 11.

[136] *Maggio and Others v. Italy*, nos. 46286/09, 52851/08, 53727/08, 54486/08 and 56001/08, 31 May 2011.

[137] ItCC, Decision No. 264/2012.

[138] ItCC, Decision No. 223/2014.

problematic (see the reconstruction of the political and legal debate surrounding the implementing law No. 65 of 2009 in Sect. 2.3.5.1).

2.12.2–2.12.3 In our view, the accommodation of important constitutional issues should occur at the *political* level both in an *ex ante* phase (trying to strengthen the influence of national parliaments upon their respective Governments voting in the Council) and in an *ex post* phase (namely during the parliamentary debates on the adoption of domestic laws transposing EU directives). While we would not recommend suspension of the application of EU law or a review of EU measures where important constitutional issues have been identified by a number of constitutional courts, we think that within the framework of an infringement proceeding constitutional arguments should be put forward in a Member State's defence and should be taken seriously both by the European Commission and by the European Court of Justice.[139]

2.13 Experts' Analysis on the Protection of Constitutional Rights in EU Law

2.13.1–2.13.2 We do not have a clear answer as to concerns about an overall reduction in the standard of protection of constitutional rights and the rule of law in the context of EU law, and this depends on the oscillating case law of the ECJ and on the different reactions of the national constitutional courts. The ECJ has alternated between very 'sensitive' (those for instance based on Art. 4(2) TEU)[140] and 'muscular' decisions (the majority now, we would say). With regard to the second group, the *Melloni* decision has been seen as a return to an 'absolute conception of primacy'.[141] This decision is in line with other recent rulings of the ECJ in which the Luxembourg Court has not shown great deference towards the national constitutional courts. We are referring for instance to the *Filipiak*[142] and *Winner Wetten*[143] cases. This does not seem to be coherent with another recent trend which sees constitutional courts more and more open to Art. 267 TFEU and with another series of decisions which can be traced back to a sort of margin of appreciation doctrine of the ECJ.[144] However, if *Melloni* represents the bad side of the coin, more recently

[139] A call for a possible *ordinary* use of the identity clause, recommending the use of Art. 4(2) TEU (requiring the EU to respect national identities) both in Member States' defences in the context of infringement proceedings and in national Parliaments' reasoned opinions in the framework of the early warning system, can already be found in Guastaferro 2012 and 2014.

[140] See Guastaferro 2012 for relevant case law.

[141] As recently suggested by Von Bogdandy and Schill 2011.

[142] Case C-314/08 *Filipiak* [2009] ECR I-11049.

[143] Case C-409/06 *Winner Wetten* [2010] ECR I-08015.

[144] Sabel and Gerstenberg 2010.

the ECJ has decided cases like *Google*,[145] *Kadi II*[146] and *Digital Rights Ireland*,[147] whereby it acted as a constitutional court that was very keen to protect fundamental rights. This combination of factors impedes us from giving a precise answer to the question, but we do think that only a more co-operative relationship between the ECJ and the national constitutional courts could improve the burning issue of the multilevel protection of fundamental rights. Perhaps the accession of the EU to the ECHR (but this is more difficult now after the delivery of Opinion 2/13[148] of the ECJ) will improve the situation at EU level, although it is difficult to foresee the effective impact that such accession will have, not only in terms of the relationship between the Strasbourg and Luxemburg Courts, but also in terms of the 'usability' of the ECHR by national judges where the direct effect of the provisions of the Convention is recognised. In this sense, *Kamberaj* seems to confirm our doubts.[149]

2.13.3–2.13.4 An example which is partially related to bringing national constitutional concerns to the ECJ is the *Berlusconi* case.[150] A recent comment on this case concerns the use of comparative arguments by the ECJ. Comparative law and a general openness towards the arguments coming from the national courts could improve the situation of fundamental rights in this field, although in *Berlusconi* the ECJ did not make any explicit reference to the national legal materials which were taken into account.

3 Constitutional Issues in Global Governance

3.1 Constitutional Rules on International Organisations and the Ratification of Treaties

3.1.1 There are two fundamental provisions in the Italian Constitution regarding the relationship between international and domestic law. Article 10 provides that '[t]he Italian legal system conforms to the generally recognised principles of international law'. Article 11 provides that

> Italy rejects war as an instrument of aggression against the freedom of other peoples and as a means for the settlement of international disputes. Italy agrees, on conditions of equality with other States, to the limitations of sovereignty that may be necessary to a world order ensuring peace and justice among the Nations. Italy promotes and encourages international organisations furthering such ends.

---

[145] Case C-131/12 *Google Spain and Google* [2014] ECLI:EU:C:2014:317.

[146] Joined cases C-584/10 P, C-593/10 P and C-595/10 P *Commission and Others v. Kadi* [2013] ECLI:EU:C:2013:518.

[147] Joined cases C–293/12 and C–594/12 *Digital Rights Ireland and Seitlinger and Others* [2014] ECLI:EU:C:2014:238.

[148] Opinion 2/13 pursuant to Article 218(11) TFEU [2014] ECLI:EU:C:2014:2454.

[149] Case C-571/10 *Kamberaj*, n. 111. See Bianco and Martinico 2014.

[150] Case C-387/02 *Berlusconi* [2005] ECR I-03565.

These two articles provide the first important distinction existing in this field in Italy, the distinction between the general rules of international law and international treaties. As for the former, Art. 10 provides for an automatic procedure of adoption, in the sense that such norms are directly incorporated into the Italian system. In this field considerations similar to those made with regard to EU law are applicable. While Art. 11 does not contain any specific reference to the North Atlantic Treaty Organization or the United Nations (although the members of the Constituent Assembly wrote Art. 11 with the possibility of joining the UN in mind), we could say that it includes some guidelines to be followed in case of limitations of sovereignty. Nevertheless, Art. 11 has been used to cover all of the relevant international memberships of the Italian Republic. Since this approach has worked so far, we do not think that it is necessary to introduce specific references to any specific international organisations in Art. 11. The intervention of the national legislature is not required for all treaties, since Art. 80 provides for the necessity of legislation enabling the ratification only with reference to some particular treaties.[151] The procedure for ratification is also governed by Art. 87, which empowers the President of the Republic to ratify international treaties.[152] When the intervention of Parliament is required, it intervenes with a normal legislative statute. According to the majority of scholars, this confers a primary force in the national hierarchy of law to norms derived from international treaties.

3.1.2 Apart from the reforms already addressed when dealing with EU law (Art. 117 of the Constitution), there have been no other constitutional reforms concerning the 'external dimension' of the Constitution.

3.1.3 Reforms relating to international law and global governance have not been at the heart of the constitutional reform agenda. This could be partly explained by the elasticity of Art. 11 and by the fact that these issues have been covered by primary norms (this is the case e.g. as regards international development co-operation policies).

3.1.4 So far, Art. 11 has proven to be broad enough to guarantee the participation of the Italian Republic in the international context. Moreover, all of the recent attempts at amending the Italian Constitution have renounced dealing with the first part of the text. There has been a kind of silent agreement about the necessity to avoid reforms concerning the very first part of the Constitution (which codifies, so

---

[151] Article 80 of the Constitution: 'Parliament shall authorise by law the ratification of such international treaties as have a political nature, require arbitration or a legal settlement, entail change of borders, spending or new legislation.'

[152] Article 87 of the Constitution:

'The President shall: …

- ratify international treaties which have, where required, been authorised by Parliament.

Article 72 Italian Constitution, provides that: 'The ordinary procedure for consideration and direct approval by the House is always followed in the case of … ratification of international treaties … .'

to say, the axiological part of the Constitution). As written in Sect. 3.1.3, we do not think it is necessary to amend Art. 11.

The Italian Constitution is based on an evident parallelism between the values inspiring the domestic activity of the Italian Republic and those inspiring the external dimension. This is because of the axiological (desired) continuity that exists between the domestic and international levels, and because of the efforts made to construct a better society, even at the international level. This double orientation (internal and external) of the constitutional project was crystal clear to the members of the Italian Constituent Assembly. There are, for instance, at least three reasons for the codification of the pacifist principle in the Italian Constitution. The first is connected to political realism: Italy could not be considered a military power, so the constitutionalisation of an imperialistic foreign policy was not an option.[153] The second reason was, in a manner of speaking, ethical, and finds expression in the words used, among others, by Don Luigi Sturzo, who defined war as 'immoral, illegitimate and prohibited'.[154] But the main reason was the intent 'to transfer, to the international level, those principles of freedom, equality and substantive respect for the human person' that were to be affirmed and implemented in the domestic order.[155]

In light of the above point on parallelism of values, one new challenge for constitutional lawyers, which has been explored in greater detail elsewhere,[156] may be how to continue the existence of an axiological continuity between the principles and values that govern the life of a given polity within its boundaries and those that should characterise the international community, while retaining constitutional values in efforts to construct a better society, even at the international level. In Italian scholarship, a number of scholars also speak about the 'weak' or 'post-modern' constitutionalism typical of the era of globalisation as something dispersed and disconnected from popular initiative rather than being entirely lost.[157]

While no immediate solutions are available, elsewhere[158] we have also noted that the idea of constitutionalism propounded by leading pluralists such as Krisch[159] does not readily correspond to what constitutional lawyers mean by the same word. In international law, 'constitutionalism may be conceived as an autonomous concept of international law rather than a concept derived by analogy from the domestic conception of constitutionalism'.[160] The problem is that some scholars in this field have too heavily emphasised only the connection between

[153] See Nenni 1946, p. 104.
[154] Sturzo 1954, p. 144.
[155] Cassese 1980, p. 519.
[156] Martinico 2014.
[157] Carrozza 2007, p. 172.
[158] Martinico 2014.
[159] Krisch 2010.
[160] Deplano 2013, p. 68.

hierarchy and constitutionalism. This may be explained by taking into account the origin of the debate at the international level, where constitutionalism has been seen as an antidote to the issue of international fragmentation.

3.2 The Position of International Law in National Law

3.2.1–3.2.2 Italy is usually seen as a country characterised by a strong dualist tradition, according to which the international and national legal systems are conceived of as autonomous.

As for international treaties, it is necessary for there to be a national act transforming the international act into national law. Another important feature of the Italian legal order is the fact that, unlike in other countries like Portugal and Spain, no specific status is accorded to treaties devoted to human rights. However, as we will show below, dualism has partly been eroded by the importance acquired by some human rights treaties (above all the European Convention on Human Rights) in the national case law of the ItCC. If one looks at the Italian Constitution, one can perceive a sort of tension between the constitutional openness of the Italian Constitution (see above) and the choice in favour of the dualist paradigm. However, the ItCC has only recently relied on external sources (primarily the ECHR and EU law) to review the constitutionality of domestic norms. In terms of protection of fundamental rights, the ECHR has been by far the international agreement with the most evident impact on our national system, which has also created tensions and disagreements between the *Corte Costituzionale* and the ECtHR. If this openness (understood as friendliness towards the international community) gives us the idea of the axiological continuity between the domestic and the external dimension, the choice made in favour of dualism seems to emphasise, on the contrary, the discontinuity and impermeability between the internal and the external spheres. Further developments (especially concerning the application of EU law and of the ECHR) have radically questioned the validity of the traditional dualist category. With regard to EU law, the position of the ItCC is emblematic of a broader trend. With regard to the ECHR, it is necessary to briefly recall its case law to appreciate the departure from the original dualism. As regards the ECHR, the original position of the *Consulta* reflected a dualist conception of the relationship between the ECHR and domestic law. Since the entry of the ECHR into the Italian legal order was enacted by an ordinary law (Law No. 848/1955), for a long time and with some exceptions,[161] the ItCC considered the ECHR as a source with primary force and the consequent application of the *lex posterior derogat legi priori* rule in case of conflict between the law regarding the ECHR and another Italian norm. This was the case until the 1990s when the *Corte Costituzionale* started to change its

[161] See, for instance, ItCC, Decision No. 10/1993, where the *Consulta* described the ECHR as an 'atypical source of law'.

approach and began to make a distinction between the content and the form of the laws giving effect to international treaties.[162] In other words, since from a material point of view the content of the ECHR aims at protecting rights codified in the Italian Constitution, it seemed necessary to readjust the previous case law. Another turning point was the reform of 2001 to adopt a new version of Art. 117(1) of the Constitution. Indeed, also on the basis of this new provision, as the literature has already stressed,[163] the Italian 'common' judges started to disapply domestic norms that conflicted with the ECHR.[164] Thus, they extended a mechanism accepted as a consequence of the *Simmenthal* judgment,[165] and aimed at solving the conflicts occurring between national norms and EU law provisions provided with direct effect. This practice induced the ItCC to give two key judgments in 2007.[166]

Without going into details,[167] the main content of these two decisions can be summarised as follows:

(a) The ECHR has a supra-legislative value (i.e. its normative ranking is halfway between statutes and constitutional norms);
(b) In some cases, the ECHR can serve as an 'interposed parameter' for reviewing the constitutionality of primary laws, since the conflict between them and the ECHR can result in an indirect violation of the Constitution (Art. 117);
(c) This (b) does not imply that the ECHR has a constitutional value; on the contrary, the ECHR itself has to respect the Constitution;
(d) The ECHR cannot be treated domestically in the same way as EU law, as we will see below;
(e) The constitutional preferential treatment accorded to the ECHR implies the necessity to interpret national law in light of ECHR provisions.

More recently, the ItCC has confirmed the preferential treatment to be acknowledged to the case law of the ECtHR.[168] Another indicator of the importance of the case law of the ECtHR in the national legal system is the recent Decision No. 113/2011 of the Constitutional Court.[169] In this judgment the *Consulta* declared Art. 630 c. 1 (a) of the Code of Criminal Procedure to be unconstitutional to the extent that it did not allow the re-opening or review of a case decided for good (and thus with a ruling covered by *res iudicata*), which was subsequently found to be in breach of the Convention.

---

[162] ItCC, Decision No. 388/1999.

[163] Biondi Dal Monte and Fontanelli 2008.

[164] See Ibid., p. 891.

[165] Case 106/77 *Simmenthal* [1978] ECR 00629.

[166] ItCC, Decisions No. 348 and No. 349/2007.

[167] For a detailed analysis of these decisions, see Biondi Dal Monte and Fontanelli 2008, and Pollicino 2008.

[168] See ItCC Decisions No. 311/2009, No. 317/2009 and No. 80/2011 amongst others. However, disagreement has not been missing. See for instance ItCC, Decision No. 49/2015.

[169] ItCC, Decision No. 113/2011.

Nevertheless, although EU law and the ECHR have partly questioned the assumptions of the dualist approach, dualism is still formally the premise of the reasoning of the ItCC in many cases. Even the counter-limits doctrine is based on a dualist fiction. In other words, the fact that, in the case of violation of the counter-limits, the ItCC would exercise its jurisdiction over the national acts giving effect to the EU treaties in our legal order, is an evident legacy of the dualist approach.

3.3 Democratic Control

3.3.1 Apart from what has been written in the section addressing EU law, as recalled above, the intervention of the national legislature is not required for all treaties, since Art. 80 provides for the necessity of legislation enabling ratification only with reference to particular treaties. As we saw above, the procedure for ratification is also governed by Art. 87, which empowers the President of the Republic to ratify international treaties. With regard to international organisations that differ from the EU, the monitoring functions performed by the national chambers have been included in their rules of procedure according to the cascade system of norms recalled above. An example is given by the provisions concerning the examination and possibly the adoption of resolutions on resolutions and recommendations adopted by international assemblies in which the national delegations of the Chamber of Deputies (Art. 125 r .C) or the Senate (Art. 143 r. S.) participate (for instance the NATO, Council of Europe and OSCE assemblies). Another important provision concerns the examination of the judgments of the European Court of Human Rights and of their national follow-up. In 2004, the Chamber set up a Permanent Observatory of judgments of the ECtHR. There is also a duty of the Government to transmit the annual report on the execution of the decisions of the ECtHR against Italy to both Houses.[170]

3.3.2 Article 75 of the Constitution prohibits referendums on laws ‘authorizing the ratification of international treaties’. Apart from what we have already recalled with regard to EU law, the only way to have a referendum on a treaty would be to cover the authorisation of the ratification with a constitutional statute which would permit a referendum according to Art. 138. We already recalled what the ItCC said in *Frontini*, but one could argue that the opinion expressed in that judgment should be limited to EU law due to its particular nature and impact on Italian constitutional law.

[170] For more info: http://leg16.camera.it/494?categoria=084; http://www.senato.it/static/bgt/listadocumenti/17/1/1323/0/index.html?static=true.

3.4 *Judicial Review*

3.4.1. According to Italian scholars, the general rules of international law (which correspond to customary international law) belong to the constitutional level.[171] According to some scholars, the international customary law that existed before the entry into force of the Italian Constitution could prevail over the constitutional provisions (because of the application of the chronological criterion), but this does not apply with regard to the principles belonging to the untouchable core recalled in Art. 139 of the Constitution,[172] as the ItCC has seemed to confirm in its recent case law.[173]

Apart from what we have already written about EU law, another interesting case is the ECHR in light of the decisions of 2007 that have already been mentioned. In those decisions, the ItCC specified that the ECHR is considered to be a particular form of public international law. From this, the Court inferred that the 'constitutional tolerance' shown by the Italian legal order towards the ECHR is weaker than that shown towards EU law. While 'counter-limits' represent, in the ItCC's case law, a selected version of the domestic constitutional principles (this implies the possibility to decide constitutional conflicts in favour of EU law provisions in some cases), in the case of the ECHR, the Italian Court seems to be less generous. It apparently asks the ECHR to respect the entire Constitution as such:

> The need for a constitutionality test on the Convention norm excludes the possibility of having a limited set of fundamental rights that could serve as a counter-limit; indeed, every norm of the Constitution shall be respected by the international norm challenged.[174]

In Judgment No. 230 of 2012, the ItCC emphasised the specific features of the domestic legal order vis-à-vis those characterising the system of the Convention,[175] and thus pointed to the possibility of episodic divergences.

According to the ItCC, an important distinction still exists between EU law and the ECHR, and this difference provided the basis of its reasoning:

> This is because, according to the constitutional judges, the ECHR legal system has distinct structural and functional legal features as compared to the European legal order. According to the Italian Constitutional Court, the ECHR is a multilateral international public law Treaty which does not entail and cannot entail any limitation on sovereignty in the terms provided by Article 11 of the Constitution.[176]

---

[171] De Vergottini 2004, p. 32.

[172] For an overview of the debate, see Cassese 1975, p. 502. According to Quadri, the automatic procedure shall be applied to the international treaties but this remains a minority view. This theory was based on the fact that one of the general rules of international law is the principle *pacta sunt servanda*. Quadri 1989, p. 64.

[173] ItCC, Decision No. 238/2014.

[174] Biondi Dal Monte and Fontanelli 2008, p. 915.

[175] Ruggeri 2012.

[176] Pollicino 2008, pp. 374–375.

This explains the different treatment reserved for the ECHR both in terms of disapplication and in terms of the necessity to be consistent with the whole Constitution rather than with the counter-limits alone.

3.5 The Social Welfare Dimension of the Constitution

3.5.1–3.5.2 Italy has never been in the position to declare a bailout and no issue has arisen with regard to IMF or World Bank conditionality. So far the most important factors to impact the constitutional welfare dimension have been the EU anti-crisis measures.

With regard to the anti-crisis measures taken at EU level, in Italy, constitutional lawyers[177] have been more interested in the impact of the anti-crisis measures on the sustainability of the welfare system, on the protection of social rights and on the effect of such measures on the relationship between the centre and the periphery.

In order to understand the case law of the ItCC, it is necessary to make a premise. As Fasone has explained,

> [t]he Italian Constitutional Court has not had the opportunity to judge directly on the constitutionality of EU and international Euro-crisis law. Nor was the constitutional review of the international Euro-crisis law measures really feasible.[178] ... The only way these agreements can become relevant within the Italian system of constitutional adjudication would be if the Constitutional Court is willing to recognize them the rank of interposed norm between ordinary legislation and the Constitution – Art. 117.1 Const.[179]

It must also be recalled that the constitutional balanced budget rule was not in full effect until 1 January 2014, and thus could not form a standard for constitutional review of legislation.[180]

The only relevant interventions of the ItCC in this field have regarded (primarily at least) the development of the Italian regional state. The Italian government introduced several cuts, and some of these measures have also impacted on the regional structures.

This discipline has been questioned before the ItCC, which, in Decision No. 151/2012[181] rejected the very centralising interpretation that the state had given of the measures in Decree Law No. 78/2010. These are just a few examples that show the risk of centralisation in the Italian system induced by the EU anti-crisis measures.[182] As Pierdominici has noted, '[i]f one can be tempted to read this last case as the symbol of a strong judicial opposition of the Constitutional Court against

[177] Gambino and Nocito 2012.

[178] See however ItCC, Decision No. 88/2013.

[179] Fasone 2014.

[180] Ibid.

[181] ItCC, Decision No. 151/2012.

[182] See also Falcon 2012, p. 11.

national legislative reforms prompted by the financial crisis, a comprehensive reading tells us, in fact, the opposite'.[183]

There are some interesting decisions concerning the protection of social rights. In Decision No. 248/2011 the ItCC deemed the right of medical assistance to be financially conditional, since its protection depends on the available resources. Another important decision is Decision No. 10/2010 concerning the so-called 'social card', a bonus accorded to guarantee the primary needs of the most disadvantaged members of the population. The ItCC upheld the constitutionality of the decree law and recognised that the intervention of the state was necessary to protect the value of human dignity in a uniform manner in light of Arts. 3, 38 and 117(2) of the Constitution, due to the extraordinary, exceptional and urgent situation following the international economic and financial crisis that in 2008 and 2009 also hit our country. In other words, as Fasone has pointed out, '[i]n a time of scarce resources even social rights must be preferably protected at State level [so] as to set [a] common standard and to decide at the centre how to use those resources.[184]

In Decision No. 80/2010, the Constitutional Court declared unconstitutional a provision of the State Financial Act of 2008 impeding public schools from contracting teachers for physically impaired students due to budgetary reasons. In another decision (No. 264/2012) about the calculation of pensions of cross-border workers, the ItCC acknowledged the possibility to limit social rights. According to the Court,

> [t]he effects of the said provision are felt within the context of a pension system which seeks to strike a balance between the available resources and benefits paid, in accordance also with the requirement laid down by Art. 81(4) of the Constitution' (old version), 'and the need to ensure that the overall system is rational', thus preventing changes to financial payments to the detriment of some contributors and to the benefit of others. In doing so it guarantees respect for the principles of equality and solidarity which, due to their foundational status, occupy a privileged position within the balancing operation against other constitutional values.[185]

Another important decision regards the so-called 'golden pensions'. In this case, the Court dealt with some decree laws aimed at collecting resources from the pensions or the incomes of the most advantaged segments of the population. The Court declared unconstitutional Decree Law No. 78/2010 concerning blockage of the salary adjustment mechanism for magistrates. On that occasion, the 'Court considered the reduction of the allowance as a form of taxation and declared them in contrast with the Constitution for the violation of the principle of equality (Art. 3) and of Art. 53, about the progressive nature of the tax system'.[186]

---

[183] Pierdominici 2014.

[184] Fasone 2014.

[185] ItCC, Decision No. 264/2012, para. 5.3.

[186] ItCC, Decision No. 223/2012, and reported by Fasone 2014.

In Decision No. 310/2013, which departed from its previous decision,[187] the ItCC dealt with Decree Law No. 78/2010, in a case concerning blockage of the salary adjustment mechanism for non-contracted workers in the public sector. The Court concluded that this blockage was a reasonable sacrifice, necessary in a phase of economic crisis. Fasone has found it interesting that the challenge of unconstitutionality was rejected by using *ad adiuvandum* (although not as the main ground for the decision), the new Art. 81 of the Constitution as amended in 2012 and Council Directive 2011/85/EU on requirements for budgetary frameworks of the Member States.[188]

3.6 *Constitutional Rights and Values in Selected Areas of Global Governance*

3.6.1 Italian scholars have questioned the compatibility between some anti-terrorist provisions and our standards of protection of fundamental rights, especially when looking at issues connected with the principle of fair trial. For instance, as Porchia and Puoti have pointed out:

> Italian scholars consider the issue of the legal proof of the terrorist purposes of an association, as a fundamental challenge for the interpreter in the struggle against terrorism, while ensuring the protection of fundamental rights of the defendants. The proof that a certain activity is pursued for terrorist purposes and not for other reasons (like belligerent actions, violent actions for criminal purposes etc.) is very difficult to achieve in a way that can be used as an admissible evidence in court.[189]

An interesting case concerning the burning issue of extraordinary renditions is the famous *Abu Omar* case which also led the ItCC to give an important decision[190] on state secrets, in which it acknowledged that the Italian 'Prime Minister' has a broad discretionary power to invoke the state secrets privilege in cases where Governmental agents are involved in extraordinary renditions. The ItCC also stated in that case 'that any review of the substantive merits of that classification [of the relevant information] was a matter for Parliament and not the courts'.[191] The referring court thus ordered the release of five members of the Italian Military Intelligence Agency involved in the kidnapping of Mr. Abu Omar. The ItCC came back to the issue of state secrets in 2014, and confirmed the essence of the decision given in 2009.[192] These decisions are part of a judicial trend which has been

---

187 Fasone 2014.

188 Fasone 2014.

189 Porchia and Puoti 2013, p. 427.

190 ItCC, Decision No. 106/2009.

191 From the website of the ItCC: http://www.cortecostituzionale.it/documenti/download/doc/recent_judgments/S2009106_Amirante_Quaranta_en.pdf.

192 ItCC, Decision No. 24/2014.

described as 'dangerous'[193] since it 'keeps the balance between security and protection of constitutional fundamental rights, leaning in favour of the needs of the former, invoking the State secret in order to hide criminal conducts of Governmental agents'.[194]

References

Avbelj M., Fontanelli F., Martinico G. (eds.) (2014) Kadi on Trial: A multifaceted analysis of the Kadi judgment. Routledge, Abingdon.

Barazzetta A. (2004) I principi di specialità e doppia incriminazione: loro rivisitazione nel mandato d'arresto europeo (The principles of specialty and dual criminality: their readjustment in the framework of the European arrest warrant). In Pedrazzi M. (ed.) Mandato d'arresto europeo e garanzie della persona (The European Arrest Warrant and guarantees for the individual). Giuffrè, Milan, pp. 91 et seq.

Barletta A. (2006) La decisione quadro sul mandato d'arresto europeo: il dibattito, l'impatto e le prospettive dell'adeguamento (The Framework Decision on the European arrest warrant: the debate, the impact and perspectives of implementation). Rivista AIC (Journal of the Italian Association of Constitutional Lawyers). http://archivio.rivistaaic.it/materiali/convegni/sirmione021003/barletta.html.

Barletta A. (2011) La legalità penale tra diritto dell'Unione europea e Costituzione (The legality principle between European Union criminal law and Italian constitutional law). Jovene, Naples.

Barletta A., Pisani M.M., Testore M. (2013) Sostegno all'effettività dei diritti della difesa per rafforzare la legittimità del processo penale in Europa (Support the effectiveness of the rights of defence to strengthen the legitimacy of the criminal process in Europe). UCPI contribution to the Conference 'Assises de la Justice: Shaping Justice Policies in Europe for the Years to Come' organised by the European Commission, Brussels, 21–22 November 2011. http://ec.europa.eu/justice/events/assises-justice-2013/index_en.htm.

Bartone N. (2003) Mandato di arresto europeo e tipicità nazionale del reato. Analisi strutturale comparata dei reati di frode/truffa nelle sovvenzioni, criminalità informatica, furto, racket/estorsione, riciclaggio, corruzione, associazione per delinquere in Italia, Francia, Germania, Spagna (The European arrest warrant and the typicity of national crime. A comparative structural analysis of the crimes of fraud in subsidies, computer crime, theft, racketeering, money laundering, corruption and criminal association in Italy, France, Germany and Spain). Giuffrè, Milan.

Bernatt M. (2014) The Compatibility of Deferential Standard of Judicial Review in the EU Competition Proceedings with Article 6 of the European Convention on Human Rights. Paper presented at the 9th ASCOLA Conference on Procedural Fairness in Competition Proceedings, University of Warsaw, Warsaw, 26–28 June 2014. Draft paper cited with the author's permission. http://www.ascola-conference-2014.wz.uw.edu.pl/conference_papers/Maciej_Bernatt_EU_Courts.pdf.

Bianco G., Martinico G. (2014) Dialogue or Disobedience? On the domestic effects of the ECHR in light of the Kamberaj decision. EPL 20:435–450.

Bin R. (2004) *Lo stato di diritto* (The rule of law). Il Mulino, Bologna.

Biondi Dal Monte F., Fontanelli F. (2008) The Decisions No. 348 and 349/2007 of the Italian Constitutional Court: The Efficacy of the European Convention in the Italian Legal System. German Law Journal 9:889–932.

---

193 Porchia and Puoti 2013, p. 427.

194 Ibid.

Bruno F. (1980) I giuristi alla Costituente: l'opera di Costantino Mortati (Lawyers at the Constituent Assembly: the work of Costantino Mortati). In: De Siervo U. (ed.) Scelte della Costituente e cultura giuridica. II: Protagonisti e momenti del dibattito costituzionale (Choices of the Constituent Assembly and legal culture. II: Protagonists and moments of the constitutional debate). Il Mulino, Bologna, pp. 59–178.

Caianiello V., Vassalli G. (2002) Parere sulla proposta di decisione-quadro sul mandato d'arresto europeo (Opinion on the proposal for a Framework Decision on the European arrest warrant). Cassazione Penale, pp. 462 et seq.

Calamandrei P. (1965) La Costituzione e le leggi per attuarla (The Constitution and its implementing laws). In: Calamandrei P. (ed.) Opere giuridiche, III (Legal works III). Morano, Naples, pp. 553 et seq.

Calamandrei P. (1966) Cenni introduttivi sulla Costituente e i suoi lavori (Introductory remarks on the Constituent Assembly and its work). In: Calamandrei P. (ed.) Scritti e discorsi politici (Writings and political speeches), vol. II. La Nuova Italia, Florence, pp. 421 et seq.

Calvano R. (2007) Legalità costituzionale e mandato d'arresto europeo (Constitutional legality and the European arrest warrant). Jovene, Naples.

Carrozza P. (2007) Constitutionalism's Post-modern Opening. In: Loughlin M., Walker N. (eds.) The Paradox of Constitutionalism: Constituent Power and Constitutional Form. Oxford University Press, Oxford, pp. 169–188.

Cartabia M. (1995) Principi inviolabili e integrazione europea (Inviolable principles and European integration). Giuffrè, Milan.

Cartabia M. (2004) La ratifica del trattato costituzionale europeo e la volontà costituente degli Stati membri (The Ratification of the Constitutional Treaty and the constituent will of the Member States). Forum di Quaderni Costituzionali. http://www.forumcostituzionale.it/.

Cartabia M., Celotto A. (2002) La giustizia costituzionale in Italia dopo la Carta di Nizza (Constitutional justice in Italy after the Charter of Fundamental Rights of the EU). Giurisprudenza Costituzionale 47(6):4477–4507.

Cartabia M., Weiler J.H.H. (2000) L'Italia in Europa (Italy within the European Union). Il Mulino, Bologna.

Caruso B. (2009) Diritti sociali e libertà economiche sono compatibili nello spazio europeo? (Are social rights and economic freedoms compatible in the European space?). In Andreoni A., Veneziani B. (eds.) Libertà economiche e diritti sociali nell'Unione Europea dopo le sentenze Laval, Viking, Rüffert e Lussemburgo (Economic freedoms and social rights in the EU after Laval, Viking, Rüffert and Luxembourg). Eddiesse, Rome, pp. 101–120.

Casetti L. (2005) Profili costituzionali (Constitutional apects). Diritto penale e processo 7:812 et seq.

Cassese A. (1975) Commento art.10 della Costituzione (Art. 10 of the Constitution. A commentary). In: Branca G. (ed.) Commentario della Costituzione, Vol. I. Principi fondamentali, Artt.1–12 (Commentary of the Constitution. Vol. I. Fundamental principles, Arts. 1–12). Zanichelli, Bologna, pp. 485 et seq.

Cassese A. (1980) Politica estera e relazioni internazionali nel disegno emerso alla Assemblea Costituente (Foreign Policy and international relations in the mind of the Constituent Assembly). In: De Siervo U. (ed.) Scelte della Costituente e cultura giuridica. II: Protagonisti e momenti del dibattito costituzionale (Choices of the Constituent Assembly. Protagonists and moments of the constitutional debate). Il Mulino, Bologna, pp. 505–549.

Cavallini F. (2007) Mandato d'arresto europeo: le sezioni unite cambiano orientamento sui limiti della carcerazione preventiva (European Arrest Warrant. The Supreme Court of Cassation changes the orientation on the maximum period of preventive detention). Diritto penale. http://www.diritto.it/docs/23651-mandato-d-arresto-europeo-le-sezioni-unite-cambiano-l-orientamento-sui-limiti-massimi-della-carcerazione-preventiva.

Chieppa R. (2007) Nuove prospettive per il controllo di compatibilità comunitaria da parte della Corte costituzionale (New Perspectives for the control of compatibility with EU law in the case law of the Constitutional Court). Il Diritto dell'Unione Europea 3:175– 204.

Court of Justice of the European Union (2015) Annual Report 2014, Luxembourg 2015. http://curia.europa.eu/jcms/upload/docs/application/pdf/2015-03/en_ra14.pdf.

Dani M. (2011) Assembling the fractured European consumer. In: LSE 'Europe in Question' Discussion Paper Series, LEQS Paper No. 29/2011. http://www.lse.ac.uk/europeanInstitute/LEQS/LEQSPaper29.pdf.

Del Tufo M.V. (2005) La doppia punibilità (Dual criminalilty). In: Pansini G., Scalfati A. (eds.) Il mandato d'arresto europeo (The European Arrest Warrant). Jovene, Naples, pp. 111 et seq.

Delledonne G. (2009) La Resistenza in Assemblea costituente e nel testo costituzionale italiano del 1948 (Resistance in the Constituent Assembly and in the text of the 1948 Italian Constitution), Historia Constitucional 10:217–241.

De Marco E. (1996) Valore attuale del principio della divisione dei poteri (Current meaning of the division of powers). Riv. amm. della Rep. it. 147:1247–1269.

Deplano R. (2013) Fragmentation and Constitutionalisation of International Law: A Theoretical Inquiry. European Journal of Legal Studies 6:67–89.

De Vergottini G. (2004) Diritto costituzionale (Constitutional law). Cedam, Padua.

Di Martino A. (2006) La frontiera e il diritto penale. Natura e contesto delle norme di 'diritto penale transnazionale' (The border and criminal law: the nature and context of 'transnational criminal law'). Giappichelli, Turin.

Falcon G. (2012) Editoriale: La crisi e l'ordinamento costituzionale (Editorial: Crisis and Constitutional Order), Le Regioni XL 1–2:9–20.

Fasone C. (2010) Quale è la fonte più idonea a recepire le novità del Trattato di Lisbona sui parlamenti nazionali? (How to implement the novelties of the Lisbon Treaty concerning national parliaments?) Osservatorio sulle Fonti. http://www.osservatoriosullefonti.it.

Fasone C. (2014) The reaction of Constitutional Courts towards the Euro-crisis law. The protection of social rights in Italy, Portugal and Spain. Paper presented at the IACL Conference, Oslo, 12 June 2014. http://www.jus.uio.no/english/research/news-and-events/events/conferences/2014/wccl-cmdc/wccl/papers/ws4/w4-fasone.pdf.

Ferrajoli L. (2009) Diritto e ragione. Teoria del garantismo penale (Reason and law. The theory of criminal guarantism). Laterza, Rome-Bari.

Ferreres Comella V. (2005) La Constitución española ante la clausola de primacia del Derecho de la Unión europea. Un comentario a la Declaración 1/2004 del Tribunal Constitucional 1/2004 (The Spanish Constitution and the primacy clause in EU law). In: Lopez Castillo A., Saiz Arnaiz A., Ferreres Comella V. (eds.), Constitución española y Constitución europea (The Spanish Constitution and the European Constitution). Centro de Estudios Políticos y Constitucionales, Madrid, pp. 80–89.

Ferro G.A. (2014) Riflessioni sul cammino "costituzionale" della Corte di giustizia dell'Unione europea (Reflections on the constitutional path of the Court of Justice of the EU), AmbienteDiritto. http://www.ambientediritto.it/home/dottrina/riflessioni-sul-cammino-%E2%80%9Ccostituzionale%E2%80%9D-della-corte-di-giustizia-dell%E2%80%99unione-europea.

Fichera M. (2011) The Implementation of the European Arrest Warrant in the European Union: law, policy and practice. Intersentia, Cambridge.

Flore D. (2009) Droit pénal européen. Les enjeux d'une justice pénale européenne. Larcier, Brussels.

Fusaro C. (2005) The Constitutional Reform: a Summary. The main changes that might be introduced into the Italian system by the constitutional reform voted by the Chamber of deputies: a summary. http://www.carlofusaro.it/in_english/constitutional_reform.html.

Galetta D. (2005) Il principio di proporzionalità comunitario e il suo effetto di spill over negli ordinamenti nazionali (Proportionality in EU law and its spillover effect on national systems). Nuove Autonomie, pp. 541–555.

Gambino S. (2014) Livello di protezione dei diritti fondamentali (fra diritto dell'Unione, convenzioni internazionali, Costituzione degli Stati membri) e dialogo fra le Corti. Effetti politici nel costituzionalismo interno ed europeo (Level of protection of fundamental rights (Between EU law, international conventions, constitutions of the Member States) and judicial dialogue. The political effect of domestic and European constitutionalism). Federalismi No. 13. http://www.federalismi.it.

Gambino S., Nocito W. (2012) Crisi dello Stato, governo dell'economia e diritti fondamentali: note costituzionali alla luce della crisi finanziaria in atto (State crisis, economic governance and fundamental rights in the light of the ongoing financial crisis). http://www.astrid-online.

Giubboni S. (2009) Dopo Viking, Laval e Rüffert. In cerca di un nuovo equilibrio fra i diritti sociali e mercato (After Viking, Laval and Rüffert. In search of a new equilibrium between social rights and the market). In Andreoni A., Veneziani B. (eds.) Libertà economiche e diritti sociali nell'Unione Europea dopo le sentenze Laval, Viking, Rüffert e Lussemburgo (Economic freedoms and social rights in the EU after Laval, Viking, Rüffert and Luxembourg). Eddiesse, Rome, pp. 121–132.

Groppi T. (2012) Editorial: The Impact of the Financial Crisis on the Italian Written Constitution. Italian Journal of Public Law 4:1–14.

Gualtieri P. (2004) Mandato d'arresto europeo: davvero superato (e superabile) il principio di doppia incriminazione? (European arrest warrant: has it really outdone (and overcome) the principle of double criminality?) Diritto Penale e Processo, pp. 115–121.

Guarino G. (2014) Cittadini europei e crisi dell'Euro (European citizens and the euro crisis). Editoriale Scientifica, Naples.

Guastaferro B. (2012) Beyond the Exceptionalism of Constitutional Conflicts: The Ordinary Functions of the Identity Clause. Yearbook of European Law 31:263–318.

Guastaferro B. (2014) Coupling National Identity with Subsidiarity Concerns in National Parliaments Reasoned Opinions. MJ 2:320–340.

Harbo T.I. (2010) The Function of the Proportionality Principle in EU Law. ELJ 16:158–185.

Herlin-Karnell E. (2013) From Mutual Trust to the Full Effectiveness of EU Law: 10 Years of the European Arrest Warrant. E.L.Rev. 38:79–91.

Hofmann H.C.H., Mihaescu C. (2013) The Relation between the Charter's Fundamental Rights and the Unwritten General Principles of EU Law: Good Administration as the Test Case. EuConst 9:73–101.

Iuzzolino G. (2002) Mandato d'arresto e garanzie costituzionali (Arrest warrants and constitutional guarantees). Il Giusto Processo 4:173 et seq.

Klip A. (2012) European criminal law. An integrative approach. Intersentia, Cambridge-Antwerp-Portland.

Krisch N. (2010) Beyond Constitutionalism. The Pluralist Structure of Postnational Law. Oxford University Press, Oxford.

Lavenex S. (2007) Mutual recognition and the monopoly of force: limits of the single market analogy. Journal of European Public Policy 14:762–779.

Luciani M. (1991) Antifascismo e nascita della costituzione (Antifascisim and the origin of the Constitution) Politica del diritto 2:183 et seq.

Manacorda S. (2004) Il mandato di arresto europeo nella prospettiva sostanzialpenalistica: implicazioni teoriche e ricadute politico-criminali (The European arrest warrant in the substantive criminal law perspective: theoretical and political implications). Rivista italiana di diritto e procedura penale, pp. 789–845.

Manacorda S. (2007) La deroga alla doppia punibilità nel mandato di arresto europeo e il principio di legalità (Note a margine di Corte di Giustizia, Advocaten voor de Wereld, 3 maggio 2007) (The exception to double criminality in the European arrest warrant and the principle of legality (A case note on Court of Justice, Advocaten voor de Wereld, 3 May 2007)). Cassazione Penale, pp. 318–335.

Martinico G. (2014) Constitutionalism, Resistance and Openness: Comparative Law Reflections on Constitutionalism in Global Governance. STALS (Sant'Anna Legal Studies) Research Paper, 5/2015, http://www.stals.sssup.it/files/martinicoSTALS.pdf.

Mastroianni R., Arena A. (2011) Media Law in Italy. Kluwer Law International, Alphen Aan den Rijn, New York.

Mirkine-Guetzévitch B. (1931) Les Nouvelles tendances du droit constitutionnel. Giard, Paris.

Mitsilegas V. (2006) The constitutional implications of mutual recognition in criminal matters in the EU. CML Rev 43:1277–1311.

Mitsilegas V. (2009) EU Criminal Law. Hart Publishing, Oxford.

Modugno F. (1966) Poteri (divisione dei) (Powers. Division of). Novissimo Digesto italiano, XIII:472 et seq.
Mortati C. (1973) Lezioni sulle forme di governo (Lessons on the form of government). Cedam, Padua.
Mostl M. (2010) Preconditions and limits of mutual recognition. CML Rev 47:405–436.
Nenni P. (1946) Una battaglia vinta (A battle won). Avanti, Rome.
Olivetti M. (2004) Foreign influences on the Italian Constitutional System. Paper submitted to the 6th World Congress of the International Association of Constitutional Law, Santiago, Chile, 12–16 January 2004. http://www.giurisprudenza.unifg.it.
Pajno A. (2003) Il rispetto dei vincoli derivanti dall'ordinamento comunitario come limite alla potestà legislativa nel nuovo Titolo V della Costituzione (Compliance with EU law obligations as a limit to the legislative power in Title V of the Constitution). Le Istituzioni del federalismo 5:814 et seq.
Passaglia P. (2010) Diritto di accesso ad Internet e giustizia costituzionale. Una (preliminare) indagine comparata (Right to internet access and constitutional justice. A (preliminary) comparative study). http://www.giurcost.org/studi/passaglia.htm.
Pastena R. (2014) Internet e privacy: una relazione complicata (A margine della sentenza della Corte di Giustizia del 13 maggio 2014) (The Internet and privacy: A complicated relationship. Comment on the decision of the CJEU dated 13 May 2014)), Rivista AIC (Journal of the Italian Association of Constitutional Lawyers) 2:1–13.
Paterniti F. (2004) La riforma dell'art. 117, 1° co. della Costituzione e le nuove prospettive dei rapporti tra ordinamento giuridico nazionale e Unione Europea (The reform of Art. 117, p. 1, of the Constitution and new prospects of the horizons in the relationship between national and EU law). Giurisprudenza Costituzionale 3:2101 et seq.
Peers S. (2014) Reverse discrimination against rape victims: a disappointing ruling of the CJEU. EU Law Analysis. http://eulawanalysis.blogspot.it/2014/03/compensation-for-crime-victims.html.
Picotti L. (2005) Il mandato d'arresto europeo tra principio di legalità e doppia incriminazione (The European arrest warrant between the principle of legality and double criminality). In Bargis M. and Selvaggi E. (eds.) Mandato d'arresto europeo. Dall'estradizione alle procedure di consegna (European Arrest Warrant. From extradition to surrender procedures). Giappichelli, Turin, pp. 46–65.
Pierdominici L. (2014) Constitutional Change through Euro Crisis Law. Report on Italy. http://eurocrisislaw.eui.eu/italy/.
Pinelli C. (2001) I limiti generali alla potestà legislativa statale e regionale e i rapporti con l'ordinamento comunitario (The general limits of the regional and state legislative power and the relationship with EU law). Il Foro italiano V:194 et seq.
Pinelli C. (2012) La tutela multilivello dei diritti fondamentali nella prospettiva della giurisprudenza italiana. Una ricostruzione (The multilevel protection of fundamental rights in the Italian case law. An overview). In: AA VV (eds.) Scritti in Onore di Alessandro Pace (Writings in Honour of Alessandro Pace), III. Editoriale Scientifica, Napoli, pp. 2377 et seq.
Pisa P. (1973) Previsione bilaterale del fatto nell'estradizione (Bilateral provision of the act in extradition policy). Giuffrè, Milan.
Pizzorusso A. (1981) Organizzazione dei pubblici poteri (Organization of public power). Enciclopedia del diritto XXXI (Encyclopedia of Law XXXI). Giuffrè, Milan, pp. 83 et seq.
Pollicino O. (2008) The Italian Constitutional Court at the Crossroads between Constitutional Parochialism and Co-operative Constitutionalism. Judgments Nos. 348 and 349 of 22 and 24 October 2007. EuConst 4:363–382.
Porchia O., Puoti P. (2013) Italy. In: Laffranque J. (ed.) The Area of Freedom Security and Justice, Including Information Society Issues, Reports of the XXV FIDE Congress Tallinn 2012, Vol. 3. Tartu University Press, Tallinn, pp. 423–460.
Quadri R. (1989) Diritto internazionale pubblico (Public international law). Priulla, Palermo.
Quattrocolo S. (2014) Il contumace cede la scena processuale all'assente, mentre l'irreperibile l'abbandona (The contumacious surrenders the procedural stage to the absent). Diritto Penale Contemporaneo 2:97–107.

Ruggeri A. (2012) Penelope alla Consulta: tesse e sfila la tela dei suoi rapporti con la Corte EDU, con significativi richiami ai tratti identificativi della struttura dell'ordine interno e distintivi rispetto alla struttura dell'ordine convenzionale ('a prima lettura' di Corte cost. n. 230 del 2012) (Penelope at the Italian Constitutional Court: she weaves and pulls the canvas of its relations with the Court of Human Rights, with special attention given to the main features of the domestic legal structure and its peculiarity when compared with the ECHR legal system. A First Reading of decision No. 230 of 2012 of the Italian Constitutional Court)). http://www.diritticomparati.it/2012/10/penelope-alla-consulta-tesse-e-sfila-la-tela-dei-suoi-rapporti-con-la-corte-edu-con-significativi-ri.html.

Sabel F., Gerstenberg O. (2010) Constitutionalising an Overlapping Consensus: The ECJ and the Emergence of a Coordinate Constitutional Order. ELJ 16(5):511–550.

Safjan M. (2012) Areas of Application of the Charter of Fundamental Rights of the European Union: Fields of Conflict? EUI Working Paper LAW 2012/22. http://cadmus.eui.eu/bitstream/handle/1814/23294/LAW-2012-22.pdf.

Saiz Arnaiz A., Alcoberro Llivina C. (eds.) (2013) National constitutional identity and European integration. Intersentia, Cambridge.

Salazar L. (2002) Il mandato d' arresto europeo: un primo passo verso il mutuo riconoscimento delle decisioni penali (The European arrest warrant: a first step towards mutual recognition in criminal matters). Diritto penale e processo pp. 1041 et seq.

Scaccia G. (2007) Gli strumenti della ragionevolezza nel giudizio (The tools of reasonableness before courts). Giappichelli, Turin.

Selvaggi E., De Amicis G. (2005) La legge sul mandato europeo d'arresto tra inadeguatezze attuative e incertezze applicative (The law on the European arrest warrant in between inadequacies and uncertain application). Cassazione Penale VI:1813 et seq.

Selvaggi E., Villoni O., (2002) Questioni reali e non sul mandato d'arresto europeo (Reality and myth of the European Arrest Warrant) Cassazione Penale:449 et seq.

Sorrentino F. (2007) Lezioni sul principio di legalità. (Lessons on the principle of legality). Giappichelli, Turin.

Spitaleri F. (2011) Le discriminazioni alla rovescia nel diritto dell'Unione europea e nell'ordinamento interno (Reverse discrimination in EU law and domestic law). http://asgi.it/wp-content/uploads/public/materiali_seminario_sassomarconi_sett_2011_spitaleri.pdf.

Sturzo L. (1954) La guerra, l'Italia e l'intervistato (The War, Italy and the interviewee). In: Sturzo L. (ed.) Politica di questi anni (Politics of these years). Zanichelli, Bologna, pp. 144–146.

Tridimas T., Gari G. (2010) Winners and losers in Luxembourg: A statistical analysis of judicial review before the European Court of Justice and the Court of First Instance (2001–2005). E.L. Rev. 35:131–173.

Vecchio F. (2014) L'ingloriosa fine della direttiva Data retention, la ritrovata vocazione costituzionale della Corte di giustizia e il destino dell'art. 132 del Codice della privacy (The inglorious end of the Data Retention Directive and the rediscovered constitutional vocation of the Court of Justice and the destiny of Art. 132 of the so called Privacy Code). http://www.diritticomparati.it/2014/06/lingloriosa-fine-della-direttiva-data-retention-la-ritrovata-vocazione-costituzionale-della-corte-di.html#sthash.IMJXMXWP.dpuf.

Von Bogdandy A., Schill S. (2011) Overcoming absolute primacy: Respect for national identity under the Lisbon Treaty. CML Rev. 48:1417–1453.

Further Reading

Calamandrei P. (1955a) Introduzione (Introduction). In: Garrone A.G., Calamandrei P. (eds.) Questa nostra Costituzione (Our Constitution). Giuffrè, Milan, pp. 1 et seq.

Calamandrei P. (1955b) Discorso sulla Costituzione (Speech on the Constitution). Speech given at the Salone degli Affreschi della Società Umanitaria (English translation), Milano, 26 January 1955. http://www.calamandrei-vc.it/web/index.php?option=com_content&task=view&id=233&Itemid=124.

Carlotto I. (2010) I giudici comuni e gli obblighi internazionali dopo le sentenze n. 348 e n. 349 del 2007 della Corte costituzionale: un'analisi sul seguito giurisprudenziale (Italian judges and international obligations after decisions nos. 348 and 349/2007 of the Italian Constitutional Court: a case law based analysis). http://archivio.rivistaaic.it/dottrina/giustizia_costituzionale/ilaria%20carlotto%20sent.348_349_2007.pdf.

Carlotto I. (2013) I giudici italiani e il divieto di applicazione diretta della convenzione europea dei diritti dell'uomo dopo il Trattato di Lisbona (Italian judges and the prohibition on the direct application of the ECHR after the Lisbon Treaty). In: Cappuccio L., Lamarque E. (eds.), Dove va il sistema italiano accentrato di controllo di costituzionalità? (Where is the Italian centralised system of control of constitutionality going?). Editoriale Scientifica, Naples, pp. 177–240.

Cheli E. (1973) Il problema storico della Costituente (The historical problem of the Constituent Assembly). Politica del diritto, pp. 485–530.

Costanzo P., Mezzetti L., Ruggeri A. (2006) Lineamenti di diritto costituzionale dell'Unione europea (European constitutional law). Giappichelli, Turin.

Croce B. (1944) Per una nuova Italia. Scritti e discorsi (1943–44) (For a new Italy. Writings and speeches (1943–44)). Ricciardi, Naples.

Fontanelli F., Martinico G. (2010) Between Procedural Impermeability and Constitutional Openness: The Italian Constitutional Court and Preliminary References to the European Court of Justice. ELJ 16(3):345–364.

Martinico G. (2012) Multiple loyalties and dual preliminarity: The pains of being a judge in a multilevel legal order. ICON 10:871–896.

Pizzorusso A. (1990) Italian and American Models of the Judiciary and of Judicial Review of Legislation: A Comparison of Recent Tendencies. Am.J.Comp.L 38:373–386.

Pollicino O. (2014) From partial to full dialogue with Luxembourg: The last cooperative step of the Italian Constitutional Court. EuConst 10:143–153.

Volterra S. (1980) La Costituzione italiana e i modelli anglosassoni con particolare riguardo agli Stati Uniti (The Italian Constitution and Anglo-Saxon models with particular reference to the United States). In: De Siervo U. (ed.) Scelte della Costituente e cultura giuridica. II: Protagonisti e momenti del dibattito costituzionale (Choices of the Constituent Assembly. II. Protagonists and moments of the constitutional debate). Il Mulino, Bologna, pp. 117–292.

Permissions

All chapters in this book were first published in NCEGGDRRL, by Springer Nature; hereby published with permission under the Creative Commons Attribution License or equivalent. Every chapter published in this book has been scrutinized by our experts. Their significance has been extensively debated. The topics covered herein carry significant findings which will fuel the growth of the discipline. They may even be implemented as practical applications or may be referred to as a beginning point for another development.

The contributors of this book come from diverse backgrounds, making this book a truly international effort. This book will bring forth new frontiers with its revolutionizing research information and detailed analysis of the nascent developments around the world.

We would like to thank all the contributing authors for lending their expertise to make the book truly unique. They have played a crucial role in the development of this book. Without their invaluable contributions this book wouldn't have been possible. They have made vital efforts to compile up to date information on the varied aspects of this subject to make this book a valuable addition to the collection of many professionals and students.

This book was conceptualized with the vision of imparting up-to-date information and advanced data in this field. To ensure the same, a matchless editorial board was set up. Every individual on the board went through rigorous rounds of assessment to prove their worth. After which they invested a large part of their time researching and compiling the most relevant data for our readers.

The editorial board has been involved in producing this book since its inception. They have spent rigorous hours researching and exploring the diverse topics which have resulted in the successful publishing of this book. They have passed on their knowledge of decades through this book. To expedite this challenging task, the publisher supported the team at every step. A small team of assistant editors was also appointed to further simplify the editing procedure and attain best results for the readers.

Apart from the editorial board, the designing team has also invested a significant amount of their time in understanding the subject and creating the most relevant covers. They scrutinized every image to scout for the most suitable representation of the subject and create an appropriate cover for the book.

The publishing team has been an ardent support to the editorial, designing and production team. Their endless efforts to recruit the best for this project, has resulted in the accomplishment of this book. They are a veteran in the field of academics and their pool of knowledge is as vast as their experience in printing. Their expertise and guidance has proved useful at every step. Their uncompromising quality standards have made this book an exceptional effort. Their encouragement from time to time has been an inspiration for everyone.

The publisher and the editorial board hope that this book will prove to be a valuable piece of knowledge for researchers, students, practitioners and scholars across the globe.

List of Contributors

Madis Ernits, Carri Ginter, Saale Laos, Marje Allikmets, Paloma Krõõt Tupay, René Värk and Andra Laurand
Faculty of Law, University of Tartu, Tartu, Estonia

Constantinos Kombos
Law Department, University of Cyprus, Nicosia, Cyprus

Stéphanie Laulhé Shaelou
School of Law, University of Central Lancashire, Pyla, Cyprus

Samo Bardutzky
University of Ljubljana, Ljubljana, Slovenia

Giuseppe Martinico
Scuola Superiore Sant'Anna, Pisa, Italy

Barbara Guastaferro
University of Naples 'Federico II', Naples, Italy
Durham Law School, Durham, England

Oreste Pollicino
Bocconi University, Milan, Italy

Index

CPSIA information can be obtained
at www.ICGtesting.com
Printed in the USA
LVHW080923010922
727359LV00003B/100

9 781639 891931